# THE TRANSFORMATION OF EUROPE

Joseph Weiler's *The Transformation of Europe* is one of the most influential works in the history of European studies. Twenty-five years after its original publication, this new collection of essays pays tribute to Weiler's legacy by discussing some of the most pressing issues in contemporary European Union law, policy and constitutionalism. The book does not intend to be a simple expression of intellectual esteem for Weiler's seminal work; instead, the collection honours it by critically engaging with some of its assumptions and theses. Overall, this volume shows how a study written in 1991 can still be fundamental to the present and future of the European Union, including the challenges presented by Brexit and by the Eurozone crises.

MIGUEL POIARES MADURO is Director of the School of Transnational Governance at the European University Institute, Florence.

MARLENE WIND is Professor and Director for the Centre for European Politics (CEP) at the Department of Political Science and Professor at iCourts (Centre of Excellence for International Courts) at the Faculty of Law, both at the University of Copenhagen.

'This inspiring interdisciplinary, international and inter-generational collection of essays reinforces how Joseph Weiler's vivid writing and intriguing arguments energise the minds of scholars from diverse fields even today.'

Karen J. Alter, Professor of Political Science and Law,
Northwestern University


'A superb exercise of self-reflection and reappropriation of knowledge. A unique way of rethinking Europe in our time.'

Loïc Azoulai, Professor of Law, Sciences Po


'A classic always provides us with a lens through which we understand the world. Weiler's "The Transformation of Europe" certainly meets these criteria and, as such, deserves the attention it gets here from a group of distinguished scholars.'

Renaud Dehousse, President, EUI

# THE TRANSFORMATION
# OF EUROPE

## Twenty-Five Years On

Edited by

### MIGUEL POIARES MADURO
*European University Institute, Florence*

### MARLENE WIND
*University of Copenhagen*

CAMBRIDGE
UNIVERSITY PRESS

# CAMBRIDGE
## UNIVERSITY PRESS

University Printing House, Cambridge CB2 8BS, United Kingdom

One Liberty Plaza, 20th Floor, New York, NY 10006, USA

477 Williamstown Road, Port Melbourne, VIC 3207, Australia

4843/24, 2nd Floor, Ansari Road, Daryaganj, Delhi – 110002, India

79 Anson Road, #06-04/06, Singapore 079906

Cambridge University Press is part of the University of Cambridge.

It furthers the University's mission by disseminating knowledge in the pursuit of
education, learning, and research at the highest international levels of excellence.

www.cambridge.org
Information on this title: www.cambridge.org/9781316610480
DOI: 10.1017/9781316662465

© Cambridge University Press 2017

First published 2017

Printed in the United Kingdom by Clays, St Ives plc

*A catalogue record for this publication is available from the British Library.*

*Library of Congress Cataloging-in-Publication Data*
Names: Maduro, Miguel Poiares, editor.
Title: The transformation of Europe: twenty-five years on / edited by Miguel Poiares Maduro,
European University Institute, Florence, Marlene Wind, University of Copenhagen.
Description: Cambridge, United Kingdom; New York, NY: Cambridge University Press, [2017] |
Includes bibliographical references and index.
Identifiers: LCCN 2017006123 | ISBN 9781107157941 (hardback) |
ISBN 9781316610480 (paperback)
Subjects: LCSH: Europe – Economic integration. | European Union. |
Constitutional law – European Union countries.
Classification: LCC JN30.T695 2017 | DDC 341.242/2–dc23
LC record available at https://lccn.loc.gov/2017006123

ISBN 978-1-107-15794-1 Hardback
ISBN 978-1-316-61048-0 Paperback

# CONTENTS

v

# CONTRIBUTORS

JULIO BAQUERO CRUZ – European Commission

GRÁINNE DE BÚRCA – New York University, USA

DANIELA CARUSO – Boston University, USA

DANIEL HALBERSTAM – University of Michigan, USA

TÜRKÜLER ISIKSEL – Columbia University, USA

R. DANIEL KELEMEN – Rutgers University, USA

PETER L. LINDSETH – University of Connecticut, USA

MIGUEL POIARES MADURO – European University Institute, Italy

FRANZ C. MAYER – University of Bielefeld, Germany

HANS W. MICKLITZ – European University Institute, Italy

KALYPSO NICOLAÏDIS – Oxford University, UK

GIANLUIGI PALOMBELLA – University of Parma, Italy

ALEXANDER SOMEK – University of Vienna, Austria

ALEC STONE SWEET – National University of Singapore, Singapore

ARMIN VON BOGDANDY – Max Planck Institute, Germany

NEIL WALKER – Edinburgh University, UK

J. H. H. WEILER – New York University, USA

MARLENE WIND – University of Copenhagen, Denmark

~

# The Transformation of Europe

## J. H. H. WEILER

## Introduction

In 1951, France, Germany, Italy, and the Benelux countries concluded the Treaty of Paris establishing the European Coal and Steel Community. Lofty in its aspirations, and innovative in some of its institutional arrangements, this polity was perceived, by the actors themselves – as well as by the developers of an impressive academic theoretical apparatus, who were quick to perceive events – as an *avant garde* international organization ushering forth a new model for transnational discourse. Very quickly, however, reality dissipated the dream, and again quickly following events, the academic apparatus was abandoned.[1]

Forty years and more later, the European Community is a transformed polity. It now comprises more than double its original Member States, has a population exceeding 350 million citizens, and constitutes the largest trading bloc in the world. But the notion of "transformation" surely comes from changes deeper than its geography and demography. That Europe has been transformed in a more radical fashion is difficult to doubt. Indeed, in the face of that remarkable (and often lucrative) growth industry, 1992 commentary, doubt may be construed as subversion.

The surface manifestations of this alleged transformation are legion, ranging (in the eyes of the beholder, of course) from the trivial and ridiculous[2] to the important and sublime. Consider the changes in the following:

[1] For a review of integration theory and its demise, see, e.g., Greilsammer, "Theorizing European Integration in its Four Periods," *Jerusalem Journal of International Relations* 2 (1976), 129; Krislov, Ehlermann, and Weiler, "The Political Organs and the Decision-Making Process in the United States and the European Community," in M. Cappelletti, M. Seccombe, and J. H. H. Weiler (eds.), *Integration through Law* (Walter de Gruyter: Berlin, New York, 1985), vol. II, book 1, 3 at 6–11.

[2] The winning song in the popular Eurovision Song Contest of 1990 was entitled "Altogether 1992," *The Times* (London) (May 7, 1990) at 6, col. 8.

1

1. The scope of Community action. Notice how naturally the Member
   States and their Western allies have turned to the Community to take
   the lead role in assisting the development and reconstruction of eastern Europe.[3] A mere decade or two ago, such an overt foreign policy
   posture for the Community would have been bitterly contested by its
   very own Member States.[4]
2. The mode of Community action. The European Commission now
   plays a central role in dictating the Community agenda and in shaping
   the content of its policy and norms. As recently as the late 1960s, the
   survival of supranationalism was a speculative matter,[5] while in the
   1970s, the Commission, self-critical and demoralized, was perceived
   as an overblown and overpaid secretariat of the Community.[6]

---

[3] See "European Commission Defines a General Framework for Association Agreements
('European Agreements') between the EEC and the Countries of Eastern and Central
Europe," *Europe*, Doc. No. 1,646/47 (September 7, 1990) at 1 (reprint of Commission com-
munication to the Council and the Parliament). The evolution is limited, however. For
example, the absence of a true Community apparatus for foreign policy rendered the political (not military) initiative in relation to the Iraqi crisis no more than hortatory. See, e.g.,
"Gulf Crisis: Positions Taken by the Twelve and the Western European Union," *Europe*,
Doc. No. 1,644 (August 23, 1990) at 1 (statements of August 2, 10, and 21, 1990); "Gulf/
EEC: The Foreign Ministers of the Twelve Confirm Their Position and Intend to Draft
an 'Overall Concept' for their Relations with the Region's Countries," *Europe*, Doc. No.
5,413 (January 19, 1991) at 3–4. The Community has, however, taken a leading role in the
Yugoslav crisis. On the evolving foreign policy posture of the Community in the wake of
1992, see generally R. Dehousse and J. Weiler, "EPC and the Single Act: From Soft Law to
Hard Law" (European University Institute Working Papers of the European Policy Unit,
No. 90/1).

[4] In 1973, the French Foreign Minister, M. Jobert, pressed the separateness (of the Framework
for European Political co-operation which dealt with foreign policy) from the Community
to a point of forcing the ministers to meet in EPC in Copenhagen in the morning, and to
assemble the same afternoon in Brussels as a Community Council to deal with Community
business: Stein, "Towards a European Foreign Policy? The European Foreign Affairs System
from the Perspective of the United States Constitution," in Cappelletti, Seccombe, and
Weiler, *Integration through Law*, vol. I, book 3 at 63.

[5] See, e.g., Heathcote, "The Crisis of European Supranationality," *Journal of Common Market
Studies* 5 (1966), 140.

[6] See, e.g., B. Biesheuvel, E. Dell, and R. Marjolin, "Report on European Institutions" (1980),
10–12, 49–56 (report of the Committee of Three to the European Council, October 1979)
(hereinafter "Report on European Institutions"); see also "Proposal for Reform of the
Commission of the European Communities and its Services" (1979) (report made at the
request of the Commission by an independent review body under the Chairmanship of Mr.
Dirk Spierenburg) (report requested in part because of sense of malaise in Commission)
(hereinafter "Spierenburg Report"). For a self-mocking but penetrating picture, see M. von
Donat, *Europe: Qui Tire les Ficelles?* (Presses d Europe: Paris, 1979).

3. The image and perception of the European Community. Changes in these are usually more telling signs than the reality they represent. In public discourse, "Europe" increasingly means the European Community in much the same way that "America" means the United States

But these surface manifestations are just that – the seismographer's telltale line reflecting deeper, below-the-surface movement in need of interpretation. Arguably, the most significant change in Europe, justifying appellations such as "transformation" and "metamorphosis," concerns the evolving relationship between the Community and its Member States.[7]

How can this transformation in the relationship between the Member States and the Community be conceptualized? In a recent case, the European Court spoke matter-of-factly of the EC Treaty[8] as "the basic constitutional charter" of the Community.[9] On this reading, the Treaties have been "constitutionalized" and the Community has become an entity whose closest structural model is no longer an international organization but a denser, yet non-unitary polity, principally the federal state. Put differently, the Community's "operating system" is no longer governed by general principles of public international law, but by a specified interstate governmental structure defined by a constitutional charter and constitutional principles.

This judicial characterization, endlessly repeated in the literature,[10] underscores the fact that not simply the content of Community-Member

---

[7] The juxtaposition of Community and Member States is problematic. The concept of the Community, analogous to the concept of the Trinity, is simultaneously both one and many. In some senses, the Community is its individual Member States: in other senses, it is distinct from them. This inevitable dilemma exists in all federal arrangements. Moreover, the notion of an individual state itself is not monolithic. When one talks of a Member State's interests, one usually sacrifices many nuances in understanding the specific position of that state: "[D]ifferent, conflicting and often contradictory interests, either objective or subjective, are frequently expressed as unified, subjective 'national' interests. Behind these articulated, subjective national interests, however, lie a variety of sets of social, economic and political relations, as well as different relationships between private and public economic organisations and the state.": F. Snyder, *New Directions in European Community Law* (Wiedenfeld and Nicolson: London, 1990) at 90 (footnote omitted); see also *ibid.* at 32, 37. While the danger of sacrificing these many voices within a state cannot be avoided, I shall try to minimize it by referring to the interest of the Member States in preserving their prerogatives as such in the Community polity.

[8] EEC Treaty, as amended by the Single European Act (SEA).

[9] Case 294/83, *Parti Ecologiste, ""Les Verts""* v. *European Parliament* [1986] ECR 1,339, 1,365 (hereinafter "*Les Verts*").

[10] For fine recent analyses, see Lenaerts, "Constitutionalism and the Many Faces of Federalism," *American Journal of Comparative Law* 38 (1990), 205; Mancini, "The Making

State discourse has changed. The very architecture of the relationship, the group of structural rules that define the mode of discourse, has mutated. Also, the characterization gives us, as analytical tools, the main concepts developed in evaluating non-unitary (principally federal) polities. We can compare the Community to known entities within meaningful paradigms.

This characterization might, however, lead to flawed analysis. It might be read (and has been read[11]) as suggesting that the cardinal material *locus* of change has been the realm of law and that the principal actor has been the European Court. But this would be deceptive. Legal and constitutional structural change have been crucial, but only in their interaction with the Community political process.

The characterization might also suggest a principal temporal *locus* of change, a kind of "Big Bang" theory. It would almost be natural, and in any event very tempting, to locate such a temporal point in that well-known series of events that have shaken the Community since the middle of the 1980s and that are encapsulated in that larger-than-life date, 1992.[12] There is, after all, a plethora of literature which hails 1992 as the key seismic event in the Community geology.[13] But, one should resist that

---

of a Constitution for Europe," *Common Market Law Review* 26 (1989), 595; and literature cited in both. The importance of the legal paradigm as a characterizing feature of the Community is recognized also in the non-legal literature. See, e.g., Keohane and Hoffmann, "Conclusions: Community Politics and Institutional Change," in W. Wallace (ed.), *The Dynamics of European Integration* (Pinter: London, New York, 1990), 276, 278–82.

[11] "Tucked away in the fairyland Duchy of Luxembourg and blessed, until recently, with benign neglect by the powers that be and the mass media, the Court of Justice of the European Communities has fashioned a constitutional framework for a federal-type structure in Europe.": Stein, "Lawyers, Judges and the Making of a Transnational Constitution," *American Journal of International Law* 75 (1981), 1; see also A. W. Green, *Political Integration by Jurisprudence* (Sijthoff: Leyden, 1969).

[12] 1992 actually encapsulates, in a game which resembles some new Cabala of Community life, a temporal move to an ever-increasing higher celestial sphere. The key dates in this game of numbers are: the 1984 European Parliament Draft Treaty on European Union and the 1985 Commission White Paper ("Completion of the Internal Market"), endorsed by the 1986 Single European Act (which entered into force in July 1987), and to which was added the April 1988 Commission (Delors) Plan of Economic and Monetary Union, endorsed in the 1989 Madrid Summit and strengthened by the Dublin 1990 decision to hold two Intergovernmental Conferences leading to the Maastricht Treaty, which came into force on 1 January 1993.

[13] "The Single European Act ... represents the most comprehensive and most important amendment to the EEC Treaty to date.": Ehlermann, "The '1992 Project': Stages, Structures, Results and Prospects," *Michigan Journal of International Law* 11 (1990), 1,097, 1,103 (hereinafter "1991 Project"). Although I agree with Ehlermann that the SEA is the

temptation too. This is not to deny the importance of 1992 and the changes introduced in the late 1980s to the structure and process of Community life and to the relationship between Community and Member States. But even if 1992 is a seismic mutation, explosive and visible, it is none the less in the nature of an eruption.

My claim is that the 1992 eruption was preceded by two deeper, and hence far less visible, profound mutations of the very foundational strata of the Community, each taking place in a rather distinct period in the Community's evolution. The importance of these earlier subterranean mutations is both empirical and cognitive. Empirically, the 1992 capsule was both shaped by, and is significant because of, the earlier Community mutations. Cognitively, we cannot understand the 1992 eruption and the potential of its shockwaves without a prior understanding of the deeper mutations that conditioned it.

Thus, although I accept that the Community has been transformed profoundly, I believe this transformation occurred in three distinct phases. In each of the phases a fundamental feature in the relationship of the Community to its Member States mutated; only the combination of all three can be said to have transformed the Community's "operating system" as a non-unitary polity.

These perceptions condition the methodological features of this chapter. One feature is a focus on evolution. I shall chart the principal characteristics of the new "operating system" in an historical framework. In other words, I shall tell a story of evolution over time. This approach will enable me not only to describe but also to analyze and explain. Each evolving facet of the new system will be presented as a "development" that needs systemic and historical analysis.

Second, in this analysis I shall focus on what I consider to be the two key *structural* dimensions of constitutionalism in a non-unitary polity: (1) the relationships between political power in the center and the periphery and between legal norms and policies of the center and the periphery; and (2) the principle governing the division of material competences between Community and Member States, usually alluded to as the doctrine of enumerated powers. The structure and process of the Community will thus occupy pride of place rather than substantive policy and content.

most important formal amendment, I contend that earlier developments without formal amendment should be considered even more important. For a recent comprehensive bibliography of 1992 literature, see *Michigan Journal of International Law* 11 (1990), 571.

The final feature of my methodological approach relates to the position of law in the evolution of the Community. In a sharp critique of a classic study of the European Community legal order, Martin Shapiro made the following comments, which could be leveled against much of the legal literature on the Community:

> [The study] is a careful and systematic exposition of the judicial review provisions of the "constitution" of the European Economic Community, an exposition that is helpful for a newcomer to these materials. But ... [i]t is constitutional law without politics ... [I]t presents the Community as a juristic idea; the written constitution as a sacred text; the professional commentary as a legal truth; the case law as the inevitable working out of the correct implications of the constitutional text; and the constitutional court as the disembodied voice of right reason and constitutional theology ... such an approach has proved fundamentally arid in the study of [national] constitutions ... it must reduce constitutional scholarship to something like that early stage of archeology that resembled the collection of antiquities ... oblivious to their context or living matrix.[14]

The plea for a "law and ..." approach is of course *de rigueur*, be it law and economics, law and culture, law and society, that is, in general, law in context. At one level, a goal of this chapter will be precisely to meet aspects of this critique of, and challenge to, European legal literature. I shall try to analyze the Community constitutional order with particular regard to its living political matrix; the interactions between norms and norm-making, constitution and institutions, principles and practice, and the Court of Justice and the political organs will lie at the core of this chapter.

And yet, even though I shall look at relationships of legal structure and political process, at law and power, my approach is hardly one of law in context – it is far more modest. In my story, de Gaulle and Thatcher, the economic expansion of the 1960s, the oil crisis of the 1970s, socialists and Christian Democrats, and all like elements of the political history of the epoch play pithy parts. It is perhaps ironic, but my synthesis and analysis are truly in the tradition of the "pure theory of law" with the riders

---

[14] Shapiro, "Comparative Law and Comparative Politics," *Southern California Law Review* 53 (1980), 537, 538. In his comment Shapiro alludes to what in its own terms is a model analysis: Barav, "The Judicial Power of the European Economic Community," *Southern California Law Review* 53 (1980), 461. And, of course, not all constitutional scholarship of the Community falls into this trap. See, e.g., Snyder, *New Directions*; Lenaerts, "Constitutionalism"; Mancini, "The Making of a Constitution."

that "law" encompasses a discourse that is much wider than doctrine and norms and that the very dichotomy of law and politics is questionable.

The shortcomings of this "purism" (not total to be sure) are self-evident: my contribution cannot be but a part of a more totalistic and comprehensive history. But, if successful, the "pure" approach has some virtues, as its ultimate claim is that much that has happened in the systemic evolution of Europe is self-referential and results from the internal dynamics of the system itself, almost as if it were insulated from those "external" aspects.[15]

### 1958 to the Middle of the 1970s: the Foundational Period: Towards a Theory of Equilibrium

The importance of developments in this early period cannot be overstated.[16] They transcend anything that has happened since. It is in this period that the Community assumed, in stark change from the original conception of the Treaty, its basic legal and political characteristics. But understanding the dynamics of the foundational period is of more than historical interest; the patterns of Community-Member State interaction that crystallized in this period conditioned all subsequent developments in Europe.

In order to explain the essentials of the foundational period, I would like to make recourse to an apparent paradox, the solution to which will be my device for describing and analyzing the European Community system.

---

[15] The "insulation" cannot be total. External events are mediated through the prism of the system and do not have a reality of their own. *Cf.* Teubner, "Introduction to Autopoietic Law," in F. Teubner (ed.), *Autopoietic Law: A New Approach to Law and Society* (Walter de Gruyter: Berlin, New York, 1988) (the autopoietic approach to law, pioneered by Niklas Luhmann and elaborated by Gunther Teubner, acknowledges a much greater role to internal discourse of law in explaining its evolutionary dynamics; autopoiesis also gives a more careful explanation of the impact of external reality on legal system, a reality which will always be mediated by its legal perception).

[16] The intellectual genesis of this chapter is rooted in my earlier work on the Community. See Weiler, "The Community System: The Dual Character of Supranationalism," *Yearbook of European Law* (Clarendon Press: Oxford; Oxford University Press: New York, 1981), vol. I, 267. It was later developed in J. Weiler, *Il sistema comunitario europeo* (Il Mulino: Bologna, 1985) (an attempt to construct a general theory explaining the supranational features of the European Community). In the present work I have tried, first, to locate my construct, revised in the light of time, within a broader context of systemic understanding; and, second, to use it as a tool to illuminate the more recent phenomenon of 1992.

## A paradox and its solution: Exit and Voice

If we were to ask a lawyer during the foundational period to compare the evolution of the European Community with the American experience, the lawyer would say that the Community was becoming "more and more like a federal (or at least pre-federal) state." By contrast, if we were to ask a political scientist at the same point in time to compare the European system with, say, the American system, the political scientist would give a diametrically opposite answer: "They are growing less and less alike."

The paradox can be phrased in non-comparative terms: from a legal-normative point of view, the Community developed in that first phase with an inexorable dynamism of enhanced supranationalism. European legal integration moved powerfully ahead. From a political-decisional-procedural point of view, the very same period was characterized by a counter-development towards intergovernmentalism and away from European integration. It is not surprising, therefore, that lawyers were characterizing the Community of that epoch as a "constitutional frame-work for a federal-type structure," [17] whereas political scientists were speculating about the "survival of supranationalism." [18]

Identifying the factual and conceptual contours of this paradox of the Community and explaining the reasons for it will be the key to explaining the significance of the foundational period in the evolution of the Community. What then are the contours of this legal-political puzzle? How can it be explained? What is its significance?

In *Exit, Voice and Loyalty*,[19] Hirschman identified the categories of Exit and Voice with the respective disciplines of economics and politics. Exit corresponded to the simplified world of the economist, whereas Voice corresponded to the messy (and supposedly more complex) world of the political scientist. Hirschman stated:

> Exit and Voice, that is, market and non-market forces, that is, economic and political mechanisms, have been introduced as two principal actors of strictly equal rank and importance. In developing my play on that basis I hope to demonstrate to political scientists the usefulness of economic concepts *and to economists the usefulness of political concepts.* This reciprocity has been lacking in recent interdisciplinary work.[20]

[17] Stein, "Towards a European Foreign Policy?" at 1.
[18] Heathcote, "The Crisis of European Supranationality."
[19] A. Hirschman, *Exit, Voice and Loyalty – Responses to Decline in Firms, Organizations and States* (Harvard University Press: Cambridge, MA, 1970).
[20] *Ibid.* at 19 (emphasis in original).

The same can be said about the interplay between legal and political analysis. The interdisciplinary gap there is just as wide.

The interplay of Exit and Voice is fairly clear and needs only a brief adjustment for the Community circumstance. Exit is the mechanism of organizational abandonment in the face of unsatisfactory performance. Voice is the mechanism of intra-organizational correction and recuperation. Apart from identifying these two basic types of reaction to malperformance, Hirschman's basic insight is to identify a kind of zero-sum game between the two. Crudely put, a stronger "outlet" for Voice reduces pressure on the Exit option and can lead to more sophisticated processes of self-correction. By contrast, the closure of Exit leads to demands for enhanced Voice. And although Hirschman developed his concepts to deal with the behavior of the marketplace, he explicitly suggested that the notions of Exit and Voice may be applicable to membership behavior in any organizational setting.

Naturally I shall have to give specific characterizations to Exit and Voice in the Community context. l propose first to discuss in legal categories the Exit option in the European Community. I shall then introduce Voice in political categories.

### Exit in the European Community: formal and selective

Formal (or total) Exit is of course an easy notion, signifying the withdrawal of a Member State from the European Community. Lawyers have written reams about the legality of unilateral Member State withdrawal.[21] The juridical conclusion is that unilateral withdrawal is illegal. Exit is foreclosed. But this is precisely the type of legal analysis that gives lawyers a bad name in other disciplines. It takes no particular insight to suggest that should a Member State consider withdrawing from the Community, the legal argument will not be the critical or determining consideration. If Total Exit is foreclosed, it is because of the high enmeshment of the Member States and the potential, real or perceived, for political and economic losses to the withdrawing state.

Whereas the notion of Total Exit is thus not particularly helpful, or at least it does not profit from *legal* analysis, I would introduce a different notion, that of Selective Exit: the practice of the Member States of

---

[21] For further discussion, see Weiler, "Alternatives to Withdrawal from an International Organization: The Case of the European Economic Community," *Israel Law Review* 20 (1985), 282, 284–8.

retaining membership but seeking to avoid their obligations under the Treaty, be it by omission or commission. In the life of many international organizations, including the Community, Selective Exit is a much more common temptation than Total Exit.

A principal feature of the foundational period has been the closure, albeit incomplete, of Selective Exit with obvious consequences for the decisional behavior of the Member States

## The closure of Selective Exit

The "closure of Selective Exit" signifies the process curtailing the ability of the Member States to practice a selective application of the *acquis communautaire*, the erection of restraints on their ability to violate or disregard their binding obligations under the Treaties and the laws adopted by Community institutions. In order to explain this process of "closure" I must recapitulate two dimensions of EC development: (1) the "constitutionalization" of the Community legal structure; and (2) the system of legal/judicial guarantees.

## The foundational period: the "constitutionalization" of the Community legal structure

Starting in 1963 and continuing into the early 1970s and beyond,[22] the European Court in a series of landmark decisions established four doctrines that fixed the relationship between Community law and Member State law and rendered that relationship indistinguishable from analogous legal relationships in constitutional federal states.

**The doctrine of direct effect** The judicial doctrine of direct effect, introduced in 1963 and developed subsequently,[23] provides the following presumption: Community legal norms that are clear, precise, and self-sufficient (not requiring further legislative measures by the authorities of the Community or the Member States) must be regarded as the law of the land in the sphere of application of Community law. Direct effect

---

[22] The process of constitutionalization is an ongoing one. I suggest the 1970s as a point of closure since, as shall be seen, by the early 1970s all major constitutional doctrines were already in place. What followed were refinements.

[23] On the doctrine of direct effect and its evolution, see T. Hartley, *The Foundations of European Community Law* (Clarendon Press: Oxford; Oxford University Press: New York, 2nd edn., 1988), 183–218.

(a rule of construction in result) applies to all actions producing legal effects in the Community: the Treaty itself and secondary legislation. Moreover, with the exception of one type of Community legislation,[24] direct effect operates not only in creating enforceable legal obligations between the Member States and individuals, but also among individuals *inter se*. Critically, being part of the law of the land means that Community norms may be invoked by individuals before their state courts, which must provide adequate legal remedies for the EC norms just as if they were enacted by the state legislature.

The implications of this doctrine were and are far reaching. The European Court reversed the normal presumption of public international law whereby international legal obligations are result oriented and addressed to states. Public international law typically allows the internal constitutional order of a state to determine the method and extent to which international obligations may, if at all, produce effects for individuals within the legal order of the state. Under the normal canons of international law, even when the international obligation itself, such as a trade agreement or a human-rights convention, is intended to bestow rights (or duties) on individuals within a state, if the state fails to bestow the rights, the individual cannot invoke the international obligation before national courts, unless internal constitutional or statutory law, to which public international law is indifferent, provides for such a remedy. The typical remedy under public international law in such a case would be an interstate claim. The main import of the Community doctrine of direct effect was not simply the conceptual change it ushered forth. In practice, direct effect meant that Member States violating their Community obligations could not shift the *locus* of the dispute to the interstate or Community plane. They would be faced with legal actions before their own courts at the suit of individuals within their own legal order.

Individuals (and their lawyers) noticed this practical implication, and the number of cases brought on the basis of this doctrine grew exponentially. Effectively, individuals in real cases and controversies (usually against state public authorities) became the principal "guardians" of the legal integrity of Community law within Europe similar to the way that

---

[24] Community directives may produce direct effects in the vertical relationship between public authority and individuals but not in the horizontal relationship of individuals *inter se*. See Case 148/78, *Pubblico Ministero v. Tullio Ratti* [1979] ECR 1,629; Case 152/84, *Marshall v. Southampton and South-West Hampshire Area Health Authority* [1986] ECR 723.

individuals in the United States have been the principal actors in ensuring the vindication of the Bill of Rights and other federal law.

**The doctrine of supremacy**    The doctrine of direct effect might not strike all observers as that revolutionary, especially those observers coming from a monist constitutional order in which international treaties upon ratification are transposed automatically into the municipal legal order and in which some provisions of international treaties may be recognized as "self-executing." The full impact of direct effect is realized in combination with the second "constitutionalizing" doctrine, supremacy. Unlike some federal constitutions, the Treaty does not include a specific "supremacy clause." However, in a series of cases[25] starting in 1964 the Court has pronounced an uncompromising version of supremacy: in the sphere of application of Community law, any Community norm, be it an article of the Treaty (the constitutional Charter) or a minuscule administrative regulation enacted by the Commission, "trumps" conflicting national law whether enacted before or after the Community norm. Additionally, although this has never been stated explicitly, the Court has the "*Kompetenz-Kompetenz*" in the Community legal order, i.e., it is the body that determines which norms come within the sphere of application of Community law.[26]

In light of supremacy, the full significance of direct effect becomes transparent. Typically, in monist or quasi-monist states like the United

---

[25] For a particularly subtle analysis of the supremacy of Community law and its evolution, see J. Usher, *European Community Law and National Law – The Irreversible Transfer* (1981), 30–8. For a more skeptical view, see De Witte, "Retour à Costa: La primauté du droit Communautaire à la lumiére du droit international," *Revue trimestrielle du droit européenne* 20 (1984), 425. For a survey and analysis of the most recent constitutional developments, see Jacobs, "Constitutional Developments in the European Community and the Impact of the Single European Market after 1992," *Michigan Journal of International Law* 11 (1990), 887. Recently, the final resistance to supremacy was removed with the decision of the French Conseil'd Etat in *Raoul Georges Nicolo and Others* [1990] CMLR 173.

[26] The principle of supremacy can be expressed, not as an absolute rule whereby Community (or federal) law trumps Member State law, but instead as a principle whereby each law is supreme within its sphere of competence. This more accurate characterization of supremacy renders crucial the question of defining the spheres of competence and in particular the concomitant institutional question of which court will have the final decision as to the definition of spheres, i.e., the question of *Kompetenz-Kompetenz*. The European Court has never addressed this issue squarely, but implicit in the case law is the clear understanding that the Court has, as a matter of Community law, the ultimate say on the reach of Community law. See, e.g., Case 66/80, *Spa International Chemical Corp.*

States, although treaty provisions, including self-executing ones, may be received automatically into the municipal legal order, their normative status is *equivalent* to national legislation. Thus the normal rule of "later in time" (*lex posteriori derogat lex anteriori*) governs the relationship between the treaty provision and conflicting national legislation. A national legislature unhappy with an internalized treaty norm simply enacts a conflicting national measure and the transposition will have vanished for all internal practical effects.[27] By contrast, in the Community, because of the doctrine of supremacy, the EC norm, which by virtue of the doctrine of direct effect must be regarded as part of the law of the land, will prevail even in these circumstances. The combination of the two doctrines means that Community norms that produce direct effects are not merely the law of the land but the "higher law" of the land. Parallels to this kind of constitutional architecture may, with very few exceptions, be found only in the internal constitutional order of federal states.

**The doctrine of implied powers**    One possible rationale underlying the Court's jurisprudence in both direct effect and supremacy has been its

v. *Amministrazione delle Finanze dello Strato* [1981] ECR 1,191; Case 314/85, *Firma Foto Frost* v. *Hauptzollamt Lubeck-Ost* [1987] ECR 4,199, cases in which the Court reserved to itself the prerogative of declaring Community law invalid. In principle, under the EEC Treaty, Art. 173, there are several reasons for annulling a measure of Community law: for example, infringement of an essential procedural requirement under EEC law. This issue, clearly, seems to belong in the exclusive province of the European Court. On second look, however, one of the grounds for annulment, indeed the first mentioned in Art. 173, is "lack of competence." If the issue of competence relates only to the respective competence of the various Community institutions, there is no problem in regarding this issue too as falling exclusively in the hands of the European Court of Justice. But the phrase "lack of competence" clearly applies also to the question of general competence of the Community *vis-à-vis* its Member States. The question as to what part of legislative competence was granted the Community by the Member States is, arguably, as much an issue of Member State constitutional law as it is of Community law. By claiming in the aforementioned cases exclusive jurisdiction to pronounce on these issues, the Court was implicitly, but unquestionably, asserting its *Kompetenz-Kompetenz*, its exclusive competence to determine the competence of the Community. Of course, one rationale of these decisions is to ensure the uniform application of Community law throughout its legal space. But this rationale, functionally persuasive as it may be, does not necessarily override from the perspective of a Member State the interest in the integrity of a state's constitutional order.

[27] Of course, on the international plane, a wrong, for which state responsibility would lie, would have been committed. The remedies for this wrong would be on the international plane as well.

attempt to maximize the efficiency by which the Community performs the tasks entrusted to it by the Treaty. As part of this rationale, one must consider the question of specific powers granted to the Community to perform these tasks. Direct effect and supremacy will not serve their functions if the Community does not have the necessary instruments at its disposal. The issue in which this consideration came to the fore, in 1970, was the treaty-making power of the Community. The full realization of many EC internal policies clearly depended on the ability of the Community to negotiate and conclude international treaties with third parties. As is the case with Member States, the problems facing the Community do not respect its internal territorial and jurisdictional boundaries. The Treaty itself was rather sparing in granting the Community treaty-making power, limiting it to a few specified cases.

In its landmark decision of that period[28] (the period *circa* 1971) the European Court held that the grant of internal competence must be read as implying an external treaty-making power. The European Court added that Community international agreements would be binding not only on the Community as such, but also, as appropriate, on and within the Member States.[29] The significance of this ruling goes beyond the issue of treaty-making power. With this decision, subsequently replicated in different contexts,[30] the European Court added another rung in its constitutional ladder: powers would be implied in favor of the Community where they were necessary to serve legitimate ends pursued by it. Beyond its enormous practical ramifications, the critical point was the willingness of the Court to sidestep the presumptive rule of interpretation typical in international law, that treaties must be interpreted in a manner that minimizes encroachment on state sovereignty. The Court favored a teleological, purposive rule drawn from the book of constitutional interpretation.

[28] Case 22/70, *Commission of the European Communities* v. *Council of the European Communities* [1971] ECR 263 (hereinafter "*ERTA*").

[29] For the evolution of the foreign-relations power of the Community, see J. Groux and P. Manin, *The European Communities in the International Order* (Commission of the European Communities: Brussels, 1985); Lachmann, "International Legal Personality of the EC: Capacity and Competence," in *Legal Issues of European Integration* 3 (1984); Weiler, "The External Legal Relations of Non-Unitary Actors: Mixity and the Federal Principle," in H. G. Schermers and D. O' Keeffe (eds.), *Mixed Agreements* (Kluwer: Deventer, Boston, 1983) at 35.

[30] The doctrine of implied powers is discussed fully in A. Tizzano, "Les compe tences de la Communaute," in *Trente ans de droit Communautaire* (European Commission, Perspectives Europe ennes, 1982), 45, 49–52.

In a parallel, although much less noticed, development, the European Court began to develop its jurisprudence on the relationship between areas of Community and Member State competence. The Treaty itself is silent on this issue. It may have been presumed that all authority granted to the Community was to be shared concurrently with the Member States, subject only to the emerging principle of supremacy. Member States could adopt national policies and laws, provided these did not contradict Community law in the same sphere.

In a bifurcated line of jurisprudence laid in place in the early 1970s and continued thereafter, the European Court developed two complementary doctrines: exclusivity and preemption.[31] In a number of fields, most importantly in common commercial policy, the European Court held that the powers of the Community were exclusive. Member States were precluded from taking any action *per se*, whether or not their action conflicted with a positive measure of Community law. In other fields the exclusivity was not an *a priori* notion. Instead, only positive Community legislation in these fields triggered a preemptive effect, barring Member States from any action, whether or not in actual conflict with Community law, according to specific criteria developed by the Court.

Exclusivity and preemption not only constitute an additional constitutional layer on those already mentioned but also have had a profound effect on Community decision-making. Where a field has been preempted or is exclusive and action is needed, the Member States are pushed to act jointly.

**The doctrine of human rights**     The last major constitutional tremor was in the field of human rights.[32] The Treaty contains no Bill of Rights and there is no explicit provision for judicial review of an alleged violation of human rights. In a much discussed line of cases starting in 1969, the Court asserted that it would, none the less, review Community measures for any violation of fundamental human rights, adopting for its criteria the constitutional traditions common to the Member States and the international

---

[31] See Waelbroeck, "The Emergent Doctrine of Community Pre-emption – Consent and Redelegation," in T. Sandalow and E. Stein (eds.), *Courts and Free Markets* (Clarendon Press: Oxford; Oxford University Press: New York, 1982), vol. II, 548.

[32] See Weiler, "Eurocracy and Distrust: Some Questions Concerning the Role of the European Court of Justice in the Protection of Fundamental Human Rights within the Legal Order of the European Communities," *Washington Law Review* 61 (1986), 1,103.

human-rights conventions to which the Member States subscribed. This enormously complex jurisprudence will be discussed later in this chapter, but its symbolic significance in a "constitution-building" exercise deserves mention here. The principal message was that the arrogation of power to the Community implicit in the other three doctrines would not be left unchecked. Community norms, at times derived only from an implied grant of power, often directly effective, and always supreme, would be subjected to a human-rights scrutiny by the Court. This scrutiny is important given the "democracy deficit" in Community decision-making.

If nothing else, this jurisprudence was as clear an indication as any of the audacious self-perception of the European Court. The measure of creative interpretation of the Treaty was so great as to be consonant with a self-image of a constitutional court in a "constitutional" polity. It should be noted further that the human-rights jurisprudence had, paradoxically, the hallmarks of the deepest jurists' prudence. The success of the European Court's bold moves with regard to the doctrines of direct effect, supremacy, implied powers, and human rights ultimately would depend on their reception by the highest constitutional courts in the different Member States.

The most delicate issue in this context was that of supremacy. National courts were likely to accept direct effect and implied powers, but found it difficult to swallow the notion that Community law must prevail even in the face of an explicit later-in-time provision of a national legislature to whom, psychologically, if not in fact constitutionally, Member State courts owed allegiance. Accepting the supremacy of Community law without some guarantee that this supreme law would not violate rights fundamental to the legal patrimony of an individual Member State would be virtually impossible. This would be especially true in Member States like Italy and Germany where human rights enjoy constitutional protection. Thus, even if protection of human rights *per se* need not be indispensable to fashioning a federal-type constitution, it was critical to the acceptance by courts in the Member States of the other elements of constitution-building. One by one, the highest jurisdictions in the Member States accepted the new judicial architecture of Europe.[33]

---

[33] The story of the acceptance of the principle of supremacy by national courts is charted in H. Schermers and D. Waelbroeck, *Judicial Protection in the European Communities* (Kluwer: Deventer, Boston, 4th edn., 1987), 115–24. See also M. van Empel, *Leading Cases on the Law of the European Communities* (Kluwer: Deventer, Boston, 1990), 203–39.

The skeptic may, however, be justified in challenging the "new legal order" I have described incorporating these doctrines,[34] especially the sharp lines it tries to draw in differentiating the "new" Community order from the "old" public international law order. After all, a cardinal principle of international law is its supremacy over national law. The notion of direct effect, or at least self-execution, is also known to international law, and implied-powers jurisprudence has operated in the jurisprudence of the International Court of Justice as well.[35] If international law shares these notions of supremacy, direct effect, and implied powers,[36] the skeptic may be correct in challenging the characterization of Community development in the foundational period as something out of the ordinary.

One reply is that the Community phenomenon represents a quantitative change of such a magnitude that it is qualitative in nature. Direct effect may exist in international law but it is operationalized in so few instances that it must be regarded as the exception which proves the general rule of its virtual non-existence. In the Community order direct effect is presumptive.[37] The question of supremacy, however, brings the key difference between the two systems into sharp relief. International law is as uncompromising as Community law in asserting that its norms are supreme over conflicting national norms. But, international law's horizontal system of enforcement, which is typically actuated through the principles of state responsibility, reciprocity, and counter-measures, gives the notion of supremacy an exceptionally rarified quality, making it difficult to grasp and radically different from that found in the constitutional orders of states with centralized enforcement monopolies.

The constitutionalization claim regarding the Treaties establishing the European Community can only be sustained by adding one more layer of analysis: the system of judicial remedies and enforcement. It is this system,

---

[34] See, e.g., Wyatt, "New Legal Order, or Old?" *European Law Review* 7 (1982), 147; see also De Witte, "Retour a Costa."

[35] See, e.g., *Reparations for Injuries Suffered in the Service of the United Nations* [1949] ICJ 174.

[36] One could also argue that the protection of fundamental human rights has become part of the customary law patrimony of international law. Cf., *Filartiga v. Pen-a-Irala*, 630 F. 2d 876 (2d Cir. 1980) (deliberate torture under color of official authority violates universally accepted norms of international law of human rights).

[37] See Pescatore, "The Doctrine of 'Direct Effect': An Infant Disease of Community Law," *European Law Review* 8 (1983), 155.

as interpreted and operationalized by the European judicial branch, that truly differentiates the Community legal order from the horizontality of classical public international law.

## The Community system of judicial review

As mentioned above, the hierarchy of norms within the European Community is typical of a non-unitary system. The higher law of the Community is, of course, the Treaty itself. Neither Community organs nor the Member States may violate the Treaty in their legislative and administrative actions. In addition, Member States may not violate Community regulations, directives, and decisions. Not surprisingly, then, the Community features a system of judicial review, operating on two levels. Two sets of legislative acts and administrative measures are subject to judicial review: (1) the measures of the Community itself (principally acts of the Council of Ministers, the Commission, and the European Parliament), which are reviewable for conformity with the Treaties; and (2) the acts of the Member States, which are reviewable for their conformity with Community law and policy, including the above-mentioned secondary legislation.

Needless to say, in the context of my discussion of the closure of Exit and of Member States' attempts to disregard those obligations they dislike, the effectiveness of review of the second set of measures assumes critical importance. Therefore, I focus only on that aspect of judicial review here.

**Judicial review at the Community level**   Either the Commission or an individual Member State may, in accordance with Articles 169–72 of the EC Treaty, bring an action against a Member State for failure to fulfill its obligations under the Treaty. Generally, this failure takes the form of either inaction in implementing a Community obligation or enactment of a national measure contrary to Community obligations. The existence of a mandatory and *exclusive* forum for adjudication of these types of disputes sets the Community apart from many international organizations.

The role of the Commission is even more special. As one commentator noted: "Under traditional international law the enforcement of treaty obligations is a matter to be settled amongst the Contracting Parties themselves. Article 169, in contrast, enables an independent Community body, the Commission, to invoke the compulsory jurisdiction of the European Court against a defaulting Member State." [38]

At the same time, the "intergovernmental" character of this procedure and the consequent limitations on its efficacy are clear. Four weaknesses are particularly glaring:

1. the procedure is political in nature; the Commission may have appropriate non-legal reasons not to initiate a prosecution;
2. a centralized agency with limited human resources is unable adequately to identify, process, and monitor all possible Member State violations and infringements;
3. Article 169 may be inappropriate to apply to small violations; even if small violations are properly identified, dedicating Commission resources to infringements that do not raise an important principle or create a major economic impact is wasteful; and
4. finally, and most importantly, no real enforcement exists; proceedings conclude with a "declaratory" judgment of the European Court without enforcement sanctions.

**Judicial review at the Member State level**    The weaknesses of Articles 169–172 are remedied to an extent by judicial review within the judicial systems of the Member States in collaboration with the European Court. Article 177 provides, *inter alia*, that when a question concerning the interpretation of the Treaty is raised before a national court, the court may suspend the national proceedings and request a preliminary ruling from the European Court in Luxembourg on the correct interpretation of the Treaty. If the national court is the court of last resort, then it must request a European Court ruling. Once this ruling is made, it is remitted back to the national court which gives, on the basis of the ruling, the opinion in the case before it. The national courts and the European Court are thus integrated into a unitary system of judicial review.

The European Court and national courts have made good use of this procedure. On its face the purpose of Article 177 is simply to ensure uniform interpretation of Community law throughout the Member States. That, apparently, is how the framers of the Treaty understood it. [39]

---

[38] Evans, "The Enforcement Procedure of Article 169 EEC: Commission Discretion," *European Law Review* 4 (1979), 442, 443.

[39] Pescatore, "Les travaux du 'Groupe Juridique' dans la négociation des Traités de Rome," *Studia diplomatica* 34 (1981), 159, 173 ("Pour autant que je m'en souvienne, l'acceptation

However, very often the factual situation in which Article 177 comes into play involves an individual litigant pleading in national court that a rule, measure, or national practice should not be applied because it violates the Community obligations of the Member State. In this manner the attempts of Member States to practice selective Community membership by disregarding their obligations have become regularly adjudicated before their own national courts. On submission of the case, the European Court has rendered its interpretation of Community law within the factual context of the case before it. Theoretically, the European Court may not itself rule on the *application* of Community law. But, as one scholar notes:

> [I]t is no secret ... that in practice, when making preliminary rulings the Court has often transgressed the theoretical border line ... [I]t provides the national judge with an answer in which questions of law and of fact are sufficiently interwoven as to leave the national judge with only little discretion and flexibility in making his final decision.[40]

The fact that the national court renders the final judgment is crucial to the procedure. The binding effect and enforcement value of such a decision, coming from a Member State's own court, may be contrasted with a similar decision handed down in declaratory fashion by the European Court under the previously discussed Article 169 procedure. A national court opinion takes care of the most dramatic weakness of the Article 169 procedure: the ability of a Member State, *in extremis*, to disregard the strictures of the European Court. Under the Article 177 procedure this disregard is impossible. A state, in our Western democracies, cannot disobey its own courts.

The other weaknesses of the Article 169 procedure are also remedied to some extent: individual litigants are usually not politically motivated in bringing their actions; small as well as big violations are adjudicated; and, in terms of monitoring, the Community citizen becomes, willy nilly, a decentralized agent for monitoring compliance by Member States with their Treaty obligations.

---

de cette idée dans son principe, ne fit pas de difficultes: je penche a croire que tous, peut-être, n'avaint pas conscience de l' importance de cette innovation." Translated: "As far as I can remember, the acceptance of that idea as to its principle did not face any difficulties: I am inclined to think that perhaps not everybody was aware of the importance of that innovation.").

[40] Rasmussen, "Why is Article 173 Interpreted against Private Plaintiffs?" *European Law Review* 5 (1980), 112, 125.

The Article 177 system is not complete, however. Not all violations come before national courts; the success of the system depends on the collaboration between national courts and the European Court; and Member States may, and often have, utilized the delays of the system to defer ruling.

On the other hand, the overall effect of the judicial remedies cannot be denied. The combination of the "constitutionalization" and the system of judicial remedies to a large extent *nationalized* Community obligations and introduced on the Community level the *habit of obedience* and the respect for the rule of law which traditionally is less associated with international obligations than national ones.[41]

It is at this juncture that one may speculate about the most profound difference between the Community legal order and international law generally. The combined effect of constitutionalization and the evolution of the system of remedies results, in my view, in the removal from the Community legal order of the most central legal artifact of international law: the notion (and doctrinal apparatus) of exclusive state responsibility with its concomitant principles of reciprocity and counter-measures. The Community legal order, on this view, is a truly self-contained legal regime with no recourse to the mechanism of state responsibility, at least as traditionally understood, and therefore to reciprocity and counter-measures, even in the face of actual or potential failure.[42] Without these features,

---

[41] See H. L. A. Hart, *The Concept of Law* (Clarendon Press: Oxford, 1961) (especially chapters 3 and 10); see also Jones, "The Legal Nature of the European Community: A Jurisprudential Analysis Using H. L. A. Hart's Model of Law and a Legal System," *Cornell International Law Journal* 17 (1984), 1.

[42] The argument for treating the Community as a fully self-contained regime in which states cannot resort to counter-measures rests, briefly, on two lines of reasoning. First, the Treaty itself provides for a comprehensive system of compulsory judicial dispute resolution and remedies, akin to that in a federal state, which would exclude the apparatus of state responsibility and counter-measures, a creature of the self-help horizontality of international law. *Cf.* Submissions of the Commission cited approvingly by the Court in Joined Cases 142 and 143/80, *Amministrazione Delle Finanze Dellostato* v. *Essevi* [1981] ECR 1,413, 1,431 ("Above all, it must be pointed out that in no circumstances may the Member States rely on similar infringements by other Member States in order to escape their own obligations under the provisions of the Treaty."); Joined Cases 90 and 91/63, *EEC Commission* v. *Luxembourg* [1964] ECR 625; Case 232/78, *EEC Commission* v. *France* [1979] ECR 2,729. See also *Ministere Public* v. *Guy Blanguernon* [1990] 2 CMLR 340; [1990] I-ECR 83 at 92, recital 7 ("[A]ccording to settled case law, a Member State cannot justify failure to fulfill its obligation ... by the fact that other Member States have also failed to fulfill theirs ... Under the legal system laid down by the Treaty the implementation of Community law by Member States cannot be subject to a condition of reciprocity."). Second, even in an extreme case in which a Member State failed to execute a judgment of the European Court,

so central to the classic international legal order, the Community truly becomes something "new."

At the end of the day the debate about the theoretical difference between international law and Community law may have the relevance of some long-lasting theological disputes, i.e., none at all. Whatever the differences in theory, there can be no argument that the Community legal order as it emerged from the foundational period appeared in its operation much closer to a working constitutional order, a fact which, as will shortly emerge, had a fundamental impact on the way in which it was treated by its Member States.

## The dynamics of Voice in the foundational period

I return to the main theme of this part of the analysis: the relationship between Voice and Exit. The closure of Exit, in my perspective, means that Community obligations, Community law, and Community policies were "for real." Once adopted (the crucial phrase is "once adopted"), Member States found it difficult to avoid Community obligations. If Exit is foreclosed, the need for Voice increases. This is precisely what happened in the European Community in the foundational period. In what may almost be termed a ruthless process, Member States took control over Community decision-making.

We may divide the Community decision-making process into the following phases: (1) the political impetus for a policy; (2) the technical elaboration of policies and norms; (3) the formulation of a formal proposal; (4) the adoption of the proposal; and (5) the execution of the adopted proposal.

The Treaty's original decision-making process had strong supranational elements. The European Commission, the Community body *par excellence*, had virtually exclusive proposal-making competence (the nearly exclusive "right of initiative"), essentially enabling it to determine the agenda of the Community. The Commission was also responsible for

the recourse to counter-measures would inevitably affect individuals removed from the dispute, militating against the very notion of a "new legal order of international law ... the subjects of which comprise not the only Member States but also their nationals." Case 26/62, *NV Algemene Transport-en Expeditie Oderneming van Gend and Loos v. Nederlandse administratie der belastingen* [1963] ECR 1, recital 3 (hereinafter "*van Gend and Loos*"). *Contra* Simma, "Self Contained Regimes," *Netherlands Yearbook of International Law* 16 (1985), 111, 123–9 (sustains the ultimate recourse, even for the Community, to public law and classical state responsibility).

preparing the proposals for formal adoption by the Council of Ministers (comprising the representatives of the Member States) and for acting as the secondary legislature of the Community. The adoption process was supranational, especially in relation to most operational areas, in that it foresaw, by the end of the transitional period, decision by majority voting. Finally, execution (by administrative regulation) was, again, the preserve of the Commission.

During the foundational period, in every phase of decision-making, the Member States, often at the expense of the Commission, assumed a dominant say. The cataclysmic event was the 1965 crisis brought about by France, which objected to the entry into force of the Treaty provisions that would actually introduce majority voting at the end of the transitional period. The crisis was "resolved" by the legally dubious Luxembourg Accord,[43] whereby, *de facto*, each and every Member State could veto Community proposed legislation. This signaled the rapid collapse of all other supranational features of Community decision-making.

The European Council of Ministers, an organ *dehors* the Treaties, assumed the role of giving impetus to the policy agenda of the Community. The Commission formally retained its exclusive power of proposal, but in reality was reduced to something akin to a secretariat. Technical elaboration became infused with Member State influence in the shape of various groups of national experts.[44] In the proposal-formulation process the Commission commenced a practice of conducting a first, unofficial round of negotiations with COREPER, the sub-organ of Council.[45] In addition, as mentioned, the Luxembourg Accord debilitated the Council's voting process, giving each Member State control over proposals and their adoption. Even in the execution of policies, the Commission and Community were "burdened" with a vast range of management and other regulatory

---

[43] The text may be found in H. R. Simmonds (ed.), *Encyclopaedia of European Community Law* (Sweet & Maxwell: London; Green: Edinburgh; Bender: New York), vol. B:2, para. B10-336. Although the Accord does not as such sanction the veto power, "a convention giving each Member State, in effect, a right of veto in respect of its 'very important interests' was established by the practice of the Council after 1965": *ibid.* at para. B10-337.

[44] See, e.g., "Report On European Institutions"; A. Spinelli, *Towards the European Union* (1983).

[45] COREPER, the Committee of Permanent Representatives, is composed of permanent representatives of the Member States to the Community who fulfill the essential day-to-day role of State representatives to the Council. On the role of COREPER within the work of the Council of Ministers, see, e.g., "Report on European Institutions" at 39–41.

committees composed of Member State representatives who controlled that process as well.[46]

Increased Voice is thus a code for a phenomenon of the Member States jointly and severally taking control of decision-making, leading to the process by which the original institutional structures foreseen in the Treaties broke down. It caused the so-called *lourdeur*[47] of the Community process and is believed by many to be the source of much of the Community malaise of that period and beyond.

## *The relationship between Exit and Voice in the foundational period*

How then do we explain these conflicting developments on the legal and political planes? I suggest explanations at three overlapping levels. The combination captures the richness and significance of the Community experience in the foundational period.

First, the developments in each of the respective political and legal domains can be explained as entirely self-referential and self-contained. Thus, for example, the very advent of de Gaulle had a major negative impact in the political realm.[48] Within the realm of law there was a clear internal legal logic which led the Court from, for example, the doctrine of direct effect to the doctrine of supremacy.[49]

The second explanation is that in the face of a political crisis already manifest in the 1960s, resulting from, *inter alia*, a new posture of France under de Gaulle and declining political will among the Member States to follow the decision-making processes of the Treaty and to develop a

---

[46] In passing, I should note that Member State control meant governmental-executive control. One net effect of this process was the creation of the so-called democracy deficit, which I discuss at pp. 77–86 below.

[47] The heaviness of the decisional process, debilitating to the efficiency of the Council and the Community as a whole. See, e.g., "Report on European Institutions" at 27–9, 37–8.

[48] "Throughout the eleven years during which General de Gaulle [who was 'allergic' to anything supranational] remained in power, no notable progress could be made in integration, either in the political domain, the institutional domain, the monetary domain or in the geographical extension of the common market.": Greilsammer, "Theorizing European Integration" at 141.

[49] If one accepts, as one must, the principle of the uniform application of Community law throughout the Community, a clear link exists whereby a holding of direct effect compels a holding of supremacy. In *van Gend and Loos* [1963] ECR 1, recital 2, the Commission and the Advocate-General differed as to whether direct effect existed. The Advocate-General argued that, since the Community had no principle of supremacy, there was no direct effect. The Commission argued that direct effect would compel supremacy. Thus, although they disagreed on the result, they acknowledged the linkage between the two.

loyalty to the European venture, the European Court stepped in to hold the construct together.[50] In this second level of analysis the relationship is unidirectional. The integrating federal legal development was a response and reaction to a disintegrating confederal political development.

The most fascinating question in this regard is how to explain the responsiveness of the Member State courts to the new judicial architecture. We have already noted that absent such responsiveness – normatively in accepting the new constitutional doctrines and practically in putting them into use through the application of the preliminary reference procedure of Article 177 – the constitutional transformation ushered by the European Court would have remained with all the systemic deficiencies of general public international law. One could hardly have talked with credibility about a new legal order.

Due to its nature, a reply to the question must remain speculative. In addition, probably no one answer alone can explain this remarkable phenomenon. The following are some possible explanations in brief, all of which may have contributed to the overall enlistment of the judicial branch in Europe.

The first reply, one which holds considerable force, is the most obvious. Courts are charged with upholding the law. The constitutional interpretations given to the Treaty of Rome by the European Court carried legitimacy derived from two sources: first, from the composition of the Court, which had as members senior jurists from all Member States; and, second, from the legal reasoning of the judgments themselves. One could cavil with this or that decision,[51] but the overall construct had an undeniable coherence, which seemed truly to reflect the purposes of the Treaty to which the Member States had solemnly adhered.

Secondly, it is clear that a measure of transnational incrementalism developed. Once some of the highest courts of a few of the Member States endorsed the new constitutional construct, their counterparts in other Member States heard more arguments that those courts should do the

---

[50] The most radical challenge to the Court as an integrationist activist transcending the political will of the Member States is H. Rasmussen, *On Law and Policy in the European Court of Justice* (Martinus Nijhoff: Dordrecht, Boston, 1986), which also critiques most books on the Court that support this approach. But see Cappelletti, "Is the European Court of Justice Running Wild?" *European Law Review* 12 (1987), 3; Weiler, "The Court of Justice on Trial," *Common Market Law Review* 24 (1987), 555 (review essay of Rasmussen's book).

[51] Indeed, in several of the key cases, such as *van Gend and Loos*, the Court's own Advocate-General differed from the Court. For an analysis, see Stein, "Towards a European Foreign Policy?" See also Rasmussen, *On Law and Policy*.

same, and it became more difficult for national courts to resist the trend with any modicum of credibility. The fact that the idea of European integration in itself held a certain appeal could only have helped in this regard.

Last, but not least, noble ideas (such as the rule of law and European integration) aside, the legally driven constitutional revolution was a narrative of plain and simple judicial empowerment. The empowerment was not only, or even primarily, of the European Court, but of the Member State courts, of lower national courts in particular. Whereas the higher courts acted diffidently at first, the lower courts made wide and enthusiastic use of the Article 177 procedure. This is immediately understandable both on a simple individual psychological level and on a deep institutional plane. Lower courts and their judges were given the facility to engage with the highest jurisdiction in the Community and thus to have *de facto* judicial review of legislation. For many this would be heady stuff. Even in legal systems such as that of Italy, which already included judicial review, the EC system gave judges at the lowest level powers that had been reserved to the highest court in the land. Institutionally, for courts at all levels in all Member States, the constitutionalization of the Treaty of Rome, with principles of supremacy and direct effect binding on governments and parliaments, meant an overall strengthening of the judicial branch *vis-à-vis* the other branches of government. And the ingenious nature of Article 177 ensured that national courts did not feel that the empowerment of the European Court was at their expense.[52]

Finally there is a third, critical layer that explains the relationship between the contrasting legal and political developments during the foundational period. It might be true that the Court of Justice stepped in in the face of a political decline. But it would be wrong to consider the relationship in exclusively unidirectional terms. The relationship has been bi-directional and even circular. The integrating legal developments at least indirectly influenced the disintegrating political ones.

I suggest a tentative thesis, which perhaps could even be part of a general theory of international law-making. This thesis meshes neatly with Hirschmans notion of Exit and Voice and posits a relationship between "hard law" and "hard law-*making*." The "harder" the law in terms of its binding effect both on and within states, the less willing states are to give up their prerogative to control the emergence of such law or the law's "opposability" to them. When the international law is "real," when it is

---

[52] In some areas, such as human rights, the high courts of at least some of the Member States needed some judicial persuasion. See pp. 23–5 above and pp. 45–6 below.

"hard" in the sense of being binding not only on but also in states, and when there are effective legal remedies to enforce it, decision-making suddenly becomes important, indeed crucial.[53] This is a way of explaining what happened in the Community in that period.

What we called, in Hirschmanian terms, the closure of Selective Exit was just that: the process by which Community norms and policy hardened into binding law with effective legal remedies. The increase in Voice was the "natural reaction" to this process. The Member States

---

[53] For example, in the United Nations, the following structure exists: in the General Assembly, resolutions (in principle, not binding) may be adopted by majority vote: in the Security Council, resolutions (binding) may be vetoed by the permanent members. The permanent members must be seen, at least partially, as representative of the major interests of the different political groupings in the General Assembly. The Council of Europe, to a certain extent, with the exception of the human-rights apparatus, has a similar construction. Year after year, the Council of Europe passes resolutions and treaties in a seemingly effort-less stream. This is so because resolutions and draft treaties of the Council of Europe do not, as such, bind the Member States. Members can always "go home," think about indi-vidual proposals, and decide to accept or reject them. A similar linkage exists in relation to the conclusion of multilateral treaties and the permissible regime of reservations. Under the old regime, texts of multilateral treaties were adopted, unless otherwise provided, by unanimous vote of the contracting parties (Enhanced Voice). The corollary was that states were highly restricted in their ability to make reservations; these had to be accepted by all parties to the Treaty (Limited Exit). Under the new treaty law – ushered by the *Reservation to the Convention on Genocide Case* [1951] ICJ 15, and later by the Vienna Convention on the Law of Treaties (1969), Arts. 9(2) and 19–21 – the text of a multilateral treaty could be adopted by the vote of two-thirds of the states present and voting (Reduced Voice); but the corollary was the greater ease with which States could make reservation to such texts. In some modern conventions, such as the 1982 Law of the Sea Convention, the unani-mous adoption (Enhanced Voice) was again accompanied by a prohibition on reservations (Reduced Exit). A similar development may be noted in relation to the doctrine of the per-sistent objector in the formation of customary law. It is clear that the modern approach to custom is more lenient towards the formation of custom with more limited participation of states in that formation (Reduced Voice), It has been predicted that this in turn will lead to a greater invocation by states of the doctrine of persistent objector (Enhanced Exit), See Stein, "The Approach of the Different Drummer: The Principle of the Persistent Objector in International Law," *Harvard International Law Journal* 26 (1985), 457. The relationship between decision-making and normative outcomes exists beyond the realm of public law and may be found in private law institutions as well. Thus Gilmore, in discussing the evolu-tion of contract theory, contrasts the nineteenth-century model, which embraced a narrow consideration theory (whereby it was difficult to enter into a contract), but also a narrow excuse theory (difficult to get out). In our terms, this would correspond to High Voice and Restricted Exit. Twentieth-century contract theory saw "a move towards a free and easy approach to the problem of contract formation" (Reduced Voice), which "goes hand in hand with a free and easy approach to the problem of contract dissolution or excuse" (Easy Exit): G. Gilmore, *The Death of Contract* (Ohio State University Press: Columbus, OH, 1974), 48.

realized the critical importance of taking control of a decision-making process, the outcome of which they would have to live with and abide by. By "natural reaction" I do not mean to imply a simplistic causal relationship. I do not suggest that, as a direct result of the decisions of the Court, in say, *van Gend and Loos*[54] (in 1963) or *Costa* v. *ENEL*[55] (in 1964), the French government decided (in 1965) to precipitate the crisis that led to the Luxembourg Accord. I suggest that the constitutionalization process created a normative construct in which such a precipitous political development becomes understandable. Because Community norms in terms of substance were important,[56] and because they were by then situated in a context that did not allow selective application, control of the creation of the norm itself was the only possible solution for individual states.[57]

Historically (and structurally) an equilibrium was established. On the one hand stood a strong constitutional integrative process that, in radical mutation of the Treaty, linked the legal order of the Community with that of the Member States in a federal-like relationship. This was balanced

---

[54] [1963] ECR 1.

[55] Case 6/64, *Flaminio Costa* v. *ENEL* [1964] ECR 585.

[56] Even if the Community did not, in its initial phases, affect the lives of many citizens, it was crucial in some important economic and political sectors, for example, agriculture.

[57] It is difficult to adduce hard proof for this thesis, but the following is evocative. In the United Kingdom's White Paper presented to Parliament by the Prime Minister in July 1971 advocating the UK's accession to the Community, the linkage is rather clear. See "The United Kingdom and the European Communities" (Cmnd. 4715, 1971), paras. 29–30. In "Membership of the European Community: Report on Renegotiation" (Cmnd. 6003, 1975), the linkage is actually made. In a section entitled "The Special Nature of the Community" (para. 118), one finds first an explanation of the "direct applicability of Community law in member countries" (para. 122), corresponding to our analysis of the constitutionalization and the closure of Selective Exit. Immediately afterwards, in "Power of Member Governments" (paras. 123–5), one finds: "[T]he importance of accommodating the interests of individual member states is recognised in the Council's general practice of taking decisions by consensus, so that each member state is in a position to block agreement unless interests to which it attaches importance are met" (para. 124). The authoritative *Encyclopaedia of European Community Law*, in interpreting the Luxembourg Accord and the veto power, states: "the existence of that convention [veto power] was a significant factor in the decision by Denmark and the United Kingdom, and subsequently by Greece, to enter the Communities.": *Encyclopaedia of European Community Law*, vol. B:2 at 11, B10-337. In *ERTA*, one of the key "constitutionalizing" cases, Advocate-General Dutheillet de Lamothe seems to suggest the same type of linkage: "Finally, from the point of view of the development of common policies, are there not grounds for fearing that the Ministers would resist the adoption of regulations which would result in the loss, in cases not provided for by the Treaty, of their authority in international matters?": *ibid.* at 292.

by a relentless and equally strong process, also deviating radically from the Treaty, that transferred political and decision-making power into a confederal procedure controlled by the Member States acting jointly and severally.

The linkage between these two facets of the Community may explain and even resolve several issues regarding the process of European integration. The first issue relates to the very process of constitutionalization in the 1960s and early 1970s, a phenomenon that has been, as noted, at the center of legal discourse about the Community. Indeed, insiders refer to this period, especially in the jurisprudence of the European Court, as the "heroic period." But, as we observed, these profound constitutional mutations took place in a *political* climate that was somewhat hostile to, and suspicious of, supranationalism. How then – and this is the dilemma – could changes so profound, which would normally require something akin to a constitutional convention subject to elaborate procedures of diplomatic negotiation and democratic control, occur with a minimal measure of political (i.e., Member State) opposition?[58] Part of the answer rests, of course, in the fact that constitutionalization during the foundational period was judicially driven, thus attaching to itself that deep-seated legitimacy that derives from the mythical neutrality and religious-like authority with which we invest our supreme courts.

The explanation I suggest is derived from the hard law/hard law-making theorem, from the interplay of Exit and Voice. Instead of a simple (legal) cause and (political) effect, this subtler process was a circular one. On this reading, the deterioration of the political supranational decisional procedures, the suspension of majority voting in 1966, and the creation and domination of intergovernmental bodies such as COREPER and the European Council constituted the political conditions that allowed the Member States to digest and accept the process of constitutionalization. Had no veto power existed, had intergovernmentalism not become the order of the day, it is not clear to my mind that the Member States would have accepted with such equanimity what the European Court was doing. They could accept the constitutionalization because they took real control of the decision-making process, thus minimizing its threatening features.

---

[58] Our confusion is enhanced if we consider that the changes introduced by the Single European Act in 1986 were *per se* less radical, and yet necessitated a tortuous political process, including a constitutional challenge in the supreme court of one of the Member States. See *Croty* v. *An Taoiseach* [1987] CMLR 666 (Irish Supreme Court).

Our speculation should not stop here: while this description of the legal-political equilibrium may explain how and why the Member States were willing to digest, or accept, the constitutional revolution, it does not explain their interest in doing so. A theory of state action without interest analysis is incomplete. What, then, was the interest of the Member States in not simply accepting the changing morphology of the Community but actually pursuing it?

The fundamental explanation is that the Member States, severally and jointly, balanced the material and political costs and benefits of the Community. Both the Community vision and its specific policy agenda were conceived as beneficial to the actors. It may, at first sight, seem reasonable when thinking about the Community and its Member States to conceive of this relationship as a zero-sum game: the strengthening of the Community must come "at the expense" of the Member States (and *vice versa*). However, the evolution of the Community in its foundational period ruptures this premise of zero-sum. The strengthening of the Community was accompanied by the strengthening of its Member States.[59] Stanley Hoffmann gave a convincing political explanation of this phenomenon.[60] But the phenomenon also derives from the unique legal-political equilibrium of the Community structure.

The interplay between the Community normative and decision-making regimes, as explained above, gave each individual Member State a position of power brokerage it never could have attained in more traditional fora of international intercourse. The constitutional infrastructure "locked" the Member States into a communal (read "Community") decision-making forum with a fairly rigorous and binding legal discipline. The ability to "go it alone" was always somewhat curtailed and, in some crucial areas, foreclosed. The political superstructure, with its individual veto power and intergovernmental discourse, gave each Member State a decisive position of influence over the normative outcome.

---

[59]  It is easy to identify the interest that the small states would have in this structure: their weight in, and power over, decision-making in inherently interdependent policy areas becomes incomparably larger compared to outside arm's-length negotiations. In principle this is true also for larger Member States. *Cf.* "The United Kingdom and the European Communities" at 7–14. In addition, the larger Member States had particular interests that could be vindicated effectively through the Community. Examples are the French interest in a European-wide common agricultural policy and the German interest in relegitimation.

[60]  Hoffman, "Reflection on the Nation-State in Western Europe Today," in L. Tsoukalis (ed.), *The European Community: Past, Present and Future* (Basil Blackwell: Oxford, 1983), 21, 22.

Finally, in at least an indirect way, these basic features of the foundational period accentuate and explain a permanent feature of the Community: its so-called democracy deficit.[61]

As already mentioned, the reference to "Member State" as a homogeneous concept or actor is misleading in several ways,[62] increasingly so in an ever more complex Community.[63] In discussing the democracy deficit it is more accurate to speak instead of the "government," i.e., the executive branch, of each Member State. Admittedly, the Treaty itself laid the seeds for the democracy deficit by making the statal executive branch the ultimate legislator in the Community. The decision-making Council members are first of all members of their respective executive branches and thus directly representative of their home-state governments. The only democratic check on Council decisions is a submission to the meek control of the European Parliament. Direct democratic accountability, by design or by default, remains vested in national parliaments to whom the members of the Council are answerable.

The mutations of the legal structure and the political process in the foundational period impacted this basic deficiency in a variety of ways.

The process of constitutionalization, hardening Community measures into supreme, often directly effective laws, backed with formidable enforcement mechanisms, meant that once these laws were enacted, national parliaments could not have second thoughts or control their content at the national, implementing level. The only formal way in which accountability could be ensured would be by tight *ex ante* control by national parliaments on the activities of ministers in Community fora. This has proved largely not feasible.[64] The net result is that the executive branches of the Member States often act together as a binding legislator outside the decisive control of any parliamentary chamber.

The changes in the decision-making processes meant that it was not simply the Voice of the Member States that was enhanced, but the Voice of "governments." It is not entirely fanciful to surmise that the acceptability

---

[61] See D. Marquand, *Parliament for Europe* (Jonathan Cape: London, 1979), 64–6; see also "Report Drawn up on behalf of the Committee on Institutional Affairs on the Democratic Deficit in the European Community," PE Doc. No. A 2-276/87 (February 1, 1988).

[62] See note 7, p. 12 above.

[63] See Snyder, *New Directions* at 32–6.

[64] See Sasse, "The Control of the National Parliaments of the Nine over European Affairs," in A. Cassese (ed.), *Parliamentary Control over Foreign Policy* (Sijthoff and Noordhoff: Alphen aan den Rijn, Germantown, MD, 1980), 137. Denmark may be the exception: see Mendel, "The Role of Parliament in Foreign Affairs in Denmark," in *ibid.* at 53, 57.

of the Community system in the foundational period was not simply
because it vindicated the interests of Member States but also because it
enhanced the power of governments (the executive branch) *per se*.

## Conclusions to the foundational period

The foundational period has been characterized by legal scholars as an
heroic epoch of constitution-building in Europe, as a time of laying the
foundation for a federal Europe. It has been described by political scientists as a nadir in the history of European integration, as an era of crum-
bling supranationalism. The thrust of my argument has been that a true
understanding of this period can only be achieved by a marriage of these
two conflicting visions into a unified narrative in which the interaction of
the legal and the political, and the consequent equilibrium, constitute the
very fundamental feature of the Community legal structure and political
process.

This very feature helps explain the uniqueness and stability of the
Community for much of its life: a polity that achieved a level of integration similar to that found only in fully fledged federal states and yet that
contained unthreatened and even strengthened Member States.

## 1973 to the Middle of the 1980s: Mutation of Juris
## Diction and Competences

### Introduction

The period from the middle of the 1970s to the middle of the 1980s is
traditionally considered a stagnant epoch in European integration. The
momentum created by the accession of the UK, Ireland, and Denmark
did not last long. The oil crisis of late 1973 displayed a Community unable
to develop a common external posture. Internally the three new Member
States, two of which, the UK and Denmark, were often recalcitrant partners, burdened the decision-making process, forcing it to a grinding pace.
It is not surprising that much attention was given in that period to proposals to address a seriously deteriorating institutional framework and to
relaunch the Community.[65]

---

[65] See "Report on European Institutions"; Spierenburg Report; the six Reports and Resolution
of the European Parliament on Institutions of July 9, 1981 (Hänsch, Diligent Baduel,
Glorioso, van Miert, Elles, Antoniozzi); "The Institutional System of the Community:
Restoring the Balance," *Bulletin of the European Communities* (Supp. 3/82), 5; "French

And yet it is in this politically stagnant period that another large-scale mutation in the constitutional architecture of the Community took place, a mutation that has received far less attention than the constitutional revolution in the foundational period. It concerned the principle of division of competences between Community and Member States.

In most federal polities the demarcation of competences between the general polity and its constituent units is the most explosive of federal battlegrounds. Traditionally, the relationship in non-unitary systems is conceptualized by the principle of enumerated powers. The principle has no fixed content and its interpretation varies from system to system; in some it has a stricter and in others a more relaxed construction. Typically, the strength by which this principle is upheld (or, at least, the shrillness of the rhetoric surrounding it) reflects the strength of 'the belief in the importance of preserving the original distribution of legislative powers as a defining feature of the polity. Thus, there can be little doubt about the very different ethos that underscored the evolution of, for example, the Canadian and US federalisms, in their formative periods and beyond, regarding enumeration. Nowhere is this different ethos clearer than in the judicial rhetoric of enumeration. The *dicta* of Lord Atkin[66] and Chief Justice Marshall[67] concerning powers are the theater pieces of this rhetoric. Likewise, the recurring laments over the "death of federalism" [68] in this or that federation are typically associated with a critique of a relaxed

---

Government Memorandum on Revitalization of the Community," *Bulletin of the European Communities* 14 (11–1981), 92; German-Italian Initiative: Draft European Act, *Bulletin of the European Communities* 14 (11–1981), 87 (Genscher-Colombo Initiative); and Report on European Political Cooperation, *Bulletin of the European Communities* (Supp. 3/81), 14. See generally, on that epoch and these proposals, Weiler, "The Genscher-Colombo Draft European Act: The Politics of Indecision," *Journal of European Integration* 6 (1983), 129.

[66] On enumeration, Lord Atkin stated: "No one can doubt that this distribution [of legislative powers between the Dominion and the Provinces] ... is one of the most essential conditions, probably the most essential condition [in the Canadian federal arrangement] ... While the ship of state now sails on larger ventures ... she still retains the watertight compartments which are an essential part of her original structure.": *A.-G. Canada v. A.-G. Ontario* (1937) 1 DLR 673 at 682–4 (PC).

[67] Over a century before, Chief Justice Marshall asserted: "Let the end be legitimate, let it be within the scope of the Constitution, and all means which are appropriate, which are plainly adapted to that end, which are not prohibited, but consist with the letter and spirit of the [C]onstitution, are constitutional.": *McCulloch v. Maryland*, 17 US (4 Wheat.) 316 (1819) at 421.

[68] E.g., van Alstyne, "The Second Death of Federalism," *Michigan Law Review* 83 (1985), 1, 709.

attitude towards enumeration and an inevitable shift of power to the center at the expense of the states.

The different views about the strictness or flexibility of enumeration reflects a basic understanding of federalism and integration. Returning to the Canadian-US comparison, we find the Atkin and Marshall *dicta* reconceptualized as follows. Wade, in the context of the Canadian experience, suggests that:

> The essential elements of a federal constitution are that powers are divided between the central and provincial governments and that neither has legal power to encroach upon the domain of the other, except through the proper process of constitutional amendment ... [T]he spirit ... which is inherent in the whole federal situation [is] that neither side, so to speak, should have it in its power to invade the sphere of the other.[69]

In contrast, Sandalow, reflecting on the US experience, suggests that:

> The disintegrative potential of [questions concerning the legality of governmental action] is especially great when they [challenge] the distribution of authority in a divided or federal system ... [Where] Congress determines that a national solution is appropriate for one or another economic issue, its power to fashion one is not likely to be limited by constitutional divisions of power between it and the state legislatures.[70]

These differences in approach could be explained by formal differences in the structure of the British North American Act (which predated the current Canadian Constitution) as compared to the US Constitution. But they also disclose a principled difference in the way the two systems value enumerated powers within the federal architecture, a difference between ends and means, functions and values. In the Wade conception of the Canadian system the division of powers was considered a *per se* value, an end in itself. The *form* of divided governance was considered to be on par with the other fundamental purposes of a government, such as obtaining security, order, and welfare, and was viewed as part of its democratic architecture. In the United States, the federal distribution retained its constitutional importance as the system evolved. In practice, however, it would seem that the principle of division was subjected to higher values

---

[69] Wade, "Amendment of the Constitution of Canada: The Role of the United Kingdom Parliament," in *British North America Acts: The Role of Parliament*, 2 HC 42 (1981) at 102, 108 (memorandum and evidence submitted to the Foreign Affairs Committee of the House of Commons).

[70] Sandalow, "The Expansion of Federal Legislative Authority," in Sandalow and Stein, *Courts and Free Markets*, 49 at 49–50 (I have reversed the order of quoted sentences).

and invoked as a useful *means* for achieving other objectives of the US union. To the extent that the division became an obstacle for the achievement of such aims it was sacrificed.[71] We may refer to this approach as a functional one. The dichotomy is, of course, not total; we find strands of both the functional and *per se* approaches in each of the systems. Nevertheless, clear differences exist in the weight given to each of the strands and in the evolution of the two federations. In addition, the legal debate about division of powers was (and remains) frequently the code for battles over raw power between different *loci* of governance, an aspect ultimately of crucial importance.

In Europe, the Treaty itself does not precisely define the material limits of Community jurisdiction.[72] But it is clear that, in a system that rejected a "melting pot" ethos and explicitly in the preamble to its constituent instrument affirms the importance of "an ever closer union among the *peoples* of Europe," that saw power being bestowed by the Member State on the Community (with residual power thus retained by the Member States) and consecrated in an international Treaty containing a clause that effectively conditions revision of the treaty on ratification by parliaments of all Member States,[73] the "original" understanding was that the principle of enumeration would be strict and that jurisdictional enlargement (*rationae materia*) could not be lightly undertaken. This understanding was shared not only by scholars,[74] but also by the Member States and the political organs of the Community, as evidenced by their practices,[75] as well as by the Court of Justice itself. In its most famous decision, *van Gend and Loos*, the Court affirmed that the Community constitutes "a new legal order of international law for the benefit of which the states have limited their sovereign rights, *albeit in limited fields*." [76] And earlier, in even more

---

[71] These developments have had their critics: e.g., van Alstyne, "The Second Death of Federalism"; *cf.* Amar, "Of Sovereignty and Federalism," *Yale Law Journal* 96 (1987), 1, 425.

[72] Arts. 2 and 3 of the EEC Treaty set out the "tasks" or "purposes" of the Community, from which its competences are derived in rather open-textured language.

[73] EEC Treaty, Art. 236.

[74] Judge Pescatore, who later became one of the formidable champions of an expansive and evolutive view of the Community, offered a classic endorsement of this original narrow understanding in at least some of its aspects: Pescatore, "Les relations extérieures des Communautés européenne," *Receuils des cours* (1961-II), 1.

[75] For example, in the enactment of Council Regulation No. 803/68, 1968 OJ (L 148), 6 (June 28, 1968), relating to the customs value of goods, a matter at the heart of the common market and the economic sphere of Community activity, the Council resorted to Art. 235 of the Treaty as the legal basis, not believing it had inherent authority in the customs-union provisions of the Treaty.

[76] *van Gend and Loos* [1963] ECR 1 (emphasis added).

striking language, albeit related to the Coal and Steel Community, the Court explained that:

> The Treaty rests on a derogation of sovereignty consented by the Member States to supranational jurisdiction for an object strictly determined. The legal principle at the basis of the Treaty is a principle of limited competence. The Community is a legal person of public law and to this effect it has the necessary legal capacity to exercise its functions but only those.[77]

In light of the Member States' vigorous reaction to the constitutional mutation of the Community during the foundational period, seizing effective control of Community governance, and the fact that a lax attitude to enumeration would indeed seem to result in a strengthening of the center at the expense of the states, we would expect that this "original" understanding of strict enumeration would be tenaciously preserved.

I characterize the period of the 1970s[78] to the early 1980s as a second and fundamental phase in the transformation of Europe. In this period the Community order mutated almost as significantly as it did in the foundational period. In the 1970s and early 1980s, the principle of enumerated powers as a constraint on Community *material* jurisdiction (absent Treaty revision) was substantially eroded and in practice virtually disappeared.[79] Constitutionally, no core of sovereign state powers was left beyond the reach of the Community. Put differently, if the constitutional revolution was celebrated in the 1960s albeit "in limited fields," the 1970s saw the erosion of these limits. As an eminent authority assesses the Community today: "There simply is no nucleus of sovereignty that the Member States can invoke, as such, against the Community." [80]

The 1970s mutation I describe went largely unnoticed by the interpretive communities in Europe: the Member States and their governments,

---

[77] Joined Cases 7/56 and 3 to 7/57, *Dinecke Algera* v. *Common Assembly of the European Coal and Steel Community* [1957–8] ECR 39 (hereinafter "*Algera*").

[78] 1973 seems an appropriate signpost, since it followed the European Council meeting of October 1972 in which an explicit decision was made to make full (and, on my reading, expansive) use of Art. 235 as part of the general reinvigoration of the Community. This process coincided with the accession of the three new Member States. Declaration of Paris Summit, *Bulletin of the European Communities* (10–1972).

[79] I should emphasize that my analysis is confined to the question of material competences. Organic and institutional changes are jealously guarded. That, as shall emerge, is part of my thesis. In other words, it is the fact that organic and institutional changes are kept under tight control (essentially conserving the prerogatives of the Member States gained in the foundational period) that enables the Member States to be lax about material demarcation.

[80] Lenaerts, "Constitutionalism" at 220. Note that Lenaerts refers in this statement to what I have termed in this article "absorption."

political organs of the Community, the European Court and, to an extent, academia.[81] This lack of attention is all the more ironic and striking when it is noted that the interaction among those interpretive communities brought about this fundamental mutation. To be sure, the expansion of Community jurisdiction in the 1970s and early 1980s was widely observed. Indeed, this growth was, as mentioned above, willed by all actors involved.

What was not understood was that, during this process of growth and as a result of its mechanics, the guarantees of jurisdictional demarcation between Community and Member States eroded to the point of collapse. This cognitive dissonance in accounts of the period is so striking that I shall attempt to explain not only the legal-political process by which strict enumeration eroded and practically disappeared, but also the reasons so fundamental a change in the Community architecture was not obvious to all.[82]

Naturally, because the process itself went largely unnoticed when it occurred, its far-reaching consequences and significance were not appreciated at the time. It is a general theme of this article that the first series

---

[81] But see Tizzano, "Lo sviluppo delle competenze materiali delle comunita europee, *Rivista di diritto europeo*" 139 (1981); Sasse and Yourow, "The Growth of Legislative Power of the European Communities," in Sandalow and Stein, *Courts and Free Markets*, 92.

[82] The erosion of jurisdictional limits did not mean that the Community and its Member States would never resort to Treaty amendment. Clearly changes as to the method of exercising jurisdiction such as the shift from unanimity to majority voting under Art. 100 would require such amendment. Not all Treaty amendment concerns jurisdictional limits. More interestingly, even in areas where jurisdiction was already clearly asserted, such as in the environmental field, the Member States would, for example in the Single European Act, "reinvent the wheel." And in matters concerning monetary and economic union, they are now negotiating Treaty amendments to give effect to the new monetary constructs. My claim is that this has become their choice, and if they had wished they could have introduced the new monetary regime under Art. 235, easily showing, in the light of other practice concerning 235, that it was necessary for the good functioning of the common market. There are, however, many advantages to pursuing the Treaty amendment route: to mention just two, the new regime becomes entrenched and cannot be changed by simple legislation (something important for, say, the independence of the proposed central European bank), and it enjoys a higher level of political legitimacy since it calls for ratification by all Member State parliaments. It is also important to understand that I am not claiming that in this period jurisdictional expansion was *quantitatively* impressive. This would be strange in a Community that was decisionally stagnant. In fact, there were many areas of explicit Community competence, such as transport regulation, where nothing was done. The interesting tale concerns the variety of new fields into which the Community moved, each on its own of relatively little importance. In fact, it could be argued that these activities emerged as a distraction, given the Community's inability to deal with its truly pressing problems. But the cumulative effect of all these activities was significant.

of mutations in the foundational period conditioned those that followed
in the 1970s. I additionally argue that the consequences and significance
of the then-unnoticed mutations in the 1970s are becoming acutely transparent today in the final phase of Community evolution. Together with
the early mutations, the mutations of the 1970s define the very significance of the Community's evolution.

## A typology of jurisdiction in the European Community

In mapping the original understanding of the distribution of competences
of the Community and Member States in schematic terms, the following
picture emerges.

1. there are areas of activity over which the Community has no
   jurisdiction;
2. there are areas of activity that are autonomous to the Community
   (therefore beyond the reach of the Member States' jurisdiction as
   such); and
3. there are large areas of activity where Community and Member State
   competences overlap.

A very strict concept of enumeration would suggest that this jurisdictional
demarcation, whatever its precise content, could and should change only in
accordance with the provisions for Treaty amendment. Jurisdictional mutation in the concept of enumeration would occur where there is evidence of
substantial change in this map without resort to Treaty amendment.

In fact, during the period in question, mutation thus defined occurred.
Moreover, it was not occasional or limited, but happened in a multiplicity of forms, the combination of which leads to my claim of erosion
of constitutional guarantees of enumeration. The picture may best be
grasped by thinking of mutation as occurring in four distinct categories
or proto-types.

## The categories of mutation

### Extension

Extension is mutation[83] in the area of autonomous Community jurisdiction. The most striking example of this change is the well-known evolution

---

[83] It is important that we do not use the term "mutation" loosely. As a "Framework
Document," the Treaty itself often calls for, or allows, change without Treaty amendment.

of a higher law of human rights in the Community. As already mentioned, the Treaty contains elaborate provisions for review of Community measures by the European Court.[84] It does not include a "Bill of Rights" against which to measure Community acts, nor does it mention, as such, human rights as a grounds for review. Yet, as mentioned earlier, in a process starting in 1969 but consolidated in the 1970s,[85] the Court constructed a formidable[86] apparatus for such review. Despite legal and policy rationales, such a development could not have occurred had the Court taken a strict view of permissible change in the allocation of competences and jurisdiction. Had the Court taken such a view, such a dramatic change could have taken place only by Treaty amendment.

An equally striking example from an area of autonomous Community jurisdiction concerns the standing of the European Parliament. The plain and simple language of the Treaty would seem to preclude both action against and by the European Parliament.[87] Yet the Court, in an expansive, systemic (and, in my view, wholly justified[88]) interpretation of the Treaty, first allowed Parliament to be sued[89] and then, after some hesitation,[90] granted Parliament standing to sue other Community institutions.[91]

The category of extension requires four ancillary comments. First, it must be emphasized that the analysis of extension (and indeed the other categories of mutation) is intended, for the time being, to be value-neutral. I do not present these examples as a critique of the Court "running wild"

---

I want to reserve the term "mutation" to those instances where the change is fundamental. Obviously, as shall be seen, when mutation does occur it is always justified by some reference to the Treaty and its "implicit" principles. It is important to understand that I do not make a normative or interpretative argument for some construction of a "legal" basis in the Treaty. The strict legal evaluation is of little interest in my view. My point is that the relevant interpretative communities, by choosing to opt for the wide and flexible reading of the Treaty, have transformed strict enumeration into a very flexible notion, practically emptied of material content in the Community.

[84] See pp. 26–9 above.
[85] For a comprehensive description and analysis of human-rights jurisprudence in the Community, see Clapham, "European Union – The Human Rights Challenge," in A. Clapham (ed.), *Human Rights and the European Community: A Critical Overview* (Nomos: Baden-Baden, 1991), vol. I.
[86] For a critique, see *ibid.*; and Weiler, "The External Legal Relations of Non-Unitary Actors."
[87] See EEC Treaty, Art. 173.
[88] Weiler, "Pride and Prejudice – Parliament v. Council," *European Law Review* 14 (1989), 334.
[89] *Parti Ecologiste "Les Vertes" v. European Parliament* [1986] ECR 1,339.
[90] Case 302/87, *Comitology* [1988] ECR 5615.
[91] Case 70/88, *Parliament v. Council* [1990] ECR 2,041.

or exceeding its own legitimate interpretative jurisdiction. Evaluating these developments, to which I shall return later, involves considerations far wider and weightier than the often arid discussion of judicial propriety. What is important, if there is any force in my argument, is the recasting of known judicial developments, usually analyzed in other legal contexts,[92] as data in the analysis of jurisdictional mutation.

Second, in the case of extension, the principal actor instigating extension was the Court itself, although, of course, at the behest of some plaintiff. Other actors played a more passive role. The action of the Court must be viewed simultaneously as reflective of a flexible, functional approach to enumeration and constitutive of such an ethos in the Community.

Third, this jurisdictional mutation, despite the radical nature of the measures themselves, was rather limited, since it was confined to changes within the autonomous sphere of the Community and did not have a direct impact on the jurisdiction of the Member States. Indeed, the human-rights jurisprudence actually curtailed the freedom of action of the Community.[93] The changes of standing concerning the Parliament were similar in potentially chilling the legislative power of Commission and Council, although in a more muted form.

Finally, and perhaps not altogether surprisingly, these developments and others like them were, with limited exceptions, both welcomed and accepted by the different interpretative communities in Europe, partly because they were seen as pertaining to the other legal categories and partly because they did not encroach directly on the Member State jurisdiction. In any event, these developments were hardly perceived as pertaining to the question of jurisdictional demarcation.

### Absorption

Absorption is a far deeper form of mutation. It occurs, often unintentionally, when the Community legislative authorities, in exercising substantive legislative powers bestowed on the Community, impinge on areas of Member State jurisdiction outside the Community's explicit competences.

---

[92] Thus the human-rights jurisprudence has been discussed essentially as part of a debate on judicial review and not seen as an issue of enumerated powers. Likewise, the issue of parliamentary standing has been seen as an issue of procedure and institutional balance but, again, not as one of enumeration ethos.

[93] Indirectly, of course, this curtails the freedom of the Member States acting *qua* Council of the Community.

One of many striking illustrations[94] is offered by the events in the *Casagrande* case.[95] Donato Casagrande, an Italian national, son of Italian migrant workers, lived all his life in Munich. In 1971 and 1972 he was a pupil at the German Fridtjof-Nansen-Realschule. The Bavarian law on educational grants (BayAföG) entitles children who satisfy a means test to receive a monthly educational grant from the Länder. The city of Munich refused his application for a grant relying on Article 3 of the same educational law, which excluded from entitlement all non-Germans except stateless people and aliens residing under a right of asylum.

Casagrande, in an action seeking a declaration of nullity of the educational law, relied principally on Article 12 of Council Regulation 1612/68.[96] The article provides that the children of a national of a Member State who is or has been employed in the territory of another Member State shall be admitted to that State's general educational, apprenticeship, and vocational training courses under the same conditions as the nationals of that State, if such children are residing in its territory." Further, the Member States must encourage "all efforts to enable such children to attend these courses under the best possible conditions." [97]

The Bayerisches Verwaltungsgericht, in an exemplary understanding of the role of review of the European Court, sought a preliminary ruling on the compatibility of the Bavarian educational provision with Article 12 of the Council Regulation.

The submission of the Bavarian public prosecutor's office (Staatsanwaltschaft), which intervened in the case, illustrated the issue of powers and mutation well. It was submitted that the Council exceeded its powers under Articles 48 and 49 of the EC Treaty.[98] These Articles concern the conditions of workers. "Since individual educational grants come under the sphere of educational policy [in respect of which the Council has no jurisdiction] ... it is to be inferred that the worker can claim the benefit of assimilation with nationals [as provided in Article 12] only as regards social benefits which have a direct relation with the conditions of work itself and with the family stay." [99]

---

[94] See, e.g., Joined Cases 6 and 11/69, *EEC Commission v. France* [1969] ECR 523 and the discussion thereof in Lenaerts, "Constitutionalism."

[95] Case 9/74, *Casagrande v. Landeshauptstadt Mu•nchen* [1974] ECR 773 (hereinafter "*Casagrande*").

[96] 1968 OJ (L 257), 2.

[97] *Ibid.* at Art. 12.

[98] *Casagrande* [1974] ECR 773 at 776.

[99] *Ibid.*

Under this view, Article 12 of the Regulation must be read as entitling children of migrants to be admitted to schools under the same conditions as children of citizens, but not to receive educational grants. If we give the Bavarian public prosecutor's assertion its strongest reading, he denied the very possibility of a conflict between Article 12 and the Bavarian BayAföG, since Article 12 simply could not apply to educational grants. Under a weaker interpretation, he was pleading for a narrow interpretation of the Article 12 provision because of the jurisdictional issue. Underlying this submission was the deeper ground that if education is outside the Community competence, then the Regulation itself transgressed the demarcation line. In any event, the interpretation sought by Casagrande could not stand.

How then did the Court deal with the question? One can detect two phases in the process of judicial consideration. The first phase consisted of an interpretation of the specific Community provision in an effort to understand its full scope. While engaging in this phase the Court acted as if it were in an empty jurisdictional space with no limitations on the reach of Community law. Not surprisingly, the Court's rendering of Regulation 12 led it to the conclusion that the article did cover the distribution of grants.[100]

In the second phase of analysis the Court addressed the jurisdictional mutation problem.[101] We must remember that the primary ground for the illegality of a measure, the infringement of the Treaty, certainly includes jurisdictional competence.[102] The Court first acknowledged that "educational and training policy is not *as such* included in the spheres that the Treaty had entrusted to the Community institutions."[103] The allusion to the Community institutions is important: the case after all deals with an issue of "secondary legislation" enacted by the political organs. But, in the key, although oblique, phrase the Court continued, "it does not follow that the exercise of powers transferred to the Community," enlarging thus the language from Community institutions to the Community as a whole and hence from secondary legislation to the entire Treaty, "*is in some way limited if it is of such a nature as to affect ... [national] measures taken in the execution of a policy such as that of education and training.*"[104] Now we understand the importance of the two-phased judicial analysis.

---

[100]  *Ibid.* at judgment recitals 8 and 9.
[101]  *Ibid.* at judgment recitals 10–15.
[102]  See EEC Treaty, Art. 173.
[103]  *Casagrande*, at judgment recital 12 (emphasis added).
[104]  *Ibid.* (emphasis added).

In phase one the Court explained the meaning of a Community measure. The interpretation may be teleological but not to the same extent as the Court's performance in the evolution of the higher law of human rights. Absorption is in this way distinguishable from extension. In the second phase, the Court stated that, to the extent that national measures, even in areas over which the Community has no competence, conflict with the Community rule, these national measures will be absorbed and subsumed by the Community measure. The Court said that it was not the Community policy that was encroaching on national educational policy; rather, it was the national educational policy that was impinging on Community free-movement policy and thus must give way.

The category of absorption also calls for some interim commentary. First, in this higher form of mutation at least two interpretative communities are playing a role in the erosion of strict enumeration: principally the legislative interpretative community, comprising in this case the Commission, Parliament, and the Council (with a decisive role for the governments of the Member States), and the judicial one.[105] This is important in relation to the question of the acceptance of the overall mutation of jurisdictional limits. As a simple examination of extension might have indicated, it cannot be seen as a judicially led development, although legal sanctioning by the Court plays an important role in encouraging this type of legislation in future cases.

Second, the limits of absorption are important. Although absorption extends the effect of Community legislation outside the Community jurisdiction, it, critically, does not give the Community original legislative jurisdiction (in, for example, the field of education). The Community could not, in light of *Casagrande*, directly promulgate its own fully fledged educational policy.

This distinction should not diminish the fundamental importance of absorption and its inclusion as an important form of mutation. This can be gauged by trying to imagine the consequences of a judicial policy that would deny this possibility of absorption. The scope of effective execution of policy over which the Community had direct jurisdiction would, in a society in which it is impossible to draw neat demarcation lines between areas of social and economic policy, be significantly curtailed. But at the same time there is a clear sacrifice and erosion of the principle

---

[105] The case highlights the fiction of assimilating government with Member State. Bavaria is as much a part of the Federal Republic of Germany as the central German government.

of enumeration. And, of course, the absorption doctrine invokes a clear preference for Community competence over Member State competence. In a sense the language of the Court suggests a simple application of the principle of supremacy. But this is not a classical case of supremacy. After all, in relation to issues of jurisdiction, supremacy may only mean that each level of government is supreme in the fields assigned to it. Here we have a case of conflicts of competences. The Court is suggesting that in such conflicts Community competence must prevail. This is the doctrinal crux of absorption.

## Incorporation

The term "incorporation" [106] is borrowed from the constitutional history of the United States and denotes the process by which the federal Bill of Rights, initially perceived as applying to measures of the federal government alone, was extended to state action through the agency of the Fourteenth Amendment. The possibility of incorporation within the Community system appears at first sight improbable. We noted already the absence of a Community "Bill of Rights." Community incorporation would entail not one but two acts of high judicial activism. First, the creation of judge-made higher law for the Community, and then its application to acts of the Member States.

Looking at this issue not through the prism of human-rights discourse, but as a problem of jurisdictional allocation, suggests that incorporation may not, after all, be so inconceivable. In the field of human rights, incorporation invokes no more than a combination of extension and absorption. The frequency and regularity by which these two other forms of Community mutation are exercised suggest that incorporation is a distinct possibility.

The interplay of the actors in pushing for this form of mutation is interesting. In an early case, the Court, of its own motion, seemed to open the door to this development. In subsequent cases, the Commission pushed hard for such an outcome, but the Court's responses have been mixed. In some cases it seemed to be nodding in this direction, while in other cases it firmly rejected the possibility.[107]

---

[106] I dealt with this issue extensively in Weiler, "The European Court at a Cross Roads: Community Human Rights and Member State Action," in F. Capotorti (ed.), *Du droit international au droit de l'intégration* (Nomos: Baden-Baden, 1987), 821 and present here merely the bare bones of the argument.

[107] For cases and analysis, see Weiler, "The European Court at a Cross Roads."

I cannot therefore present incorporation as a *fait accompli* in the evolving picture of mutation of jurisdictional limits. But the concept, even in its current embryonic Community form, is important for two reasons. First, it shows again the internal interplay of the various actors in pushing the frontiers of Community jurisdiction. At times it is the Court; at other times the legislative organs in conjunction with the Court; at other times still the Commission trying, as in the *Cinéthèque* case, to enlist the Court's support (in this case rather unsuccessfully[108]). Second, it shows the dynamics of the enumeration. That incorporation could be tried, more than once – at first causing a split between the opinions of the Court and its Advocate-General, which later developed into a somewhat bifurcated jurisprudence[109] – is only conceivable in a legal-political environment which has already moved, through the agencies of extension and incorporation, far away from a strict concept of enumeration.

## Expansion and its causes

Expansion is the most radical form of jurisdictional mutation. Whereas absorption concerned Community legislation in a field in which the Community had clear original jurisdiction, and describes a mutation occurring when the effects of such legislation spill over into fields reserved to the Member States, expansion refers to the case in which the original legislation of the Community "breaks" jurisdictional limits.

I have already alluded to the expansive approach to implied powers adopted by the Court as part of the constitutionalization process in the foundational period. If expansively applied, the implied-powers doctrine may have the *de facto* consequence of permitting the Community to legislate and act in a manner not derived from clear grants of power in the Treaty itself. This would not constitute veritable expansion. The implied-powers doctrine is not veritable expansion because typically the powers implied are in an area in which the Community clearly is already permitted to act, and the powers to act would be construed precisely as "instruments" enabling effective action in a permissible field. Thus, in the leading case of implied powers,[110] there was no question that the Community could act in the field of transport policy; what the Court did was to enable it, within this field, to conclude international agreements.

---

[108] See Cases 60 and 61/84, *Cinéthèque SA v. Federation National des Cinémas Français* [1985] ECR 2,605.

[109] For discussion, see Weiler, "The European Court at a Cross Roads" at 824–30.

[110] See *ERTA* at 273, 290.

Even though the implied-powers doctrine cannot be construed strictly as true expansion as defined above, it is important in this context. First, the way a court approaches the question of implied powers is in itself an indirect reflection of its attitude toward enumeration. Even if implying powers as such does not constitute a mutation, a court taking a restrictive approach to enumeration will tend to be cautious in implying powers, whereas a court taking a functional, flexible approach to enumeration will be bolder in its implied-powers jurisprudence. It is interesting that the European Court itself has changed its attitude toward implied powers and, by implication, toward enumeration. In its very early jurisprudence, it took a cautious and reserved approach to implied powers; it was really only in a second phase that it changed direction on this issue as part of the process of constitutionalization.[111]

Second, even though, strictly speaking, the implied-powers doctrine is intended to give the Community an instrument in a field within which it already has competence, these distinctions often break down in reality. When the Court in the 1970s considered and construed the powers that flowed from the common commercial policy, it did, even on a very conservative reading, extend the jurisdictional limits of the Community.[112]

It is, however, in the context of Article 235 of the Treaty that we find the *locus* of true expansion. Article 235 is the "elastic clause" of the Community – its necessary and proper provision. Article 235 provides that:

> if action by the Community should prove necessary to attain, in the course of the operation of the common market, one of the objectives of the Community and this Treaty has not provided the necessary powers, the Council shall, acting unanimously on a proposal from the Commission and after consulting the European Parliament, take the appropriate measures.

---

[111] Compare *Algera* (denying the right to set aside administrative measures) with *ERTA* (establishing the right to enter into agreements with third countries).

[112] See, e.g., Opinion 1/78, Opinion given pursuant to the second subparagraph of Art. 238(1) of the EEC Treaty [1979] ECR 2,871; [1979] 3 CMLR 639 ("*Rubber*"). The Council (and France and the UK as interveners) claimed that the conclusion of the Rubber Agreement, as an instrument of co-operation and development which also impinges on broader strategic concerns of the Member States, was outside the scope and competence of the Community's Common Commercial Policy. The Court gave an extensive reading to the limits of the exclusive (!) Common Commercial Policy and held that: "it is clear that a coherent commercial policy would no longer be practicable if the Community were not in a position to exercise its powers also in connexion with a category of agreements which are becoming, alongside traditional commercial agreements, one of the major factors in the regulation of international trade": *ibid.* at 2,912, recital 43.

On its face, this is no more than a codified version of an implied-powers doctrine; clearly, Article 235 should not be used to expand the jurisdiction of the Community (which derives from its objectives and functional definition as explicitly and implicitly found elsewhere in the Treaty) by adding new objectives or amending existing ones. Since, however, the language of the article is textually ambiguous, and concepts such as "objectives" are by their nature open-textured, there has been a perennial question how far beyond the literal Treaty definition of the Community's spheres of activities and powers the use of Article 235 will permit without actually amending the Treaty.

The history of Article 235 in legislative practice, judicial consideration, and doctrine includes several changes which reflect the changes in the development of the Community itself. In the period from 1958 to 1973, Article 235 was used by Community institutions relatively infrequently[113] and, when used, was usually narrowly construed. Under the restrictive view, shared by all interpretative communities at the time,[114] the function of Article 235 was to compensate *within an area of activity explicitly granted by the Treaty* for the absence of an explicit grant of legal power to act. Two examples demonstrate the early conception of the article. One was the enactment on the basis of Article 235, in 1968, of Regulation 803/68 on customs valuation, setting out the criteria by which the value of imported goods to the Community for the purpose of imposing customs duties would be calculated. Implicit in this recourse to Article 235 was the belief that:

1. customs valuation was necessary to attain the objectives of the Treaty; but
2. since the reach of the Community spheres of activity had to be narrowly construed, one could not use the common commercial policy or Article 28 as a legal basis, as these did not explicitly cover customs valuation.

A second example is the use of Article 235 as a legal basis for extending the list of food products in Annex II to the Treaty.[115] Here it was clear that

---

[113] For quantitative analysis, see Weiler, *Il sistema comunitario europeo* at 195.

[114] E.g., Usher, "The Gradual Widening of European Community Policy on the Basis of Article 100 and 235 of the EEC Treaty, "in J. Schwarze and H. G. Schermers (eds.), *Structure and Dimensions of European Community Policy* (Nomos: Baden-Baden, 1988), 30 ("Article 235 was obviously intended as an exceptional measure").

[115] Art. 38(3) of the EEC Treaty provides, *inter alia*, that "products subject to [the Common Agricultural Policy of the EEC] are listed in Annex II to this Treaty." It also explicitly

the sphere of activities did cover the measure in question, but that there was no specific grant of power in relation to new products. Recourse to Article 235 seemed necessary. The explanation for this restrictive quantitative and qualitative usage is simple. Quantitatively, in that phase of establishing the basic structures of the Community system, the Treaty was relatively explicit in defining the legislative agenda and granting legal powers. The initial legislative program simply did not call for frequent recourse to Article 235. Qualitatively, that period, especially since the middle of the 1960s, was characterized by a distinct decline in the "political will" of at least some of the Member States to promote expansion of Community activity.

Following the Paris Summit of 1972, where the Member States explicitly decided to make full use of Article 235 and to launch the Community into a variety of new fields, recourse to Article 235 as an exclusive or partial legal basis rose dramatically. Therefore from 1973 until the entry into force of the Single European Act (the SEA), there was not only a very dramatic quantitative increase in the recourse to Article 235, but also a no less dramatic understanding of its qualitative scope. In a variety of fields, including, for example, conclusion of international agreements, the granting of emergency food aid to third countries, and creation of new institutions,[116] the Community made use of Article 235 in a manner that was simply not consistent with the narrow interpretation of the article as a codification of the implied-powers doctrine in its instrumental sense. Only a truly radical and "creative" reading of the article could explain and justify its usage as, for example, the legal basis for granting emergency food aid to non-associated states.[117] But this wide reading, in which

---

foresees that this list should be enlarged by adding new products. And yet despite this explicit invitation the political organs did not believe that they had the power to amend the list without recourse to Art. 235.

[116] For fuller accounts of the wide use and wide construction, see, e.g., Usher, "The Gradual Widening" at 114; H. Smit and P. Herzog, Law of the European Community (Bender: New York, 1991), vol. VI, 269.

[117] The Community Framework Regulations on food-aid policy and food-aid management were initially based jointly on Art. 43 (Common Agricultural Policy) and Art. 235 of the EEC Treaty. See Council Food Aid First Framework Regulation No. 3,391/82, 1982 OJ (L 352), 1; Council Food Aid Second Framework Regulation No. 3,972/86, 1986 OJ (L 370), 1, as amended by Regulation No. 1930/90, 1990 OJ (L 174), 6, is based exclusively on Art. 235. Before the adoption of Framework Regulations, there were a few decisions on emergency operations which were based exclusively on Art. 235. See, e.g., Council Regulation No. 1,010/80, 1980 OJ (L 108), 1; Council Regulation No. 3,827/81, 1981 OJ (L 392), 1 (both concerning the supply of sugar to UNRWA as food aid for refugees); Council

all political institutions partook,[118] meant that it would become virtually impossible to find an activity which could not be brought within the "objectives of the Treaty." [119] This constituted the climax of the process of mutation and is the basis for my claim not merely that no core activity of state function could be seen any longer as still constitutionally immune from Community action (which really goes to the issue of absorption), but also that no sphere of the material competence could be excluded from the Community acting under Article 235. It is not simply that the jurisdictional limits of the Community expanded in their content more sharply in the 1970s than they did as a result of, for example, the Single European Act. The fundamental systemic mutation of the 1970s, culminating in the process of expansion, was that any sort of constitutional limitation of this expansion seemed to have evaporated.

It is important to emphasize again that, for this inquiry, the crucial question is not the *per se* legality of the wide interpretation of Article 235.[120] In the face of a common understanding by all principal interpretative communities, that question has little if any significance and perhaps

---

Regulation No. 3,723/81, 1981 OJ (L 373), 11 (concerning the supply of exceptional food aid to the least developed countries). So long as the food aid is a mechanism for the disposal of Common Agricultural Policy (CAP) surpluses there is no question of legal basis and competence based on Art. 43 of the EEC Treaty. The inclusion of Art. 235 would cover the incidence of food aid that is not so tied to CAP objectives and mechanisms. The current exclusive reliance on Art. 235 is deliberate in order to disconnect food aid from the CAP and to emphasize that it is not an instrument of the CAP. Laudable as the granting of food aid is, it is difficult to see how the functioning of the common market, a condition for the recourse to Art. 235, is served by granting humanitarian food aid to non-associated countries. But see Marenco, "Les conditions d'application de l'Article 235 du Traité CEE," *Revue du marché commun* 12 (1970), 147.

118  Parliament has pushed for the usage of Art. 235 as well, since, *inter alia*, it is one of the provisions under which consultation with Parliament is obligatory.

119  Elsewhere I have argued, tongue in cheek, that, on this reading defense would also be a permissible usage of Art. 235, since the common market could hardly function with the territories of the Member States under occupation: Weiler, *Il sistema comunitario europeo* at 188. For broad interpretation of the "objectives" of the Community, see Case 242/87, *Commission v. Council* [1989] ECR 1,425 (hereinafter "*Erasmus*").

120  The Court tacitly sanctioned this wide usage. Broadly speaking, two principal conditions must be fulfilled to invoke Art. 235. The measure must be "necessary," in the course of the operation of the common market, to attain one of the objectives of the Treaty. In addition, Art. 235 may be used when the Treaty does not provide the "necessary" powers. The Court addressed both conditions liberally in the leading case of the early period, Case 8/73, *Hauptzollamt Bremerhaven v. Massey Ferguson GmbH* [1973] ECR 897 (hereinafter "*Massey Ferguson*"). Regarding the second, the Court was explicit. In an action for annulment of the regulation adopting the above-mentioned Community customs-valuation regime, the Court had to decide whether reliance on Art. 235 as an exclusive basis was

no meaning.[121] Far more intriguing and far more revealing is to explore the explanation for and the significance of the phenomenon. One should not, after all, underestimate its enormity in comparison to other non-unitary (federal) systems. Not only did the Community see in this second phase of its systemic evolution a jurisdictional movement as profound

justified. While acknowledging that a proper interpretation of the alternative legal bases in the EEC Treaty (Arts. 9, 27, 28, 111, and 113) would provide an adequate legal basis, and thus, under a strict construction, render Art. 235 not "necessary," the Court, departing from an earlier statement, none the less considered that the Council's use of Art. 235 would be "justified in the interest of legal certainty": *Massey Ferguson* [1973] ECR 897 at 908. Legally, this might have been an unfortunate formulation since an aura of uncertainty almost *ipso facto* attaches to a decision to make recourse to Art. 235. Politically, it may have been wise, for a more rigid interpretation could have thwarted the desire of the Member States, consonant with the Treaty objectives, to expand greatly the areas of activity of the Community, even if by the dubious use of Art. 235. Practically speaking, recourse to Art. 235 in that period made little difference in the content of measures adopted, because virtually all measures were adopted under the penumbra of *de facto* unanimity. Taking their cue from this case, Community institutions henceforth made liberal use of Art. 235 without exhaustively considering whether other legal bases existed. Regarding the first requirement that the measure be "necessary" to attain one of the objectives of the Treaty, the Court was willing to construe Community legal reach and the notion of objectives very widely, not only in a whole range of cases not directly concerned with Art. 235, but also in *Massey Ferguson* itself. Since Member States had the ability to control the usage of Art. 235, disagreements, often acrimonious, on the proper scope to be given to the first condition were resolved within the Council and not brought before the Court.

[121] The doctrinal writing continues the attempt to ascribe material limitations on the usage of Art. 235 even in the face of this overwhelming practice. *The Encyclopaedia of European Community Law* is a typical example: Art. 235 does not open unlimited opportunity to increase the powers of the Community. In the first place, recourse to "Art. 235 is limited by the objectives of the Treaty." Then comes the retreat: "Extensive interpretation as to the nature of these objectives is, of course, always possible, but the strongest guarantee against abuse is the required unanimity of the Council.": *The Encyclopaedia of European Community Law*, vol. B:2 at B10/70/19, General Note to Article 235 (Release 40:23-ix-86). The learned commentator implicitly admits the futility of the task and then, abandoning an analytical attempt to circumscribe the article in normative terms, resorts to an institutional guarantee, as if the Council could not itself, even if acting unanimously, abuse Art. 235. Where writers try to insist on material limits, they end up flying in the face of the legislative practice. See, e.g., "Les guillons, extension des competence de la CEE par l'Article 235 du Traité de Rome," *Annuaire Fran,cais de droit internationale* (1974), 996; Lachmann, "Some Danish Reflections on the Use of Article 235 of the Rome Treaty," *Common Market Law Review* 18 (1981), 447. For other more or less successful attempts, see Giardina, "The Rule of Law and Implied Powers in the European Communities," *Italian Yearbook* 1 (1975), 99; Marenco, "Les conditions d'application"; Olmi, "La place de l'Article 235 CEE dans le système des attribution de competence de la Communauté," in *Melanges Fernand Dehousse* (Nathan: Paris; Labor: Brussels, 1979), 279; Waelbroeck, "Article 235," in J. Megret, J.-V. Louis, D. Vignes, and M. Waelbroeck (eds.), *Le droit de la Communauté economique européenne* 15 (Presses Universitaires: Brussels, 1987), 521, 530.

as any that has occurred in federal states, but even more remarkable, indeed something of a double riddle, this mutation did not, on the whole, ignite major "federal" political disputes between the actors (for example, between the Member States and the Community).

No one factor can explain a process so fundamental in the architecture of the Community. I suggest the following as some of the more important factors of this change.

**Incrementalism**    Part of the explanation to the riddles can be found already in the very description I offered of the process of jurisdictional mutation. There is no single event, no landmark case, that could be called the focal point of the mutation. Even some of the important cases I mentioned, such as those in the field of human rights, were not seen through the prism of jurisdictional mutation. Instead, there was a slow change of climate and ethos whereby strict enumeration was progressively, relentlessly, but never dramatically, eroded. Extension, absorption, incorporation, and powers implied by the Court, all feed on each other in cog-and-wheel fashion so that no dissonances are revealed within the constitutional architecture itself as it is changing. When the Court is very activist in an area, in extension, for example, it is so toward the Community as such and not the more sensitive Member States.[122] By contrast, in the cases of absorption and expansion, areas where the mutative effect impinges on Member State jurisdiction, the role of the Court is in a kind of "active passivism," reacting to impulses coming from the political organs and opting for the flexible rather than strict notion of enumeration. In its entire history there is not one case, to my knowledge, where the Court struck down a Council or Commission measure on grounds of Community *lack of competence*.[123] The relationship between the Court

---

[122]  The exception to this institutional "coziness" is the case law concerning the "exclusive" competence of the Community. See Weiler, "The External Legal Relations" at 71–2.

[123]  There have been many cases of annulment of Council and Commission measures, but not on grounds that the Community exceeded its competences. In Joined Cases 281, 283 to 285, and 287/85, FRG v. *Commission of the European Communities* [1987] ECR 3,203 (concerning the immigration of non-Community workers), the Court annulled a Commission decision as going beyond the scope of the Commission's powers under Art. 118. The parties invited the Court to consider the social sector as being the preserve of the Member States, "from which it follows that, like all the other fundamental choices made in the Treaty, that choice may only be amended by use of the procedure provided for in Article 236": *ibid.* at 3,232. The Court, however, pointedly refrained from endorsing that proposition, gave a wide reading to the scope of action of the Community in the social field, and annulled the decision on the grounds that the Commission exceeded its powers,

and the political organs was a bit like the offense in American football.[124] The Court acted as the "pass protectors" from any constitutional challenge; the political organs and the Member States made the winning pass.

Nevertheless, incrementalism alone cannot explain a change so radical and a reaction so muted. Politically, the Community architecture at the end of the foundational period was unlike any other federal polity. Therein lies one emphatically important aspect of this development. Even if the judicial signals indicated that strict enumeration would not be enforced by the Court, these could, after all, have remained without a response by the political organs and the Member States.

Two factors, one historical and one structural, combine to explain the aggressiveness with which the political process rushed through the opening judicial door. Both factors are rooted in the heritage of the foundational period.

**A strategy of revival** In a determined effort commencing in 1969,[125] the end of the de Gaulle era, and culminating in the successful negotiation of the UK, Danish, and Irish accessions in 1973, the Community sought ways to revitalize itself, to shake off the hangovers of the Luxembourg Crisis, to

---

not that the Community had no competence in the field. In recitals 23 and 24 of the judgment the Court said: "[M]igration policy is capable of falling within the social field within the meaning of Article 118 only to the extent to which it concerns the situation of workers from non-member countries as regards their impact on the Community employment market and working condition. As a result, in so far as Decision 85/ 381/EEC includes the promotion of cultural integration as a whole among the subjects for consultation, it goes beyond the social field in which, under Article 118, the Commission has the task of promoting co-operation between Member States." This judgment has been read as a decision implicitly excluding cultural integration from Community competence: Bradley, "The European Court and the Legal Basis of Community Legislation," *European Law Review* 13 (1988), 379, 384. I disagree with this reading. The Court specifically mentions that it is interpreting the meaning of the social field within the meaning of Art. 118, which is special in that it gives certain powers to the Commission. In the light of the broad reading given by the Court to the scope of Community objectives in the context of Art. 235 in a case such as *Erasmus* (where the Court construed the objectives of the Community to include the enhancement of the quality of teaching and information furnished by Community universities with a view to ensuring the competitiveness of the Community in world markets and also "the general objective" of creating a citizens' Europe) I submit that, had the same decision been made by the *Council* rather than the Commission on the legal basis of Arts. 118 *and* 235, the Court would have held it to be within *Community* competences.

[124] Of which, despite five years in the Midwest, I am still happily ignorant of most nuances.

[125] Prompted by and reflected in the "Report of the Working Party Examining the Problem of the Enlargement of the Powers of the European Parliament," *Bulletin of the European Communities* (Supp. 4/72), 1 (the "Vedel Report").

extricate itself from the traumas of the double UK rejection, and to launch itself afresh. The Paris Summit of 1972, in which the new Member States participated, introduced an ambitious program of substantive expansion of Community jurisdiction and a revival of the dream of European union. Article 235 was to play a key role in this revival. In retrospect this attempt was a failure, since the Community was unable to act in concert on the issues that really mattered during the 1970s, such as developing a veritable industrial policy or even tackling with sufficient vigor Member State obstacles to the creation of the common market. The momentum was directed to a range of ancillary issues, such as environmental policy, consumer protection, energy, and research, all important of course, but a side game at the time. Yet, although these were not taken very seriously in substance (and maybe because of that), each required extensive and expansive usage of Article 235 and represented part of the brick-by-brick demolition of the wall circumscribing Community competences.

**Structuralism: the abiding relevance of Exit and Voice**    But the structural, rather than historical, explanation of the process of expansion and its riddles is the critical one. The process of decline in the decisional supranational features of the Community during the foundational period, demonstrated by the enhanced Voice of the Member States in the Community policy-making and legislative processes, was the key factor giving the Member States the confidence to engage in such massive jurisdictional mutation and to accept it with relative equanimity.

In federal states, such a mutation would by necessity be *at the expense* of Member State government power. In the post-foundational period Community, in contrast, by virtue of the near total control of the Member States over the Community process, the community appeared more as an instrument in the hands of the governments rather than as a usurping power. The Member State governments, jointly and severally, were confident that their interests were served by any mutative move.[126] If the governments of the Member States could control each legislative act, from inception through adoption and then implementation, why would they fear a system in which constitutional guarantees of jurisdictional change were weakened? Indeed, they had some incentive, in transferring competences to the Community, to escape the strictures, or nuisance,

---

[126] To be sure, Art. 235 provides for unanimity: Member State confidence was boosted because of the knowledge that also in the implementation of any measure their interests would be guaranteed.

of parliamentary accountability. In federal states, the classical dramas of federalism in the early formative periods presuppose two power centers: the central and the constituent parts. In the Community, in its post-foundational period architecture, the constituent units power *was* the central power.

As we see in several cases from that period, it was hardly feasible politically, although it was permissible legally, for a Member State to approve an "expansive" Community measure and to challenge its constitutionality as *ultra vires*.[127] It is easy also to understand why the Commission (and Parliament) played the game. The Commission welcomed the desire to reinvigorate the Community and to expand its (and the Commission's own) fields of activity. Since most Community decision-making at that time was undertaken in the shadow of the veto consecrated by the dubiously legal Luxembourg Accord, the Commission found no disadvan- tage, and in fact many advantages, in using Article 235. Neither the Commission nor Parliament, which was to be consulted under the Article 235 procedure, were likely to challenge judicially the usage. Moreover, since Article 235 enabled the adoption of "measures," whether regulations, directives, or decisions, it provided a flexibility not always available when using other legal bases.

### Evaluating the mutation of jurisdictional limits and the erosion of strict enumeration in the 1970s

The process of mutation is evidence of the dynamic character of the Community and its ability to adapt itself in the face of new challenges. It is also evidence that what were perceived as negative and debilitating political events in the 1960s had unexpected pay-offs. I do not believe that the Community would have developed such a relaxed and functional approach to mutation had the political process not placed so much power in the hands of the Member States. Yet even then at least two long-term problems were taking root.

---

[127] A Member State may challenge an act even if it voted in favor of it: Case 166/78, *Government of the Italian Republic* v. *Council of the European Communities* [1979] ECR 2,575, 2,596. But it will normally not choose to challenge on the grounds of lack of competence. In Case 91/79, *Commission* v. *Italy* [1980] ECR 1,099, Italy was sued by the Commission for its failure to implement an environmental-protection directive the *vires* of which (pre-SEA) could have been challenged in defense; Italy explicitly elected not to do so.

### The question of constitutionality

I have argued that the *de facto* usage of Article 235, from 1973 until the Single European Act, implied a construction, shared by all principal interpretive communities, that opened up practically any realm of state activity to the Community, provided the governments of the Member States found accord among themselves. This raised two potential problems of a constitutional nature.

From the internal, autonomous legal perspective, it is clear that Article 235 could not be construed simply as a procedural device for unchecked jurisdictional expansion. Such a construction would empty Article 236 (Treaty revision) of much of its meaning and would be contrary to the very structure of Article 235. Legal doctrine was quick to find autonomous internal constructions which would not empty the article of meaning, but which would emphasize its virtually limitless substantive scope. Thus it has been suggested that Article 235 cannot be used in a way that would actually violate the Treaty.[128] Few writers (or actors) sought to check the expansive use of the article.[129] The general view had been (and in many quarters remains) that the requirement of unanimity does effectively give the necessary guarantees to the Member States. If there has been a debate over the article's meaning, it concerns the analytical construction of the article. The Community is no different from any other legal polity. Language, especially such contorted language as found in Article 235, has never been a serious constraint on a determined political power.

The constitutional problem with an expansive interpretation of Article 235, and in general with the entire erosion of strict enumeration, does not thus rest in the realm of autonomous positivist legalisms.

The constitutional danger is of a different nature. As we saw, results of the constitutional "revolution" of the Community in the 1960s and the system of judicial remedies upon which they rest depend on creating a relationship of trust, a new community of interpretation, in which the European Court and Member State courts play complementary roles.

The overture of the European Court toward the Member State courts in the original constitutionalizing decisions, such as *van Gend and Loos*, was based on a judicial-constitutional contract idea. Suggesting that the

---

[128] As mentioned earlier, institutional and organic changes would in principle require Treaty amendment, though Usher, "The Gradual Widening" gives examples of institutional changes under Art. 235.

[129] See Lachmann, "Some Danish Reflections" (detailing strong Danish principled opposition to the wide use of Art. 235).

new legal order would operate "in limited fields," [130] the European Court was not simply stating a principle of Community law, which, as the maker of that principle, it would later be free to abandon. It was inviting the supreme Member State courts to accept the new legal order with the understanding that it would, indeed, be limited in its fields.

The acceptance by the Member State legal orders was premised, often explicitly, on that understanding. Thus the Italian Constitutional Court, when it finally accepted supremacy, did so "on the basis of a *precise criterion of division of jurisdiction.*" [131]

The danger in this process is now clear. Whereas the principal political actors may have shared a common interest in the jurisdictional mutation, it was, like still water, slowly but deeply boring a creek in the most important foundation of the constitutional order, the understanding between the European Court and its national counterparts about the material limits to Community jurisdiction. The erosion of enumeration meant that the new legal order, and the judicial-legal contract which underwrote it, was to extend to all areas of activity – a change for which the Member State legal orders might not have bargained. With the addition of the SEA, what was an underground creek will become one of the more transparent points of pressure of the system.

There is another, obvious sense in which erosion of enumeration is problematic from a constitutional perspective. The general assumption that unanimity sufficiently guarantees the Member States against abusive expansion is patently erroneous. First, it is built on the false assumption that conflates the government of a state with the state. Constitutional guarantees are designed, in part, to defend against the political wishes of this or that government, which government after all, in a democratic society, is contingent in time and often of limited representativeness. Additionally, even where there is wall-to-wall political support, there will not necessarily be a recognition that constitutional guarantees are intended to protect, in part, individuals against majorities, even big ones. It is quite understandable why, for example, political powers might have a stake in expansion. One of the rationales, trite yet no less persuasive, of enumeration and divided powers is to anticipate that stake to prevent concentration of power in one body and at one level. When that body and that level operate in an environment of reduced public accountability (as is the case of the Commission and the

---

[130]  *van Gend and Loos* [1963] ECR 1.
[131]  *Frontini v. Amministrazione Delle Finanze* [1974] CMLR 372, 385 (emphasis added).

Council in the Community environment) the importance of the constitutional guarantee even increases.

### Mutation and the question of the democratic character of the expansion

Treaty amendment by Article 236 satisfies the constitutional requirement all Member States have that calls for assent of national parliaments. The expansive usage of Article 235 evades that type of control. At a very formal level, the jurisdictional mutation of the nature that occurred in the 1970s accentuates the problems of democratic accountability of the Community. This deficit is not made up by the non-binding consultation of the European Parliament in the context of Article 235.

The "democratic" danger of unchecked expansion is not, however, in the formal lack of Member State parliamentary ratification: the structure of European democracies is such that it is idle to think that governments could not ram most expansive measures down willing or unwilling parliamentary throats. After all, in most European parliamentary democracies, governments enjoy a majority in their national parliaments and members of parliaments tend to be fairly compliant in following the policies of the party masters in government. The danger of expansion rests in a more realistic view of European democracies.

The major substantive areas in which expansion took place were social: consumer protection, environmental protection, and education, for example. These are typically areas of diffuse and fragmented interests. Whether we adopt a traditional democratic or a neo-corporatist model,[132] we cannot fail to note that the elaboration of the details of such legislation in the Community context had the effect of squeezing out interest groups representing varying social interests, which had been integrated to one degree or another into national policy-making processes.[133] The Community decision-making process, with its lack of transparency and

---

[132] Parliament is only one of the actors in the outplay of the democratic choices. *Cf.* P. Schmitter, "Democratic Theory and Neo-Corporatist Practice" (European Union Institute Working Papers, No. 83/74).

[133] On the ambivalent position of pressure groups at the EC level, see, e.g., Loosli-Surrans, "Quelle sécurité pour les consommateurs europe ens?"; Micklitz, "Considerations Shaping Future Consumer Participation in European Product Safety Law," in C. Joerges, *Product Liability and Product Safety in the European Community* (European Union Institute Working Papers, No. 89/404). See generally A. Philip, "Pressure Groups in the European Community" (University Association for Contemporary European Studies Occasional Papers, No. 2, 1985).

tendency to channel many issues into "state interests," tends to favor certain groups well placed to play the Community-Member State game and disfavor others, especially those that depend on a parliamentary chamber and the "principle of reelection" to vindicate diffuse and fragmented interests.

Expansion thus did not simply underscore the perennial democracy deficit of the Community, but actually distorted the balance of social and political forces in the decisional game at both the Member State and Community level.

## Conclusion

The principal feature of the period lasting from the middle of the 1970s into the 1980s is that precisely in this period, one of political stagnation and decisional malaise, another important, if less visible, constitutional mutation - the erosion of the limits to Community competences – took place. The full importance of this mutation and some of its inherent dangers and risks come to light only now, in the 1992 epoch. And yet a final word is called for. Unlike the constitutional revolution in the foundational period, which seems irreversible and which constitutes the very foundation of the Community, the mutation of the 1970s can perhaps be checked. I shall return to this theme below.

## 1992 and Beyond

### Introduction

The 1992 program and the Single European Act determine both the current agenda of the Community and its *modus operandi*.[134] Neither

---

[134] See generally J. Deruyt, *L'acte unique européen* (1989); R. Bieber *et al.* (eds.), *1992: One European Market* (Nomos: Baden-Baden, 1988); Berman, "The Single European Act: A New Constitution for the Community?" *Columbia Journal of Transnational Law* 27 (1989), 529; Dehousse, "1992 and Beyond: The Institutional Dimension of the Internal Market Programme," *Legal Issues of European Integration* 1 (1989), 109; Ehlermann, "The Internal Market Following the Single European Act," *Common Market Law Review* 24 (1987), 361; Ehlermann, 1992 Project; Glaesner, "The Single European Act," *Yearbook of European Law* (Clarendon Press: Oxford; Oxford University Press: New York, 1986), vol. VI, 283; Glaesner, "L'Article 100A: Un novel instrument pour la realisation du marché commun," *Cahiers de droit européen* 25 (1989), 615; Moravcsik, "Negotiating the Single European Act: National Interests and Conventional Statecraft in the European Community," *International Organization* 45 (1991), 19.

instrument is on its face functionally radical; the White Paper[135] goal of achieving a single market merely restates, with some nuances, the classical (Treaty of Rome) objective of establishing a common market. The bulk of the 1992 program is little more than a legislative timetable for achieving in seven years what the Community should have accomplished in the preceding thirty. The SEA is even less powerful.[136] Its forays into environmental policy and the like fail to break new jurisdictional ground, and its majority-voting provisions, designed to harmonize non-tariff barriers to trade, seem to utilize such restrictive language, and open such glaring new loopholes,[137] that even some of the most authoritative commentators believed the innovations caused more harm than good in the Community.[138] Clearly, the European Parliament and the Commission were far from thrilled with the new Act.[139]

[135] "Completing the Internal Market" (Milan, June 28–9, 1985) Com (85) 310 (White Paper from the Commission to the European Council). In this White Paper, the Commission outlined its internal-market strategy, later to be called the 1992 program.

[136] "Measured against Parliament's Draft Treaty of European Union and other recent reform proposals, as well as against the stated preferences of the Commission and certain Member States, the Single European Act is not a revolutionary product.": Berman, "The Single European Act" at 586.

[137] See, e.g., SEA, Art. 100A(4) (supplementing the EEC Treaty, Art. 100).

[138] See, e.g., Pescatore, "Some Critical Remarks on the Single European Act," *Common Market Law Review* 24 (1987), 9 (describing the SEA as a "severe setback" for the European Community); see also Pescatore, "Die 'Einheitliche Europäische Acte,' Eine ernste Gefahrfür den Gemeinsamen Markt," *Europarecht* 21 (1986), 153.

[139] See Address by Commission Vice-President Frans Andriessen, Signing Ceremony for SEA (1986) *Bulletin of the European Communities* (2-1986), point 1.1.1 (giving the SEA a decidedly cool reception); see also Address by Jacques Delors, Programme of the Commission for 1986, reprinted in *Bulletin of the European Communities* (Supp. 1/86). Delors gave the Act a cool reception but put on a brave face: "You [Parliament] have your reservations, we have ours; but it would be a mistake to be *overly* pessimistic" (emphasis added). Ehlermann, in his 1987 paper, comments that: "Comparing the final text of the Single European Act with the Commission's original ideas shows that the differences are greatest in the area of the internal market. Nowhere does the end result depart so radically from the Commission's original paper.": Ehlermann, "Internal Market" at 362. This is revealing since it suggests that, at its core, the internal market, the SEA seemed at first disappointing. Ehlermann's comments are particularly authoritative since he was Director-General of the Commission's Legal Service and privy to most developments from the inside. His assessments also reflect the Commission's moods. See Parliament Fights On for More Say," *European Parliament News* (UK edn., January 1986) at 1, col. 1 (a report on the Parliament's negative reaction to the outcome of the intergovernmental conference). See the following debates of the European Parliament: Resolution following the Debate on the Statement by the Council and the Commission after the Meeting of the European Council on December 2–3, 1985, in Luxembourg, 1985 OJ (C 352), 60; Resolution on the Position of the European Parliament on the Single Act Approved by the Intergovernmental Conference on December 16–17, 1985, 1986 OJ (C 36), 144;

And yet, with the hindsight of just three years, it has become clear that 1992 and the SEA do constitute an eruption of significant proportions.[140] Some of the evidence is very transparent. First, for the first time since the very early years of the Community, if ever, the Commission plays the political role clearly intended for it by the Treaty of Rome. In stark contrast to its nature during the foundational period and the 1970s and early 1980s, the Commission in large measure both sets the Community agenda and acts as a power broker in the legislative process.[141]

Second, the decision-making process takes much less time. Dossiers that would have languished and in some cases did languish in impotence for years in the Brussels corridors now emerge as legislation often in a matter of months.[142]

For the first time, the interdependence of the policy areas at the new-found focal point of power in Brussels creates a dynamic resembling the almost forgotten predictions of neo-functionalist spillover.[143] The

Resolution on European Union and the Single Act, 1986 OJ (C 120), 96; Resolution on Relations between the European Parliament and the Council, 1986 OJ (C 283), 36; Resolution on Relations between the European Parliament and the Commission in the Institutional Context of the Treaties, 1986 OJ (C 283), 39; Resolution on the Ratification Procedure for the Single Act in National Parliaments and on the Attainment of European Union, 1986 OJ (C 29), 119; Resolution on the Single European Act, 1987 OJ (C 7), 105; Resolution on the Strategy of the European Parliament for Achieving European Union, 1987 OJ (C 190), 71; Resolution on the Results Obtained from Implementation of the Triple Act, 1988 OJ (C 309), 93; and Resolution on Relations between Parliaments and the European Parliament, 1989 OJ (C 69), 149.

[140] Again Ehlermann can serve as our barometer. Writing in 1990 he comments: "The '1992 Project' has radically changed the European Community. It has given the 'common market' new impetus and has lifted the Community out of the deep crisis in which it was bogged down in the first half of the 1980s." He adds: "[The] Single European Act ... represents the most comprehensive and most important amendment to the EEC Treaty to date ... [T]he core and the 'raison d'être' of the [SEA] are the provisions on the internal market.": Ehlermann, "1992 Project" at 1,097, 1,103. This change in nuance in assessing the SEA reflects a general shift in opinion in Community institutions. My own assessment has been that the dynamics generated by the SEA and 1992 surprised most observers and actors.

[141] This development is the expected result of "returning" to majority voting. Amendments to Commission proposals must be unanimous: EEC Treaty, Art. 149(1). But the Commission "may alter its proposal at any time during the procedures [of decision-making]": EEC Treaty, Art. 149(3). The Commission may amend its own proposal, finding a *via media* among contrasting amendments. None of the amendments on its own could gain unanimity, but a compromise version, in the form of the Commission's altered proposal, may gain a majority. This prerogative of the Commission obviously gives it considerable power it did not have under the shadow of the veto.

[142] See Ehlermann, "1992 Project" at 1,104–6.

[143] *Cf.* Keohane and Hoffmann, "Conclusions: Community Politics and Institutional Change," in W. Wallace (ed.), *The Dynamics of European Integration* (Pinter: London,

ever-widening scope of the legislative and policy agenda of the Community manifests this dynamic. The agreement to convene two new intergovern-mental conferences to deal with economic and monetary union just three years after the adoption of the SEA symbolizes the ever-widening scope of the agenda, as does the increased perception of the Community and its institutions as a necessary, legitimate, and at times effective *locus* for dir-ect constituency appeal.

But if the instruments themselves (especially the SEA) are so meager, how can one explain the changes they have wrought? In the remainder of this chapter I shall do the following: first, I shall take a closer look at the impact of the SEA on the elements of Community structure and process analyzed in the preceding sections of this chapter. I shall try to show that the changes are greater than meet the eye. I believe that their significance, analyzed in the light of the transformation effected in the previous two periods in the Community evolution, is far reaching. Then, instead of elaborating further on the promise inherent in this last period in Community evolution, a subject on which there has been no shortage of comment and celebration, I shall attempt to point out dangers and raise critical questions.

### *Structural background to 1992 and the Single European Act:*
### *the tension and its resolution*

The balance of constitutionalism and institutionalism, of reduced Exit and enhanced Voice, was the heritage of the foundational period and explains much of the subsequent strength and stability of the Community polity.[144] But the foundational period equilibrium was not without its costs. Those costs are the ones inherent in consensus politics: the need to reach unani-mous agreement in policy-making and governance.

From the little empirical evidence available, we know that consensus politics did not significantly impede policy management during the 1960s, 1970s, and into the 1980s.[145] However, the Community became increas-ingly unable to respond to new challenges, that called for real policy choices. Thus, while consensus politics (the manifestation of enhanced Voice) explains the relative equanimity with which the jurisdictional

---

New York, 1990), 276, 282*ff.* For a review of neo-functionalist spillover, see Greilsammer, "Theorizing European Integration."

[144] See pp. 34–9 above.

[145] See Krislov, Ehlermann, and Weiler, "The Political Organs" at 30–57.

limits of the Community broke down in the 1970s, this very consensus model also explains why, within the Community's expanded jurisdiction, it was unable to realize its most traditional and fundamental objectives, such as establishing a single market in the four factors of production.[146] From a structural point of view, one critical impediment to these goals was the growth in the number of Member States. In just over a decade the number of Member States doubled. But the new Member States entered a Community with decisional processes that were created in the foundational period and that were not changed to accommodate the increased number of participants. Achieving consensus among the original six was difficult enough. It became substantially more difficult with the first enlargement to nine and virtually debilitating when the number grew to twelve. In addition, the entry first of the UK, Ireland, and Denmark and then of Greece, Spain, and Portugal caused the Community to lose a certain homogeneity of policy perception and cultural orientation. This loss of homogeneity accentuated a problem that would exist in any event by the pure numbers game. Community decision-making fell into deep malaise. It is not surprising that almost every initiative between 1980 and the SEA recognized the need to change processes of decision-making, usually by moving to some form of majority voting.

Another structural element encouraged change. The evolving rules concerning the free movement of goods and other factors of production between the Member States created a regulatory gap in the European polity. A rigorous (and courageous[147]) jurisprudence of the Court of Justice seriously limited the ability of the Member States to adopt protectionist measures *vis-à-vis* each other.[148] Indeed, it went further. The Court held that once the Community enacted measures regulating non-tariff barriers to movement of goods, such measures would preempt any subsequently enacted Member State legislation that frustrated the design of the extant

---

[146] For an analysis of the fragmented market despite close to three decades of a common market regime, see J. Pelkmans and A. Winters, *Europe's Domestic Market* (Royal Institute of Internatioanl Affairs: London; Routledge: New York, 1988).

[147] Unlike those of most other systems in Europe, judges on the European Court serve for renewable terms (EEC Treaty, Art. 167). This rule compromises the appearance of independence. Currently the intergovernmental conference holds a proposal to extend the terms of judges to twelve years and make them non-renewable. See "Resolution of European Parliament on the Intergovernmental Conference," PE 146.824, Art. 167.

[148] The famous line of the decision from Case 8/74, *Procureur du Roi* v. *Benoit and Gustave Dassonville* [1974] ECR 837 and its progeny. See generally L. Gormley, *Prohibiting Restrictions on Trade within the EEC* (North Holland: Amsterdam, New York, 1985).

Community measures.[149] In addition, it is important to remember that this was an area in which the Treaty provided for unanimous decision-making. The Treaty rule on decision-making and the Court's jurisprudence on the preemptive effect of such decision-making combined to chill the climate in which the Community and its Member States were to make critical decisions to eliminate the numerous barriers to a true common market. Not only was it difficult to achieve consensus on one Community norm to replace the variety of Member State norms, but also there was the growing fear that once such a norm was adopted, it would lock all Member States into a discipline from which they could not exit without again reaching unanimity. If the Community once agreed on a norm on, for example, the permissible level of lead in gasoline, no Member State could subsequently reduce the level further without the consent of all twelve Member States within the Community decision-making process. The combination of legal structure and political process militated against easy consensus even on non-protectionist policy.

The deep political subtlety of the Commission White Paper outlining the 1992 program becomes clear in this context, as does its ultimate success. Unlike all earlier attempts and proposals to revive the Community, the 1992 White Paper, although innovative in its conception of achieving a Europe without frontiers,[150] was entirely functional. It delineated the ostensibly uncontroversial goal of realizing an internal market, and, in the form of a technical list of required legislation, the uncontroversial means necessary to achieve that goal. Critically, it eschewed any grandiose institutional schemes. These were to come as an inevitable result, once 1992 was in place. Because of this technocratic approach, the White Paper apparently appealed to those with different, and often opposing, ideological conceptions of the future of Europe. To some, it represented the realization of the old dream of a true common marketplace, which, because of the inevitable connection between the social and the economic in modern political economies, would ultimately yield the much vaunted "ever closer union among the peoples of Europe." To others, it offered a vision of the European dream finally lashed down to the marketplace, and, importantly, a market unencumbered by the excessive regulation that had built up in the individual Member States. Dismantling regulation

---

[149] See, e.g., Case 148/78, *Pubblico Ministero* v. *Ratti* [1979] ECR 1,629, 1,643 (recital 27); Case 5/ 77, *Tedeschi* v. *Denkavit Commerciale* [1977] ECR 1,555, 1,576–7 (recital 35) (hereinafter "*Denkavit*").

[150] Ehlermann, "1992 Project" at 1,099.

that impeded intra-Community trade would, on this reading, yield the dismantling of regulation altogether.

The key to the success of the 1992 strategy occurred when the Member States themselves agreed to majority voting. They took this step clearly not as a dramatic political step toward a higher level of European integration in the abstract, but rather as a low-key technical necessity in realizing the "non-controversial" objectives of the White Paper. This movement found expression in the single most important provision of the SEA, Article 100A.

As indicated above, this provision at face value seems minimalist and even destructive. First, the move to majority voting in Article 100A is couched as a residual measure and derogation from the principal measure, which requires unanimity, namely old Article 100.[151] Second, the exception to Article 100A, Article 100A(4), was drafted in an even more restrictive form by the heads of state and government themselves.[152] The exception states that for enactments by majority voting a Member State may, despite the existence of a Community norm, adopt national safeguard measures.[153] Indeed, this exception may be seen as an ingenious attempt by the Member States to retain the equilibrium of the foundational period in the new context of majority voting.

The essence of the original equilibrium rested on the acceptance by the Member States of a comprehensive Community discipline on the condition that each would have a determinative Voice, the veto, in the establishment of new norms. In Article 100A, the Member States, by accepting a passage to majority voting, seemed to be destroying one of the two pillars of the foundational equilibrium. But, by allowing a Member State to derogate from a measure even in the face of a Community norm (adopted by a majority!) the other pillar of comprehensive Community jurisdiction seems to be equally eroded, thereby restoring the equilibrium. The

---

[151] See Art. 100A(1) ("By way of derogation from Article 100 ...").

[152] See Ehlermann, "Internal Market" at 381.

[153] Art. 100A(4): "If, after the adoption of a harmonization measure by the Council acting by a qualified majority a Member State deems it necessary to apply national provisions on grounds of major needs referred to in Article 36 ... it shall notify the Commission of these provisions. The Commission shall confirm the provisions involved after having verified that they are not a means of arbitrary discrimination or a disguised restriction on trade between Member States. By way of derogation from the procedure laid down in Articles 169 and 170, the Commission or any Member State may bring the matter directly before the Court of Justice if it considers that another Member State is making improper use of the powers provided for in this article."

exception breaks, of course, the rule of preemption established by the Court in cases where harmonization measures were adopted.[154]

Finally, as an indication of the low-key attitude toward the new voting procedure, a proposal to formally "repeal" the Luxembourg Accord was rejected by the Member States. Indeed, when presenting the SEA to their national parliaments, both the French and British ministers for foreign affairs claimed that the Single European Act left the Luxembourg Accord intact. Thus the French Foreign Minister solemnly declared in the *Assemblée Nationale*, responding to concerns that the SEA gave too much power to the Community at the expense of the Member States that, *"en toute hypothèse, même dans les domaines où s'applique la règle de la majorité qualifiée, l'arrangement de Luxembourg de janvier 1966 demeure et conserve toute sa valeur."* Likewise, in the House of Commons the British Foreign Secretary assured the House that "as a last resort, the Luxembourg compromise remains in place untouched and unaffected." [155]

These three elements together may have given the Member States the feeling that the step they took was of limited significance and the outside observer the impression that the basic equilibrium was not shattered. It is most striking in this connection to note that even Mrs. Thatcher, the most diffident head of government among the large Member States, character- ized the Single European Act on the morrow of its adoption by the European Council as a "modest step forward." [156] But shattered it was, since each of these precautions was either ill-conceived or rendered impracticable because of open-textured drafting and a teleology that traditionally presaged for construing derogations to the Treaty in the narrowest possible way.

Although the language of the provision suggests the new system was intended as a derogation, the prevailing view is that Article 100A has become the "default" procedure for most internal market legislation, and that the procedure of other articles is an exception.[157] Significantly, the

---

[154] See *Denkavit* [1977] ECR 1,555.

[155] On the failure of the proposal to repeal the Accord, see Ehlermann, "1992 Project" at 1,106. For declarations in the UK Parliament and the French Parliament on the continued existence of the Luxembourg Accord even after the SEA, see 96 *Parliamentary Debates*, HC (5th series, 1986), 320 (debates of the House of Commons of April 23, 1986); Séance of the Assemblée Nationale (November 20, 1986), JO No. 109, 111 AN (CR), 8th Législature, 81st Séance, 6,611 (November 21, 1986).

[156] *Washington Post* (December 4, 1985) at A29, col. 1.

[157] "Article 100A thus gives the Council enormous scope for action, which is limited principally, I suspect, only by the existence of other enabling provisions": Ehlermann, "Internal Market," 134 at 384. Ehlermann argues convincingly that Art. 100A will be used in most cases, even in amending old Art. 100 legislation, a case in which Art. 235 s provision for

connection between Article 100A and Article 8A means that majority voting should take place, except where specifically excluded,[158] for all measures needed to achieve the objective of an internal market. The internal market is defined "as an area without internal frontiers in which the free movement of goods, persons, services and capital is ensured." [159] This requirement of majority voting extends the scope of the Article 100A procedure beyond the harmonization of technical standards affecting the free movement of goods. The net result is that few cases exist that would *compel* resort to the old legal basis and its unanimity requirement. The Commission proposes the legal basis of decisions; any change of such basis would be subject itself to a unanimous Council vote, which would be difficult to achieve. In any event, even if the Council could change the legal basis, the Court, if a challenge were brought, would tend to side with the Commission on issues of legal basis.[160]

Likewise, and contrary to some of the doomsday predictions,[161] the derogation to the principle of preemption in Article 100A(4), so carefully crafted by prime ministers and presidents, has had and must have very little impact. It allows a Member State to adopt, under strict conditions and subject to judicial review, unilateral derogations of Community harmonizing measures when the Member State seeks to uphold a higher level of protection. But that does not seem to be the real battlefield of majority voting. The real battlefield is regulation by the Community in areas in which Member States may feel that they do not want any regulation at all, let alone a higher Community standard.[162]

unanimity may have been used in the past. He says it will be used also for legislation of a scope that goes beyond the grounds of Art. 100, which was limited to harmonization of national measures that affected the establishment or functioning of the common market. Thus, Art. 100A will be used, in most cases, when new legislation to achieve the common market is needed: *ibid.*

[158] E.g., SEA, Art. 100A(2).

[159] SEA, Art. 8A.

[160] In a series of cases, starting with Case 45/86, *Commission of the European Communities v. Council of the European Communities* [1987] ECR 1,493 (general tariff preferences), the Commission has challenged the Council's use of Art. 235 (which provides for unanimity) rather than alternative legal bases in the Treaty. In a clear departure from its precedent, which would have allowed the Council to do so, in *Massey Ferguson*, the Court sided with the Commission. See also Case 51/87, *Commission of EC* v. *Council of EC* [1988] ECR 5,459; Case 165/87, *Commission of EC* v. *Council of EC* [1988] ECR 5,545; Case 275/87, *Commission of EC* v. *Council of EC* [1989] ECR 259; Case 288/87. But see Case 242/87, *Commission of EC* v. *Council of EC* [1989] ECR 1,425.

[161] See, e.g., Pescatore, "Some Critical Remarks."

[162] The UK strongly opposed, on principle, the adoption of Council Directive No. 89/662 on the approximation of the laws, regulations, and administrative provisions of the Member

The sharpest impact, however, of majority voting under the SEA does not turn on these rather fine points. Earlier I explained that, although the language of the Luxembourg Accord suggested its invocation only when asserting a vital national interest, its significance rested in the fact that practically all decision-making was conducted under the shadow of the veto and resulted in general consensus politics.[163]

Likewise, the significance of Article 100A was its impact on *all* Community decision-making. Probably the most significant text is not the SEA, but the consequently changed rules of procedure of the Council of Ministers, which explain the rather simple mechanism for going to a majority vote.[164] Thus, Article 100A's impact is that practically all Community decision-making is conducted under the shadow of the vote (where the Treaty provides for such vote). The Luxembourg Accord, if not eliminated completely, has been rather restricted. For example, it could not be used in the areas in which Article 100A provides the legal basis for measures. In addition, to judge from the assiduousness with which the Member States argue about legal bases, which determine whether a measure is adopted by majority or unanimity,[165] it is rather clear that they do not feel free to invoke the Luxembourg Accord at whim. If the Accord persists at all, it depends on the assertion of a truly vital national interest, *accepted as such* by the other Member States, and the possibility of any Member State forcing a vote on the issue under the new rules of procedure. In other words, in accordance with the new rules, to invoke the Luxembourg Accord a Member State must persuade at least half the Member States of the "vitality" of the national interest claimed.

States concerning the labeling of tobacco products, 1989 OJ (L 359). It did not oppose the low standard of the regulation but argued that the Community did not have competence in the field of health. The derogation in Art. 100A(4) was useless in the face of this type of opposition. The UK had recourse only if it wanted a higher standard of protection against the danger of smoking.

163 The only habitual prior exception concerned decisions within the process of adopting the Community budget.

164 See amendment of the Council's Rules of Procedure adopted by the Council on July 20, 1987, 1987 OJ (L 291), 27. New Art. 5(1) provides: The Council shall vote on the initiative of its President. "The President shall, furthermore, be required to open voting proceedings on the invitation of a member of the Council or of the Commission, provided that a majority of the Council's members so decides." The new rules do not differentiate between votes under Art. 100A and any other legal basis which provides for majority voting in the Treaty.

165 See Art. 235 cases listed in note 160, pp. 70–1 above.

## Under the shadow of the vote

Majority voting thus becomes a central feature of the Community in many of its activities.[166] A parallel with the opposite (Luxembourg Accord veto) practice of the past exists: today, an actual vote by the majority remains the exception. Most decisions are reached by consensus. But reaching consensus under the shadow of the vote is altogether different from reaching it under the shadow of the veto. The possibility of breaking deadlocks by voting drives the negotiators to break the deadlock without actually resorting to the vote. And, as noted above, the power of the Commission as an intermediary among the negotiating members of Council has been considerably strengthened.

This chapter has emphasized the relationships between the transformations of each of the definitional periods of the Community. In discussing each of the earlier periods, I have already pointed out the evolution of some important structural elements, such as the growth in the number of the Member States, that partially caused this return to majority voting.

But, of course, the crucial linkage to the past is not cause but effect. The (re)turn to majority voting constitutes a transformation as momentous as those that occurred earlier in the life of the Community because of those earlier changes. It is trite but worth repeating that, absent the earlier process of constitutionalization, a process that gave a real bite to Community norms, adoption by majority would be of far lesser significance. What puts the Community and its Member States in a new defining situation is the fact that the foundational equilibrium, despite attempts to rescue it in the actual drafting of the SEA, seems to be shattered.[167] Unlike any earlier

---

[166] Several important Community areas remain that require unanimity. Art. 100A(2) provides for exceptions from majority voting in the field of the movement of persons, fiscal provisions, and the rights and interests of employed persons.

[167] If the Member States did not want to be in this situation, why did they, in practice, construe the SEA as they did? One can only speculate as to the answer. Critically, Member States differ in relation to the turn to majority voting. Some feel that the reality of interdependence is such that a blocking possibility pays less than the ability to force a recalcitrant major player in certain circumstances. In addition, it seems that, as in earlier episodes, some simply did not appreciate the significance of their constitutionalizing moves and unwittingly found themselves in the "trap" of Community discipline, where the stakes of rupture are possibly very high. It always seems difficult to root an explanation in ignorance by, or mistake of, major state actors. But how else does one explain the statements made by the UK and French Foreign Ministers in their respective parliamentary assemblies? See note 155, pp. 69–70 above. Or how does one explain Thatcher's early evaluation of the SEA as a "modest" step – a step which later has come to be regarded as

era in the Community,[168] and unlike most of their other international and transnational experience, Member States are now in a situation of facing binding norms, adopted wholly or partially against their will, with direct effect in their national legal orders.

Likewise, the erosion of enumeration is far more significant in the environment of majority voting. There is something almost pitiful in the rude awakening of some of the Member States. For example, in 1989, the Council, in a hotly contested majority vote on the basis of Article 100A, adopted the new Community cigarette-labeling directive, which specifies a menu of mandatory warnings. Manufacturers must choose a warning to print on all cigarette packets.[169] The directive was hotly contested not because of the content of the warnings or even the principle of warnings, but because one of the Member States challenged the competence of the Council (meeting as a Council of Health Ministers) to adopt legislation pursuing the *objective* of health. Strictly speaking, to achieve a common market in tobacco products, it would be enough to pass a measure providing that cigarette packages carrying any of the warnings agreed upon could not be impeded in its intra-Community free movement. This directive goes much further, however. Instead of stopping at the market rationale, its legal basis includes the European Council meeting of June 1985, which launched a European action program against cancer, and the resolution of July 1986 on a program of action of the European Communities against cancer.[170]

What, in June 1985 (prior to the SEA), may have seemed a totally banal resolution under which Member States could control any operationalization of the action program against cancer, attained an altogether different

the most comprehensive and "most important amendment to the EEC Treaty to date"? Was she deliberately underestimating the nature of change brought about by, in particular, the shift to majority voting, or was she, as I argue in the text, not fully aware of the limits to the safeguards built into the revised Art. 100A? Failure of Member States to appreciate the full impact of their action is not new. As indicated above, it would appear that in negotiating Art. 177 the Member States were not fully aware of its far-reaching constitutional implications. See pp. 27–8 above.

[168] There were a few episodes in which the Luxembourg Accord did not "save" a Member State. The agricultural-price-increase episode in 1982 is an example. See *The Times* (London) (May 19, 1982) at 1, 5, 30 (articles on EEC override of UK veto); "A Failure for Europe," *ibid.* at 15; see also "Editorial Comments: The Vote on the Agricultural Prices: A New Departure?" *Common Market Law Review* 19 (1982), 371.

[169] See Council Directive No. 89/662 on the approximation of the laws, regulations, and administrative provisions of the Member States concerning the labelling of tobacco products, 1989 OJ (L 359).

[170] 1986 OJ (C 184), 19.

meaning in 1989, when the measures could be, and were, adopted by majority vote. However, in the light of the erosion of the principle of enumeration in the 1970s, a challenge to the constitutionality of the measure as *ultra vires* would likely fail.

Member States thus face not only the constitutional normativity of measures adopted often wholly or partially against their will, but also the operation of this normativity in a vast area of public policy,[171] unless the jurisprudence changes or new constitutional amendments are intro- duced.[172]

---

[171] Admittedly, legislating on the outer reaches of Community jurisdiction requires resorting to Art. 235, which does provide for unanimity. But, as discussed at pp. 70–1 above, Art. 100A could be used in some instances instead of Art. 235, especially given the new Commission strategy, supported by the Court, of limiting the use of Art. 235 whenever another Treaty legal basis exists; the cigarette labeling directive illustrates this point quite forcefully.

[172] In fact, in this new decisional climate, a heightened sensitivity to demarcation of competences exists, one which hardly existed in the past. See "Resolution of Parliament of July 12, 1990, on the principle of Subsidiarity," PE 143.504: "[H]aving regard to the future development of the Community, in particular its commitment to draw up a draft constitution for European Union and the fact this process of transforming the European Community *requires a clear distinction to be made between the competences of the Union and those of the Member States ...*": preamble to Resolution, at 13 (emphasis added); see also "27th Report of the Select Committee on the European Communities [of the UK House of Lords] on Economic and Monetary Union and Political Union of October 30, 1990" (HL Paper 88-I) at paras. 143–4, 204 ("There is also a more general fear that the Community is taking collective decisions in areas where such choices could perfectly well be left to the member States"). See generally Jacqué and Weiler, "On the Road to European Union – A New Judicial Architecture: An Agenda for the Intergovernmental Conference," *Common Market Law Review* 27 (1990), 185, 199–206; and "Editorial Comments," *Common Market Law Review* 27 (1990), 181. For a recent harsh critique of the unchecked expansion of jurisdiction, see Hailbronner, "Legal-Institutional Reforms of the EEC: What Can We Learn from Federalism Theory and Practice?" *Swiss Review of International Economic Relations* 46 (1991), special issue 3/4. In the leaked "Non-Paper" of the Luxembourg Presidency of April 15, 1991, setting out the state of negotiation of the Intergovernmental Conference, the principle of subsidiarity has been inserted as an operational part of the Treaty. The proposal is included as an amendment to EEC Treaty, Art. 3 and reads as follows: "La Communauté agit dans les limites des compétences qui lui sont conférées et des objectifs qui lui sont assignés par le present traité. Dans les domaines que ne relévent pas de sa competénce exclusive, la Communauté intervient conformément au principe de la subsidiarité, si et dans la mesure où les objectifs qui lui sont assignes peuvent être mieux réalisés au niveau Communautaire qu'au niveau des états membres oeuvrant isolément, en raison des dimensions ou des effets de l'action envisagée.": "Non-paper: project d'articles de Traité, en vue de la mose en place d'une union politique" (Luxembourg. April 15, 1991) at 12. This proposal, which was ultimately adopted as Art. 3B, on my reading, provides a new criterion for judicial review by the Court under Arts. 173 and 177(b). The fact that subsidiarity, often thought of as a principle incapable of

## *The challenge of majority voting*

As indicated above, I think enough has been written about the promise of the enhanced "efficiency" of the decisional process and the internal dynamic generated and manifested, for example, in the current intergovernmental conferences.[173] In contrast, I wish to explore less visible implications of the change. Since the SEA does rupture a fundamental feature of the Community in its foundational period, the equilibrium between constitutional and institutional power, it would follow from the analysis of the foundational period that the change should have implications that go beyond simple legislative efficiency. On this reading, the SEA regime does truly constitute a defining experience for the Community. The lack of any temporal perspective suggests great caution in this part of the analysis, and I pose my points as questions and challenges rather than affirmations.

## The challenge of compliance[174]

Although the problem of compliance with Community norms by the Member States is not new, the context of the SEA regime changes our evaluation. In reading the explanation earlier that the Community has developed effective mechanisms for the enforcement of Community law, one should not be misled to think that no violations, by Member States, Community institutions, or individuals, occur. They occur regularly and, as Community activities and impact expand, increasingly.[175] In this respect the Community is no different (in principle) than, for example, any state of equivalent size and complexity. Indeed, that was the critical factor in our analysis. When violation takes place it does so in a constitutional context with an ethos of domestic rather than international law. Since the Member States were able to control the elaboration of Community legislation in all its phases and were able to block any measure not to their liking, the non-compliance reflex would tend to operate at a surface and convenience level and thus would not indicate fundamental discontent.[176]

---

translation into an operative positive obligation, has been included is an indication of the strength of feeling concerning the question of erosion of jurisdictional limits.

[173] For the "bright side of the moon," see Ehlermann, "1992 Project."

[174] See generally Weiler, "The White Paper and the Application of Community Law," in Bieber, *1992: One European Market?* at 337.

[175] The White Paper raises the issue explicitly in section 152.

[176] The Commission drew a bleak picture in the White Paper: "Of the total number of complaints received by the Commission, some 60 percent, i.e., on average 255 each year, relate to Articles 30–36 of the Treaty, but because of the lack of resources it can, in a given year,

Under the new regime non-compliance could become more of a strategy. If the equilibrium of Voice and Exit is shattered by reducing the individual power of Member State Voice, the pressure might force a shift to strategies of Exit, which, in the Community context, means selective application rather than withdrawal. There are some signs that this may be happening.[177] In any event, although the Community is impressively on course in "implementing" the 1992 legislative program, a "black hole" of knowledge exists regarding the true level of Member State implementation.[178]

This problem of compliance is merely one manifestation of the deep dilemma involved in dismantling the foundational equilibrium. It is useful here, albeit in a very loose manner, to introduce Hirschman's third notion,

settle only one hundred cases. The resulting delays and backlogs benefit the infringing States, impede systematic action, proceedings, and frustrate the confidence of industry as well as that of the man in the street. Measures have to be taken to remedy the situation.": *ibid.* at section 153. One should not minimize the pragmatic nature of the problem, accentuated by the ability of Member States to disregard judgments of the Court in direct Art. 169 actions. None the less, it is interesting to note that the protectionist violation the Commission points out has been in some measure at least a response to the jurisprudence of the Court and not to consensual legislation. As far as directives are concerned, in most cases, non-incorporation is a result of objective constitutional and procedural difficulties at the national level (especially in Italy and Belgium) and not from an evasive or defiant strategy by a Member State.

[177] The problem was considered sufficiently grave to merit specific mention in the conclusions of the Dublin Summit of June 25–6, 1990, which set up the new Intergovernmental Conferences. Thus, in Annex I, mention was made of the need to give consideration to the automatic enforceability of Arts. 169 and 171 judgments of the European Court and of Member States ensuring the implementation and observance of Community law and European Court judgments: Dublin Summit, Annex I, reprinted in "Conclusions of the European Council Dublin 25 and 26 June 1990," *Europe*, Doc. No. 1,632/1,633 (June 29, 1990) at 9. The European Parliament, in its proposed Treaty amendments submitted to the Intergovernmental Conference, suggested amending Art. 171 to read: "The court may combine its judgments with financial sanctions against the Member State that has been found to be in default. The amount and method of collection of such sanctions shall be determined by a regulation adopted by the Community in accordance with the procedure laid down pursuant to Art. 188(b). The Court may also impose on recalcitrant states other sanctions such as suspension of right to participate in certain Community programs, to enjoy certain advantages or to have access to certain Community funds.": Art. 171, PE 146.824. The Select Committee of the House of Lords observed: "[T]here are Member States which seem to treat their obligation to translate Directives into national law by a certain date as little more than a vague guideline": "27th Report of the Select Committee on the European Communities [of the UK House of Lords] on Economic and Monetary Union and Political Union of October 30, 1990" (HL Paper 88-I) at para. 146: see also *ibid.* paras. 45–8, 205.

[178] On the general picture of implementation, see "Septième rapport annuel au parlement européen sur le controle de l'application du droit Communautaire," Com (90) 288 Final (May 22, 1990). See also Commission Reports on the Implementation of the White Paper.

Loyalty. Two possible readings of the future present themselves. On one reading, the dismantling of the foundational equilibrium will constitute a destabilizing act of such dimension that it threatens the acceptance not simply of a particular Community measure but of the very constitutional foundation. Alternatively, acceptance of Community discipline may have become the constitutional reflex of the Member States and their organs.[179] A Loyalty to the institution may have developed that breaks out of the need for constant equilibrium. The two decades of enhanced Voice thus constitute a learning and adaptation process resulting in socialization; at the end of this period decisional changes affecting Voice will not cause a corresponding adjustment to Exit. Time will tell, but there are signs that Loyalty with a large mixture of expediency may prevent or at least reduce the otherwise destabilizing effect of the new change.

### Challenges of "democracy" and "legitimacy"[180]

1992 also puts a new hue on the question of the democracy deficit. A useful starting point could indeed be a focus on the European Parliament and its role. It is traditional to start an analysis of the role of the European Parliament in the governance structure of the Community with a recapitulation of the existing democracy deficit in EC decision-making. This deficit informs, animates, and mobilizes the drive to change the powers of the European Parliament. In addition, to the extent that the governments of the Member States have responded, weakly and grudgingly, to this drive, it is surely because even they recognized the compelling power of the democracy deficit argument.

---

[179] For suggestions that this issue may be not quite as settled as one may wish, not even among the courts of the Member States, see, e.g., Cartabia, "The Italian Constitutional Court and the Relationship between the Italian Legal System and the European Community," *Michigan Journal of International Law* 12 (1990), 173; Szyszczak, "Sovereignty: Crisis, Compliance, Confusion, Complacency?" *European Law Review* 15 (1990), 480.

[180] See Weiler, "Parlement européen, intégration européenne, démocratie et légitimité," in J.-V. Louis and D. Waelbroeck (eds.), *Le parlement européen* (Editions de Université de Bruxelles: Brussels, 1988), 325, in which I have elaborated these points more expansively. I have been considerably helped by, and have drawn in particular on, the following works: L. Brilmayer, *Justifying International Acts* (Cornell University Press: Ithaca, NY, 1989): T. Franck, *The Power of Legitimacy among Nations* (Oxford University Press: New York, 1990); J. Habermas, *Legitimation Crisis* (Beacon Press: Boston, 1975); L. Henkin, *Constitutionalism, Democracy and Foreign Affairs* (Columbia University Press: New York, 1990); Dahl, "Federalism and the Democratic Process," in J. R. Pennock and J. W. Chapman (eds.), *Liberal Democracy*, XXV Nomos (New York University Press: New York, 1983) at 95. My own synoptic presentation cannot do justice to the richness of the works cited.

The typical argument views the European Parliament as the only (or at least principal) repository of legitimacy and democracy in the Community structure. The phrase most often used in this context is "democratic legitimacy."[181] The Commission, in this view, is an appointed body of international civil servants, and the Council of Ministers represents the executive branch of each national government which, through Community structures, has legislative powers it lacks on respective national scenes.

Thus, the Council, a collectivity of ministers, on a proposal of the Commission, a collectivity of non-elected civil servants, could, and in some instances must, pass legislation which is binding and enforceable even in the face of conflicting legislation passed by national parliaments. This occurs without corresponding parliamentary scrutiny and approval. Indeed, the Council could pass the legislation in the face of the European Parliament's disapproval. This happens often enough to render the point not simply theoretical. What is more, the Council can legislate in some areas that were hitherto subject to parliamentary control at the national level. We have already seen how the constitutionalization process in the foundational period and the erosion of enumerated powers in the second period accentuated this problem.

According to this view of the Community, the powers of the European Parliament are both weak and misdirected. They are weak in that the legislative power (even post-SEA) is ultimately consultative in the face of a determined Council. Even the Parliament's budgetary powers, though more concrete, do not affect the crucial areas of budgetary policy: revenue raising and expenditure on compulsory items.[182] The power to reject the budget *in toto* is a boomerang which has not always proved effective, although in 1984 the budget ultimately was amended in a direction that took account of some of the Parliament's concerns. The possibility of denying a discharge on past expenditure lacks any real sanction power.

---

[181] The problem of democratic structures is addressed this way by the Dublin Summit in "Conclusions of the European Council Dublin 25 and 26 June 1990," Annex I at 8.

[182] Parliament has a final say (within limits set by the Commission) only on expenditure items which are not mandated by the Treaty itself. For the best explanation of the Parliament's powers in this field, see J. Jacqué, R. Bieber, V. Constantinesco, and D. Nickel, *Le parlement européen* (Economica: Paris, 1984), 178. See also Case 34/86, *Council v. Parliament* [1986] ECR 2,155 (concerning the 1986 Budget) (especially the opinion of Advocate-General Mancini). Parliament was granted real approval control as regards association agreements under Art. 238 and the accession of new Member States under Art. 237. It has no formal powers, even of consultation as regards trade agreements under Art. 113.

Those parliamentary powers that are real, the powers to dismiss the Commission, to ask questions of the Commission, and to receive answers, are illusory at best and misdirected at worst. They are illusory because the power to dismiss is collective and does not have the accompanying power to appoint. They are misdirected because the Council is the "villain of the peace" in most European Parliament battles. All these well-known factors taken together constitute the elements of the democracy deficit and create the crisis of legitimacy from which the Community allegedly suffers.

Although the democracy deficit is prominent in Parliamentary rhetoric, the day-to-day complaint of Parliament especially in the pre-SEA days was not that the Community legislator (the Council) was over-vigorous and violated democratic principles, but rather that it failed to act vigorously enough. Critics argued that the Council had incapacitated itself and the entire Community by abandoning Treaty rules of majoritarian decision-making by giving a *de facto* veto to each Member State government that asserts a "vital national interest."

The veto power arrogated by the Member States produced another facet of the democracy deficit: the ability of a small number of Community citizens represented by their minister in the Council to block the collective wishes of the rest of the Community.

Parliamentarians almost uniformly claim that both facets of the malaise could be corrected by certain institutional changes, which on the one hand would "de-block" the Council by restoring majority voting, but which would also significantly increase the legislative and control powers of Parliament. Increased powers to the Parliament, directly elected by universal suffrage, would, so it is claimed, substantially reduce the democracy deficit and restore legitimacy to the Community decision-making process. It is further argued that, regarding the decisional malaise, Parliament has over the years boasted a *communautaire* spirit which would, if given effective outlet, transcend nationalistic squabbles and introduce a dynamism far more consonant with the declared objectives of the Treaties. The large majority accorded to the draft Treaty Establishing the European Union is cited as a typical example of this dynamism. Although these points seem obvious, they receive little critical analysis.

The absence of a critical approach derives in part from a loose usage of the notions of democracy and legitimacy. Very frequently in discourse about the Parliament and the Community the concepts of democracy and legitimacy have been presented interchangeably although in fact they do not necessarily coincide. To be sure, today, a non-democratic government or political system in the West could not easily attain or maintain legitimacy, but it is still possible for a democratic structure to be illegitimate - either *in toto* or in certain aspects of its operation.[183]

In spite of all the conceptual difficulties of dealing with "legitimacy," [184] even in this brief excursus it may be useful to draw one classical distinction between formal (legal) legitimacy and social (empirical) legitimacy. The notion of formal legitimacy in institutions or systems implies that all requirements of the law are observed in the creation of the institution or system. This concept is akin to the juridical concept of formal validity. In today's Europe, as in the West generally, any notion of legitimacy must rest on some democratic foundation, loosely stated as the People's consent to power structures and process. A Western institution or system satisfies formal legitimacy if its power structure was created through democratic processes.[185] Thus, in the Community context, I simply point out that the Treaties establishing the Community, which gave such a limited role to the European Parliament, were approved by the national parliaments of all founding Member States and subsequently by the parliaments of six acceding Member States. Proposals to give more power to the European Parliament have failed, for a variety of reasons, to survive the democratic processes in the Member States.[186] This definition of formal legitimacy is thus distinct from that of simple "legality." Formal legitimacy is legality understood in the sense that democratic institutions and processes created the law on which it is based (in the Community case, the Treaties).

Thus, in this formal sense, the existing structure and process rests on a formal approval by the democratically elected parliaments of the Member

---

[183] A stark example may drive the point home better than an abstract explication: Germany during the Weimar period was democratic but the government enjoyed little legitimacy. Germany during National Socialism ceased to be democratic once Hitler rose to power, but the government continued to enjoy widespread legitimacy well into the early 1940s. *Cf.* G. Craig, *Germany 1866–1945* (Oxford University Press: New York, 1978) at chapters 15 and 18.

[184] See generally Hyde, "The Concept of Legitimation in the Sociology of Law," *Wisconsin Law Review* (1983), 379.

[185] Franck's synthesis of "legitimacy" as it applies to the rules applicable to states is: "Legitimacy is a property of a rule or rule-making institution which itself exerts a pull toward compliance on those addressed normatively because those addressed believe that the rule or institution has come into being and operates in accordance with generally accepted principles of right process.": Franck, *The Power of Legitimacy among Nations* at 24.

[186] The SEA, which touches only slightly the so-called democracy deficit, was ratified by the parliaments of all the Member States. Likewise, with each Community enlargement, in 1973, 1981, and 1986, national parliaments had the opportunity to protest the non-democratic character of the Community, but instead reconfirmed the governance system.

States; and yet, undeniably, the Community process suffers from a clear democracy deficit in the classical sense outlined above.

"Social legitimacy," on the other hand, connotes a broad, empirically determined, societal acceptance of the system. Social legitimacy may have an additional substantive component: legitimacy occurs when the government process displays a commitment to, and actively guarantees, values that are part of the general political culture, such as justice, freedom, and general welfare.[187]

An institution, system, or polity, in most, but not all, cases, must enjoy formal legitimacy to enjoy social legitimacy. This is most likely the case in Western democratic traditions, which embody the rule of law as part of their political ethos. But a system that enjoys formal legitimacy may not necessarily enjoy social legitimacy. Most popular revolutions since the French Revolution occurred in polities whose governments retained formal legitimacy but lost social legitimacy. These admittedly primitive distinctions will become relevant to our discussion with one further excursus into the notions of integration and democracy.[188]

Obviously, democracy cannot exist in a modern polity as in "the Greek polis" or "the New England town." Representative democracy replaces direct participation. None the less, democracy can be measured by the closeness, responsiveness, representativeness, and accountability of the

---

[187] Franck usefully sorts legitimacy theories into three groups. The first group regards legitimacy as process. He cites Weber: "Weber postulates the validity of an order in terms of its being regarded by the obeying public 'as in some way obligatory or exemplary' for its members because, at least, in part, it defines 'a model' which is 'binding' and to which the actions of others 'will in fact conform …' At least, in part, this legitimacy is perceived as adhering to the authority issuing an order, as opposed to the qualities of legitimacy that inhere in an order itself.": Franck, *The Power of Legitimacy among Nations* at 16–18, 250 note 29 (quoting from M. Weber, *Economy and Society: An Outline of Interpretive Sociology* (Bedminster Press: New York, 1968) at 31). The second group mixes process and substance. This notion "is interested not only in how a ruler and a rule were chosen, but also in whether the rules made, and commands given, were considered in the light of all relevant data, both objective and attitudinal:" Franck, *ibid.* at 17. Franck quotes Habermas: "Legitimacy means that there are good arguments for a political order's claim to be recognized as right and just:" *ibid.* at 248 note 27 (quoting J. Habermas, *Communication and the Evolution of Society* (Beacon Press: Boston, 1979) at 178–9). His third group, primarily neo-Marxist, focuses on outcomes: "In this view, a system seeking to validate itself … must be defensible in terms of the equality, fairness, justice, and freedom which are realized by those commands": *ibid.* at 18. We do not have to choose among these different conceptualizations of legitimacy, since all three support my simple proposition distinguishing social legitimacy from both democracy and legal validity *simpliciter*.

[188] See generally Dahl, "Federalism and the Democratic Process."

governors to the governed. Although this formula is vague, it is sufficient for present purposes.

Imagine three independent polities, each enjoying a representative democracy. Let us further assume that each government enjoys legislative and regulatory power in the fields of education, taxation, foreign trade, and defense. In relation to each of these four functions the electors can influence directly their representatives, through elections and the like, as to the polity's education policy, level of taxation, type of foreign trade (e.g., protectionist or free), and defense-force composition and policy. Assume finally that for a variety of reasons the three polities decide to integrate and "share their sovereignty" in the fields of taxation, foreign trade and defense.

If this decision to integrate was democratically reached within each polity, the integrated polity certainly enjoys formal legitimacy. However, by definition, initially the new integrated polity's "responsiveness" will be less than that of the three independent polities. Prior to the integration, the majority of electors in polity A would have a controlling influence over their level of taxation, the nature of their foreign trade policy, and the size and posture of their army. In the integrated polity, even a huge majority of the electors in polity A can be outvoted by the electors of polities B and C.[189] This will be the case even if the new integrated polity has a perfectly democratically elected "federal" legislator. The integrated polity will not be undemocratic but it will be, in terms of the ability of citizens to influence policies affecting them, less democratic.[190]

This transformation occurs, in reverse form, when a centralized state devolves power to regions, as in the cases of Italy, Spain, and recently France. Regionalism, "the division of sovereignty" and granting of it to more or less autonomous regions is in some respects the opposite of integration. One of the prime motivations for regionalism is to enhance democracy in the sense of giving people more direct control of areas of public policy that affect their lives.

To suggest that in the process of integration there is a loss, at least in one sense, of democracy, does not, as such, condemn the process of integration. The electors in polities A, B, and C usually have formidable

---

[189] The dilution in Voice operates on two levels: a diminution in the specific gravity of each voter's weight in the process, and a diminution in the gravity of each voter's state.

[190] Different federal options will of course have consequences also for the allocation choices of voters and substantive policy outcomes. For a sustained discussion of this issue, see Rose-Ackerman, "Does Federalism Matter? Political Choice in a Federal Republic," *Journal of Political Economy* 89 (1981), 152.

reasons for integrating despite this loss of some direct control over policy when it is made in the larger polity. Typically the main reason is size. By aggregating their resources, especially in the field of defense, total welfare may be enhanced despite the loss of the more immediate influence of their government's policies. Similar advantages may accrue in the field of foreign trade. Phenomena such as multinational corporations, which may manage to escape the control of any particular polity, may exist, and only an integrated polity can tax or regulate them effectively. In other words the independence and sovereignty of the single polities may be illusory in the real interdependent world. None the less, the ability of the citizens of polity A, B, or C directly to control and influence these areas will have diminished.

Even within each polity the minority was obliged to accept majority decisions. So why do I claim that in the enlarged, integrated polity, in which an equally valid majoritarian rule applies, a loss of democracy occurs? This is among the toughest aspects of democratic theory.

What defines the boundary of the polity within which the majority principle should apply? No theoretical answer to this question exists. Long-term, very long-term, factors such as political continuity, social, cultural, and linguistic affinity, and a shared history determine the answer. No one factor determines the boundaries; rather they result from some or all of these factors. People accept the majoritarian principle of democracy within a polity to which they see themselves as belonging.[191]

The process of integration – even if decided upon democratically – brings about at least a short-term loss of direct democracy in its actual process of governance. What becomes crucial for the success of the integration process is the social legitimacy of the new integrated polity despite this loss of total control over the integrated policy areas by each polity.

How will such legitimacy emerge? Two answers are possible. The first is a visible and tangible demonstration that the total welfare of the citizenry is enhanced as a result of integration. The second answer is ensuring that the new integrated polity itself, within its new boundaries, has democratic structures. But more important still is giving a temporarily enhanced Voice to the separate polities. It is not an accident that some

---

[191] "Thus it does not seem possible to arrive at a defensible conclusion about the proper unit of democracy by strictly theoretical reasoning: we are in the domain not of theoretical but of practical judgment.": Dahl, "Federalism and the Democratic Process" at 106; see also Brilmayer, *Justifying International Acts* at 13–27, 52–78 (chapter 1, "Political Legitimacy and Jurisdictional Boundaries" and chapter 3, "Boundary Assumptions in Domestic Political Theory").

of the most successful federations which emerged from separate polities – the United States, Switzerland, Germany – enjoyed a period as a confederation prior to unification. This does not mean confederation is a prerequisite to federation. It simply suggests that in a federation created by integration, rather than by devolution, there must be an adjustment period in which the political boundaries of the new polity become socially accepted as appropriate for the larger democratic rules by which the minority will accept a new majority.[192]

From the political, but not legal, point of view the Community is in fact a confederation. The big debate is therefore whether the time is ripe for a radical change toward a more federal structure, or whether the process should continue in a more evolutionary fashion.

These answers about the possible emergence of legitimacy can be at odds with each other. Giving an enhanced Voice to each polity may impede the successful attainment of the goals of integration. Denying sufficient Voice to the constituent polities (allowing the minority to be overridden by the majority) may bring about a decline in the social legitimacy of the integrated polity with consequent dysfunctions and even disintegration. In terms of democratic theory, the final objective of a unifying polity is to recoup the loss of democracy inherent in the process of integration. This "loss" is recouped when the social fabric and discourse are such that the electorate accepts the new boundary of the polity and then accepts totally the legitimacy – in its social dimension – of being subjected to majority rule in a much larger system comprised of the integrated polities.

We can now see how these notions play out in a reconstructed analysis of the democracy issue in the Community. As stated above, a premise of the traditional analysis is that the Community suffers from a legitimacy crisis. Is the absence of legitimacy formal? Surely not. The Community, including its weak Parliament, appointed Commission, and unaccountable Council, enjoys perfect formal legitimacy. The Treaties all have been approved by the Community electorate through their national parliaments in accordance with the constitutional requirement of each Member State. In addition, the Treaties have been approved several times more with the accession of each new Member State and most recently with the adoption of the Single European Act.

If there is a crisis of legitimacy, it must therefore be a crisis of social (empirical) legitimacy. What is the nature of this crisis of social legitimacy,

---

[192] We do not have to take the formal transfer as the actual transfer. Arguably, the United States became truly federal only after the Civil War.

if indeed it exists? The traditional view is that the absence of legitimacy is rooted in the democracy deficit. As stated above, the implication is that any increase in the legislative and control powers of the European Parliament at the expense of the Council contributes to an elimination of this legitimacy crisis. I challenge the premise and the conclusion. I believe that Parliament should be given enhanced powers, because I acknowledge the democracy deficit in the formal sense explained above. But I think that it is at least questionable whether this will necessarily solve the legitimacy problems of the Community. It may even enhance them.

The legitimacy problem is generated by several factors, which should be discussed separately. The primary factor is, at least arguably, that the European electorate (in most Member States) only grudgingly accepts the notion that crucial areas of public life should be governed by a decisional process in which their *national* voice becomes a minority which can be overridden by a majority of representatives from other European countries. In theoretical terms there is, arguably, still no legitimacy to the notion that the boundaries within which a minority will accept as democratically legitimate a majority decision are now European instead of national. It is interesting, and significant, that for the first time national parliaments are taking a keen interest in the structural process of European integration and are far from enamored with the idea of solving the democracy deficit by simply enhancing the powers of the European Parliament.[193]

At its starkest, this critical view claims that in terms of social legitimacy no difference exists between a decision of the Council of Ministers and a decision of the European Parliament. To the electorate, both chambers present themselves as legislative, composed of Member States' representatives. In both cases, until time and other factors resolve this dimension of legitimacy, the electorate of a minority Member State might consider it socially illegitimate that they have to abide by a majority decision of a redefined polity.

On this view, the most legitimating element (from a "social" point of view) of the Community was the Luxembourg Accord and the veto power. To be sure, a huge cost in terms of efficient decision-making and progress was paid. But this device enabled the Community to legitimate its program and its legislation. It provided the national electorates an *ex ante* "insurance policy" that nothing could pass without the electorate

---

[193] See, e.g., "27th Report of the Select Committee on the European Communities [of the UK House of Lords] on Economic and Monetary Union and Political Union of October 30, 1990" (HL Paper 88-I) at paras. 157, 158, and 210.

Voice having a controlling say. The "insurance policy" also presented an *ex post* legitimation as well: everything the Community did, no matter how unpopular, required the assent of national ministers. The legitimacy of the output of the Community decisional process was, thus, at least partially due to the public knowledge that it was controllable through the veto power. The current shift to majority voting might therefore exacerbate legitimacy problems. Even an enhanced European Parliament, which would operate on a co-decision principle, will not necessarily solve the legitimacy problem. The legitimacy crisis does not derive principally from the accountability issue at the European level, but from the very redefinition of the European polity.

Pulling all the threads together, the conclusion provides at least food for thought: in a formal sense, majority voting exacerbates the democracy deficit by weakening national parliamentary control of the Council without increasing the powers of the European Parliament. But even increasing the powers of the European Parliament (to full co-decision on the most ambitious plan) does not wholly solve the problem. It brings to the fore the intractable problem of redefining the political boundaries of the Community within which the principle of majority voting is to take place. It is an open question whether the necessary shift in public loyalty to such a redefined boundary has occurred even if we accept the formalistic notion of state parliamentary democracy.

## Beyond 1992: Two Visions of the Promised Land: the Ideology, Ethos, and Political Culture of European Integration

By way of conclusion I would like to examine, far more tentatively, another facet of the transformation of Europe: the ideology, ethos, and political culture of European integration, particularly in relation to 1992.[194]

---

[194] In the earlier parts of this chapter I rested my interpretation, as much as possible and at least in its factual matrix, on an "objective" reality rooted in "empirical" and consequently "refutable" data. Likewise, my analytical moves were transparent enough to open them to rational critique. Obvious and inevitable limitations on the resulting "scientific objectivity" of the chapter exist. Clearly, to give the most banal example, my own prejudices, overt and less overt, shaped the selection of factual data, and, of course, their perception and analysis. Readers are always better placed than the writer to expose those prejudices and discount them in assessing the overall picture. In turning to ethos, ideology, and political culture, the screening process of the "self" (my "self") plays an even bigger role in the narrative. To try to "document" my assertions and conclusions here would be to employ the semblance of a scholarly apparatus where it is patently not merited. I do not, and cannot, claim to root this part of the chapter on the kind of painstaking research and complex

Ideological discourse within the Community, especially in the pre-1992 period, had two peculiar features. On the one hand, despite the growing focus of Community activity on important issues of social choice, a near absence of overt debate on the left-right spectrum existed. 1992 (as a code for the overall set of changes) represents a break from this pattern. On the other hand, there was abundant discourse on the politics and choices of the integration model itself. But this discourse was fragmented. In specialized political constituencies, especially those concerned with Community governance, public discourse was typically a dichotomy between those favoring the Community (and further European integration) and those defending "national sovereignty" and the prerogatives of the Member State. The outcome of the debate was curious. In the visible realm of political power from the 1960s onwards, it seemed that the "national interest" was ascending.[195] The "high moral ground" by contrast, seemed to be occupied fairly safely by the "integrationists."

So far as the general public was concerned, the characterizing feature of public discourse was a relatively high level of indifference, disturbed only on rare occasions when Community issues caught the public imagination. Although opinion polls always showed a broad support for the Community, as I argued earlier, it was still possible to gain political points by defending the national interest against the threat of the faceless "Brussels Eurocracy."

Here, the importance of 1992 has not been only in a modification of the political process of the Community, but also in a fascinating mobilization of wide sections of general public opinion behind the "new" Europe. The significance of this mobilization cannot be overstated. It fueled the momentum generated by the White Paper and the Single European Act,

---

tools that characterize the work of the social historian or the historical sociologist. Caveat lector! None the less, my brief narrative will, I hope, serve a function. Compared to the plethora of systemic and substantive theories and analyses of the processes of European integration, a real dearth of ideological and cultural scrutiny exists. Two recent extremely illuminating reflections on these issues are Snyder, *New Directions*; and J. Orstrom Moller *Technology and Culture in a European Context* (Nyt Nordisk Forlag: Copenhagen, 1991). By offering my perspective on these issues I hope the reader is drawn to reflect, and thereby, challenged to take position.

[195] The constitutional revolution was not immediately apparent even to relatively informed audiences. See Weiler, "Attitudes of MEPs towards the European Court," *European Law Review* 9 (1984), 169. One of the interesting conclusions of this survey of attitudes is that even those Members of the European Parliament strongly opposed to the dynamics of European integration and the increase in power of the Commission and Parliament regarded the Court with relevant equanimity.

and laid the ground auspiciously for creating Community initiatives to push beyond 1992. These Community initiatives included the opening in December 1990 of two new Intergovernmental Conferences designed to fix the timetable and modalities of economic and monetary union, as well as the much more elusive task of political union. Although no one has a clear picture of "political union,"[196] with open talk about Community government, federalist solutions, and other such codes,[197] even if the actual changes to the existing structure will be disappointing, in the ideological "battle" between state and Community, the old nationalist rhetoric has become increasingly marginalized and the integrationist ethos has fully ascended. The demise of Prime Minister Thatcher symbolizes this change.

The impact of 1992, however, goes well beyond these obvious facts of mobilization and "European ascendancy." Just below the surface lurk some questions, perhaps even forces, which touch the very ethos of European integration, its underlying ideology, and the emergent political culture associated with this new mobilization. Moreover, in some respects the very success of 1992 highlights some inherent (or at least potential) contradictions in the very objectives of European integration.

I shall deal first with the break from the Community's supposed ideological neutrality, and then turn to the question of the ethos of European integration in public discourse.

---

[196] The term has no fixed meaning and is used to connote a wide variety of models from federalist to intergovernmentalist. See generally R. Mayne and J. Pinder, *Federal Union: The Pioneers* (St. Martin's Press: New York, 1990); R. Pryce (ed.), *The Dynamics of European Union* (Croom Helm: London; Methuen: New York, 1987) (usefully tracing the evolution of the concept of political union over the history of European integration up to the Single European Act): J. Lodge (ed.), *European Union: The European Community in Search of a Future* (Macmillan: London, 1986).

[197] See, e.g., President Delors' speech to the European Parliament of January 17, 1990: "Cet exécutif [of the future Community on which Delors was speculating – the Commission according to the logic of the founders] devra être responsable, bien entendu, devant les institutions démocratique de la future *féderation* …"(Translated: "It is self-evident that this executive has to be responsible to the democratic institutions of the future *federation* …"):

"Jacques Delors presente de programme de la Commission et dessine un profit de l'Europe de demain," *Europe* Doc. No. 1,592 (January 24, 1990) at 7 (emphasis added). Likewise, when speaking approvingly of Mitterrand's idea of an "all-European confederation," Delors adds:

"Mais ma conviction est qu'une telle confédération ne pourra voir le jour qu'une fois réalisé l'Union politique de la Communauté!" (Translated: "But my conviction is that such a federation cannot emerge once the political Union of the Community is realised!"): *ibid.* at 4.

### *1992 and the "ideological neutrality" of the Community*

The idea of the single market was presented in the White Paper as an ideologically neutral program around which the entire European polity could coalesce in order to achieve the goals of European integration. This idea reflected an interesting feature of the pre-1992 Community: the relative absence of ideological discourse and debate on the right-left spectrum. The chill on right-left ideological debate derived from the governance structure of the Community.[198]

Since in the Council there usually would be representatives of national governments from both right and left, the desired consensus had to be one acceptable to all major political forces in Europe. Thus, policies verged towards centrist pragmatic choices, and issues involving sharp right-left division were either shelved[199] or mediated to conceal or mitigate the choice involved. The tendency towards the lowest common denominator applied also to ideology.

Likewise, on the surface, the political structure of the European Parliament replicates the major political parties in Europe. National party lists join in Parliament to sit in European political groups. However, for a long time the politics of integration itself, especially on the issues of the European Parliament's power and the future destiny of the Community, were far more important than differences between left and right within the chamber. The clearest example was the coalescing of Parliament with a large majority behind the Independent Communist Spinelli and his draft Treaty for European Union.[200]

Most interesting in this perspective is the perception of the Commission. It is an article of faith for European integration that the Commission is not meant to be a mere secretariat, but an autonomous political force shaping the agenda and brokering the decision-making of the Community. And yet at the same time, the Commission, as broker, must be ideologically neutral, not favoring Christian Democrats, Social Democrats, or others.

This neutralization of ideology has fostered the belief that an agenda could be set for the Community, and the Community could be led towards

---

[198] Of course I do not suggest that choices with ideological implications were not made. But they were rarely perceived as such.

[199] Thus, the proposed European company statute was shelved for many years because of the inability to agree, especially on the role of labor in the governance structure of the company.

[200] Typically, right and left have differed sharply in Parliament on issues of foreign affairs and extra-Community policies.

an ever closer union among its peoples, without having to face the normal political cleavages present in the Member States. In conclusion, the Community political culture which developed in the 1960s and 1970s led both the principal political actors and the political classes in Europe to an habituation of all political forces to thinking of European integration as ideologically neutral in, or ideologically transcendent over, the normal debates on the left-right spectrum. It is easy to understand how this will have served the process of integration, allowing a non-partisan coalition to emerge around its overall objectives.

1992 changes this in two ways. The first is a direct derivation from the turn to majority voting. Policies can be adopted now within the Council that run counter not simply to the perceived interests of a Member State, but more specifically to the ideology of a government in power. The debates about the European Social Charter and the shrill cries of "socialism through the back door," as well as the emerging debate about Community adherence to the European Convention on Human Rights and abortion rights are harbingers of things to come. In many respects this is a healthy development, since the real change from the past is evidenced by the ability to make difficult social choices and particularly by the increased transparency of the implications of the choice. At the same time, it represents a transformation from earlier patterns with obvious dysfunctional tensions.

The second impact of 1992 on ideological neutrality is subtler. The entire program rests on two pivots: the single market plan encapsulated in the White Paper, and its operation through the new instrumentalities of the Single European Act. Endorsing the former and adopting the latter by the Community and its Member States – and more generally by the political class in Europe – was a remarkable expression of the process of habituation alluded to above. People were successfully called to rally behind and identify with a bold new step toward a higher degree of integration. A "*single European* market" is a concept which still has the power to stir. But it is also a "single European *market*." It is not simply a technocratic program to remove the remaining obstacles to the free movement of all factors of production. It is at the same time a highly politicized choice of ethos, ideology, and political culture: the culture of "the market." It is also a philosophy, at least one version of which – the predominant version – seeks to remove barriers to the free movement of factors of production, and to remove distortion to competition as a means to maximize utility. The above is premised on the assumption of formal equality of individuals.[201] It is an ideology the contours of which have been the subject of intense debate within the Member States in terms of their own political choices. This is not the place to explicate these. Elsewhere, two slogans, "The One Dimensional Market" and "Big Market as Big Brother," have been used to emphasize the fallacy of ideological neutrality.[202] Thus, for example, open access, the cornerstone of the single market and the condition for effective non-protectionist competition, will also put pressure on local consumer products in local markets to the extent these are viewed as an expression of cultural diversity. Even more dramatic will be the case in explicit "cultural products," such as television and cinema. The advent of Euro-brands has implications, for better or for worse, which extend beyond the bottom line of national and Community economies. A successful single market requires widespread harmonization of standards of consumer protection and environmental protection, as well as the social package of employees. This need for a successful market not only accentuates the pressure for uniformity, but also manifests a social (and hence ideological) choice which prizes market efficiency and Europe-wide neutrality of competition above other competing values.

It is possible that consensus may be found on these issues, and indeed that this choice enjoys broad legitimacy. From my perspective, it is important to highlight that the consensus exudes a powerful pressure in shaping the political culture of the Community. As such, it is an important element of the transformation of Europe.

### The ethos of European integration: Europe as unity and Europe as Community

As indicated above, 1992 also brings to the fore questions, choices, and contradictions in the very ethos of European integration. I shall explore these questions, choices, and contradictions by construing two competing visions of the promised land to which the Community is being led in 1992

---

[201] There is an alternative construction of the Community political ideology also present in the European debate, one which recognizes "inequalities but deploring their inequities, considers the market to be just one of several basic means of governing society.": Snyder, *New Directions* at 89.

[202] Biener, Dehousse, Pinder, and Weiler, "Back to the Future: Policy, Strategy and Tactics of the White Paper on the Creation of a Single European Market," in Bieber, *1992: One European Market?* at 18–20.

and beyond. The two visions are synthetic constructs, distilled from the discourse and praxis of European integration.

Unitarian and communitarian visions share a similar departure point. If we go back in time to the 1950 Schuman Declaration and the consequent 1951 Treaty of Paris establishing the European Coal and Steel Community, these events, despite their economic content, are best seen as a long-term and transformative strategy for peace among the states of western Europe, principally France and Germany.[203] This strategy tried to address the "mischief" embodied in the excesses of the modern nation-state and the traditional model of statal intercourse among them that was premised on full "*sovereignty*," "*autonomy*," "*independence*," and a relentless defense and maximization of the national interest. This model was opposed not simply because, at the time, it displayed a propensity to degenerate into violent clashes, but also because it was viewed as unattractive for the task of reconstruction in times of peace.[204] The European Community was to be an antidote to the negative features of the state and statal intercourse; its establishment in 1951 was seen as the beginning of a process[205] that would bring about their elimination.

At this point, the two visions depart. According to the first vision, unity, the process that started in 1951 was to move progressively through the steps of establishing a common market and approximating economic policies[206] through ever tighter economic integration (economic and monetary union), resulting, finally, in full political union, in some version of a federal United States of Europe. If we link this vision to the governance process and constitutional structure, the ultimate model of the

---

[203] See, e.g., Schuman Declaration of May 9, 1950, reprinted in *Bulletin of the European Communities* 13 (1980), 14, 15 (hereinafter "Schuman Declaration") ("The gathering of the nations of Europe requires the elimination of the age-old opposition of France and the Federal Republic of Germany."); and the preamble to 1951 Treaty of Paris, reprinted in European Community Information Service, *Treaties Establishing the European Communities* (1987) ("Considering that world peace can be safeguarded only by creative efforts commensurate with the dangers that threaten it ...").

[204] This does not mean that states and leaders were engulfed in some teary-eyed sentimentalism. Signing on to the Community idea was no doubt also a result of cool calculation of the national interest. See A. Milward, *The Reconstruction of Western Europe 1945–51* (University of California Press: Berkeley, CA; Methuen: London, 1984). But this does not diminish the utility of seeking the overall ethos of the enterprise that they were joining.

[205] On the one hand: "In taking upon [it]self for more than 20 years the role of champion of a united Europe, France has always had as [its] essential aim the service of peace." On the other hand: "Europe will not be made all at once, or according to a single ... plan." Schuman Declaration at 15.

[206] EEC Treaty, Art. 2.

Community and the constitutionalized treaties stands as the equivalent, in the European localized context, of the utopian model of "world government" in classical international law. Tomorrow's Europe in this form would indeed constitute the final demise of Member State nationalism and, thus, the ultimate realization of the original objectives through political union in the form of a federalist system of governance.[207]

The alternative vision, community, also rejects the classical model of international law which celebrates statal sovereignty, independence, and autonomy and sees international legal regulation providing a "neutral" arena for states to prosecute their own ("national") goals premised on power and self-interest.[208] The community vision is, instead, premised on limiting, or sharing, sovereignty in a select albeit growing number of fields, on recognizing, and even celebrating, the reality of *interdependence*, and on counterpoising to the exclusivist ethos of statal autonomy a notion of a *community* of states and peoples sharing values and aspirations.

Most recently, it has been shown convincingly, not for the first time, how the classical model of international law is a replication at the international level of the liberal theory of the state.[209] The state is implicitly treated as the analogue, on the international level, to the individual within a domestic situation. In this conception, international legal notions such as self-determination, sovereignty, independence, and consent have their obvious analogy in theories of the individual within the state. The idea of community is thus posited in juxtaposition to the international version of pure liberalism and substitutes a modified communitarian vision.

Since the idea of "community" is currently in vogue and has become many things to many people, I would like to explain the meaning I attach to it in this transnational European context.[210] The importance of the

---

[207] Of course, even in this vision, one is not positing a centrist unified Europe but a federal structure of sorts, in which local interests and diversity would be maintained. Thus, although Delors speaks in his October 17, 1990, speech of Europe as a federation, he is – in good faith – always careful to maintain respect for "pluralism." See "Jacques Delors at the College of European in Bruges," reprinted in *Europe* Doc. No. 1,576 (October 21, 1989), 1 at 5 (hereinafter "Delors Speech of October 17, 1990").

[208] This, of course, is the classical model of international law. It is not monolithic. There are, in international law, voices, from both within and without, calling for an alternative vision expressed in such notions as the "common heritage of humankind." See, e.g., R. Sands, *Lessons Learned in Global Environmental Governance* (World Resources Institute: Washington, DC, 1990).

[209] M. Koskenniemi, *From Apology to Utopia* (Finnish Lawyers' Publishing Co.: Helsinki, 1989) at xvi, *passim*.

[210] I certainly do not find it useful to make an explicit analogy to the theories of community of domestic society, although I would not deny their influence on my thinking. See, e.g.,

EEC interstatal notion of *community* rests on the very fact that it does not involve a negation of the state. It is neither state nor community. The idea of community seeks to dictate a different type of intercourse among the actors belonging to it, a type of self-limitation in their self-perception, a redefined self-interest, and, hence, redefined policy goals. To the interest of the state must be added the interest of the community. But crucially, it does not extinguish the separate actors who are fated to live in an uneasy tension with two competing senses of the polity's self, the autonomous self and the self as part of a larger community, and committed to an elusive search for an optimal balance of goals and behavior between the community and its actors. I say it is crucial because the unique contribution of the European Community to the civilization of international relations – indeed its civilizing effect on intra-European statal intercourse – derives from that very tension among the state actors and between each state actor and the Community. It also derives from each state actor's need to reconcile the reflexes and ethos of the "sovereign" national state with new modes of discourse and a new discipline of solidarity.[211] Civilization is thus perceived not in the conquering of Eros but in its taming.[212]

Moreover, the idea of Europe as community not only conditions discourse among states, but it also spills over to the peoples of the states, influencing relations among individuals. For example, the Treaty provisions prohibiting discrimination on grounds of nationality, allowing the free movement of workers and their families, and generally supporting a rich network of transnational social transactions may be viewed not simply as creating the optimal conditions for the free movement of factors of production in the common market. They also serve to remove nationality and state affiliation of the individual, so divisive in the past, as the principal referent for transnational human intercourse.

---

M. Sandel, *Liberalism and the Limits of Justice* (Cambridge University Press: Cambridge, New York, 1982); M. Walzer, *Spheres of Justice* (Basic Books: New York, 1983); and the fierce debates about these, e.g., Dworkin, "To Each His Own," *New York Review of Books* (April 14, 1983); "Spheres of Justice: An Exchange," *New York Review of Books* (July 21, 1983).

[211] *Cf.* EEC Treaty, Art. 5.

[212] This tension between actor and community finds evocative expression in the preamble and the opening article of the EEC Treaty, the foundation of the current Community. The preamble speaks of "an ever closer union among the *peoples* of Europe" (emphasis added); whereas Art. 2 speaks of "closer relations between the *States* belonging to it" (emphasis added). Note, too, that the preamble speaks about the peoples of Europe rejecting any notion of a melting pot and nation-building. Finally, note the "ever closer union": something which goes on for "ever" incorporates, of course, the "never." See EEC Treaty, preamble.

The *unity* vision of the promised land sees then as its "ideal type" a European polity, finally and decisively replacing its hitherto warring Member States with a political union of federal governance. The *community* vision sees as its "ideal type" a political union in which Community and Member State continue their uneasy co-existence, although with an ever-increasing embrace. It is important also to understand that the voice of, say, Thatcher is not an expression of this community vision. Thatcherism is one pole of the first vision, whereby Community membership continues to be assessed and reevaluated in terms of its costs and benefits to a Member State, in this case the UK, which remains the ultimate referent for its desirability. The Community is conceived in this way of thinking not as a redefinition of the national self but as an arrangement, elaborate and sophisticated, of achieving long-term maximization of the national interest in an interdependent world. Its value is measured ultimately and exclusively with the coin of national utility and not community solidarity.

I do not think that 1992 can be seen as representing a clear preference and choice for one vision over the other. But there are manifestations, both explicit and implicit, suggesting an unprecedented and triumphal resurgence and ascendancy of the unity vision of Europe over the competing vision of community: part and parcel of the 1992 momentum. If indeed the road to European union is to be paved on this unity vision, at the very moment of ascendancy the Community endangers something noble at its very core and, like other great empires, with the arrival of success may sow the seeds of self-destruction.

Why such foreboding? Whence the peril in the unity vision? At an abstract logical level it is easy to challenge the unity vision which sets up a fully united Europe as the pinnacle of the process of European integration. It would be more than ironic if a polity with its political process set up to counter the excesses of statism ended up coming round full circle and transforming itself into a (super)state. It would be equally ironic that an ethos that rejected the nationalism of the Member States gave birth to a new European nation and European nationalism. The problem with the unity vision is that its very realization entails its negation.

But the life of the Community (like some other things) is not logic, but experience. And experience suggests that with all the lofty talk of political union and federalism we are not about to see the demise of the Member States, at least not for a long time. The reports leaking out of the Intergovernmental Conference suggest fairly modest steps on this road.

That being the case, the unease with the unity vision none the less remains. For if the unity ethos becomes the principal mobilizing force of the polity, it may, combined with the praxis and rhetoric of the 1992 single market, compromise the deeper values inherent in the community vision, even if the Community's basic structure does not change for years to come. I suggested above that these values operated both at the interstate level by conditioning a new type of statal discourse and self-perception and at the societal and individual level by diminishing the importance of nationality in transnational human intercourse. How then would the unity vision and the 1992 praxis and rhetoric corrode these values?

The successful elimination of internal frontiers will, of course, accentuate in a symbolic and real sense the external frontiers of the Community. The privileges of Community membership for states and of Community citizenship for individuals are becoming increasingly pronounced. This is manifest in such phenomena as the diffidence of the Community towards further enlargement (packaged in the notion of the concentric circles),[213] in the inevitable harmonization of external border controls, immigration, and asylum policies, and in policies such as local European content of television-broadcasting regulation. It assumes picaresque character with the enhanced visibility of the statal symbols already adopted by the Community: flag, anthem, Community passport. The potential corrosive effect on the values of the community vision of European integration are self-evident. Nationality as referent for interpersonal relations, and the human alienating effect of *us* and *them* are brought back again, simply transferred from their previous intra-Community context to the new inter-Community one. We have made little progress if the *us* becomes European (instead of German or French or British) and the *them* becomes those outside the Community or those inside who do not enjoy the privileges of citizenship.

There is a second, slightly more subtle, potentially negative influence in this realm. A centerpiece of the agenda for further integration is the need of Europe to develop the appropriate structures for a common foreign and defense policy.[214] It has indeed been anomalous that despite the repeated calls since the early 1970s for a Europe that will speak with one voice,[215]

---

[213] See Delors Speech of October 17, 1990.

[214] *Ibid.*; see also "Proposals of European Parliament to Intergovernmental Conference," PE 146.824, new Art. 130U (proposing full-fledged apparatus for European foreign and security policy).

[215] On the history of European political co-operation and the idea of Europe speaking with one voice, see Stein, "Towards a European Foreign Policy?"

the Community has never successfully translated its internal economic might to commensurate outside influence. There could be much positive in Europe taking such a step to an enhanced common foreign and security policy. The potential corrosive element of this inevitable development rests in the suspicion that some of the hearkening for a common foreign policy is the appeal of strength and the vision of Europe as a new global superpower. Europe *is* a political and economic superpower and often fails to see this and discharge its responsibilities appropriately. But the ethos of strength and power, even if transferred from the Member State to the European level, is closer to the unity rather than community notion of Europe and, as such, partakes of the inherent contradiction of that vision.

All these images and the previous question marks are not intended as an indictment of 1992 and the future road of European integration. Both in its structure and process, and, in part, its ethos, the Community has been more than a simple successful venture in transnational co-operation and economic integration. It has been a unique model for reshaping transnational discourse among states, peoples, and individuals who barely a generation ago emerged from the nadir of Western civilization. It is a model with acute relevance for other regions of the world with bleak histories or an even bleaker present.

Today's Community is impelled forward by the dysfunctioning of its current architecture. The transformation that is taking place has immense, widely discussed promise. If I have given some emphasis to the dangers, it is not simply to redress a lacuna in the literature. It is also in the hope that as this transformation takes place, that part, limited as it may be, of the Community that can be characterized as the modern contribution of Europe to the civilization of interstatal and intrastatal intercourse shall not be laid by the wayside.

## The Trans Formation of Europe: An Afterword

### Infranationalism

The central thesis of the preceding essay concerned a relationship – complex at times – between Community legal structure (constitutionalism, normative supranationalism, "Exit") and Community political process (institutionalism, decisional supranationalism, "Voice"). These two poles were used simultaneously as a narrative device (that is, a way of telling the story) and as an analytical device (that is, a way of explaining it). Critically, the relationship was neither one-dimensional in its direction (from law to politics or from politics to law) or in its causality (this legal development explains this political process or *vice versa*). Instead, both description and analysis were circular – political process explaining and conditioning legal structure and legal structure conditioning and explaining political process.

One important pay-off in my view was the ability to assess the key relationship of Community and Member States in an equally complex and partially circular manner. The picture of transformation presented is at odds with two theses which have had some currency in the literature.

One thesis, finding, perhaps, its louder expression in Euroskeptic rather than Europhile circles, views the march of Community evolution as representing a continued net loss of sovereignty.[216] Implicitly, this view regards European integration as a zero-sum game between the Member States and the Community as power brokers in the public square. The history of most federal states, in which centralization has taken place at the expense of local power, lends credibility aplenty to this view. The analysis in "Transformation" militates against this evaluation and attempts to dispel a straightforward zero-sum analysis.

An alternative thesis argues in different guises[217] that the Member States have all along remained the central players in Community evolution and that most evolution, even in the critical field of constitutionalization, was willed and served the interest of the Member States. A more nuanced version of this thesis unpacks the concept of Member State and argues that, at a minimum, governments, the executive branch, of Member States have been empowered by the Community structure and process at the expense of, say, other branches of Member State government. The analysis in "Transformation" sustains some part of this thesis but also qualifies it substantially. Even the enhanced "Voice" of the Member States prior to the shift to majority voting took place in an institutional and constitutional environment which was quite unlike classical intergovernmental fora, even in an increasingly interdependent and "globalized" world. As to the thesis of executive branch empowerment, whilst this is largely

---

[216] See, e.g., Schmidt, "National Patterns of Governance under Siege: The Impact of European Integration," in B. Kohler-Koch (ed.), *The Transformation of Governance in the European Union* (Routledge: 1998).

[217] See, e.g., A. Moravcsik, "Preference and Power in the European Community: A Liberal Intergovernmentalist Approach," in S. Bulmer and A. Scott (eds.), *Economic and Political Integration in Europe: Internal Dynamics and Global Context* (Blackwell: Oxford, Cambridge, MA, 1994); and A. Moravcsik, "Why the European Community Strengthens the State: Domestic Politics and International Cooperation" (Harvard University CES Working Paper Series No. 52, 1994).

true in general formal terms and also true in the big Newtonian events of Community life such as intergovernmental conferences (where big events take place at low speed), it has to be qualified by an Einsteinian perspective of the Community – its day-to-day atomistic management (where small events happen at large speed). There,[218] governments often find themselves as impotent as other national or even Community actors.

Further, even if there is much force to the executive branch empowerment argument, it has been over a shrinking public policy domain. Nowhere will this be as visible as in the area of economic and monetary union.

With a distance of six years or so since the publication of "Transformation," I am able to be more decisive in characterizing the third period of European integration which, in my analysis, comes after the watershed of the SEA and the restoration of qualified majority voting in widespread areas of Community life. The foundational period was one which saw the emergence of constitutionalism and with it the basic equilibrium between legal structure and political process which, in my view, was the key to explaining that dimension of the polity for its first decades. The 1970s and the period leading up to the adoption of the SEA were times which, I argued, were not "stagnant" from a structural point of view, but saw a major constitutional quiet revolution: the collapse of an effective system of enumeration and constitutional guarantees to the limits of Community legislative and other action.

What, then, would be the hallmark of the last decade from a constitutional and institutional perspective?

It is, in my view, the emergence of *infranationalism* as a central feature of Community governance.[219] Infranationalism is explained in a couple of essays in the second part of this volume. It is based on the realization that increasingly large sectors of Community norm creation are done at a meso-level of governance. The actors involved are middle-range officials of the Community and the Member States in combination with a variety of private and semi-public bodies players. Comitology[220] and the

---

[218] See, e.g., Alexander Ballmann, "Infranationalism and the Community Governing Process," Annex to J. H. H. Weiler, Alexander Ballmann, Ulrich Haltern, Herwig Hofmann, Franz Mayer and Sieglinde Schreiner-Linford, "Certain Rectangular Problems of European Integration" (Project IV/95/02, Directorate General for Research, European Parliament, http://www.iue.it/AEL/EP/fpp.html, 1996).

[219] See José de Areilza, "Sovereignty or Management?: The Dual Character of the EC's Supranationalism – Revisited" (Harvard Jean Monnet Working Paper No. 2/95, 1995; http://www.law.harvard.edu/Programs/JeanMonnet/); and Ballmann, "Infranationalism."

[220] See, e.g., R. H. Pedler and G. F. Schaefer (eds.), *Shaping European Law and Policy – The Role of Committees and Comitology in the Political Process* (European Centre for Public

remaining netherworld of Community committees are the arena, and the political science of networks is the current analytical tool which tries to explain the functioning of this form of governance. From a constitutional point of view, my argument is simple: infranationalism is not constitutional or unconstitutional. It is outside the constitution. The constitutional vocabulary is built around "branches" of government, around constitutional functions,[221] around concepts of delegation, separation, checks, and balances among the arms of government etc. Infranationalism is like the emergence of viruses for which antibiotics, geared towards the control of microbes and germs, were simply ill-suited. Infranationalism renders the nation and state hollow and its institutions meaningless as a vehicle for both understanding and controlling government – hence my choice of this appellation.

I believe that increasingly both academia and the political process itself will turn towards the phenomena associated with infranationalism as meriting most attention in understanding and improving the quality and transparency of Union governance.

## The Community equilibrium in the 1990s and beyond

"Transformation" left open the question concerning the potential consequences of the introduction of relatively widespread majority voting on the institutional and constitutional architecture of the Community with the coming into force of the SEA in the late 1980s.

If we revert to the equilibrium theorem which underlies "Transformation," the introduction of majority voting (for reasons explained in the essay itself), which in some ways limits the individual voice of individual Member States, should have resulted in challenges to the Exit pole of the equilibrium, that is, the constitutional architecture of the Community. Alternatively, one could look for evidence that the sustained period of equilibrium between Voice and Exit helped foster a loyalty to the new emergent polity in which Voice achieved through the normal channels of Community decision-making would be considered adequate.

Affairs, European Institute of Public Administration Maastricht: 1996); Vos, "The Rise of Committees," *European Law Journal* 3 (1997), 210; Bradley, "The European Parliament and Comitology: On the Road to Nowhere?," *European Law Journal* 3 (1997), 230; and Joerges and Neyer, "From Intergovernmental Bargaining to Deliberative Political Processes: The Constitutionalisation of Comitology," *European Law Journal* 3 (1997), 273.

[221] E. U. Petersmann, *Constitutional Functions and Constitutional Problems of International Economic Law: Foreign Trade Law and Policy in the USA, the EC and Switzerland* (1991).

Several essays in the second part of this volume provide what could be considered as evidence that such a loyalty, if it exists at all, is precarious and argue that it is precarious because there is a legitimacy dissonance between the constitutional claims of the polity and its social reality. They also provide some evidence that the constitutional architecture is, indeed, coming under challenge. Let me present briefly some of that evidence:

1. There are challenges from the collectivity of states. Consider first the Maastricht Treaty itself under the shadow of which we are still operating. EMU aside, in a praiseworthy and deservedly famous article reflecting on the constitutional dimensions of Maastricht, "The Constitutional Structure of the Union: A Europe of Bits and Pieces," Deidre Curtin criticized the fragmentation and constitutional incoherence of the Union structure and had, too, harsh words for a certain assault on the ECJ in the Maastricht process.[222] Amsterdam is generally even more anemic, but whilst expanding somewhat the role of the European Parliament in the decisional process, one cannot but notice a growing reticence towards the constitutional architecture on issues such as majority voting, the role of the Commission, and, arguably, foreign policy.

2. There are challenges from individual Member States. In the Maastricht process it was the UK and Denmark. In the Amsterdam IGC there was the Franco-German (!) initiative which introduced such variable geometry as to make the Community pillar itself one of bits and pieces. The final version, under strenuous pressure from small Member States, emasculated much of the original initiative. But its very proposal is of some significance. In the same breath one could mention the breathtaking proposal which surfaced during the IGC to amend Article 189A which requires unanimity to modify a Commission proposal. A better targeted attack on the constitutional powers of the Commission is more difficult to imagine. This proposal was blocked – a deal-breaker for the Commission – but it is a sign of the attack on the constitutional-institutional balance.

3. There are challenges from constitutional actors within Member States. Most interesting are the challenges coming from the national judiciary and in particular the highest courts. The German Constitutional Court and its Belgian counterpart have been most explicit on the issue of

---

[222] D. Curtin, "The Constitutional Structure of the Union: A Europe of Bits and Pieces," *Common Market Law Review* 30 (1993), 65.

jurisdiction. The Italian Court which has declared that it was under no duty to make references to the ECJ under Article 177 since it was not a "jurisdiction" in the sense of the Treaty has been more subtle but even more insidious at the same time. There are signs from others as well, challenging precisely the hegemony of the ECJ.[223] There has been an understandable reaction trying to minimize and paper over the cracks. But it is there for anyone who wishes to look. Also at lower levels of the judiciary, the *Francovich* jurisprudence, for example, is not receiving quite the same welcome as earlier constitutional advances of the ECJ.[224]

4. There are challenges from, yes, new constituencies within the ECJ. (We should not commit the error of imagining the ECJ as an homogeneous actor free of internal factions, disagreements and internal conflicting views on many issues, including the contours of constitutionalism. The oft-deep divisions on fundamental issues between Advocates-General – full members of the ECJ – and the ECJ itself surely mirror similar divisions within the College of Judges.) Consider the post-Maastricht jurisprudence of the ECJ itself – for example its famous (or, to some, infamous) *Keck* decision which shifted the balance back to the Member States in the critical area of the internal market. Assailed by many champions of the single market as a heresy, Norbert Reich used that decision among those justifying his analysis of a veritable economic constitutional *revolution*.[225] But there were others such as the controversial decisions which cut the role and power of the Community in the World Trade Organization or the one which denied the Union the competence to adhere to the European Convention on Human Rights.

5. Most important, in my view, are the challenges from general public opinion in several Member States. Maastricht, refreshingly, gave the lie to years of a Eurobarometer ostrich syndrome. It is clear that Euro-skepticism is not just another English vice. At a minimum, "Europe" is no longer part of consensus, non-partisan politics in many

---

[223] For a sober account of the evolving relationship between the European Court of Justice and national courts, see generally, Slaughter, Stone and Weiler (eds.), *The European Court of Justice and National Courts* (Hart Publishing: Oxford, 1998).

[224] See Caruso, "The Missing View of the Cathedral: The Private Law Paradigm of European Legal" (Harvard Jean Monnet Working Paper 9/96, 1996; http://www.law.harvard.edu/Programs/JeanMonnet/); and Harlow, "Francovich and the Problem of the Disobedient State," *European Law Journal* 2 (1996), 199.n Market Law Review 31 (1994), 459.

[225] Reich, "The November Revolution of the European Court of Justice: Keck, Meng and Audi Revisited," *Common Market Law Review* 31 (1994), 459.

Member States, not least the new ones. Politicians can no longer count on automatic approval of their architectural changes to Community and Union.

As in "Transformation" itself, I cannot overemphasize that my argument is not about a direct causal relationship: "Majority voting? Let's attack the constitutional foundation" is no more my point than "Supremacy and direct effect? Let's insist on a veto" was in "Transformation." What I am arguing is that there is a nexus between the two spheres of politics and law where developments in one create a climate, act as a catalyst, help sustain developments, and moves in the other.

Put differently, my argument is that the current political processes of Community governance offer a much less hospitable environment for the continued development or even the sustaining of the constitutional architecture. A new transformation is called for. What it may be like and on what basis it may be forged is part of the subtext of many of the essays in the second part of this book.

~

# Introduction: *The Transformation of Europe*
# Twenty-Five Years After

MIGUEL POIARES MADURO AND MARLENE WIND

What made *The Transformation of Europe* (ToE) a profoundly original contribution was the deep diagnosis of the legal and political interplay in the construction of a supranational Europe. It was original in how it presented the process of European integration and reinvented its narrative, but it was equally original in how it reached that result: by a unique methodology combining law and political science to challenge the conclusions on European integration each discipline had reached on its own.

The originality of Weiler's approach allowed him to question the dominant narratives of European integration. It was, as Neil Walker puts it in his contribution to this volume, not an insider's tale that defended European constitutionalism as inevitable and as a 'good thing'. Rather, ToE 'presented a picture of European integration that was more dynamic, but also more precarious and less insular than the received wisdom'. ToE describes the process of constitutionalisation in an overall positive light, but, at the same time, highlights the extent to which the success of European integration is founded on an inherent and unstable tension between state polities and the emerging European polity. Combining the legal and the political development as genuinely interdependent, ToE captured the essence of the European experiment and challenged the so far preached narrative of a European integration process that was orchestrated by politicians aided by law and lawyers. As Weiler presented it in ToE, things were much less intentional and much more structural with politics being locked into a gradually more and more binding legal structure. Thus if you wake a law or political science student up in the middle of the night and ask 'what are the central points in Weiler's *The Transformation of Europe?*' most would probably still say: 'the gradual "locking-in" of a constitutional legal structure manifesting itself as a "silent revolution" only realised by the political sphere after the fact'. As the student becomes slightly more awake, however, she will most likely add something rather important, namely, the prediction or anticipation in ToE that as majority voting becomes the dominant decision mode in the EU and as EU law gets 'harder' in terms of its binding effect, the less willing member states will be to give up their control with the process. Or as Weiler puts it himself: 'The "harder" the law in terms of binding effect both on and within states, the less willing states are to give up their prerogative to control the emergence of such law or the law's "opposability" to them … decision making suddenly become important.' The paradox is, in other words, that the more successful the constitutionalisation becomes, the more stalemate in the political decisions. If exit is no longer possible, voice and loyalty are the only options; however, voice does not necessarily mean progress in terms of more integration, as Weiler posits. The question is, of course, how we today twenty-five years later judge Weiler's diagnosis and his theoretical contribution to both law and political science? Has stalemate occurred as predicted, or has the power of law and of the EU legal regime been so strong that politics succumbed? As it will be discussed in many of the contributions to this celebratory volume, there are in fact different views on this.

Another important contribution of ToE was the normative concern of democracy and of constitutional tolerance. In that respect, ToE seems to anticipate the success of constitutional pluralism as both a descriptive theory of how the relationship between national constitutional law and EU law has evolved without a determination of final authority, and a normative theory arguing for that question of final authority to be left open as that is what best aligns with a vision of democracy and constitutionalism in an interdependent Europe. This tension is not easy to manage, however, and the ever-embarrassing nature of European integration (highlighted by Weiler) has put it under increased stress. There is thus a normative conflict or tension between the demand of constitutional discipline coupled with an increasing awareness of a lacking constitutional authority in Weiler's writings. We have on the one hand the doctrines established by the ECJ instituting supremacy, direct effect, and judicial remedies which effectively have subjected member states to a constitutional discipline. On the other hand the EU's lack of a traditional Demos and of genuine electoral politics has led some to argue for limits to either the strength and/or the scope of that constitutional discipline and others to push for the emergence of true European parliamentarianism and even the creation of a European Demos (albeit of a different nature from a national Demos). Weiler himself has increasingly highlighted the absence of values from the process of European integration. The paradox is that all these different approaches depart from the inherent tension and incrementalism that Weiler identified as the foundation of the success of European integration.

How to solve the problems that this foundational tension has created without eliminating the tension itself has, perhaps, become the crucial issue of European integration, one that ToE partly anticipated but was not focused on solving.

This book is structured in the following manner:

**Gráinne de Búrca** argues in her 'The Transformation of Europe Revisited: Civilising Interstatal Relations' that Weiler's piece, aside from changing the usual understanding of the legal and political processes of European integration, drew attention to the problems which have come to be recognised as the biggest challenges faced by the EU: the political and democratic deficits, the ineffectiveness in protecting its own values, and the erosion of the legitimacy of its institutions and the entire process of European integration. However, instead of concluding from these challenges the demise of the EU, de Búrca argues that the EU can draw on a strength also identified by Weiler to find a future-oriented raison d'être. Its aim of civilising interstate relations, that has governed it internally, can now assume a stronger international role. According to de Búrca, it is in this that the Union may find the public engagement and support necessary for its legitimacy. In other words, it will be the successful transfer of the community vision to shape an effective but distinctive external policy of the EU that may allow it to overcome its current internal challenges.

**Peter L. Lindseth** writes in 'Disequilibrium and Disconnect: On Weiler's (Still Robust) Theory of European Transformation' that the essential message embodied in the equilibrium theory Weiler articulated in ToE remains valid today. This message, according to Lindseth, is one of caution regarding the nature and scope of integration: when the integration process assumes that it enjoys resources of legitimacy beyond those it in fact possesses, the essential equilibrium of European integration is put into question. In this light, Europe's challenges cannot be solved by legal and institutional engineering as they are not founded on a democratic deficit, but on a genuine 'democratic disconnect'. In this way, while seeing himself as in line with Joseph Weiler's original message in ToE, Lindseth argues that an administrative model provides a better framework for understanding the EU than a constitutional model. The latter would assume the possibility of an autonomous democratic and constitutional legitimacy that the Union does not have.

**Julio Baquero Cruz** calls his essay 'Joseph Weiler and the Experience of Law' and takes a very personal route explaining how Weiler influenced him as a legal scholar. Baquero Cruz describes very vividly how he struggled with his legal studies in Spain as a twenty-year-old, but also how he almost entirely transformed as he met Joseph Weiler and discovered what he calls the 'enhanced view of law'. Baquero Cruz links ToE with the work of Joseph Weiler as a teacher of law. The focus is his enormous contribution to a view of law that is respectful and knowledgeable of the text and dogmatics, but inclusive of justice and subject to the perspectives of multiple disciplines. Baquero Cruz's personal recognition of the impact of Joseph Weiler does not prevent him from challenging Weiler's description in ToE of the foundational and consolidating periods. He believes Weiler's points are overstated. The changes were more gradual than they are presented in ToE, and the relation between exit and voice is not descriptively adequate for Baquero Cruz. In his view, the evidence does not support the thesis that the political developments towards consensus decision-making were an answer to the legal developments towards the constitutionalisation of EU law. The opposite, however, might be more likely. In Baquero Cruz's view, the political inter-governmental developments might have impacted the 'self-perception of judges, their mission and their decisions'. This more gradualist perspective without profound transformations likely also supports Baquero Cruz's view on the community and unity visions. Contrary to Joseph Weiler, he does not see a necessary choice between them. In his view, the community vision may, instead, be the path to the unity vision.

In her chapter '*The Transformation of Europe* in US Legal Academia and Its Legacy in the Field of Private Law' **Daniela Caruso** explains that the rise of EU law in US legal scholarship was closely tied to the 'professional itinerary of Joseph Weiler' and the impact of ToE. She explains the success of ToE with the power of its narrative, but also with the historical context ('when and where the story is told'). ToE coincides with a period of renewed interest in federalism in American scholarly and political debates. Europe, as ToE explained, was doing federalism, but a different kind of federalism. The timing and power of ToE allowed a transatlantic dialogue on constitutionalism to emerge. European integration was used to bring new insights into the American debate, but also to allow a less ideological discussion on federalism. This decade of success of European integration studies in American universities is now over, according to Caruso. The failure of the constitutional treaty and the European crisis following the financial crisis have contributed to the demise of European studies in the

United States. EU law thus eventually migrated back to where it came from: comparative and international law. Caruso highlights a second aspect: the impact of ToE and EU law on her own field of private law. She recalls the ambivalence with which Joseph Weiler describes the single market project. Weiler notes the deep political nature of this project. It is a project that prizes market efficiency above other values. Caruso argues that Weiler was proved right and that many conflicts emerged between national private law and EU law by virtue of the political project embodied in the rationality of the single market. But she also contends that time has changed the political values of the single market project that, nowadays, is less about deregulation of private autonomy and more about the uniformity of private law regulation. This does not prevent, however, the asymmetry of costs that private law uniformity may have in different economies within the EU, something that Caruso believes ought to get more salience.

**Neil Walker** argues in his 'A European Half-Life? A Retrospective on Joseph Weiler's *The Transformation of Europe*' that ToE not only was a landmark in European legal scholarship, but also marked a watershed in Weiler's own approach to the European project. Walker describes how Weiler's work evolved from the sharp, almost clinical diagnosis of EU law (and politics) in ToE to a much more normative strand of writings in his later work. This was the consequence of the transformation described in ToE itself. In fact, Weiler's works become increasingly pessimistic in light of the 'failure to meet the challenge of political renewal, which the 1990s – the original age of transformation – presented in such stark form'. The emergence of supranational politics, depicted at the end of ToE (mostly with majority voting), and the increased irrelevance of the original motivational ideals of peace and prosperity brought challenges that the EU has not been successful in addressing. Weiler's later work focuses, precisely, on the diagnosis of that failure, the incapacity of the EU 'to provide a context for the inculcation of the very virtues which would allow the sustained realization or renewal of these values'. As Walker notes, Weiler is, however, sceptical of institutional moves and fearful of doing too little or too much. There is a risk, Walker argues, that the diagnosis, even if correct, will simply be left hanging with no obvious course of treatment. The consequence would be Europe entering 'half-life'. Is it, asks Walker, in the process of irreversible decline and fragmentation? He claims that there is actually more that can be done, in hard institutional terms, to pursue constructed European common goods generated through mechanisms of voice and decision at the continental scale.

**Gianluigi Palombella** delivers his perspectives on ToE in 'On the Past and the Future of *The Transformation of Europe*: Law, Governance, Rights, and Politics in the EU Evolution'. He writes that even twenty-five years after ToE was published, the EU still fails to trigger the 'awaited political mobilisation' expected of a true democracy. Palombella argues that Weiler's framework of analysis (institutions/politics interplay, legitimacy, ideological neutrality, the unity/community alternative) is still valid in assessing progress and focuses on three domains to assess such progress: European public (law), rights, and governance. He states that there is a potential in rights and governance for the EU to become a privileged space for European citizens to deal with the excesses of globalisation and the risks of managerialism. However, as Weiler himself has pointed out, 'European institutions have worked in such a way as to prevent Europe from cultivating the proper virtues that are necessary to pursue the foundational ideals.'

**R. Daniel Kelemen and Alec Stone Sweet** embark on a different route in their 'Assessing *The Transformation of Europe*: A View from Political Science'. They start by saying that ToE 'is arguably the most influential paper ever published on the European Court of Justice' and highlight the different ways in which it has been so. But they focus on how ToE developed a theory of how the Court's doctrinal actions related to state power and the development of the integration process. The core of this theory is the equilibrium thesis (that the legitimacy of the process of constitutionalisation undertaken by the Court rested on an equilibrium between a supranational legal system and an intergovernmental legislative system). The authors argue that, while this thesis explains the foundational period, the evidence does not support its impact on subsequent developments. The juridically driven constitutionalisation of the treaties was simply too self-reinforcing.

**Armin von Bogdandy** starts by arguing in his 'The Lisbon Treaty as a Response to *Transformation*'s Democratic Scepticism' that ToE teaches how systematic legal thought today requires interdisciplinary insights to develop the powerful concepts necessary to give meaning to all relevant legal materials and fact. But Bogdandy's focus is not the social science theory that Joseph Weiler develops in ToE, but rather the democratic deficit issue. The author argues that Weiler's community vision requires a unique conception of democracy for the EU that has, in fact, made its way into the Treaties. This democratic conception of EU democracy is based on notions of citizenship and representation that do not copy or question state notions and on developing new forms of participatory and deliberative democracy at the EU level. In an optimist tone, von Bogdandy argues, in particular, that much of Title II of the Treaty on the EU in the Lisbon Treaty can be read as a political response to the concerns expressed in ToE.

**Daniel Halberstam's** essay: 'Joseph Weiler, Eric Stein, and the Transformation of Constitutional Law', argues that pursuing ToE's transformation idea today requires nothing less than the transformation of constitutional law itself. Halberstam concludes his essay by noting a tension in ToE: it embraces constitutionalism, but also denies it by explaining it away. ToE warned that the move to majority voting would endanger the constitutional structure of the EU, but Halberstam argues in his piece that constitutionalisation of the Union critically depended on the loss of member state control. Halberstam contends that Weiler's account of the constitutionalisation of the European Union lacks a generative space of governance at the European level. The latter is crucial for the project of European integration to be genuinely constitutional. The challenge, for the future, is how to make Joseph Weiler's vision of 'community, not unity' compatible with a constitutional European Union. This requires transforming constitutional law itself, a project in which Halberstam sees himself engaged together with a third generation of scholars who work on the 'house' that Eric Stein built and that Joseph Weiler thoroughly remodelled.

In 'Perils of Unity, Promise of Union', **Kalypso Nicolaïdis** praises ToE for being a pioneering contribution making it possible for both political scientists and lawyers to see themselves in the equilibrium theory. The ToE offers, as Nicolaïdis puts it, a new analytical lens through which the integration process could be comprehended. But, even more importantly, the equilibrium between voice and exit constitutes a normative imperative and not simply an empirical observation. That is the community vision put forward by Weiler even if Nicolaïdis might prefer the expression Union, not Unity, to that of community. According to Nicolaïdis, it is natural for the equilibrium dynamics to change, but the task ahead is precisely that of identifying the new form of equilibrium. She fears that current political and economic dynamics are missing the essential normative imperative identified in ToE and argues for a renewal of the EU that could reinstate that equilibrium. She advances three conditions linked to the respect, but also rescuing, of national democracies, equal ownership of EU decisions by states and citizens, and, above all, 'a true transnational ambition towards progressive maturing of European citizens inspired by virtues of transnational mutuality and capacity to own others' plights and democratic traditions'.

**Alexander Somek** in his 'Unity and Community: A Tale of Two Monsters and One Unanswered Question' expresses deep gratitude for the contribution ToE made to his own 'discovery' of EU law and integration, but doesn't shy from a deep challenge to the core of Weiler's community vision. Somek's contribution starts by highlighting how the community vision conceives the supranationality of European integration as a way to rescue the nation from the state. European supranationality would prevent the abuses of the internal and external boundaries of the states. It would be the instrument to make states behave responsibly. According to Somek, there is, however, an ambivalence in Weiler's vision that has been reinforced by the practice of European integration: is it the abuse or the existence of the boundaries that is the problem? Using, in particular, the example of the internal market, Somek argues that the obstacle-based approach to free movement demonstrates how the question of abuse inevitably becomes a question of the existence of the boundaries itself. Boundaries, however, are crucial for political control and effective distributive justice. As such, the real question is where the relevant lines of those boundaries are to be drawn today.

'How Transformative Is the European Project? asks **Türküler Isiksel** in her essay. She argues that ToE poses two bold questions about transformation: 'can we view European integration as a transformative project' and 'has it achieved the transformation that it set out to achieve?' Isiksel argues that the answer is ambivalent, but largely negative. The transformation embodied in Weiler's supranationalism and community vision would require the self-understanding of states to have changed but, instead, the forces of voice and exit that compose Weiler's equilibrium model and the continued practice of European integration remain linked to the traditional understanding of the state. Weiler himself has criticised the loss of purpose of the Union. For him, the telos of European integration required a disentanglement of the exercise of political power from exclusivist notions of culturally, racially, linguistic, or religiously defined communities, but this was not achieved. Only such transformation would have made it possible for European citizens to remain committed to European integration even when it fails to deliver the promised results. This loyalty did not emerge, and without it the changes undertaken in Europe are not really transformative.

**Franz C. Mayer** in his essay '*The Transformation of Europe*: Loyalty Lost, Democracy Lost?' investigates what happed after ToE with concepts like loyalty and democracy. Mayer has looked into Weiler's republished version of ToE from 1999 where he added an afterword on exactly loyalty and the democratic deficit. Mayer notes that it was not an optimist afterword based on the growing Euroscepticism of MS populations. A new transformation is required involving the concepts of democracy and loyalty at the core of ToE. Mayer presents both pessimist and optimist accounts on the evolution of those themes and the role of law in addressing them. There have been instances of loyalty such as the Eurozone members' acceptance to join the fiscal treaty or other Eurozone measures or the European supreme/constitutional courts dialogue with the ECJ through preliminary references. But there are also confrontational instances such as the German *Bundesverfassungsgericht*'s recent rulings. One thing seems clear to Mayer: there has been a shift from democracy talk to identity talk. Where will that take the Union, and can the insistence on national identity be addressed through the prism of 'constitutional tolerance' (another Weiler concept)? These are open questions. Mayer concludes by appealing again to Hirschman's concepts (exit, voice, and loyalty) in foreseeing the role of EU law scholars. The challenges faced required loyalty to their discipline.

**Hans W. Micklitz's** essay is called 'The Transformation of Private Law'. Joseph Weiler's ToE is silent on the role of private law, but this does not – argues Micklitz – make it irrelevant. It is contended that exit vs. voice has become an integral part of the private law-making process. Micklitz sees those variables as operating differently in two different 'forms' of private law. Member states are willing to promote integration through the development of European *regulatory* private law, but those same member states voice critique and resistance 'whenever the EU via law making or via judicial interference tends to Europeanise *traditional* private law'. Micklitz argues that the EU is developing out of regulatory private law a largely autonomous European private law that is managed by regulatory agencies where the courts have only a limited say. Ultimately, this risks the provincialisation of member states' private legal orders. If so, according to Micklitz, 'the legitimacy of European private law as such is in jeopardy.'

**Marlene Wind** focuses on four lessons to be learned from ToE in her chapter '*The Transformation of Europe* and of Selective Exit Twenty-Five Years After'. The first is interdisciplinary. Why did ToE end up as a classic contribution to integration theory in both political science and law? A lot, she argues, has to do with the polarisation of the discipline in the 1960s, 1970s, and 1980s, when lawyers ignored political strategy altogether and political scientists hardly took any notice of law. ToE bridged the divide and even opened a flood of new research combining law and political science perspectives on the EU. The second theme that this article deals with is the central point in ToE about unintended consequences. Wind draws on her own research in describing how supremacy and direct effect as doctrines were adopted through tacit contract with the member states, but nevertheless over time produced a European order that was much more powerful than intended by the sovereignty-fixated capitals. The author explains how this striking insight has helped us to get away from narrow intergovernmentalist as well as simplistic neofunctionalistic perspectives dominating the political science field. A third and fourth theme deals with the issue of selective exit – understood here as noncompliance with EU law at the national level. Wind argues that selective exit is 'back' and should be taken seriously by researchers of European integration. When directives, and to some degree even regulations, are disregarded or deliberately implemented too late or wrongly, it is a form of 'selective exit' that Weiler did not anticipate in ToE. Whether it is a direct cause of majority voting is, however, hard to say argues Wind, but we should be much more aware of how the 'hardening of law' effects compliance structures in the member states. One good example of 'selective exit' is the interaction – or lack thereof – by national courts with the European Court of Justice. Wind draws again on her own research to exemplify how Nordic courts and judges have discretely avoided forwarding cases to the CJEU for decades. She argues that attention should be drawn to this type of practice, which also helps us understand much better the politics of law at the member state level.

In his essay, 'Europe Transformed. Exit, Voice . . . and Loyalty?' **Miguel Poiares Maduro** revisits the equilibrium between exit and voice in light of how Europe has evolved. In ToE, Weiler presents the foundational equilibrium as the explanation for the success of legal integration. But it is also on this equilibrium that Joseph Weiler seems to base much of the legitimacy of European integration. Poiares Maduro argues that the original equilibrium is no longer possible in light, in particular, of the evolution of the Union into a majoritarian polity. This evolution is described by linking the processes of constitutionalisation and Europeanisation and highlighting the extent of the transformation on the scope and nature of power in Europe. This is then linked to four different dimensions of the legitimacy crisis faced by Europe. Poiares Maduro argues that a new foundational equilibrium is required and can be found by looking at the third element of Hirschman's *Exit, Voice and Loyalty*. Loyalty is not, however, a substitute for exit or voice, but rather a way to understand and reconstruct exit and voice. The concept of systemic voice is then put forward as crucial to reinstate the unstable equilibrium on which the process of European integration can succeed.

This book closes with Joseph Weiler's revisitation of his own work. In a way, and true to Weiler's constant intellectual restlessness, his chapter presents the greatest challenge to *The Transformation of Europe*. Weiler provocatively announces this at the beginning of the chapter, when he describes the relationship between ToE and what followed in his scholarship as that of a 'slow dismantling'. The reality is, however, more ambiguous. This piece is strongly influenced by a diagnosis of the current crisis of European integration, a crisis that has led him to understand what he defines as 'the tragic nature of the European construct': for European integration to be truly democratically legitimated, the foundational equilibrium described in ToE (later normatively expressed in terms of the principle of constitutional tolerance) will have to be put into question. Weiler identifies and critically reviews three legitimating strategies in the history of European integration: input (process) legitimacy; output (result) legitimacy; and political messianism (something on which Weiler has elaborated in his most recent works). He concludes that all have failed to provide the European Union with the legitimacy necessary to withstand the present crisis and react appropriately. The depletion of Europe's legitimating resources does not lead to a conclusion, however, that less Europe is necessary. On the contrary: Weiler makes clear that the current challenges require European answers that only the European Union can develop. The tragedy is that European integration no longer seems to have the necessary legitimacy resources to successfully do what it needs to do. The only hope would be for national processes and structures to lend the Union the legitimacy it needs, something that is difficult when national legitimacy resources are running low.

This book's contributions have been selected from two conferences celebrating 'The Transformation of Europe' at the EUI in Florence (2010) and at Yale University, USA (2011). We are grateful to these two institutions for having hosted these events.

# 1

## *The Transformation of Europe* Revisited: Civilising Interstatal Relations

GRÁINNE DE BÚRCA

Joseph Weiler's magisterial article on *The Transformation of Europe*[1] was published at what has since come to be recognised as a crucial moment – perhaps the crucial turning point – in the trajectory of the European Union. Appearing in 1991, his essay took as its core theme a retrospective assessment of the path of European integration, published just as the successful 1992 Single Market program launched by the Single European Act was reaching its target date. While much of the article contained a subtle and insightful tracing of the unexpected and – prior to Weiler's path-breaking body of work – inadequately understood legal and political processes by which the early European Community system evolved, the last part of the article featured hints of the challenges to come. It posed some of the most persistent and challenging normative questions about the evolving European polity: What kind of democracy could it comprise? What kind of legitimacy might it enjoy? What would happen once its image of ideological neutrality faded and the emerging opposition between social Europe and market Europe became more evident? And finally – the 'ethos' question – would Europe's vision continue to be a distinctive one of supranational community or would it move towards a federal-state-like unity?

The main part of the article, in other words, reflected the dominant emphasis of the best interdisciplinary scholarship on European integration until that time – an emphasis also evident in Weiler's earlier major collaborative work *Integration through Law*[2] – which sought to explain and understand the fascinating, novel, and until then largely successful project of European integration. And yet it was the prognosis of significant

---

[1] J. H. H. Weiler, 'The Transformation of Europe', *Yale Law Journal*, 100, 8 (1991), 2403–83.
[2] M. Cappelletti, M. Seccombe and J. H. H. Weiler (eds.), *Integration through Law* (Berlin: W. de Gruyter, 1986).

challenges to come, contained in the latter part of *The Transformation of Europe*, which has proven all too accurate. It was not clear, at the time the article was written, what was likely to emerge from the two inter-governmental conferences of the early 1990s which were taking place at that time. In retrospect, however, we know that the publication of *The Transformation of Europe* coincided not just with the 1992 target date of the single market project, but also with the moment of enactment of the Maastricht Treaty which laid the legal foundations of economic and monetary union, and which has come to mark a turning point in the history of European integration.

Since the Maastricht Treaty was adopted, and even before it came into force, the European Union has been more or less continuously in what external observers and EU insiders alike have described as crisis mode.[3] The Maastricht Treaty moment is now associated with the end of the era of 'permissive consensus',[4] the beginning of vocal popular opposition to the EU as reflected in referenda and otherwise, and the rise of political Euroscepticism.[5] The Maastricht Treaty on European Union precipitated an era of backlash against the perceived return to the misplaced ambition of early 1950s European federalism and the turn away from the cautiously incremental functionalism of the ECSC and EEC treaties.[6] The leap taken in the Maastricht Treaty was simultaneously too great and too little: ambitious new policies like economic and monetary union, justice and home affairs, and a common foreign and security policy were introduced, but their shaping was deliberately removed from parliamentary control and placed in the hands of executives and intergovernmental actors. Twenty-five years on from the publication of *The Transformation of Europe* and the negotiation of the Maastricht Treaty, the European Union has, since the

[3] For an analysis of the crisis narrative, see V. Della Sala, 'Crisis, What Crisis? Narration, Crisis and Decline in the European Union', euce.org/eusa/2011/papers/8f_dellasalla.pdf.

[4] The term was coined by L. Lindberg and S. Scheingold in *Europe's Would-Be Polity: Patterns of Change in the European Community* (Englewood Cliffs, NJ: Prentice Hall, 1970). See also L. Hooghe and G. Marks, 'A Postfunctionalist Theory of European Integration: From Permissive Consensus to Constraining Dissensus', *British Journal of Political Science*, 39 (2008), 1–23.

[5] See P. Taggart and A. Szczerbiak, *The Comparative Party Politics of Euroscepticism*, Volumes 1 and 2 (Oxford University Press, 2008).

[6] For an account of the failed European Political Community treaty and the European Defence Community, see R. T. Griffiths, *Europe's First Constitution: The European Political Community, 1952–1954* (London: Federal Trust, 2000) and K. Ruane, *The Rise and Fall of the European Defence Community: Anglo–American Relations and the Crises of European Defence*, 1950–55 (Basingstoke: Macmillan, 2000).

onset of the banking crisis in 2007, been in the midst of what many view as an existential crisis. The dividends of relative prosperity and peace have been taken for granted and no longer supply a *raison d'être* for a closely integrated European polity sufficient to command popular support, and the idea of supranationality is too ambiguous, too thin, or perhaps too controversial to take their place.

The three major criticisms of the EU Joseph Weiler articulated in the second part of *The Transformation of Europe* were of (i) the democratic and (closely linked) political deficit; (ii) the lack of hard capacity and resolve to defend the values it holds dear; and (iii) the continued slide in the legitimacy of the EU and its institutions. Each of these criticisms remains equally, if not even more relevant today. The political and democratic deficits remain a matter of significant ongoing concern, the EU's legitimacy has continued to slide, and the lack of hard EU capacity and resolve in foreign policy is as evident as ever, even as the financial and debt crisis has shaken the Union's foundations. In terms of its democratic and political deficits, the EU seems to repeat if not to exacerbate its earlier failings. Each occasion of popular critique appears to have the effect, instead of inducing EU leaders to confront the political deficit more directly or to endeavour to be more democratically responsive, of prompting them to remove issues ever further from public and democratic debate.[7] When the Constitutional Treaty was rejected by referendum in 2005, the EU leaders chose, during a hasty and secretive intergovernmental conference, to repackage it with little substantive change as a legally complex amending Treaty (the Lisbon Treaty) to avoid the likelihood of it being put to a popular vote in any state.[8] More recently, a turn away from democratic institutions and towards technocratic solutions has characterised the EU's response to the banking and sovereign debt crisis.

In other words, the picture of the EU today is a very gloomy one, with the challenges and critiques articulated by Weiler in *The Transformation of Europe* having grown ever more challenging. And yet, rather than joining the many plausible voices predicting the continued decline and even demise of the EU, I want to return to another suggestion made in the

---

[7] Compare S. Bartolini, 'Should the Union Be Politicized? Problems and Risks', with S. Hix, 'Why the EU Needs (Left-Right) Politics: Policy Reform and Accountability Are Impossible without It', Notre Europe, Policy Paper No. 19 (2006).

[8] See G. de Búrca, 'The Lisbon Treaty No-Vote: An Irish Problem or a European Problem?' *Irish Yearbook of International Law*, 3 (2008), 3.

concluding passages of Weiler's article about the European Community's vision of 'civilising interstatal relations'. I will argue that this suggestion, despite its appearance as part of a warning about the EU's future, offers the germ of an argument from which a more optimistic vision of the EU's possible future path might be drawn.

Towards the end of *The Transformation of Europe*, Weiler argued that there is a risk that the possible development of Europe as a global power could move the EU in the troubling direction of a vision of 'unity' or super-statehood, rather than continuing with the community vision and its aim of 'civilising interstatal relations'. Contemplating the EU twenty-five years on, however, I suggest that it may be precisely in the development of a stronger international role to complement its internal role and policies that the EU could find a stronger, future-oriented *raison d'être*. It could do this by contributing something distinctive to transnational, global relations, while simultaneously generating some of the domestic public engagement and support which is necessary to sustain the EU as a political system.

Weiler's concern, even while he lamented the lack of EU military capacity, was that the EU's wish to develop a common foreign and security policy might herald its emergence as a global superpower in a way that would reflect a 'unity' vision rather than the distinctive community vision thus far pursued by the EU. The unity vision he described was one which saw the EU member states moving ever closer into a federal political union, gradually submerging their individual state identities into a federal (super)state. Development of a foreign and security policy, together with economic and monetary union, seemed to portend a possible move in this direction. The community vision, on the other hand, which the European Community had pursued for the first few decades of its existence, would not involve the gradual disappearance of separate sovereign states, but added the interest of the community to the interest of the state, and sought to reconcile sovereign statehood with a new discipline of interstatal cooperation and solidarity.

I suggest that the EU's gradual development of a stronger and wider role in external relations over the twenty-five years since *The Transformation of Europe* was published has not seen the emergence of a unity vision, but instead a continuation of something closer to the community vision Weiler described. Further, not only has the emergence of stronger EU external relations failed to lead to the growth of a super-state based on a unity vision, but much of the EU's international relations in fact entail the promotion beyond the EU of the complex, multi-headed, painstaking and often frustrating but also distinctive form of interstatal cooperation on which the EU has itself been built.

Until twenty years ago, the EU's international role was marginal and attracted little academic or public interest outside the field of trade. Today, however, the EU has developed a stronger and broader set of external policies in many important fields and has strengthened its presence in various international fora,[9] while consciously investing institutional effort and resources into shaping its global role and impact.[10] And despite its economic decline through the years of the banking and sovereign debt crisis, and despite the many critiques of the EU's external policies, including the damage inflicted by the colonial past of its member states,[11] the EU nonetheless still potentially represents an alternative model of global engagement to that offered by other major global actors such as the United States and China today. While the argument that the EU, unlike other important global actors, is a uniquely 'normative' actor has been robustly challenged,[12] it can nevertheless be plausibly argued that the EU is a different *kind* of international actor from other comparably sized global powers, and that this offers it the possibility of playing a distinctive kind of global role.

---

[9] Examples of this are the EU's influence within the G20, and the EU's new status at the UN. See J. Wouters and S. Van Kerckhoven, 'The EU's Internal and External Regulatory Actions after the Outbreak of the 2008 Financial Crisis', Leuven Working Paper No. 69 (July 2011).

[10] There is a vast literature in both law and political science on EU external relations, and a lively debate on the distinctiveness or otherwise of EU foreign policy. For two contrasting perspectives, see, e.g., I. Manners, 'Normative Power Europe: A Contradiction in Terms?' *Journal of Common Market Studies*, 40 (2002), 235–58 and A. Hyde Price, 'A Tragic Actor? A Realist Perspective on "Ethical Power" Europe', *International Affairs*, 84 (2008), 29–44. For an intermediate position between the 'normative EU' and 'realist EU' perspectives, see S. Keukeleire and J. MacNaughtan, *The Foreign Policy of the EU* (Basingstoke: Palgrave Macmillan, 2008) and P. Holden, *In Search of Structural Power: EU Aid Policy as a Global Political Instrument* (Aldershot: Ashgate, 2009). For recent collections on legal aspects of EU external relations, see B. Van Vooren, S. Blockmans and J. Wouters, *The EU's Role in Global Governance: The Legal Dimension* (Oxford: Oxford University Press, 2013); D Kochenov and F. Amtenbrink, *The EU's Influence on the Global Legal Order* (Cambridge: Cambridge University Press, 2013); M. Cremona and B. de Witte, *EU Foreign Relations Law: Constitutional Fundamentals* (Oxford: Hart, 2008); P. Koutrakos (ed.), *EU Foreign Policy: Legal and Political Perspectives* (Cheltenham: Edward Elgar, 2011).

[11] For some critical accounts, see S. Engle-di Mauro (ed.), *The European's Burden: Global Imperialism in EU Expansion* (New York; Oxford: Peter Lang, 2006); M. Farrell, 'A Triumph of Realism over Idealism? Cooperation between the EU and Africa', *Journal of European Integration*, 27 (2005), 263–83; and H. Behr, 'The European Union in the Legacies of Imperial Rule? EU Accession Politics Viewed from a Historical Comparative Perspective', *European Journal of International Relations*, 13 (2007), 239–62.

[12] N. Tocci (ed.), *Who Is a Normative Foreign Policy Actor? The EU and Its Global Partners* (CEPS, 2008).

   While it is unquestionably a complex and often contradictory external
actor both in its internal and its external policies,[13] the EU has nonetheless, in the arena of external relations, more consistently pursued a
collective approach than other comparably powerful global actors, opting more often for a multilateralist rather than a unilateralist approach
in its foreign relations.[14] The EU has sought to develop and project a
distinctive character as a global actor in fields such as climate change,
development, human rights, and democracy promotion, and as an actor
committed to pursuing collective and coordinated, as well as multilateral solutions to global problems.[15] In other words, the EU has pursued
a reasonably progressive set of internationally oriented policies across a
number of fields of this kind, and has generally placed more emphasis
on the pursuit of milieu than possession goals in its foreign policy.[16] This
is far from saying that the EU is a uniquely 'normative' or 'ethical' actor,
or that it does not robustly pursue its own material interests in its external relations.[17] On the contrary, the EU has regularly been criticised by
development NGOs and others for advancing its own economic interests

---

[13]  See Z. Laidi, 'European Preferences and Their Reception, in Z. Laidi (ed.), *EU Foreign
   Policy in a Globalized World: Normative Power and Social Preferences* (London: Routledge,
   2008), introduction.

[14]  See G. de Búrca, 'EU External Relations: The Governance Mode of Foreign Policy', in B. Van
   Vooren, S. Blockmans and J. Wouters (eds.), *The EU's Role in Global Governance: The Legal
   Dimension* (Oxford: Oxford University Press, 2013), 39–58. For a critique of the EU's weak-
   ening commitment to liberal internationalism and multilateralism, see R. Youngs, *The EU's
   Role in World Politics: A Retreat from Liberal Internationalism* (London: Routledge, 2010).

[15]  The European Council on Foreign Relations in its annual scorecards on European foreign
   policy has indicated that even where it is weak in bilateral relations with powerful states
   such as China and Russia, the EU has scored well on a broad range of important multilateral and global issues, notably climate change, crisis management, Bretton Woods reform,
   non-proliferation, human rights at the UN, international criminal court policy, development aid, and global health. See www.ecfr.eu/content/entry/european_foreign_policy_
   scorecard_2012 and 2013.

[16]  On milieu and possession goals, see A. Wolfers, *Discord and Collaboration: Essays on
   International Politics* (Baltimore, MD: Johns Hopkins University Press, 1965), chapter 5,
   73–6. He defines possession goals as those which focus on the protection or strengthening
   of national possessions and resources, such as territory, trade advantages, and domestic
   sovereignty. Milieu goals, on the other hand, focus on shaping and stabilising the surrounding and international environment and emphasise the promotion of long-term
   security, stability, sustainability, cooperation, and peaceful international relations.

[17]  See, e.g., for a discussion of the EU's relations with Africa, focusing on the tensions between
   its self-interested pursuit of market access on the one hand and its professed commitment
   to the interests of African countries on the other, D. Sicurelli, *The European Union's Africa
   Policies: Norms, Interests and Impact* (Ashgate, 2010).

and damaging the interests of poorer nations through its agricultural and trade policies, amongst others.

Nevertheless, the combination of a number of particular features – its own sixty-year practice and experience of messy and complex but peaceful transnational political cooperation within the EU, and its pursuit of externally-oriented goals in a generally collective way – means that the EU is potentially well-positioned to play a distinctive role in international affairs, despite its declining economic power and the rise of other powerful global actors. This distinctive position has the potential not only to help address global problems, but also to offer a new kind of *raison d'être* capable of contributing to the generation of public support and democratic engagement within the EU. This is not an argument to the effect that the EU could or should take over all or most of the external functions of member states, nor that it should seek to develop a comprehensive foreign policy to replace that of individual states. On the contrary, as has been argued elsewhere, an overextension by the EU in its international goals, and especially an assumption by the EU of functions or tasks which it is unlikely to be able to perform effectively or well – would probably further exacerbate its democratic deficit, rather than addressing the slide in EU legitimacy.[18] Yet the idea of a political system committed to civilising interstatal relations, not only between the member states of the EU amongst themselves, but between the EU and its neighbouring states, between the EU and other regions, and more generally in the EU's promotion of processes of global governance, is a vision of community rather than unity, and offers a normative ideal worthy of pursuit.

But how might this vision of civilising interstatal relations, which Weiler identified as one of the defining ideas of the early European communities, help to address one of the other major challenges identified in *The Transformation of Europe*, namely, the slide in the legitimacy of the EU? This argument is less easy to make, since it remains the case that citizens are generally far more concerned about matters of local and immediate relevance, including their social and economic welfare, than they are with global issues such as international peace and security. Nevertheless, particularly in an era of globalisation, there is much less of a sharp divide between domestic and foreign policy than before, and especially in a political system like that of the EU. The internal and external dimensions

---

[18] See A. Follesdal, 'EU's Raison d'être – Leadership, Democracy or Both? Reflections on Weiler and de Búrca', *Maastricht Journal of European and Comparative Law*, 19 (2012), 7–8.

of EU action are closely connected in a range of ways. In the first place, the EU increasingly claims to act, and is expected by Europeans to act, so as to manage the effects of globalisation on behalf of its inhabitants.[19] Secondly, as has been mentioned, the EU potentially offers an alternative geopolitical model to that of other major powers such as the United States and China. Despite the prolonged economic crisis and recession, the EU remains the largest market in the world, and a major exporter of regulatory standards as well as a major trade partner.[20] A powerful critique of the EU's primary focus on austerity throughout the economic crisis has been its negative consequences, not just for the EU and its citizens, but also for the world: 'the politics of austerity prevents Europe from offering an alternative vision of capitalism and globalization to that put forward by the United States. Gone is the idea of Europe leading a global third way between laissez-faire capitalism and managed socialism.'[21] The capacity of the EU to offer a third-way model of social democracy as an alternative means of managing economic globalisation is relevant both internally and externally to the citizens and residents of the EU, as well as to many others outside the EU who are affected by its actions.

In an increasingly interdependent world, the EU's potential to exercise global leadership on a range of crucial matters which states cannot address alone, including climate change, migration, privacy, Internet governance, financial regulation and terrorism, to mention just a few, is just as relevant to the lives of EU citizens as the EU's internal social and economic policies. Giuliano Amato and Federico Ghizzoni have argued that the capacity of the EU as an integrated political system to tackle Ian Morris's 'five horsemen of the apocalypse' (climate change, famine, migration, disease, and state failure)[22] provides a powerful reason for the EU's continued existence.[23] These challenges directly affect the lives of both European citizens and others, are not merely the remote foreign policy concerns of elites. The EU has experience, internally, of coordinating the different interests of sovereign states with a view to addressing common

---

[19]  See the special issue 'Europe and the Management of Globalization', in S. Meunier and W. Jacoby (eds.), *Journal of European Public Policy*, 17 (2010), 299–448. For a discussion of apparent public expectations that the EU should fulfil this role, see ibid, 302.

[20]  See A. Bradford, 'The Brussels Effect', *Northwestern University Law Review*, 107 (2012), 1–64.

[21]  A. Newman, 'Austerity and the End of the European Model', Foreign Affairs, 1 May 2012.

[22]  I. Morris, *Why the West Rules – For Now: the Patterns of History, and What They Reveal About the Future* (New York: Farrar, Straus & Giroux, 2010).

[23]  G. Amato and F. Ghizzoni, 'Why It's Worth Keeping the EU Dream Alive', Financial Times, 31 October 2011.

problems, and this experience equips it to promote and support similar collective problem-solving processes internationally.

Weiler's *The Transformation of Europe* drew attention in a characteristically prescient way to the problems which have since come to be recognised as some of the biggest challenges facing the EU, including the slide in its legitimacy. However, in cautioning against a move from the EU's novel community vision to a more centralised unity vision, he also perceptively identified one of the EU's most original contributions as well as its distinctive strength, in its ideal of civilising interstatal relations. Building on this underappreciated insight, I have suggested that the continued development of the EU's external role, and its emergence as a distinctive kind of international actor, could also be relevant to strengthening its internal legitimacy. In other words, the EU's potential to exercise international leadership on a range of crucial global challenges and its capacity to manage globalisation could help to galvanise public support for the European Union today, and to provide a compelling account of what it stands for to a generation far removed from the circumstances of its origins.

# 2

# Disequilibrium and Disconnect: On Weiler's (Still Robust) Theory of European Transformation

PETER L. LINDSETH

When Miguel Maduro invited me to participate in the conference leading to this volume, I took the occasion to reread Joseph Weiler's impressive *oeuvre*. It was a salutary exercise. I admit that there were times in the past when my attitude to aspects of Weiler's work tended towards the critical.[1] After the passage of time, however, I have come to view those earlier critiques as, if not misplaced, then at least increasingly marginal. Disagreements no doubt persist, but the events of the past decade and a half or so – the Eurozone crisis especially, but also the earlier saga over the Constitutional and Lisbon Treaties – have led to a much more sympathetic understanding of Weiler's approach to the integration phenomenon.

This change in my thinking flows, in particular, from a reinvigorated appreciation of Weiler's 'equilibrium theory' as elaborated in his two most famous articles from the 1980s and early 1990s, *The Community System: The Dual Character of Supranationalism*[2] and *The Transformation of Europe*.[3] Weiler's theory focuses our attention on an essential balance in the integration process: between, on the one hand, democratic and constitutional legitimacy flowing from the national level, and, on the other, the functional shift in regulatory power to Europe's technocratic and judicial institutions in service of the goals of integration. A similar outlook animates much of my own work – detailed most comprehensively in *Power and Legitimacy: Reconciling Europe and the*

---

[1] P. L. Lindseth, 'Democratic Legitimacy and the Administrative Character of Supranationalism: The Example of the European Community', *Columbia Law Review*, 99, 3 (1999), 628–738; P. L. Lindseth, 'The "Maastricht Decision" Ten Years Later: Parliamentary Democracy, Separation of Powers, and the Schmittian Interpretation Reconsidered', *Robert Schuman Centre for Advanced Studies/EUI Working Papers*, RSC No. 2003/18. http://cadmus.eui.eu/dspace/bitstream/1814/1893/1/03_18.pdf (accessed 9 February 2009).

[2] J. H. H. Weiler, 'The Community System: The Dual Character of Supranationalism', *Yearbook of European Law*, 1, 1 (1982), 267–306.

[3] J. H. H. Weiler, 'The Transformation of Europe', *Yale Law Journal*, 100, 8 (1991), 2403–83.

*Nation-State*[4] – even if I articulate these views in different and undoubtedly less eloquent ways.

This broadly shared perspective between Weiler and myself, if I may be so bold,[5] leads to an overarching caution regarding the integration phenomenon. I am not referring to scepticism, at least about integration generally. Rather, I am referring to a deeper concern about delegating political, regulatory, and adjudicative functions that stretch beyond the capacity of European institutions to legitimise in any robust sense on their own.[6] This does not mean that conferring powers on the EU is a mistake – there are often sound functional and normative reasons to do so. But when European elites assume that integration enjoys resources of legitimacy beyond those it in fact possesses (as the Eurozone crisis has sadly demonstrated at repeated junctures), the result is a deep disruption of the essential equilibrium in European integration that Joseph Weiler so incisively understood and described in the 1980s and early 1990s.

A few months after the conference for this volume, I found myself in a conversation with a colleague who had also been a participant. I voiced the idea that Weiler's equilibrium theory remained a sound basis to understand the legitimacy dynamics in European integration. The response surprised me: 'Oh, that theory only made sense in the era of unanimity in the Council. After the SEA and Maastricht it no longer holds'. This answer puzzled me not just because it seemed to dismiss Weiler's attempt to update the theory via the notion of 'constitutional tolerance' in the 2000s.[7] It also puzzled me because it failed to appreciate how Weiler's theory suggested limits on the scope of supranational delegation that would

---

[4] P. L. Lindseth, *Power and Legitimacy: Reconciling Europe and the Nation-State.* (Oxford; New York: Oxford University Press, 2010).

[5] There are others I could of course add to this cohort, notably Kalypso Nicolaïdis and her concept of 'demoicracy'. See, e.g., K. Nicolaïdis, 'The Idea of European Demoicracy', in J. Dickson and P. Eleftheriadis (eds.), *Philosophical Foundations of European Union Law* (Oxford: Oxford University Press, 2012), 247–74. For further elaboration on the linkages of my views to those of both Weiler and Nicolaïdis, see P. L. Lindseth, 'Equilibrium, Demoicracy, and Delegation in the Crisis of European Integration', *German Law Journal*, 15, 4 (2014), 529–67.

[6] J. H. H. Weiler, 'The Political and Legal Culture of European Integration: An Exploratory Essay', *International Journal of Constitutional Law*, 9, 3–4 (2011), 678–94; P. L. Lindseth, 'Author's Reply: "Outstripping", or the Question of "Legitimate for What?" in EU Governance', *European Constitutional Law Review (EuConst)*, 8, 01 (2012), 153–64.

[7] J. H. H. Weiler, 'In Defence of the Status Quo: Europe's Constitutional *Sonderweg*', in J. H. H. Weiler and M. Wind (eds.), *European Constitutionalism Beyond the State* (Cambridge: Cambridge University Press, 2003), 7–23; J. H. H. Weiler, 'Prologue: Global and Pluralist

be helpful in understanding the sort of disequilibrium that has so afflicted the EU since the onset of the Eurozone crisis. Indeed, if one were in a particularly uncharitable mood, one could take this person's response (from someone in fact deeply admiring of the man and his work) as suggesting that integration had somehow passed Weiler by, shifting into a new stage of legal and institutional transformation that his theory could no longer comprehend.[8]

The argument of this contribution is thus quite simple: Weiler's equilibrium theory is not a creature of the past but remains a robust explanation of core characteristics of a sustainable process integration over the long term. Scholars would do well to heed the theory's central insights, both descriptively and normatively, because they serve as a healthy corrective to the widely held but mistaken idea that European legitimacy is somehow simply a matter of legal and institutional engineering (more power to the European Parliament! more transparency and participation rights! more judicially enforceable rights against the member states!). Reforms along those lines may well be attractive for all sorts of instrumental and normative reasons. But we should not confuse them for genuine 'democratic' legitimation in the proper sense of the term.

Faith in legal and institutional engineering alone, as if more complex challenges of legitimation did not exist, is indicative of another widely held but mistaken notion: that Europe's legitimacy problem is best described as a 'democratic deficit' when, in fact, it is a 'democratic disconnect'.[9] The former view places its hopes in an increase in 'input legitimacy' but ignores the deeper problems of 'demos legitimacy' in the EU, i.e., the missing sense that Europe's technocracy and courts constitute a form of self-government 'of the people'.[10] To see Europe's legitimacy problem

---

Constitutionalism – Some Doubts', in G. de Búrca and J. H. H. Weiler (eds.), *The Worlds of European Constitutionalism* (Cambridge: Cambridge University Press, 2012), 8–18.

[8] We had seen this sentiment before, of course. It was implicit in any number of dismayed commentaries of the early- to mid-2000s regarding Weiler's (ultimately well-grounded) lack of enthusiasm for what would become the failed Constitutional Treaty (again see Weiler, 'In Defence of the Status Quo'). Consider also Weiler's more recent rejection of currently popular (he might say 'faddish') theories of 'constitutional pluralism', as well as the claim he was a 'constitutional pluralist' *avant la lettre* (in this regard, see Weiler, 'Prologue' as well as his extended dialogue with Daniel Halberstam at 284–301 in the same volume).

[9] Lindseth, *Power and Legitimacy*; P. L. Lindseth, 'Delegation Is Dead, Long Live Delegation: Managing the Democratic Disconnect in the European Market-Polity', in C. Joerges and R. Dehousse (eds.), *Good Governance in Europe's Integrated Market* (Oxford: Oxford University Press, 2002), 139–63.

[10] P. L. Lindseth, 'Of the People: Democracy, the Eurozone, and Lincoln's Threshold Criterion', *Berlin Journal*, 22 (2012): 4–7.

as a 'disconnect' is not to deny the value of formal improvements in transparency and participation, or even increases in EP power. But very much consistent with Weiler's writings on the topic,[11] the idea of a disconnect keeps the categories of formal democratisation and democratic legitimacy distinct. This alternative view stresses that, for integration to be enduring and successful, it must maintain the connection to democratic and constitutional legitimacy on the national level in a realistic sense. By contrast, calls for 'more Europe', whether in the present crisis or otherwise, too often mean the displacement of integration's national democratic foundations in favour of supranational mechanisms whose socio-political/socio-cultural underpinnings are, at this point in integration history, deeply questionable.

Weiler's first attempt to come to terms with what he was then calling the 'Community System' was in *The Dual Character of Supranationalism*.[12] In many respects, this work was more descriptive than normative in its ambitions. It sought to comprehend 'the apparently paradoxical emergence of two conflicting trends' over the prior three decades – between increasing 'normative' (judicial) supranationalism, on the one hand, and much more constrained, if not outright diminishing, 'decisional' (political) supranationalism, on the other.[13] Rather than viewing these trends as anomalous, Weiler concluded more hopefully (and, in this respect, more normatively) that 'the process represents a certain balance of action and reaction' in which 'the *approfondissement* of normative supranationalism… is matched by an ever closer national control exercised in the decision-making processes'. He continued:

> Here then is one dimension of the Community formula for attaining an equilibrium between whole and part, centripetal and centrifugal, Community and Member States. It is an equilibrium which explains a seemingly irreconcilable equation: a large, surprisingly large, and effective measure of transnational integration coupled at the same time with the preservation of strong, unthreatened, national Member States. It is this equilibrium which may perhaps explain the overall stability of the system and its resilience to recurring crises generated within and outside.[14]

[11]  Weiler, 'The Political and Legal Culture of European Integration'.
[12]  Weiler, 'The Community System'.
[13]  Ibid., 273.
[14]  Ibid., 292.

Anticipating what would become the ideal of 'unity in diversity' (as opposed to 'ever closer union'), Weiler celebrated a Community characterised:

> on the one hand by a shared historical, political and cultural background which, since repeatedly threatened by strife and conflict in the past and finding common economic and political exigencies in the present, was and is being pushed and drawn towards integration. But also a Community which is, on the other hand, equally characterized by a rich diversity which has evolved in a history of separate tribal, religious, linguistic, economic and political development the complete integration of which is neither feasible [n]or desirable.[15]

But there was one question for which *Dual Character* did not really have a satisfactory answer: 'What are the ties that keep the framework together?'.[16] In some sense, this is the question that Weiler ultimately attempted to address in *Transformation*.[17] This article famously restated the equilibrium theory in terms of Hirschman's *Exit, Voice, and Loyalty*.[18] Through recourse to Exit and Voice, Weiler sought to clarify his earlier claims about the relationship between judicial and political supranationalism – the former foreclosing selective Exit by policing member state compliance under the doctrines of direct effect and supremacy (among others), but the latter ensuring ongoing national Voice in supranational decision-making via the national veto in the Council. By adding Hirschman's notion of Loyalty to the discussion, however, Weiler quite rightly focused attention on the ongoing challenge of identifying the sources of legitimacy for this system. That challenge became increasingly pressing, post-SEA, with 'the dismantling [of] the Foundational equilibrium' – i.e., eliminating the veto in key domains – thus also eliminating an essential vehicle for Voice.[19]

For those who saw the solution to the resulting 'democratic deficit' in an increase in the powers of the EP, Weiler quite rightly cautioned that such a strategy merely 'brings to the fore the intractable problem of redefining the political boundaries of the Community within which the principle of

---

[15] Ibid., 293.
[16] Ibid., 296.
[17] See Weiler, 'The Transformation of Europe', 2473–74 and more particularly Part IV of the article.
[18] A. O. Hirschman, *Exit, Voice, and Loyalty: Responses to Decline in Firms, Organizations, and States* (Cambridge, MA: Harvard University Press, 1970).
[19] Weiler, 'The Transformation of Europe', 2465–66.

majority voting is to take place', i.e., the famous problem of the European 'demos' (or lack thereof). For Weiler, it was not at all clear that 'the necessary shift in public loyalty to such a redefined boundary' would occur 'even if we [apply] the formalistic notion of state parliamentary sovereignty' to the Community via an empowerment of the EP.[20]

The problem was not 'formal (legal) legitimacy' but 'social (empirical) legitimacy' – the latter being 'a broad, empirically determined societal acceptance of the system'.[21] Achieving a robust legitimacy for integration would not simply (or even principally) be a question of formal institutional or legal engineering, particularly in augmenting the EP's role.[22] Rather, it would ultimately turn on less manageable developments in 'ideology, ethos, and political culture'.[23] Weiler sought to capture this challenge in the juxtaposition between what he was calling the 'unity' and 'community' visions of integration. And here it becomes clear that, much less than seeing the equilibrium theory as relevant only for the period before the advent of majority voting in the Council, he sees it having enduring analytical purchase for sustainable integration:

> The idea of community seeks to dictate a different type of intercourse among the actors belonging to it, a type of self-limitation in their self-perception, a redefined self-interest, and, hence, redefined policy goals. To the interest of the state must be added the interest of the community. But crucially, it does not extinguish the separate actors who are fated to live in an uneasy tension with two competing senses of the polity's self, the autonomous self and the self as part of a larger community, and committed to an elusive search for an optimal balance of goals and behavior between the community and its actors.[24]

Despite the normative language, Weiler is articulating here not merely a personal ideal for what integration *should* be; rather, as an extension of the equilibrium theory, his 'community vision' contains the rudiments of a positive analysis of the key variables – functional, political, and cultural – that would come to define successful and durable, as opposed to unstable and crisis-ridden, integration.[25] My book *Power and Legitimacy* elaborates, in effect, on those variables by offering a detailed

---

[20] Ibid., 2473–74.
[21] Ibid., 2468–69.
[22] Ibid., 2471–72.
[23] Ibid., 2474.
[24] Ibid., 2480.
[25] Cf. Weiler, 'The Political and Legal Culture of European Integration'.

historiographical and legal-theoretical framework to capture the role of balance, contestation, and reconciliation in European public law.[26] Even if terminological differences persist – notably regarding the 'administrative' vs. 'constitutional' character of integration (which I take up in the next section) – I have come to conclude that these differences do not negate more fundamental agreements over substance. It is that question to which I now turn.

Weiler's work has long accepted, perhaps reluctantly,[27] a 'constitutionalist' vocabulary to describe legal integration. I am hesitant to adopt a similar terminology, arguing instead for an 'administrative, not constitutional' understanding of the integration phenomenon. Despite the constitutionalist (messianic?) aspiration of many in the European elite, in my view the polycentric distribution of legitimacy resources in the 'constituted' bodies of the member states – in effect, 'demoicracy'[28] – has led European public law to converge around the normative principles and legitimating structures of what I call the 'postwar constitutional settlement of administrative governance'.[29]

The problem with a primarily constitutionalist terminology, even if subtly or critically deployed, is that it risks giving license to those prepared to assume what is fundamentally contested in the integration process: the capacity of European supranationalism to legitimise an ever-increasing amount of normative power in fully autonomous democratic and constitutional terms, as if integration were a site of such authority in its own right, apart from the member states that created it.[30] Whether cast in terms of 'constitutional pluralism' or in the (perhaps less in-vogue) language of European 'federalism', the assumption of this literature is that integration entails the interaction between two levels of governance that are somehow strongly legitimated in their own way, each with a robust 'constitutional' legitimacy.

---

[26] See Lindseth, *Power and Legitimacy*, especially 13–14.
[27] See, e.g., J. H. H. Weiler and J. P. Trachtman, 'European Constitutionalism and Its Discontents', *Northwestern Journal of International Law and Business*, 17 (1996), 354–97.
[28] See Nicolaïdis, 'The Idea of European Demoicracy'.
[29] Lindseth, *Power and Legitimacy*.
[30] See, e.g., M. Rosenfeld, *The Identity of the Constitutional Subject: Selfhood, Citizenship, Culture, and Community* (New York: Routledge, Taylor & Francis, 2010); D. Halberstam, 'Local, Global, and Plural Constitutionalism: Europe Meets the World', in G. de Búrca and J. H. H. Weiler (eds.), *The Worlds of European Constitutionalism* (Cambridge: Cambridge University Press, 2012), 150–202.

My countervailing 'administrative' interpretation tries to show why this is mistaken, both legally and historically.[31] But because the 'administrative' framework has often been misunderstood, let me set out some of my standard clarifications regarding what the rubric does *not* mean, whether applied to the EU or otherwise.

First and foremost, it does *not* mean that a regime so labelled is merely 'limited' or 'specialized',[32] indeed even entirely 'non-political'.[33] Administrative governance is 'deeply political', even if the opposite has been (mis-)attributed to me in the past.[34] Anyone with knowledge of the modern administrative state understands that the authority delegated to the administrative sphere is often functionally autonomous but nevertheless concerns questions of values and the allocation of scarce resources – in short, distributive justice – the very essence of politics.[35] What defines 'administrative' is not, in fact, the *nature* of the power exercised (political or not), but rather its *separation* from bodies understood to embody or express the capacity of a historical political community to rule itself in a fully demos-legitimate, i.e., 'constitutional' sense, whether legislative, executive, or judicial.

[31] See more recently Lindseth, 'Equilibrium, Demoicracy, and Delegation in the Crisis of European Integration'; see also P. L. Lindseth, 'Between the "Real" and the "Right": Explorations along the Institutional-Constitutional Frontier', in M. Adams, E. H. Ballin, and A. Meuwese (eds.), *Constitutionalism and the Rule of Law: Bridging Idealism and Realism* (Cambridge: Cambridge University Press, 2017), 60–93.

[32] See G. de Búrca, 'Reflections on the EU's Path from the Constitutional Treaty to the Lisbon Treaty', *Fordham Law Legal Studies Research Paper, No. 1124586* (2008), 8, http://papers.ssrn.com/sol3/papers.cfm?abstract_id=1124586#PaperDownload (accessed 2 June 2008), citing, *inter alia*, Lindseth, 'Democratic Legitimacy and the Administrative Character of Supranationalism'.

[33] D. Curtin, *Executive Power of the European Union: Law, Practices, and the Living Constitution* (Oxford; New York: Oxford University Press, 2009), 37, citing Lindseth, 'Democratic Legitimacy and the Administrative Character of Supranationalism'.

[34] H. H. C. Hofmann and A. H. Türk, 'The Development of Integrated Administration in the EU and Its Consequences', *European Law Journal*, 13, 2 (2007), 267, though earlier (ibid., 264), these authors suggest that I maintain the opposite, again citing Lindseth, 'Democratic Legitimacy and the Administrative Character of Supranationalism' conflating me with H. P. Ipsen, *Europäisches Gemeinschaftsrecht* (Tübingen: Mohr, 1972).

[35] In the first article in which I advanced the 'administrative' rubric for integration, I in fact stressed how the jurisdiction of administrative bodies had often been depicted as 'technical' in order to justify the delegation of power but that this depiction has never altered the essentially 'political' character of the power itself, in the sense of dealing with questions of values or the allocation of scarce resources, the very core of politics (see Lindseth, 'Democratic Legitimacy and the Administrative Character of Supranationalism', 687–88; see also P. L. Lindseth, '"Weak" Constitutionalism? Reflections on Comitology and Transnational Governance in the European Union', *Oxford Journal of Legal Studies*, 21, 1 (2001), 157, n. 51).

I am not particularly wedded to the 'administrative' label as such, as long as the substance of the framework I just described is maintained. The label causes confusion among those not familiar with the law or history of administrative governance and, for that reason, might be amended or replaced. I continue to use it, however, to stress the complexity of the challenge of reconciling 'government' and 'governance' – terms more familiar in this context – and to show how this tension is not novel. Rather, it inheres in any system of diffuse and fragmented authority in which more strongly legitimated institutions (call them historically 'constituted' bodies) interact with more weakly legitimated 'agents' at the periphery, which, despite their lack of strong autonomous legitimacy, nevertheless exercise functionally autonomous regulatory power. But autonomous regulatory power does not mean that these agents are or can be, in themselves, 'constitutionalised' (i.e., experienced as self-legitimating).[36] They remain 'administrative' because, regardless of label, they are experienced in political-cultural terms as exercising 'delegated' regulatory power.[37]

In short, what these bodies otherwise lack, despite their autonomous *power*, is autonomous democratic and constitutional *legitimacy* to exercise that power without some mechanisms of oversight by constitutional bodies residing elsewhere (what I call 'mediated legitimacy'). Legitimacy mediated through the nation-state is essential to 'equilibrium' in a Weiler sense, or as I put it in *Power and Legitimacy*, to the 'reconciliation' of modern administrative 'governance', whether within or beyond the state, with conceptions of constitutional 'government' inherited from the past. It is only through such reconciliation and mediated legitimacy that forms of administrative governance, national or supranational, are still experienced as 'democratic' and 'constitutional' in some historically and culturally recognisable way. Otherwise the danger is of 'a truly Weberian nightmare – technocratic domination without the possibility of any kind of ... legitimat[ion] via representative government, capable of breaking through the varied and often questionable claims of "expertise" (whether within or beyond the state)'.[38]

Over the course of the 1990s, my emerging sense of the 'administrative' character of European supranationalism[39] obviously placed me in

---

[36] Lindseth, 'Between the "Real" and the "Right"'.

[37] P. L. Lindseth, 'Agents Without Principals?: Delegation in an Age of Diffuse and Fragmented Governance', in F. Cafaggi (ed.), *Reframing Self-Regulation in European Private Law* (Alphen aan den Rijn, NL: Kluwer Law International, 2006), 107–30.

[38] Lindseth, *Power and Legitimacy*, 246.

[39] Culminating in Lindseth, 'Democratic Legitimacy and the Administrative Character of Supranationalism'.

tension with the dominant 'constitutional' vocabulary of European public law of that era, of which Joseph Weiler seemed to be a leading, if critical, exponent.[40] To my mind, the idea of supranational 'constitutionalisation', in whatever form, was based on a partly valid[41] but nevertheless incomplete legal-historical perspective, rooted in the comparison of European institutions to the emergence of international organisations (IOs) over the course of the twentieth century. This perspective operated, we might say, along a dimension from public international law (IOs) to purported supranational constitutionalism (the EU) – which, when applied to Europe, becomes what we might call the 'constitutional, not international' framework.

The EU and IOs are better seen, I would maintain, as denationalized expressions of the diffusion and fragmentation of regulatory power *away* from the 'constituted' bodies of self-government on the national level, which is the essential characteristic of modern administrative governance. This process of diffusion and fragmentation in fact began (at least) in the mid-nineteenth century, reflecting what two global historians have called the 'leaky' container of the modern nation-state.[42] From this perspective, neither the EU nor the IOs that emerged in the twentieth century are 'constitutional' in themselves, in the sense of representing a political community historically conscious of itself as 'entitled to effective organs of political self-government'.[43] Rather, these bodies remain fundamentally technocratic and juristocratic, possessing what is ultimately perceived to be *delegated* normative power; hence the felt need for limits on their scope

---

[40] See again Weiler and Trachtman, 'European Constitutionalism and Its Discontents'.

[41] Especially so with regard to international or supranational adjudicative authority in the protection of human rights against the excesses of state power; see J. H. H. Weiler, ' The Geology of International Law – Governance, Democracy and Legitimacy', *Zeitschrift für ausländisches öffentliches Recht und Völkerrecht*, 64 (2004), 551 (referring to 'a third stratum of [international] dispute settlement which may be called constitutional, and consists in the increasing willingness, within certain areas of domestic courts[,] to apply and uphold rights and duties emanating from international obligations. The appellation constitutional may be justified because of the "higher law" status conferred on the international legal obligation').

[42] Cf. C. Bright and M. Geyer, 'Where in the World Is America? The History of the United States in the Global Age', in T. Bender (ed.), *Rethinking American History in a Global Age* (Berkeley and Los Angeles: University of California Press, 2002), 63–99.

[43] N. MacCormick, *Questioning Sovereignty: Law, State, and Nation in the European Commonwealth* (Oxford; New York: Oxford University Press, 1999), 173. This democratic and constitutional self-consciousness need not be grounded in exclusionary ethnic, religious, or linguistic affinities but, as Neil MacCormick has also shown, can be 'civic' even if still necessarily grounded in a 'historical' and indeed 'cultural' experience: ibid, 169–74.

of authority as well as for some form of legitimating oversight by national bodies (but not full blown control).[44] The key difference between the EU and IOs, therefore, is in their relative *degree of autonomous discretion* in the exercise of delegated power (the EU enjoys much more autonomy, as is well known), which in turn intensifies its problem of legitimation. But otherwise the difference is one of degree and not of kind – both the EU and IOs are manifestations of modern administrative governance, functionally diffused and fragmented beyond the confines of the state to address certain pressing regulatory and political problems.

There is, however, a final and perhaps more fundamental drawback of the 'constitutional, not international' framework: its failure to account for the intertwined and overlapping relationship between democratic and constitutional legitimacy in modern governance. Following the lead of Jed Rubenfeld[45] and Bruce Ackerman,[46] we should recognize that democratic and constitutional legitimacy are inextricably connected in the modern era, tied to the construction of a polity's identity over time, thus emerging historically together. It is thus profoundly difficult to claim that the EU has an autonomously 'constitutional' character (except in only the most formal sense) if Europeans refuse to grant it autonomous 'democratic' legitimacy. Weiler's (correct) acknowledgment of the undoubted weakness of European supranationalism in terms of its own autonomous democratic legitimacy – the essence of the equilibrium theory – necessarily undermines any continuing assumption that the European legal order somehow 'constitutionalised' itself at some point in its past, measured along the 'constitutional, not international' dimension or otherwise. This is something Weiler has apparently been increasingly inclined to recognize: 'constitutional discipline without polity and without resembling the habits and practices of democratic legitimacy', he has recently written, 'are highly problematic ... even in the EU – *a fortiori* outside it'.[47]

My countervailing 'administrative, not constitutional' understanding of integration is in fact consistent with 'community vision' articulated in Weiler's *Transformation*. The associated 'discipline' at the core of integration's purported constitutionalisation (notably the de facto private-party

---

[44] On the control-legitimation distinction, see Lindseth, *Power and Legitimacy*.
[45] J. Rubenfeld, *Freedom and Time: A Theory of Constitutional Self-Government* (New Haven, CT: Yale University Press, 2001).
[46] B. A. Ackerman, *We the People: Foundations* (Cambridge, MA: Harvard University Press, 1991).
[47] Weiler, 'Prologue', 12.

standing to enforce directly effective and supreme EU norms via the pre-liminary reference) is best understood as an aspect of an instrumental, functionalist logic of administrative-type delegation of autonomous regulatory power. It is a way to enforce policy 'pre-commitment'[48] via supranational mechanisms such as the European Commission and the ECJ.[49] The essentially functionalist character of this discipline can in fact be traced all the way back to *Van Gend & Loos* itself.[50] Despite the fervent hopes of certain jurists since the 1960s,[51] this functionalist character has always been an inadequate basis for a genuine supranational 'constitutional' legitimacy.[52] No matter how much international lawyers see that discipline as evidence of supranational 'constitutionalisation', it has simply not given rise to the political-cultural recognition among the peoples of the EU that supranational institutions are anything but highly juridical, technocratic, and distant, falling well short of embodying or expressing the capacity of some new strongly-legitimated political community to rule itself through representative institutions 'constituted' for that purpose.

Some of Weiler's more recent writings confirm this basic insight and, in fact, deepen it. His widely-read exploration of integration as a legalistic, technocratic, but nevertheless 'messianic' project is depressing reading indeed: As he stresses, the project has never been 'particularly concerned with democracy (or, at inception, human rights). It sought its legitimacy in the nobility of its cause'.[53] As a consequence, Weiler questions whether the vaunted supranational 'rule of law' promoted by the Court of Justice in fact qualifies as such. Per Weiler, the Court's 'formalist, positivist and Kelsenian' conception of the rule of law fails because it is 'not respectful

---

[48] As Weiler has stressed, Community discipline is voluntary (ibid., 12–13), which is one additional reason it maps nicely onto the terrain of 'pre-commitment'. See also Weiler, 'In Defence of the Status Quo'.

[49] See e.g. Lindseth, *Power and Legitimacy*, 85; 117–18.

[50] Ibid., 137–38. See also J.H.H. Weiler, 'Van Gend en Loos: The Individual as Subject and Object and the Dilemma of European Legitimacy', *International Journal of Constitutional Law*, 12 (2014), 94–103.

[51] For an analysis, see M. Rasmussen, 'Establishing a Constitutional Practice of European Law: The History of the Legal Service of the European Executive, 1952–65', *Contemporary European History*, 21 (Special Issue 3) (2012), 375–97.

[52] Cf. also Weiler, 'The Political and Legal Culture of European Integration', 690, describing how this functionalist logic has been grounded in the defence of 'Community rights, which serve, almost invariably, the economic interests of individuals ... "bought" at least in some measure at the expense of democratic legitimation'. The net effect has been the vindication of 'a personal, private interest against the public good' defined through the democratic process ibid., 691.

[53] Ibid., 689.

of two conditions' in balance: 'rootedness in a democratic process of lawmaking and respectful of fundamental human rights. The European Court of Justice accepted the second of these conditions in an activist jurisprudence, beginning in 1969', but thereafter, it has never been able to develop 'a similar jurisprudence as regards the decisional processes of the Union'.[54]

That latter statement is not entirely true, of course, but it is not true in a way that actually *strengthens* Weiler's argument. In the line of cases beginning with *Roquettes Frères* (1980), the Court attempted to resolve certain 'legal basis' disputes by reference to the 'fundamental democratic principle that the peoples should take part in the exercise of power through the intermediary of a representative assembly'.[55] This reasoning simply begged the question of whether the European 'peoples' collectively constituted a demos for purposes of representative self-government.[56] Weiler's view on the topic is now clear: 'The manifestations of the so-called democracy deficit are persistent, and no endless repetition of the powers of the European Parliament will remove them'.[57] This is so because what Europe suffers from is a democratic *disconnect*, not a deficit. Increasing the power of the EP assumes the latter when it is really the former, which in turn requires very different and often more national means of democratic legitimation (or 'equilibrium', to use Weiler's terminology).

But if this is in fact the case, the question then becomes not one of 'legal basis' and associated procedures – a less pressing problem in an era of near-total co-decision via the 'ordinary legislative procedure'. Rather, it is more deeply one of the allocation of 'competences' between the national and supranational bodies themselves, i.e., the scope of delegated regulatory power in the first place. Are there any legal limits on the extent of power that can be legitimately delegated to the (technocratic, jurisocratic) EU deriving from the need to preserve the democratic and constitutional character of the member states in a historically recognizable sense? And even as to seemingly permissible delegations, are there any interpretations of supranational authority that interfere with the democratic prerogatives of member states in a constitutionally illegitimate way?

---

[54] Ibid., 691.
[55] Case 138/79, *SA Roquettes Frères v. Council* [1980] ECR 3333, 3360; see also Case C-300/89, *Commission v. Council* [1991] ECR I-2867, I-2900 (re the appropriate legal basis for the adoption of the titanium dioxide waste directive).
[56] See e.g. Lindseth, 'Democratic Legitimacy and the Administrative Character of Supranationalism', 672–83.
[57] Weiler, 'The Political and Legal Culture of European Integration', 679.

These are the sorts of questions that national high courts have found increasingly critical over the last quarter century.[58] However, the European Court of Justice has refused to address them, particularly in relation to the question of subsidiarity.[59] These are also questions that Weiler's equilibrium theory, along with sympathetic notions like 'demoicracy',[60] raise but, despite their many virtues, have not yet developed the normative traction to provide a fully satisfactory answer. Hopefully the value-added of my work[61] is that by looking to the history of administrative governance, one can gain some normative guidance for how modern democracy has sought to come to terms with delegated normative power in any form, whether within or beyond the state.[62]

This guidance may be particularly important in the context of the ongoing upheaval in the Eurozone. As of this writing (primarily February 2013, undated modestly for publication in July 2015 with a few stray references added thereafter), the Eurozone crisis still threatens national parliaments with the loss of a key prerogative of democratic self-government – the power of decision over spending and indebtedness – which some observers hope will eventually shift to supranational bodies.[63] This loss was acutely felt in the Greek crisis of the summer of 2015. Under the postwar constitutional settlement on which integration has been built, national legislatures were supposed to retain this prerogative, despite the otherwise vast expansion of administrative governance, both nationally and supranationally. In the integration process up to and including the Treaties of Maastricht and Lisbon, only delegations justifiable under formulas that supported domestic administrative delegations were generally permissible.[64] Delegation of supranational authority to impose

---

[58] See Lindseth, *Power and Legitimacy*, Chapter 4. See also the recent decision of the German Federal Constitutional Court in *Gauweiler*, BVerfG, 2 BvR 2728/13 (21 June 2016), www.bverfg.de/e/rs20160621_2bvr272813.html (accessed 12 April 2017), para. 142 (surveying the case law).

[59] Lindseth, 'Democratic Legitimacy and the Administrative Character of Supranationalism', Part VI; see also Lindseth, *Power and Legitimacy*, Section 5.1.

[60] See, e.g., Nicolaïdis, 'The Idea of European Demoicracy'.

[61] See, e.g., Lindseth, 'Equilibrium, Demoicracy, and Delegation in the Crisis of European Integration'.

[62] Lindseth, 'Agents Without Principals?'.

[63] P. L. Lindseth, 'Thoughts on the Maduro Report: Saving the Euro Through European Democratization?' *EUtopialaw* (2012b), http://eutopialaw.com/2012/11/13/1608/ (accessed 9 February 2013).

[64] Lindseth, *Power and Legitimacy*, chapter 4.

indeterminate, future taxation or debt obligations on national legislatures could not be justified by one of these formulas ('foreseeability' and 'predictability' in German parlance, or what American administrative lawyers would recognize as the requirement of an 'intelligible principle', 'standard', or 'policy' in domestic enabling legislation); hence its democratically problematic character. The evolution of the Eurozone crisis, particularly as it related to Greece in the summer of 2015, suggests a process of integration that was now deeply (and perhaps irretrievably) out of balance relative to its essential historical foundations in the postwar constitutional settlement. The result is a situation of true disequilibrium and disconnect.

Supranational governance is legitimate for certain purposes but perhaps not others – unless Europeans are prepared to change fundamentally their understanding of what democratic self-government means, or where it is located. In short, whenever we talk about the legitimacy of integration, we must always ask 'legitimate for what?'.[65] It is one thing to delegate authority to harmonize regulatory standards in various domains (important a task though that may be). It is quite another to delegate control over national spending or indebtedness in an indeterminate way. The Eurozone crisis may increase functional demands for ever-greater delegations. But those delegations still must be reconciled (balanced) with historical understandings of democratic self-government on the national level. That, I believe, is the essential implication of Weiler's still robust theory of European equilibrium, one that defines both a normative and descriptive formula for successful European transformation. It is also one I wholeheartedly endorse and in effect seek to develop, from an 'administrative, not constitutional' perspective, in my own work.

---

[65] Lindseth, 'Author's Reply'.

# Joseph Weiler and the Experience of Law

## JULIO BAQUERO CRUZ*

Change is what keeps us from ossifying.

John Cage

Il y a une violence du Neutre,

mais cette violence est inexprimable;

il y a une passion du Neutre,

mais cette passion n'est pas celle d'un vouloir-saisir.

Roland Barthes

## 1

The law is about norms, but it is also about justice. It has a form, but it never lacks substance. It is a practical discipline, but it is also part of the humanities and of the social sciences, and it can be studied as one of the various artefacts that make up a human culture. It is about arguments, but it is also about interests and power. And it is politics through other means and a mechanism of socioeconomic engineering.

That enhanced view of law is rare. Many practitioners and also academic lawyers approach it as a mere technique. The view of law as norms may be boring, but it is useful and necessary. If all lawyers had an enlarged approach to law, the legal world would perhaps be more interesting, but also too chaotic. And then the law would not perform one of its main functions: ensuring order, stability, and certainty in human relationships.

The enhanced view of law entails another danger. Beyond the technical approach, the law may become subject to ideological manipulation and hubris. But is not the technical approach subject to the even graver

* Member of the Legal Service of the European Commission and visiting professor at Sciences Po (Paris) and Universidad CEU San Pablo (Madrid). The opinions contained in this essay are personal and may not coincide with those of the European Commission.

danger of taking legal choices for granted without the critical check of an enhanced view? In a democratic system, the counter-majoritarian difficulties that plague the highest courts of every polity may actually be an issue for many lawyers. The only correction, imperfect as it may be, depends on character, self-knowledge and self-restraint, the passive virtues of inaction and neutrality, both in the Wechslerian sense of deciding cases on the basis of principles that transcend the case in hand and that will be applied in similar cases,[1] and in the Barthesian sense of acknowledging the existence of questions that are undecidable on legal grounds and of suspending our judgment regarding them.[2] Undecidable as they may be, in law the obligation for courts of justice to avoid a *non liquet* means that that suspension of judgment must come to an end at some point and produce a decision – even a decision not to decide. Which means that neutrality in law does not stand for silence, sterility, and defeat (a defeat of legal rationality), but can be a force that keeps the law moving.

Other forces that keep the law moving are the interaction between normative and institutional realities, the depth, system, and structure of law (the interconnectedness of norms, principles, and values), its open texture, the indeterminacy of language, and what I should like to call the 'excessive' character of law, that is, the fact that it is through law that justice and injustice take shape. The central grounds of law might well be order, stability, and predictability, but at its extremes the law is filled with a subversive potential. Subversive in the sense of being capable of unsettling the very constellations of power and interests that framed it in the beginning. Subversive in the sense of being capable of questioning itself, of putting itself upside down if justice requires it.

This is so and I would say even more so in the case of European Union law, which has always found itself on the difficult ground of having to connect itself with previously separate legal orders and to mediate between systems of values, principles, and interests which sometimes do not seem to be convergent or compatible. Indeed, the promise and the danger of Union law have to do with the fact that its mission may be perceived as a subversive influence and resisted by the legal orders of the Member States. Union law is meant to enlarge their horizon and to include them in a wider sphere of order, values, and principles, but that objective may

---

[1] H. Wechsler, 'Toward Neutral Principles of Constitutional Law', *Harvard Law Review*, 73, 1 (1959), 1–35.
[2] R. Barthes, *Le Neutre: Cours au Collège de France (1977–1978)* (Paris: Seuil, 2002).

unsettle the interests, powers, and legitimation structures underpinning national legal orders.

2

It took me a long time to see the law that way, with all the excitement, the dangers, and the endless movement between an internal and an external perspective attached to it. In my childhood and early youth I never saw the law like that. I only saw words, codes, and rules that seemed to have little to do with any recognisable human experience. But little by little I started to understand that law could be seen as part of a larger framework. I arrived there with the help of some people, a number of books, and curiosity. Joseph Weiler was one of the persons that helped me. Let me explain how.

The first time I saw Weiler was in a summer course that took place in El Escorial. I think it was in July 1993. The course was called *The European Constitution*.[3] It was organised by Marcelino Oreja, at the time a member of the European Parliament. I was a law student, twenty years old, sitting at the back of the conference room. I had just finished the third year of my legal studies in Madrid. Back then I didn't like the law much and I dreamed of doing something else. I felt very much like James Boswell, who had written about himself: 'Consider this poor fellow hauled away to the town of Edinburg. ... His flighty imagination quite cramp'd and he obliged to study *Corpus Iuris Civilis*.'[4] Or like Kafka, for whom his legal studies were a period during which his spiritual food was a sort of sawdust which had already been chewed by thousands of mouths.[5]

My initial dislike of the law was not wholly my fault. In view of the way in which it was (and still is) taught in Spain most of the time, the opposite would have been surprising. Most Spanish lawyers see the law as a sacred thing. It is not about arguments. It is only about rules, approached as flatly as possible. Creativity has no place in it. One must learn the codes by heart and know all the numbers. It is useless to study cases, as they are supposed to be an automatic application of those rules. Our main activity in the classroom was to copy what the

---

[3] The proceedings were published in M. Oreja and Í. Méndez de Vigo (eds.), *La Constitución Europea* (Madrid: Universidad Complutense de Madrid, 1994).

[4] *The Correspondence of James Boswell and William Johnson Temple, 1756–1795*, T. Crawford (ed.), vol. 1: 1756–77 (Edinburgh: Edinburgh University Press, 1997), 33.

[5] F. Kafka, *Brief an den Vater/Lettre au père* (Paris: Gallimard, 1995), 118–20.

professor dictated from a book or from notes. The students with faster hands, clearer handwriting, and better memories got the best grades, as they could parrot word by word the notes they took. The professors loved those students. They never asked difficult questions. They never questioned anything. The idea was not to think. The idea was to remember. Back then I had a good memory and I did well enough. But I wasn't interested in what I was doing.

Even though Spain had joined the European Community in 1986, at the time, Community law was not part of the Spanish curriculum. Even at present, in many Spanish law faculties there is only one optional class of general Union law, and there are no faculty departments of Union law, which has been divided between constitutional lawyers, administrative lawyers, and international lawyers – each school approaching it and deforming it from its own perspective. Instead, we had plenty of civil law (four years), administrative law (two years), penal law (two years), civil and penal procedure (two years), and several extremely useful things such as natural law, canon law, *Corpus Iuris Civilis*, history of Spanish law, and so on and so forth. As a result, when I arrived at the conference in El Escorial all I knew about Community law was what the professor of international law had told us in half an hour: the names of the four main institutions, the legal sources, and a rudimentary idea of the principles of direct effect and supremacy.

The two weeks in El Escorial were important for my legal education. I learned that the European Community had its own legal order, that there was an ongoing process of 'constitutionalisation', that its law was an important part of the Spanish legal system, and that the process of integration was difficult, dynamic, and exciting. Among the speakers were Francesco Capotorti, Eduardo García de Enterría, Meinhard Hilf, Antonio La Pergola, Jean-Victor Louis, Araceli Mangas, Francisco Rubio Llorente, Wolfgang Wessels, and Joseph Weiler. All of them were serious and brilliant jurists. They knew what they were talking about. They spoke with clarity, with rigour, and sometimes also with passion about the European project. What they said was very different from the dismal university lectures on *Corpus Iuris Civilis*. Most were Europhiles, but there were also some believers in national constitutional law that ended up sounding, perhaps unwittingly, like Eurosceptics, administrative lawyers who wanted to 'downsize' the Community to make it fit their doctrinal model, and a number of unreconstructed international lawyers who visibly suffered trying to come to terms with the Community 'monster'.

Joseph Weiler, who spoke towards the end of the conference, was also serious and brilliant, but he was quite another thing. First of all in his appearance. He did not wear the dark clothes and serious ties of the other speakers. He had wild hair and beard and was wearing a Hawaiian shirt, no tie, a straw hat, and rundown shoes. His way of talking and the things he said were as different as his appearance was. To my delight, he started quoting Brecht. He spoke with passion and conviction, but he didn't sound like a Eurosceptic or a Europhile. He approached European integration in a very neutral manner. His intervention, which was the embryo of 'Fin-de-siècle Europe: do the new clothes have an emperor',[6] his piece on the values of European integration, seemed to me to be about law only marginally. It sounded more like political science, or legal theory, or moral philosophy. It was one of my first experiences of the enlarged view of law. I remember thinking at the time: if this is a lawyer, if this is law, then this is something I might like to do. It was one of the things that made me stick to the law.

After that summer I spent another year in Madrid, studying law, but also reading tons of fiction, poetry, and philosophy. The next year I went to New York on an exchange programme. At some point I applied to the College of Europe and I was called for an interview in Madrid. To prepare for it, I read again Weiler's paper on values. When I quoted him at the interview, the members of the panel were interested. I was selected and received the grant.

In Bruges, in 1995–6, I learned a lot about the law of European integration. The professors were demanding and excellent. What they taught was not always the kind of approach to law that excited me, but I knew that there was also a value in what they did and that I needed to master the technical aspects of law very well before going any further. In the second semester we had a course with Joseph Weiler. It was called 'The Transformation of Europe: How the Law Changes and Why'. We were a small group of about ten students. Joseph Weiler came three or four times. All in all we might have spent fourteen hours with him. Not much, but enough to leave a deep trace on us. To begin with, we had to read *The Transformation of Europe*. The article was in the reserve, at the library of the College of Europe, as an offprint of the *Yale Law Journal*,[7] together with the first issues of the *European Law Journal*, which I also

---

[6] J. H. H. Weiler, *The Constitution of Europe* (Cambridge: Cambridge University Press, 1999), 238–63.

[7] J. H. H. Weiler, 'The Transformation of Europe', *Yale Law Journal*, 100, 8 (1991), 2403–83.

read. After four years there and having been read by countless students, the offprint was in a pitiful state, mistreated in the same way as *Le droit de l'intégration*,[8] the great little book by Pierre Pescatore, a mandatory reading for Barav's course. I photocopied Weiler's article and read it two or three times. I found it very interesting. It was more clearly about law than his piece on values, but the law constantly opened to other things.

3

*The Transformation of Europe* was another experience that transformed me as a jurist. I have often read it afterwards and it is like a good novel: you can read it several times and you always find something new in it. The style is vivid, never boring. Detailed description is kept to a minimum. Analysis thrives.

Parts I and II take stock of the previous work of Joseph Weiler,[9] summarising his main arguments and findings. Parts III and IV explore the issues on which he focused after 1991: legitimacy, democracy, identity, values, and citizenship. From the point of view of Weiler's academic legal writings, *The Transformation of Europe* can be seen as *Joseph Weiler at a Crossroads* or as *The Transformation of Joseph Weiler*. Indeed, in Parts III and IV law ceases to be the central subject and is replaced by fundamental problems of political theory applied to European integration. In examining them, the law is presented as a sort of infrastructure of complex relationships based on power and legitimacy. *The Transformation of Europe* thus marks the transition from the first Weiler, who focused on law in context, to the second Weiler, who seems more interested in the context of the law.

The main feat of the article was and remains, in my view, to posit a structural connection between the law and the politics of European integration. Weiler unveiled a curious paradox in the development of European integration during the 1960s, 1970s, and 1980s: the strange cohabitation between the increasingly federal structure of the law of integration and the increasingly intergovernmental character of its political process. And he tried to explain the paradox and the reasons behind it in light of the

---

[8] Sijthoff, Leiden, 1972.
[9] J. H. H. Weiler, 'The Community System: The Dual Character of Supranationalism', *Yearbook of European Law*, 1 (1981), 267–306; J. H. H. Weiler, *Il sistema comunitario europeo* (Bologna: Il Mulino, 1985).

interconnection between law and politics. Doing that, he was following the example of American constitutional law scholars like Alexander Bickel or John Hart Ely.[10] But he was clearly breaking new ground, for it was not at all clear how the arguments of a Bickel or an Ely could be transposed to European integration.

The second important aspect of the article was to underline that the European polity had transformed itself deeply through the years, not only or mainly through Treaty revisions, but rather through profound mutations that took place without changes in its founding texts. The view of European integration offered in the article is one of almost perpetual instability and insufficiency, of continuous change to achieve an equilibrium that is never long-lasting. Indeed, towards the end Weiler argues that the 'Community is impelled forward by the dysfunctioning of its current architecture',[11] as if crises and the very mismatch between legal and political integration were the very motor of integration.

That narrative of transformation has a strong mythopoeic force. It is in that force, which has modified the way we conceive of the relationship between law and politics in integration, that lies the main value of the article. *The Transformation of Europe* should be seen, therefore, not just as a description of something that happened, but as a performative utterance that transforms its own object.

When I read the article in Bruges I believed every word of it. Today, although I still agree with most of the analysis, some aspects seem to me less convincing: the argument about the foundational period, the notion of transformation, and the distinction between the 'community' and the 'unity' visions.

My main difficulty with Weiler's argument on the foundational period concerns precisely its descriptive accuracy. As already recalled, his main point is the famous paradox: while European legal integration moved forward and direct effect and supremacy render the Community 'indistinguishable from analogous legal relationships in constitutional federal states',[12] the decision-making process moved towards intergovernmentalism and away from integration.[13]

---

[10] A. M. Bickel, *The Least Dangerous Branch: The Supreme Court at the Bar of Politics* (New Haven, CT: Yale University Press, 1986); J. Hart Ely, *Democracy and Distrust: A Theory of Judicial Review* (Cambridge, MA: Harvard University Press, 1980).

[11] Weiler, 'The Transformation of Europe', 2483.

[12] Ibid., 2413.

[13] Ibid., 2410.

I can see both processes taking place in the period of consolidation, from 1973 to the middle of the 1980s, but I think that both points are somewhat overstated with regard to the foundational period (from 1963 to the early 1970s). In the legal dimension, direct effect and supremacy are taken at face value by Weiler in an idealised view of the system, as if both jurisprudential utterances immediately and effectively changed the normative reality and the usual legal practices in the Member States. The fact is that direct effect and supremacy are real only insofar as the national judicial and administrative practices generally follow their demands. Even today, direct effect and supremacy are not always strictly followed, be as a result of mere ignorance or of conscious resistance, and Union law remains significantly less effective than national law or than the law of a federal State, and is not always applied when and as it should be. That was also the case, perhaps even more so, back in the 1960s, which means that Weiler's argument about the 'closure of selective exit' for the Member States on the legal side, which would explain their intergovernmental reaction on the political side, is not totally correct. An effective closure of selective exit would presuppose a general habit of obedience of the law of integration and an internalisation of the common European law by all national legal actors. The closure was as imperfect as that habit and that internalisation were. It was, to be sure, no longer in the hands of national executives or legislatures, but of autonomous and sometimes unpredictable national courts. A relationship could be conceived that way, although it would be a weak one, based on national stochastic processes.

At the same time, Weiler argues, the Member States 'jointly and severally' took control of decision-making, 'leading to the process by which the original institutional structures foreseen in the Treaties broke down'.[14] He argues that the increase in the Member States' voice that resulted from these changes in the political process was 'the "natural reaction" to [the process by which Community norms and policy hardened into binding law with effective legal remedies]', positing not 'a simplistic causal relationship', but a legal context in which the intergovernmental development of the decision-making process 'becomes understandable'.[15] In other

---

[14] Ibid., 2424.
[15] Ibid., 2427. The same argument was repeated in the afterword included in the book: 'I cannot overemphasize that my argument is not about a direct causal relationship.... What I am arguing is that there is a nexus between the two spheres of politics and law where developments in one create a climate, act as a catalyst, help sustain developments, and moves in the other' (Weiler, *The Constitution of Europe*, 101).

words, the Member States 'could accept the constitutionalization because they took real control of the decisionmaking process, thus minimizing its threatening features'.[16]

Today I also have doubts about that view. I think it is accurate to see the empty chair crisis, the Luxembourg compromise, and the ensuing institutional practice as consequences of internal tensions within the political process, in particular of the forthcoming shift to qualified majority voting in a number of important areas (like the fixing of agricultural prices and of the common external tariff) after the end of the first stage of integration, and also of tensions internal to French politics – the crisis was quickly brought to an end after a weakened de Gaulle won the French presidential elections on the second round, against Mitterrand, on 19 December 1965. If there is an explanation that makes perfect sense, why look for other explanations? The legal developments were, at most, part of the wider context, but I don't think they had any real impact at the time or that in that normative context the political developments become more understandable. I think they are perfectly understandable within the political context, without any reference to legal developments.[17] The opposite, however, might be more likely: that those political developments had an impact on the self-perception of judges, their mission, and their decisions.

As a matter of fact, consensus was also sought in the few areas already formally subject to qualified majority voting before the empty chair crisis and consensus voting would probably have predominated anyway, even without the Luxembourg compromise. That was the view of the French ministry of foreign affairs. A note of the Quai d'Orsay, of 21 May 1965, explicitly says that the passage to qualified majority voting in some fields would not represent a problem to France, because decisions of political importance would always be taken by consensus among the governments.[18]

---

[16] Weiler, 'The Transformation of Europe', 2429.

[17] The French diplomatic and internal administrative records of the time do not contain a single reference to the case law of the European Court of Justice, direct effect or supremacy (see my article J. Baquero Cruz, 'The Luxembourg Compromise from a Legal Perspective: Constitutional Convention, Legal History or Political Myth?', in J. Palayret, H. Wallace and P. Winand (eds.), *Visions, Votes and Vetoes: The Empty Chair Crisis and the Luxembourg Compromise Forty Years On* (Brussels: P.I.E. Peter Lang, 2006), 251–78.

[18] Ibid., 259, referring to the document 'Règles de majorité dans le traité de Rome', No. 107/CE, MAE-DAESCE, Vol. 1111, 5.

Indeed, consensus decision-making remains the predominant decision-making practice in the European Union even at present.[19] I don't think the relative hardness of Union law explains that practice or makes it understandable. The reason for it was and remains the need to accommodate interests and to create a good climate in negotiations among actors whose level of mutual trust might not always be high.

My second remark concerns the notion of 'Transformation'. In my view it is understandable that the 1960s and 1970s were a period of *evolution* without Treaty change. On the one hand, the Community was rather homogenous and the Treaty had been signed not too long ago. On the other hand, the Treaty had been designed as a flexible instrument, a *traité cadre*, an open framework with a potential for growth, both in law and in policy terms. It is likely that there was no major need to change the Treaty until the 1980s. And there was fierce opposition to change it in order to dilute integration (consider the rejection by the Five of the French proposal to modify the voting rules during the empty chair crisis).

Weiler presents the constitutionalisation process as a 'radical mutation of the Treaty'. The changes in the political process would also be 'deviating radically from the Treaty'.[20] I disagree with the intensity of these claims. I do not think the constitutionalisation process radically 'mutated' the Treaty or 'transformed' the Community. The Court was not as *bold* and *revolutionary* as is often claimed.[21] The constitutionalisation of the Treaty was, for the most part, an evolutionary process more in tune with the constitutional structure, spirit, and seeds scattered in various parts of the founding text than the opposite reading would have been. In legal terms, direct effect and supremacy fit better with the Treaty, as it stood when the seminal cases of the 1960s were decided, and were a more natural interpretation of it than the opposite solutions of no direct effect and no supremacy.[22] The drafters of the Treaty were at least as bold as the Court, if not bolder, inter alia in their decision to establish a legislative body which

---

[19] See F. Hayes-Renshaw and H. Wallace, *The Council of Ministers*, 2nd edition (Basingstoke: Palgrave-MacMillan, 2006), 259–97.

[20] Weiler, 'The Transformation of Europe', 2428.

[21] See, for example, A. Stone Sweet, *The Judicial Construction of Europe* (Oxford: Oxford University Press, 2004) and K. J. Alter, *Establishing the Supremacy of European Law* (Oxford: Oxford University Press, 2001). Among the lawyers, D. Rossa Phelan, *Revolt or Revolution: The Constitutional Boundaries of the European Community* (Dublin: Round Hall Sweet & Maxwell, 1997).

[22] See my argument in J. Baquero Cruz, 'The Changing Role of the European Court of Justice', *International Journal of Legal Information*, 34, 2 (2006), 223–45, at 224–30.

could enact secondary law, including 'directly applicable' Regulations, and a Court of Justice endowed with a large jurisdiction, and connected with national courts through the preliminary rulings mechanism, obligatory for national courts of last resort and optional for all other national courts.[23]

As to changes in the political process, they did not deviate radically from the Treaty but were possible within the Treaty framework. The practice of consensus does not deviate from the Treaty as long as it does not involve a formal veto right and voting remains possible. The historical record shows that very often successful veto positions were invoked with the support of a blocking minority, and that is a far cry from the unilateral veto right de Gaulle claimed in 1966. A hard unilateral veto right in fields subject to qualified majority voting would have been unlawful. However, such a right hardly ever existed in fact. What existed was the natural tendency to accommodate interests and to reach consensus, and also a number of successful 'vetoes' with the support of blocking minorities, which is a lawful practice.[24]

The end of *The Transformation of Europe* is a praise of cosmopolitanism and 'community' against the 'unity' vision of integration. The 'unity' vision of European integration would have as its objective the establishment of a United States of Europe and would lead to the creation of a form of European nationalism. Instead, the 'community' vision would simply lead to a redefinition of the discourse of interstate relationships, without negating the nation-state. It would not lead to a European nationalism, but to a taming of state nationality and its consequences.

In the conclusion to the article, Weiler ceases to be neutral and clearly takes a political position. From a more neutral stance towards integration, one could see these two visions as two stages in a process rather than as opposing paradigms of integration, the community vision having the potential to lead to the union vision. Indeed, if the restructuring of interstate discourse through common institutions and law is effective, and if the taming of nationhood and nationality is also effective, a cohesive European polity could probably emerge, as could a sense of belonging, a European sense of allegiance – which does not need to be

---

[23] On the historical context, see A. Boerger-de Smedt, 'Negotiating the Foundations of European Law, 1950–57: The Legal History of the Treaties of Paris and Rome', *Contemporary European History*, 21, 3 (2012), 339–56.

[24] See J. Baquero Cruz, 'The Luxembourg Compromise from a Legal Perspective', at 258–62 and 270–2.

exclusive, as Weiler himself later argued in his piece on citizenship and the Maastricht-Urteil,[25] but may be shared among the various levels. In *The Transformation of Europe*, Weiler seems to condemn the unity vision on the basis of a presumption that the state and nationalism are intrinsically bad. But are they? Doesn't it depend on the type of polity and the kind of allegiance that takes shape in it? Is the alternative preferable, with the possible resurgence of nationalism in the Member States to occupy the political space and the processes of legitimation that the European polity has been unable or unwilling to cultivate?

## 4

Reading his work was formative but less important than listening to him. As in many traditions, with Weiler the important things were conveyed orally. That's how one learned about learning, about teaching, and about thinking. The texts were supplementary and most instructive only to those that followed his oral teaching. They are not useless for others, but they are less useful for them.

I have said that with Weiler the law opened to many other things: political science, sociology, legal theory. But sometimes it also seemed to close on itself and he would just focus on hermeneutics, on extremely detailed analysis of legal texts. Reading legal provisions and judgments with him was very much like analysing a poem or a literary work with a philologist. I was puzzled. Beforehand, I always thought that the law was the very opposite of poetry and literature, that there was a deep gap between them. At the time it never entered my mind that law and poetry had similar origins, as Vico says: *Et carmina fuisse leges, quae, scriptura nondum inventa, nullo consilio, sed natura ipsa, cantu dictatae, facilius memoriae mandabantur./Unde idem verbum* nómos *et 'legem' et 'cantum' significat./ Et sic poetas fuisse primos legislatores.*[26]

Never before had I paused to think that the law was also about words and interpretation of sometimes obscure texts, that there was poetry in law and justice, and also justice and laws in poetry, and that the law could also be a creative activity. In Bruges I started to glimpse that, and I also started to see the law as much more than the dry and boring memorisation of legal provisions: it was about structures, ideas, and arguments, and

[25] J. H. H. Weiler, 'Does Europe Need a Constitution? Demos, Telos and the German Maastricht Decision', *European Law Journal*, 1, 3 (1995), 219–58.

[26] G. Vico, *Opere giuridiche* (Florence: Sansoni, 1974), 485.

it began to have a context. And I also began to see myself, as a lawyer, as something else than a walking but at bottom inert memory.

Weiler said astonishing things in the classroom. Sometimes he sounded like a Zen master, leading us to moments of *satori*. He made us feel that the class was important to him, that he was profiting from us as much as we did from him. His class was a performance and had an experimental nature. One day a student made a very formalistic argument. Weiler asked: 'would that be fair?' 'That's what the law says', the student said, 'why should we care whether it's fair or not? That's not the lawyer's business'. Weiler seemed angry. 'If you take justice out of the law', he said, 'then the law will dry up and become an instrument of domination'. Otherwise he was most tolerant with the students. He liked discussion and being contradicted. At one point, though, he would see that the debate was not moving towards the point he wanted to make. Then he would say: 'We have to agree to disagree about that.'

I did my LL.M. thesis under his supervision, on Opinion 1/94 about the WTO Agreement. I wrote it in two months, after having read lots of things. It was a horrible essay. Towards the end of the discussion about my text Weiler told me that I could rework it over the summer and then try to publish it in a law journal. I did some more work on the essay, which was published in 1997.[27] I was twenty-four years old. It was my first legal publication. When I received it, in 1997, I was lawyering with a big corporate law firm in Madrid. I liked seeing the article in print, but it made me think that I was far away I was from my real interests. I applied to the EUI for a grant to do a PhD. Joseph Weiler wrote one of the letters that had to be sent. I was given an interview and when, in April 1997, I received an e-mail from the EUI saying that they offered me the grant I was glad to have the chance of devoting some years of my life to research, meditation, reading, and writing. I left the law firm in May 1997, spent four months in the countryside near Palencia, and left for Florence at the end of August.

In 1997, Joseph Weiler had already been away from the Institute for quite a long time, but his spirit was still present and he often visited Florence. In my first year, he gave a workshop on 'How to Write a Thesis'. The workshop was inspiring. I still remember many of the things he said. He who was so clearly full of talent told us: 'talent is cheap; work

---

[27] J. Baquero Cruz, 'Opinion 1/94 on the WTO Agreement: Disintegration of the Law of Integration in the External Economic Relations of the European Community', *Columbia Journal of European Law*, 3, 2 (1997), 257–82.

is expensive.' He gave us a very high and challenging idea of the work we had ahead of us.

After Florence we have met rarely, no more than two or three times, but he had already left in me a vivid impression of what is interesting and genuine in legal work and academic life: the view of law as something more than technique, as an intellectual endeavour involving continuous exploration, endless questioning, and also pleasure in what one does. He also taught us the active value of neutrality. In addition to that, he was an example of that distance from all national legal schools and traditions that makes him an ideal interpreter of Union law, teaching us that to be a good Union lawyer one has to transcend one's national identity and embrace a wider identity, one must overcome the weaknesses of each national legal tradition and build up a new tradition made of the best of each system, with a rich blend of argumentation, structure, form, integrity, and justice. And, finally, he taught us that one should approach the law of integration with a sense of historical meaning and responsibility, and with a deep understanding of the interaction between law, values, and political realities.

# *The Transformation of Europe* in US Legal Academia and Its Legacy in the Field of Private Law

DANIELA CARUSO*

## I  Introduction

Joseph Weiler's children loved transformer toys: the car that turns into a scorpion, the helicopter that morphs into a monster, and so on. The Weilers' home must have been cluttered with transformers at the time *The Transformation of Europe* was written, and perhaps inspiration for the project came first and foremost from the playroom. Of course, child play was only partly responsible for the catchy title of this masterpiece. In the American legal historiography of the time, 'Transformation' – with a nod to Polanyi – was code for an extended, ambitious, and critical rendition of epic legal developments. A voracious reader and himself a novelist, Joseph Weiler had learned from Ovid, Kafka, and Stan Lee that a good transformation story can grip the collective consciousness, and knew that the matrix of metamorphosis, with all its evocative power, would make the story of post-WWII European legal developments particularly compelling. He was, of course, correct.

A gripping narrative is, however, only one ingredient of success. It also matters when and where the story is told. The long-lasting fame of an extraordinary piece often depends on the impact it has on its contemporaries – those who read it for the first time and choose to pass it on to their successors as a classic. *The Transformation of Europe* was published by a top US law journal at the dawn of the 1990s and made an immediate splash. Instantly famous, it was regularly assigned in a range of American academic courses, was widely quoted and cited by US scholars across many disciplines, and became a pillar in the architecture of EU studies. Part II of this essay revisits a few traits of that place and time – US legal academia in

* Professor of law, Boston University School of Law

the 1990s – and investigates the importance of *The Transformation* in that context. I suggest that, in the heat of the 'federalist revolution' wrought by the Rehnquist court, Joseph Weiler's piece performed an important role, enabling a momentary suspension of partisan assumptions about the proper division of labour between states and federal government. I further surmise that the particular synergy between this piece and US federalism jurisprudence, in a cultural and political climate conducive to transatlantic cooperation, was a fundamental reason for the rise of EU law as an autonomous discipline in US law schools.

Part III focuses on the legacy of the transformation matrix and applies it to a subset of EU law that hardly existed when the piece was published – namely, EU private law. Precisely because, through Professor Weiler's lens, the process of Europeanisation came across as deeply transformative of the legal landscape, *The Transformation* made me wonder why EEC law had always seemed so tangential, or perhaps altogether orthogonal, to the private laws of the member states. Among the circle of *civilistes* with whom I had been acquainted since the 1980s, Europeanisation had once asserted itself in the form of a mandatory products liability regime. But not even that notable reform had prompted any real reflection on the systemic change that was happening in Brussels. How could we have missed the transformation? And how could the transformation have bypassed private law?

I began my own journey into EU law by investigating these questions, and found myself witnessing a radical change. Over the past twenty-five years, private law has moved from a parallel universe to the centre stage of integration policies; it has morphed from bulwark of state sovereignty to natural target of harmonisation. Professor Weiler's seminal article, written before the fact, gave us the tools we needed to comprehend this transformation as it unfolded.

First, *The Transformation* unearthed the philosophical premise of formal equality among individuals, which lay at the core of the Single Market agenda and allowed for the downplaying of socioeconomic differences (in this sense, the integration project had much in common with the liberal civil codes of the founding member states); second, Professor Weiler's work was a lesson in the importance of self-referential frameworks. His epistemic focus on the resiliency of thickly interwoven legal rules, insulated from political dynamics, was crucial to understanding the particular itinerary of private law within the EU architecture. Writing about the transformation of European private law in the aftermath of *The Transformation* felt like spotting new trees in a large forest, whose existence and basic bio-rules had been revealed to us with unprecedented clarity.

## II   *The Transformation of Europe* in US Legal Academia

The rise of EU law in US legal scholarship – from international lawyers' pet project to new fuel for comparative constitutional scholarship, and then on to self-contained subject matter with an independent *raison d'être* – is closely tied to the professional itinerary of Joseph Weiler.[1] Under the auspices of Eric Stein and Peter Hay, EEC law developed as a discipline at the University of Michigan, and the collaboration between US legal academia and the European University Institute (EUI) grew in quality and intensity. The year 1984 saw the birth of a massive research project sponsored by the EUI and the Ford Foundation, named 'Integration through Law'.[2] According to the vision of senior co-author Mauro Cappelletti, the project was to map the budding European legal integration onto the lessons of a mature American federalism. The blueprint of the project had a one-way direction, portraying the United States as a source of 'experience' and Europe as a wide-eyed youth in need of inspiring examples. Joseph Weiler's take on the project, however, was quite different. He was determined to avoid the trap of ephemeral similitude. Having identified a bedrock of analogies, he then set out to unearth the specific dynamics that had enabled Europe's legal change. Weiler's own contribution to *Integration through Law*, focused as it was on Europe's institutional uniqueness, found its natural sequel in *The Transformation*. This article explained Europe in terms remarkably intelligible to US lawyers, but avoided any direct reference to US federalism. This was, familiarly enough, a constitutional project based on a court-led orchestration of federal and state powers. Yet its internal analytics, shaped by the logic of free trade and by technocratic opacity, were sufficiently rich and peculiar to dispel any off-putting déjà vu effect.

The timing of *The Transformation* proved brilliant. Weiler's narrative enabled transatlantic dialogue on constitutionalism at a point in US legal history when federalism came to dominate both scholarly and political discourse. In his early years on the Court, Justice Rehnquist had reminded

---

[1] This section is adapted from D. Caruso, 'EU Law in U.S. Legal Academia', *Tulane Journal of International and Comparative Law*, 20 (2011), 175, 181–9.

[2] M. Cappelletti, M. Seccombe and J. H. H. Weiler (eds.), *Integration Through Law: Europe and the American Federal Experience* (Berlin; New York: W. de Gruyter, 1985).

his brethren that state prerogatives were enshrined in the Constitution ('the Tenth Amendment ... is not without significance'[3]) and had denounced what he perceived as an undue growth of Congress's power to regulate interstate commerce. In his view, decades of Washington-friendly constitutional adjudication had turned the doctrine of delegated powers into 'fiction'.[4] Appointed to the role of Chief Justice in 1985, Rehnquist spearheaded what we now know as the 'federalist revolution', openly aimed at restoring what he (and many others) envisioned as the proper balance between state and federal government in the US constitutional design. Sandwiched between two cases that upheld federal powers, *Garcia v. San Antonio Metropolitan Transit Authority* (1985) and *Gonzales v. Raich* (2005), were a number of remarkable pronouncements aimed at keeping Congress's legislative reach at bay. To name just a few: *New York v. United States* (1992), upholding the state's challenge of federal legislation by breathing new life into the Tenth Amendment; *United States v. Lopez* (1995), narrowing the legislative reach of the interstate commerce clause; and *City of Boerne v. Flores* (1997), limiting Congress's enforcement powers under the Fourteenth Amendment.

Predictably, this flurry of dramatic pronouncements energised US legal academia. In polarised academic debates, federalism grew into a sort of collective neurosis.[5] It is in this context that EU law gained its highest ever degree of popularity. In January 1993, in sync with the entry into force of the Treaty of Maastricht, a modern American casebook on EU law came out of the presses of West Publishing.[6] In 1994, the *Columbia Law Review* dedicated 125 pages to George Bermann's discussion of subsidiarity (a wholly European doctrine aimed at determining, politically and perhaps judicially, the distribution of powers between Brussels, states, and substate entities),[7] and Columbia University lent its flag to a new journal devoted exclusively to European law.[8] EU federalism was mainstreamed into US constitutional discourse. Top law journals made room, without

---

[3] *Nat'l League of Cities* v. *Usery*, 426 US 833, 842–3 (1976).
[4] *Hodel* v. *Va. Surface Mining & Reclamation Ass'n*, 452 US 264, 308 (1981) (Rehnquist, J., concurring).
[5] See E. L. Rubin & M. Feeley, 'Federalism: Some Notes on a National Neurosis', *UCLA Law Review*, 41 (1994), 903, 908.
[6] G. A. Bermann et al., *Cases and Materials on European Union Law* (1st edition 1993).
[7] G. A. Bermann, 'Taking Subsidiarity Seriously: Federalism in the European Community and the United States', *Columbia Law Review*, 94 (1994), 331, 423.
[8] *The Columbia Journal of European Law*, 1 (1994/95).

apologies, for EU law articles. EU law classes were taught by full-time faculty members who considered the subject their main area of research.

The European connection to the US federalist debate had been made structurally clear in *The Transformation*. The three main sources of the federalist revolution – the commerce clause of the US Constitution, the equal protection clause of the Fourteenth Amendment, and states' sovereign prerogatives per the Tenth and Eleventh Amendments – found adequate functional equivalents in the Treaty of Rome. These analogies made it possible, in turn, to understand what was different. And, for at least two reasons, such differences became a worthwhile field of scholarly investigation.

First, bringing the EU experience to bear on the American debate had the effect of mixing up, and thereby diffusing, the political stakes of the Supreme Court's case law. State prerogatives in the European context of the mid-1990s were often associated with a bulwark of social protection against the flood of neoliberal deregulation – in sharp contrast to the politics of similar arguments in US federalism. This was enough to cast state sovereignty in a different light. In the words of Ernest Young: 'Considering issues of federalism in the context of Europe ... helps us shed some of the historical baggage hindering present debate, and it demonstrates that any number of different federal settlements may be workable and legitimate.'[9] For those interested in de-ideologising the federalism question and rephrasing it in doctrinal terms, EU parallels offered an extraordinary opportunity.

Second, the very effort of searching for functional equivalence in an altogether different analytical system could prompt novel taxonomies and lead to deeper insights. A wave of academic Europhilia permeated the US judiciary. Justice Breyer's dissent in *Printz v. United States* (1997) referred to the EU edifice in order to relativize the anti-commandeering principle. This was by no means the first or the last reference to European law in the US Supreme Court, but it was by far the most structural. At stake was not just the possibility of transatlantic similarities between discrete rules, but a comprehensive overlap of two legal archetypes of federalism. There was more, here, than the academic discipline of comparative law had ever promised. For once, the legal orders of the old and new continents seemed to have reached sufficient structural convergence that dialogue could

---

[9] E. A. Young, 'Protecting Member State Autonomy in the European Union: Some Cautionary Tales from American Federalism', *New York University Law Review*, 77 (2002), 1612, 1618.

actually become relevant for the positivists. Europe seemed to be doing
federalism by other means, i.e., by other doctrines and, more importantly,
by other politics, but doing federalism nonetheless. The effort of deciphering its language was worthwhile, because it yielded fresh evidence of
good or bad practices that could somehow enrich the federalist debate at
home. It is in light of such payoffs, visibly enabled by *The Transformation*,
that EU law became an autonomous subject with status and prestige in
US law schools.

This unusual degree of US interest in the legal structure of European
integration coincided with other transatlantic synergies. The 1990s, the
golden age of EU law in American academia, were also years of unprecedented optimism among mainstream internationalists. The end of the
Cold War and the spread of the Washington Consensus had led the world
to the impression that international values might at last be converging.
This 'long decade' nurtured the 'ideal of the gradual transformation of
the world into a community governed by widely-accepted internationalist principles and institutions'.[10] Of course, reality was more complicated,
but convergence made for fashionable discourse, and the discourse recast
outrageous events as unavoidable deviations from a trajectory of steady
progress. In the aftermath of September 11, 2001, the French newspa-
per *Le Monde* proclaimed unambiguous transatlantic alliance in a famous
editorial ('Nous sommes tous Americains')[11] and three months later the
European Council issued the Laeken Declaration (the blueprint of a
Philadelphia-inspired constitutional moment for the EU). These were also
years during which the EU consolidated its eastward expansion, arguably
attesting to the demise of once insurmountable ideological divisions. This
cultural climate enabled a new rapprochement between mainstream constitutionalists and comparative lawyers. *The Transformation*, a catalyst of
transatlantic dialogue, found in that dialogue new life and importance.

The myths of the long decade soon crumbled, shattered by the divergence of member states' stances on post-9/11 strategies, the implosion of
the EU constitutional dream, and the bursting of many a financial bub-
ble. The world found itself divided again, with no consensus on how to
handle economic interdependence or how to secure peace. At the level of
transatlantic relations, the EU's statement of friendship in the aftermath
of 9/11 proved meaningless, as the United States found itself negotiating

---

[10] N. Berman, 'Intervention in a 'Divided World': Axes of Legitimacy', *European Journal of
International Law*, 17 (2006), 743, 745–6.
[11] J. Colombani, 'Nous sommes tous Americains', Le Monde, 13 September 2001.

its European allegiances one state at a time in Kissingerian mode. The EU's inability to produce a constitution rendered federalist analogies implausible. Alternative narratives of the integration project, emphasising its administrative and regulatory core, gained scholarly currency.[12] US constitutional law scholars gradually abandoned the field, and so did mainstream law journals. EU law courses saw diminishing enrolment and often came to be taught by European visitors or were simply outsourced to overseas campuses in the summer. Even before the global financial crisis, the European job market became less promising to US law students due to an inward-looking transformation of multinational firms, increasingly prone to staff their European offices with local lawyers only briefly trained in the United States.

To be sure, this was not the end of US-based interest in the European experiment. EU law as an autonomous legal system with not-quite-federal features, as outlined in *The Transformation* and since complicated by further layers of law, politics, and history, continued to feature in dedicated monographs, specialised law journal articles, and most importantly, political science literature. In legal academia, however, the comprehensive study of the dynamics of European integration migrated back to the fields it came from: comparative or international law. Within comparative law, the large-scale functionalism of the 1990s dried up and gave way to *bricolage* (a term aptly chosen by Mark Tushnet to indicate the scholarly technique of taking bits and pieces of a foreign system as tools for domestic legal inquiries).[13] The global financial crisis has certainly made the United States pay close attention to European responses, but only in a fragmented manner and with discrete regard to its many pieces (pension reform, banking regulation, or sovereign debt monitoring). The project of European legal integration as a whole, its oscillation between unity and community, and the transformation of its ethos, must now compete for attention with other phenomena of regionalisation on the world stage. In this sense, *The Transformation* is the hallmark of a period that has come to an end – a particular phase of transatlantic fame for EU law that sprang in large part from this single-authored contribution and that is now behind us. What is definitely *not* over, however, is the legacy of the piece for all those who continue – by virtue of geographic situation and/or academic

---

[12] P. L. Lindseth, *Power and Legitimacy: Reconciling Europe and the Nation-State* (Oxford: Oxford University Press, 2010).

[13] M. Tushnet, 'The Possibilities of Comparative Constitutional Law', *Yale Law Journal*, 108 (1999), 1225, 1228.

pursuit – to engage in the study of EU law. What follows is an attempt to show how, now as twenty-five years ago, *The Transformation*'s analytics continue to prove essential.

### III   *The Transformation*'s Legacy in the Context of EU Private Law

*The Transformation* famously explained how something as intensely political as the integration of Europe could be perceived, in its foundational period and beyond, as ideologically neutral. Weiler's explanation resided in the particular institutional design of the Community, in the specific modus operandi of Commission and Council of Ministers, and in the relative isolation of legal analytics from political contestation. In the final pages of his article, however, Professor Weiler observed that the era of ideological neutrality had come to an end. By his account, Jacques Delors' White Paper for the completion of the Internal Market (1985) had marked the institutional embrace of a particular ideology – one that lent primacy to the goal of transactional efficiency and that assumed formal equality among players. In his words:

'A '*single* European market' is a concept which still has the power to stir. But it is also a 'single European *market*'. It is not simply a technocratic program to remove the remaining obstacles to the free movement of all factors of production. It is at the same time a highly politicised choice of ethos, ideology, and political culture: the culture of 'the market'. It is also a philosophy, at least one version of which – the predominant version – seeks … to maximize utility [and] is premised on the assumption of formal equality of individuals. It is an ideology the contours of which have been the subject of intense debate within the Member States in terms of their own political choices. … This need for a successful market not only accentuates the pressure for uniformity, but also manifests a social (and hence ideological) choice which prizes market efficiency and European-wide neutrality of competition above other competing values.'[14]

This reading was of course correct and utterly perceptive: market efficiency – even though marbled by competing values – was a very specific cognitive framework,[15] and there was nothing ideologically neutral

---

[14] J. H. H. Weiler, 'The Transformation of Europe', *Yale Law Journal*, 100, 8 (1991), 2477–8. Footnotes omitted.

[15] M. Bartl, 'Internal Market Rationality, Private Law and the Direction of the Union: Resuscitating the Market as the Object of the Political', *European Law Journal*, 21 (2015).

about elevating *The Market* to a per se goal. But in the mid-1980s the Commission saw things differently, and had no intention of putting forth an ideological manifesto. Its emphasis on markets was heralded, and perhaps even genuinely conceived, as a renewed promise of neutrality – the conceptual opposite of an ideological move. This explicit focus on rule uniformity, efficiency, and – as per Weiler's observation – formal equality between individuals was a revival of eighteenth-century private law rhetoric. The classical private law formula that several sovereigns (most notably Napoleon) had used to build their nation-states in continental Europe was being deployed again: no state powers, no conception of the common good, no social goals would ever interfere with private property or contractual autonomy. The rules of private exchange and ownership would be distributively neutral, simple vehicles for the realisation of individual (Kantian) autonomy. This portrayal of private society as animated only by forces of its own – the aggregate results of individuals' self-interested agendas – had allowed the nascent states of the old continent to promote themselves as mere enablers of multiple pursuits of happiness. The sovereign's respect for the autonomy of private transactions had been deployed as proof of self-restraint, and had therefore contributed to legitimising the sovereign's power. In eighteenth- and nineteenth-century Europe, the conceptual separation of private law rules from politics had performed an essential state-making function. The Single Market agenda, like classical private law, could now serve the goal of solidifying the supra-nation.

It was not yet obvious, at the end of the 1980s, that deepening European integration would bring the Commission to venture into the heart of continental legal systems –namely their private laws of contract and property, whose differences might stand in the way of seamless market transactions. For a long time, European integration had seemingly remained on the 'public' side of the private/public divide: it had concerned itself mostly with trade barriers erected by national executives (a matter of state sovereignty) and agricultural or industrial policies. Both of these functions concerned background allocative choices and were therefore traditionally orthogonal to a classical understanding of private law rules. The 1985 Product Liability Directive[16] – admittedly a major break with the private-law principle of fault-based liability – had passed without much

---

[16] Council Directive 85/374/EEC of 25 July 1985 on the approximation of the laws, regulations, and administrative provisions of the Member States concerning liability for defective products.

fanfare because it was in line with the spirit of the time,[17] and had not yet manifested its transformative potential.[18] But in the 1990s, the impact of the Single Market agenda on national private laws became obvious, and Professor Weiler's intuition proved dramatically true: the Single Market *was* an ideological project that risked flattening private law under the paradigm of formal equality; and it *was* a project at odds with the reality of twentieth-century private law – now a historically mature and nuanced platform for private autonomy, informed (in some states more than others) by solid mechanisms for the protection of weaker parties.

The tone of the debate was indeed reminiscent of the analytics of *The Transformation*, which centred on the relative insulation of law from political contestation. But there was something unique, and irreducible to the pattern of incremental constitutionalisation identified by Professor Weiler, in the encounter between private law and Europeanisation. The unassailability of national private law was surprisingly stronger than constitutional statehood, as it relied on entrenched fictions of horizontality and closure, had history on its side, and was firmly rooted in Western legal thought.[19] States' civil codes had survived, with little change, profound constitutional upheavals, and might be equally resilient to Maastricht.

It is against this bulwark of resistance that the transformation of private law had to be mobilised. The White Paper of 1985 gave the Commission the mandate of building *the market*, and the Commission needed an argumentative strategy that would make its new inroads into private law seem normal and unobjectionable. This strategy was to be built on the foundations of classical private-law rhetoric. Like the coins of the late Roman Empire, private law had two sides. One side emphasised the horizontality of private exchange, its insulation from power, its apparent neutrality, and its theoretical indifference to politics. This picture was of course terribly out of date at the end of the twentieth century, but in the necessarily simplified private-law parlance of supranational fora, it was somehow acceptable and perfectly compatible with the neoliberal initiative. In the nascent debate about the harmonisation of private law, the Commission

---

[17] W. Boger, 'The Harmonization of European Products Liability Law', *Fordham International Law Journal*, 7 (1983–1984), 1.

[18] M. Reimann, 'Product Liability in a Global Context: The Hollow Victory of the European Model', *European Review of Private Law*, 11 (2003), 128. The impact of the product liability reform on state law would become obvious with such decisions as C-183/00 *Gonzáles Sánchez v Medicina Asturiana SA* [2002] ECR I-3901.

[19] D. Caruso, 'The Missing View of the Cathedral: The Private Law Paradigm of European Legal Integration', *European Law Review*, 3 (1997), 3.

kept flashing this side – and this side only – of the coin. Private law's self-contained indifference to shifts in power, as well as its philosophical origins, allowed the Commission to promote the harmonisation project as an ideologically neutral no-brainer.

The other side of the coin, by contrast, referred to the role that private law had played in continental state-making: by guaranteeing their subjects full autonomy in inter-private relations, sovereigns had justified their own rise to power, their own legitimacy, and their very existence. Private law's structural closure, internal coherence, and quasi-constitutional status armed state legislators with arguments for resisting harmonisation.

The 1990s witnessed serious clashes between the Commission's market agenda and national resistance, often motivated by social justice concerns in private law. Iconic episodes of this saga include the French reluctance to transpose the Product Liability Directive, which could (and would) reduce the protection of accident victims;[20] and the Social Justice Manifesto, an influential academic protest against the neoliberal bent of Commission proposals in contract law matters.[21] In the course of these clashes, many fictions imploded, and the two sides of the private law coin – neutrality and authority – became welded to one another. The openly political tone of parliamentary debates concerning the implementation of private law directives brought to the surface the many ideological choices hidden in private law rules – as applied by the courts in characteristically opaque judgments. The allegedly close and self-referential analytics of civil codes gave way to the realisation that many different regulatory goals could be – and had been – pursued under the cloak of neutrality.

The scene of private law harmonisation looks different today. All parties have learned from past mistakes. States no longer deploy arguments of doctrinal closure, and have come to accept that, like almost everything else, private law is now appropriate material for supranational compromise. Scholars are more attuned to stakeholders' voices and are fully aware of the politics of private law reform. Most importantly, the Commission has grown sensitive to the fact that Gierke's social oil facilitates consensus around private law proposals.[22] Much to the chagrin of efficiency-minded

---

[20] Ibid.

[21] Study Group on Social Justice in European Private Law, 'Social Justice in European Contract Law: A Manifesto', *European Law Journal*, 10 (2004), 653.

[22] N. Jabko, *Playing the Market: A Political Strategy for Uniting Europe, 1985–2005* (Ithaca, NY; London: Cornell University Press, 2006).

observers,[23] the Commission's lodestar is no longer the *de*regulation of private autonomy in the name of untrammelled commerce, but rather the uniformity of private law *regulation*. The new instruments of private law harmonisation – such as the Consumer Rights Directive[24] – are replete with mechanisms that protect the presumptively weaker party against the perils of uneven bargaining power. The philosophy of the new instruments is no longer the neoliberal presumption of equality, but rather – as in the private law of the member states – a dynamic compromise between efficiency goals and social justice.

And yet, Joseph Weiler's previously quoted prediction – that the Single Market would entail 'a highly politicized choice of ethos, ideology, and political culture', that it would seek 'to maximize utility' and would be 'premised on the assumption of formal equality of individuals' – proves totally accurate in light of the current state of private law harmonisation. The logic of the market, as interpreted by the Commission, demands that private law be uniform across the Union, with no regard for structural asymmetries between North and South, or East and West.[25] Private law rules are meant to impose identical regulatory costs on businesses in every corner: those who can pass such costs onto consumers, and those who can't. Supranational rules of private exchange may be well suited to redress the bargaining imbalance between two parties, but they may also produce perverse distributive effects when applied, without adequate macro-adjustments, to the socioeconomic periphery of the Union.[26]

It is a well-known fact in international law and politics that uniform social regulation imposes uneven burdens on struggling economies, and that corrective mechanisms (in the form of trade concessions or rule relaxations) may be necessary to redress the asymmetric costs of compliance. Within the Union, by contrast, the asymmetric costs of uniform private laws have not yet gained adequate salience, obscured as they are by the win-win narrative of harmonisation. The governments whose citizens have more to lose, or less to gain, from private-law uniformity are particularly eager to embrace it: uniformity signals health, legal maturity, and readiness to compete. The result is déjà vu. The fiction of formal equality

---

[23] See, e.g., R. Epstein, *Harmonization, Heterogeneity and Regulation: Why the Common European Sales Law Should Be Scrapped* (2012).

[24] Directive 2011/83/EU of the European Parliament and of the Council of 25 October 2011 on consumer rights.

[25] D. Kukovec, 'Law and the Periphery', *European Law Journal*, 21 (2015), 406

[26] Ibid.

between private actors controls, today as at the birth of the nation-state, the writing of private law for the supra-nation. The uniformity of private law raises important questions of distributive justice, yet it continues to be heralded as per se progress ('uniformity will drive down the cost of doing business'). Professor Weiler's take on the Single Market agenda – the prediction that it would '[prize] market efficiency and European-wide neutrality of competition above other competing values' – has a very contemporary flavour and survives the apparent demise of neoliberal rhetoric.[27] *The Transformation*'s emphasis on the power of self-referential legal frameworks is to this day affirmed by the history of EU private law, and by countless other stories of European integration.

---

[27] Weiler, 'Transformation of Europe', 2478.

# 5

# A European Half-Life?: A Retrospective on Joseph Weiler's *The Transformation of Europe*

NEIL WALKER

Joseph Weiler's *The Transformation of Europe* (*TOE*)[1] was undoubtedly a landmark in European legal scholarship, but it also marked a watershed in its author's own approach to the European project. European legal scholarship was never quite the same after *TOE*, but nor was Joseph Weiler's contribution to that body of scholarship. In some ways, a shift in his perspective is to be expected. *TOE* was an agenda-reshaping piece, and it is only natural that its author should follow the new agenda that he did so much to set. That, indeed, is a large part of the story, but still only one part. It is also the case, I believe, that the author gradually came to understand the new agenda to be less relevant, or less 'actionable' than previously he had thought, and in any case less central, either because the world had simply moved on yet again in new and unpredictable ways, or, perhaps, because the agenda had never been as open as he once believed. In this retrospective comment, I want to explore both parts of the story. I want to examine what they tell us about the evolving character of supranational Europe as a political project and also as a field of inquiry, and how this movement is both reflected in and touched by the thought of one of the leading jurists of the age.

What was the new agenda? The originality of *TOE* lay in its deep diagnosis of the legal and political condition of supranational Europe. Previous legal scholarship had tended to adopt an insider line, taking the fact and the value of the postwar new European order for granted – as something to be affirmed, defended, and incrementally developed as a 'good thing'. *TOE* told a more challenging tale. Drawing heavily on historical materials, and more lightly, but effectively, on contributions from the non-legal sciences of Europeanisation, it presented a picture of European integration that was more dynamic but also more precarious and less

---

[1] J. H. H. Weiler, 'The Transformation of Europe', *Yale Law Journal*, 100 (1991), 2403–83.

insular than the received wisdom. According to the fresh narrative, legal supranationalism was no longer to be viewed as a mere projection and epiphenomenon of concerted 'high' political will, nor was it to be understood as somehow detached or sealed off from any immediate sense of political partisanship or contestation. One or both of these perspectives, each tending to situate law in an unproblematic and settled relationship with the 'political', were implicit in the dominant model of legal scholarship. In *TOE* the legal and the political domains were instead depicted as having long been in a relationship of complex, inverted symbiosis. The stepwise 'locking in' of robust legal supranationalism, measured in terms of increase in the authority, reach, and enforcement capacity of European legal norms, was portrayed as both condition and reinforced consequence of weak political centralism, measured in terms of the maintenance of strong state-executive and so 'intergovernmental' control of the process of law-*making* at European level. That intergovernmental control went against the grain – or at least the long-term vision – of the more *communautaire* foundational texts of the Paris of 1951 and Rome of 1957, but had been vigorously reasserted by Charles De Gaulle in the events leading up to the 1966 Luxembourg Compromise and its consolidation of the national veto over key European decisions.

Yet this relationship was already unravelling by the time it was diagnosed in *TOE*.[2] The Single European Act in 1987, soon to be reinforced by the 1992 Maastricht Treaty, had altered the subtle balance between strong legal authority and modest political capability at the European centre. The introduction of qualified majority voting in the area of the 'completion' of the single market and, progressively, in other flanking areas of social and economic policy, together with the gradual empowerment of the European Parliament as an actor in the legislative process, constituted an important if partial move towards *political* supranationalism or neofederalism. This, in turn, meant that Europe was faced with a new set of possibilities, but also with a new set of dangers and constraints.

As Weiler sets out in the closing pages of *TOE*, Europe thus transformed was faced with new challenges of democracy and legitimacy, and the meeting of these challenges was bound to be further transformative. The development of majoritarian legislative authority at the centre raised the question of the deep democratic credentials of a wider Europe

---

[2] Although Weiler had in fact developed the rudiments of the *TOE* thesis in an earlier article; see J. H. H. Weiler, 'The Community System: The Dual Character of Supranationalism', *Yearbook of European Law*, 1 (1981), 267–306.

of such ample new political means. It did so as a matter of absolute standards, and, of more immediate consequence, it also did so *relative to* the much longer established and more firmly embedded democratic claims of the member states themselves, whose independent authority was eroded or threatened by these centripetal forces. What is more, the combination of the aggressive promotion of the single market under the '1992' Programme and its relocation, post-Maastricht, within a deeper framework of Economic and Monetary Union, the palpable sense of a broadening of the supranational agenda to cover other, politically controversial and only loosely single-market-implicated areas of social policy such as internal security, defence, and environmental policy, and the growing likelihood of national governments in power being bound against their will by the accumulation of regulatory initiatives at the centre, meant that the legal-technocratic cloak of ideological neutrality which had long shielded the European project from political controversy looked increasingly threadbare. Europe now had to come to terms with the higher and more controversial profile of its common institutions. And in so doing, less reliance than previously could be placed on the loyalty, quiet diplomacy, and pragmatic idealism of its officials, judges, and various national fellow-travelling elites to drive its agenda and valorise its operations. In moving forward under these altered conditions, according to Weiler, Europe was faced with starker choices. It would take either the path of Unity – of federal statehood writ large, or, as he himself would prefer, and would claim to be way more faithful to the European project's formative postwar ethos, of Community – of a novel and subtly balanced condition between internationalism and statehood.

This novel idea of Community had both 'hard' and 'soft' components. At its 'hard' material and institutional end it was premised on a limited sharing of sovereignty, and a gradually thickening structure of policy and institutional interdependence. At the 'soft' cultural and ethical end, it was premised on the development of a new political sensibility and on the altered moral horizons associated with that new political sensibility; in particular, on the mutual complementarity of a bounded idea of national identity and a more inclusive sense of a continental identity of values and aspirations. In each dimension of Community, 'hard' and 'soft', the trick lay in finding a way of political being which, crudely, was neither too little nor too much. On the one hand, the new Europe had always been more than the mere instrument of its states, its value more than the aggregation and its authority more than the delegation of their various and separate self-interests. And in the exercise of its extended, more transparent, and more potentially state-antagonising capacity, Europe would have to find ways to safeguard and justify that relative autonomy from its original sources of power. On the other hand, Europe would have to assert itself in a manner that did not destroy its own distinctive *raison d'être* as an accompaniment to rather than a new embodiment of the nation-state – as an entity that qualified rather than undermined, supplemented rather than supplanted, complemented rather than copied the constituent states of Europe.

So the new agenda set by *TOE* was one in which European law lost its rarefied, always/already quality. It was one where legal scholars were not only encouraged to take a greater interest in the historical origins of the European project as a way of understanding the contingency of the present and of accessing the framing conditions of an uncertain future. In addition, they were drawn to address directly normative questions and institutional-design puzzles about the shaping of that uncertain future.

This agenda, as already intimated, explains much of the trajectory of Weiler's own later work. The essays that formed the second part of his 1999 collection *The Constitution of Europe*[3] – a collection in which, tellingly, *TOE* reappears as the anchoring essay – were mostly taken from the post-*TOE* years. Much more than his earlier work, which, like *TOE* itself, tended to be concerned with diagnosis of the deep and distinctive structure of EU law (and, sometimes, as in his work on human rights, external relations or the free movement of goods, with its precise doctrinal implications),[4] this later seam of writing was explicitly normative. In particular, *The Constitution of Europe* was concerned to explore and deepen what Weiler meant by his preference for Community over Unity, and to do so in both 'hard' and 'soft' terms. It was the work in which he addressed the challenge of revitalising the congealing values of Peace and Prosperity – values he had identified as constituting the ethical heart of the original project of a continent devastated by war; in which he argued for supranational democracy as a vital but, finally,

---

[3] J. H. H. Weiler, *The Constitution of Europe: "Do the New Clothes Have an Emperor?" and Other Essays on European Integration* (Cambridge: Cambridge University Press, 1999), chapters 6–10. For my Review, see N. Walker, 'All Dressed Up', *Oxford Journal of Legal Studies*, 21 (2001), 563–82.

[4] See Weiler, *The Constitution of Europe*, *supra* note 3, chapters 3 and 4 on human rights and external relations respectively. On the free movement of goods, see J. H. H. Weiler, 'The Constitution of the Common-Market Place: Text and Context in the Evolution of the Free Movement of Goods', in P. Craig and G. de Búrca (eds.), *The Evolution of EU Law* (Oxford: Oxford University Press, 1999), 349–75.

instrumental good of the continental polity – empty without a reinvestment in core values; in which he developed his ideas about the 'taming' of national by European identity rather than its replacement – the one concerned with the retention of that culture of originality and belonging that is inextricable from and vital to primary political community at the state level, the other inhabiting a more cosmopolitan and so other-regarding sensibility; and in which he began to develop his notion of Tolerance, and in particular national tolerance of and *self*-discipline before the supranational edifice and its wide-ranging normative message as to the acceptance of the non-national 'other', as the lodestar of European constitutionalism – an argument which would come to form part of his later powerful opposition to the top-down imposition of a documentary Constitution for Europe against the backdrop of the failed constitutional initiative of 2003–5.[5]

Yet this is only one part of the story, and essentially the first part. In more recent years the writings of Weiler, always a healthy corrective to unthinking Euro-complacency or glib Euro-optimism, have taken a more pessimistic turn. Where once Supranationality, offered in the upper case as the animating structural ideal – the 'x' factor of integration – supplying both the institutional hardware and the ethical software for the substantive ideals of Peace and Prosperity,[6] was an elusive yet preciously defining feature of the European *Sonderweg*, now it began to look plain elusive. For the tension that Weiler identified with such acuity in *TOE* between too much and too little – between preventing the excesses of a new Unity on the one hand and avoiding a failure of Community to renew its credentials under conditions of greater political capacity, increased public profile and more diverse and more insistent political challenge on the other, now threatened, in his eyes, to collapse into a series of intractable problems.

In particular, a much emphasised and recently repeated theme of his post-*TOE* work has been the difficulty of replacing or replenishing the original motivational ideals of Prosperity and Peace in a time of relative plenty, however unevenly distributed, and in a place where the

---

[5] See, e.g., J. H. H. Weiler, 'A Constitution for Europe? Some Hard Choices', *Journal of Common Market Studies*, 40 (2002), 563; J. H. H. Weiler, 'On the Power of the Word: Europe's Constitutional Iconography', *International Journal of Constitutional Law*, 3 (2005), 173–90.

[6] See Weiler, *The Constitution of Europe, supra* note 3, chapter 7, '*Fin de Siècle Europe*: Do the New Clothes Have an Emperor?'.

sound of War is now only heard from beyond its borders.[7] In seeking to demonstrate this loss of momentum, Weiler is critical, and not without reason, of the stubborn lack of clear and democratically sensitive lines of accountability within the European institutional balance, of the sustained absence of true political contestation at the European level, and of the stark contrast between the ebbing of popular interest and participation in European elections and the ever greater mobilisation of national support behind profoundly anti-European parties. If this echoes a common catalogue of complaint, Weiler has also, more distinctively, been critical of what he sees as a gradually hardening deficit of effective political capacity and resolve on the part of the EU's leading institutions. This failure, for him, was manifest, for example, in the EU's ineffectual response to conflict amongst its near neighbours – in particular to humanitarian crises in Bosnia and Kosovo, and, more recently, in its absence from the top table in respect of intervention in Libya, and its reluctance to make common cause of the problems generated by the pressure of mass immigration from northern Africa. And, of course, more topically still and most urgently of all, this lack of resolve has also been evident in the EU's repeated failure to contain or reverse its widely ramified sovereign debt crisis, even in the face of Greece's ever downward spiral of debt and austerity and the broader threat to the member states of southern Europe. Importantly, however, unlike so many other analyses, for whom the current parlous state of the Union is quite distinct in profundity from anything that preceded it and essentially rooted in macro-economic factors, for Weiler, without in any way seeking to underplay the significance or urgency of the threat to economic and monetary union, the immediate crisis is instead viewed as essentially *continuous* with a longer and broader pattern of *political* impotence.

Weiler sees the accumulation of democratic ills and of decision-making black spots and policy haemorrhages as deeply symptomatic of political drift, as a running indictment of a failure to meet the challenge of political renewal, which the 1990s – the original age of transformation – presented in such stark form. And this critique is underscored by two additional

---

[7] See in particular J. H. H. Weiler '60 Years since the First European Community – Reflections on Political Messianism', *European Journal of International Law (EJIL)*, 22 (2011), 303–11; J. H. H. Weiler, 'The Political and Legal Culture of European Integration: An Exploratory Essay', *International Journal of Constitutional Law*, 9 (2011), 678–94; J. H. H. Weiler, 'In the Face of Crisis: Input Legitimacy, Output Legitimacy and European Integration', *Journal of European Integration*, 34 (2012), 825–41.

sceptical themes, both of which focus on the limitations of the 'hard' institutional side of the formula for Community. On the one hand, for all that he is critical of the failure of the European architecture to adapt to new challenges, there is an abiding concern in Weiler's work to avoid just the kind of institutional overreach that would either intentionally pursue or unintentionally stumble on the 'wrong road' of European Unity or statehood. Whenever the reassertion of supranational Europe is seen to involve the accoutrements of statehood, whether a written Constitution, or an unqualified sense of the supremacy of European law, or any arrangement which would elevate European citizenship above national citizenship in Europe's complex matrix of civil attachments and democratic connections, the fear is expressed that this goes too far, if not necessarily in the deed or likely consequence then certainly in the hubristic intent. On the other hand, there is a sense that the ills of Europe have become so much 'part of a deep-seated political culture'[8] that they are in any case simply not susceptible to treatment through institutional arrangements; or, in a milder version, that institutional reforms significantly *underdetermine* the possibility of genuine transformation which would allow supranational Europe to recover its sense of political purpose.[9]

By the same token, Weiler does not offer any alternative blueprint to resolve what he sees as the ills of Europe. In his work, from *Un'Europa Cristiana*[10] onwards, on the complex relationship between political values and individual virtue, and in particular the failure of the values and structures of political supranationalism to provide a context for the inculcation of the very virtues which would allow the sustained realisation or renewal

---

[8] Weiler, '60 Years Since', *supra* note 7, 309.

[9] On one interpretation of his early post-TOE work, Weiler reads like an institutional conservative, as someone who, in his own words, approaches the European constitutional design with the attitude, 'if it ain't broke, don't fix it', and who is of the view that it 'ain't (yet) broke'. See J. H. H. Weiler, 'Epilogue: Fischer: The Dark Side', in C. Joerges, Y. Meny, and J. H. H. Weiler (eds.), *What Kind of Constitution for What Kind of Polity? Responses to Joschka Fischer* (Florence: Robert Schuman Centre, 2000). This, however, would in my view be a false reading, or at least an exaggerated one. His conservatism extends only to the basic supranational ideal, and to what he understands as vital to the maintenance of that ideal, including the promotion of the idea of Tolerance, and the avoidance of Big 'C' constitutional solutions. As his consistent critique of the democratic deficit and as his frequent proposals for reform make clear, he has always been interested in institutional redesign, even if he sees this as only a modest part of the answer to Europe's problems. See, e.g., Weiler, *The Constitution of Europe, supra* note 3, chapter 10; J. H. H. Weiler, 'To Be a European Citizen: Eros and Civilization', *Journal of European Public Policy*, 4 (1997).

[10] J. H. H. Weiler, *Un' Europa Cristiana: Un saggio esplorativo* (Milan: Rezzi, 2003).

of these values, there is much reflection on how the 'soft' ethical side of the problem of Community is key, and how it must be addressed in its own terms. The danger here, however, is that the diagnosis, even if correct – or, at least, to the extent that it is correct – is simply left hanging, suggesting no obvious course of treatment beyond the kinds of institutional reforms he either resists or treats as of secondary importance.

It is that concern which lies behind the headline of my piece. 'Half-life' is a scientific term denoting the period of time it takes a substance undergoing irreversible decay to decrease by half, and is sometimes used more loosely to depict the condition of terminal decay itself. But I approach this stylisation tentatively. The question mark in my title reflects a series of genuine uncertainties. First and foremost, over whether, for Joseph Weiler, Europe today has, indeed, entered or may be on the verge of entering the half-life phase. Is the future of supranational Europe already in danger of becoming one of irreversible decline, or, put less sensationally, at least one of diffusion, defusion, dilution, and fragmentation – of mutation into something that is no longer recognisably Big-S Supranational?

And insofar as Weiler's work does contemplate the half-life thesis, further exploration is required to clarify what this means in terms of both prognosis and diagnosis. As to prognosis, even if the canonical postwar form of the European project is in secular decline, this need not imply either the expectation of or a preference for a clearly alternative geopolitical solution on the one hand, or a dystopian outcome on the other. Weiler is no flat-earth nationalist, nostalgically hankering after, still less anticipating a return to the 'Westphalian' paradigm of mutually exclusive states. His earlier enthusiasm for and pioneering justification of the supranational project makes that perfectly clear. Equally, unlike those who would view the EU's 'natural' evolution as tending towards a more inclusive and less regionally delineated complex of planetary regulation, he is no champion of ambitious models of global governance in which cosmopolitan optimism somehow trumps the opposing dangers of renewed Great Power imperialism or rudderless fragmentation. Instead, the Supranational paradigm understood as a *singular* achievement – according to which there is a common trajectory of integration in which all national polities share the same institutions and embrace the same culture of indefinite common commitment – may simply be exhausted, with no clear option either of reversion or of succession. The sense Weiler's recent work conveys, then, is that the age of Supranationality as a sufficient or even still a relevant model either for the European continent itself, or, as has often been urged or assumed, for other regions and other operations of transnational governance, may be drawing to an end,[11] and with no other political vision readily equipped to take its place.

Yet, even if, in this reading of Weiler, both steady state Supranationalism and its starkest alternatives are ruled out, that does not mean that we would be left only with a residual half-life narrowly and negatively conceived – involving nothing more than the gradual corrosion and reduction of Europe's dense and complex structure of transnational governance. Over the longer term, if we take a more optimistic view, novel vocabularies of legitimation and new expressions of collective self-authentication can often be found for emergent forms of political practice that are hardly recognised and reckoned for their novelty before the new terms are coined. For history teaches us that it is a paradoxical, Owl-of-Minervan feature of much transformative social and political change that forward-looking reflection and imagination is fired by the stirrings of new practice rather than offering its prior inspiration. This is a point, indeed, that Weiler himself once strikingly insisted upon in characterising the nascent Supranational Community of the 1950s and 1960s itself as a case of Doing before Hearkening[12] – as a series of experimental steps which only gradually discovered and revealed their deeper purpose and direction. In the recent revival of a tentative and, admittedly, still normatively impoverished language of multi-speed Europe – of flexible or differentiated Europe – we may see something similar unfolding.[13] We may observe the beginnings of a process by which today's profoundly challenged Supranationalism may come in time to be understood and articulated as mutating into a new and differently legitimated political form.

But if we focus instead on more pressing short-term realities, we may draw a less optimistic and more sobering conclusion. One of the salutary lessons of the current, already long-extended Euro crisis, with its progressively destabilising disconnect between a common monetary policy

---

[11] See my exchange with Weiler on the subject of my essay N. Walker, 'The Place of European Law', in G. De Búrca and J. H. H. Weiler (eds.), *The Worlds of European Constitutionalism* (Cambridge: Cambridge University Press, 2012), 57–104. See esp. J. H. H. Weiler in the same volume 'Dialogical Epilogue', 270–8, where he questions the continuing significance of the EU as a global archetype.

[12] Weiler, *The Constitution of Europe, supra* note 3, chapter 1, 'Introduction: "We all do, and hearten"'.

[13] See, e.g., J. Piris, *The Future of Europe: Towards a Two-Speed EU?* (Cambridge: Cambridge University Press, 2012).

that produces highly selective economic hardship and a fiscal policy which lacks either the common pan-European means and commitment or the sufficiently other-regarding resolve of the richer states to supply a more solidaristic solution, is that institutions do not readily disappear or transform themselves just because they become temporarily or even persistently dysfunctional. Repeated self-reassertion, in the manner of the extensive range and breathless pace of elite institutional initiative we have witnessed over the crisis years,[14] may be no prelude to renewal or to any kind of orderly mutation. Rather, it may simply signal obliviousness to or denial of the onset of half-life, or even a kind of weary resignation mixed with a determination not to lose out in the international blame-game – the dangers of which negative orientations I return to in the conclusion.

Before that, however, we need to attend to Weiler's deeper historical diagnosis of the present condition, for this reinforces the sense in his later work of the fading of the Supranational paradigm as a matter of waste and atrophy rather than as a productive morphosis. Of key significance here are his views about the 'messianic'[15] origins of the Union. Weiler contends, using the Schumann Declaration as Exhibit One, that the fact that certain ideals – Peace and Prosperity again – were at the centre of the original European project, both encouraged and was encouraged by a kind of top-down single-mindedness and infallibility of purpose amongst a core group of postwar European leaders.

Even if we do not fully buy into the messianic metaphor of the Promised Land for an entity which has so often, and with good reason, been accused of bureaucratic distance and of failure to ignite the passion of genuine commitment amongst the populations of its member states, Weiler is certainly correct in identifying a strongly teleological element in the initial European project. In fact, rather than contradictory forces, elite-led passion and a quotidian culture of unobtrusive, technocratic rule and quiet compliance might be said to be naturally complementary dimensions of a vast socio-political project of such early settled purpose. Taken together, moreover, these different features of teleological rule – both the impassioned grand vision and the minutely reasoned detail – reflected

---

[14] From a huge literature, see, e.g., the special issue of the *European Law Journal* edited by D. Chalmers for comprehensive documentation and incisive analysis of the early years of the financial crisis; Volume 18, Issue 5, September 2012; see also, more recently, F. W. Scharpf, 'After the Crash: A Perspective on Multilevel European Democracy', *European Law Journal*, 21 (2015), 484–505; C. Offe, *Europe Entrapped* (Oxford: Hart, 2015).

[15] See, e.g., Weiler, 'Sixty Years Since', *supra* note 7, 306.

and cultivated a sensibility which, from the early days, stood against con-
testatory democratic openness and allowed only grudging recognition
to those market-correcting rights-claims that might temper the precon-
ceived economy-centred project. Yet, it might be argued, just such a background of a more ample democratic culture and a more pluralist menu of
basic goods might have served the EU better as it entered its transformative phase in the late 1980s.

   Weiler's own take on the absence of democracy from the early EU, in
fact, turns out to be even more critical than this. His message seems to be
less one of missed opportunity than of genetic limitation or disability. He
claims that 'if political messianism is not rapidly anchored in the legitimation that comes from popular ownership, it rapidly becomes alien ...
and turns on its creators.'[16] Does this mean, perhaps, that by the time of
*1992* it was already too late for the EU to legitimise its inevitable spurt
of post-foundational expansion and transformation? But given that, for
Weiler, the messianic or teleological element is also at the root of all that
is distinctively good in the EU, namely the commitment to Peace and
Prosperity in an other-regarding transnational environment – was there
ever a moment where it would have been possible, even in principle, to
introduce democracy *early enough* to ensure that a narrow messianism,
or teleological perspective, did not take hold, but not *so early* as to destroy
the momentum and sense of common cause without which the founding
ideals would have been frustrated? In other words, perhaps on Weiler's
analysis the EU was damned to an early grave – a half-life of inexorable
deterioration – if it did democratise and diversify its basic goods, and
equally damned if it did not.

These points, to repeat, are made tentatively. I merely speculate on the
reasons for and implications of what is a distinct shift in tone and perspective from the more open sense of normative possibilities Joseph
Weiler set out in his path-breaking *TOE* agenda, and as to the extent and
precise implications of that shift. Perhaps, though, the half-life metaphor
oversteps the mark. After all, natural science has no place for the con-
tingencies of human agency, and for that reason has never been the best
model for the study of politics and society. And if the very point of the
half-life metaphor is to suggest that the path-dependent pathologies of
Europe's Supranational project may simply be beyond human remedy, we
must beware its 'scientific' capacity to reduce and distort.

[16] Ibid., 308.

Two further points might be made in clarification of Weiler's mature post-*TOE* position, each of which underlines the need to treat the half-life metaphor with great caution as a characterisation of his later work. First, the weight of his analysis has been on the past and present rather than the future – on the lessons of diagnosis rather than the vagaries of prognosis. Before we ask what is to be done, we must work out why things are as they are, and if in so doing we offer no comfortable sense either of continuity or of evolution, then that stands, not as a blanket denial of the possibility of a better future, but merely as an important warning against complacency to those in the futures business His priority has been to demonstrate why and how the EU of today, and so also the EU of tomorrow, has been reduced to a more precarious state than many of its supporters have in recent years typically been prepared to concede, and who can say that approach has not been vindicated by the depth of the current crisis.

Secondly, we should not forget that, for all he sees the European project as having eclipsed the selfish concerns of its member states, Weiler retains a distinction between generative authority and ethical purpose. For him, Supranationality was a national production that came to transcend national self-interest. Equally, his wariness about new institutional solutions at the European level is not just a product of a general institutional scepticism, but also of a more particular scepticism about the capacity of European institutions to provide the fulcrum of change when the wellsprings of legitimacy remain so firmly located in the cultural heartlands of the individual states. If Europe is to be made anew, then for Weiler the onus will once again lie with 'the national communities as the deepest source of legitimacy of the integration project'.[17] On that view, the inescapability of failure, and of its accompanying half-life, is only plausible within narrow parameters; namely, to the extent that we cleave to the belief that the Union can be *self*-transformative rather than requiring to revert to its founding parents in times of trouble.

My own view, on which I have exchanged views with Joseph before,[18] is somewhat different. I believe that that there *is* more that we can do from the hard institutional side to create the political-cultural wherewithal to pursue common continental goods; that these may not be *manifest* common goods like Peace and Prosperity – so self-evident that they do not require legitimation or discovery by democratic means, but rather *constructed* common goods – generated through mechanisms of voice and

---

[17] Weiler, 'In the Face of Crisis', *supra* note 7, 837.
[18] See Weiler, 'Dialogical Exchange', *supra* note 11.

decision at the continental scale;[19] that these processes need not tend towards a new Unity, nor even significantly endanger remaining national processes of will formation; and that the process which led to the failed Constitutional Treaty, far from an irrelevance or a hubristic conceit, was actually a missed opportunity to generate a broader debate and develop a broader commitment to a 'post-messianic' EU. This is not the place to debate these matters more fully, or to consider whether now might be a riper time than the pre-crisis mid-noughties for a process of constitutional mobilisation, but merely to acknowledge that my views involve a degree of speculation in extending faith in the transnational political process, just as Weiler's involve a degree of speculation in the curtailment of that faith.[20]

What is not a matter of speculation, however, is that the political backdrop of 2017 is not that of 1991, but an even more challenging one. In *TOE*, Weiler thought it worthy of remark, so well entrenched was the Union by then, that 'as recently as the late 1960s, the survival of supranationalism was a speculative matter.'[21] He set his transformative agenda, therefore, against a backdrop of political flux, but also long-term security. Today, no one would doubt that the threat to survival is, finally but firmly, back on the political radar,[22] however unlikely that might have seemed in the intervening years. Equally, however – and this is one final way in which the half-life label might be useful – the return of a deep-set fear of demise generates its own counterpoint. Weiler is sensitive to this, singling out those prominent members of the current European elite, institutional heads and key national leaders alike, who have played and continue to play on the sense of crisis so as to encourage a one-way climate of 'integration through fear.'[23] Without the Euro and all its works, it is proclaimed from these influential quarters, the EU simply cannot survive – a perspective which purports to justify the unprecedented range of urgent measures of

---

[19] See Walker, 'The Place of European Law', *supra* note 11 esp. 90–5.

[20] See N. Walker, 'Constitutional Pluralism Revisited', *European Law Journal*, 22 (2016), 333–55.

[21] Weiler, 'The Transformation of Europe', *supra* note 1, 2406.

[22] In his annual State of the Union speech on 28 September 2011, the previous president of the Commission, Jose Manuel Barroso, was moved to state that 'We are today faced with the greatest challenge our union has known in all its history.' www.reuters.com/article/2011/09/28/us-eu-barroso-idUSTRE78R0WG20110928. It is testimony to how widespread the language of crisis has become in such a short timeframe that what appeared unprecedented in its candour only five and a half years ago has so quickly become unremarkable, even commonplace, in EU institutional discourse.

[23] J. H. H. Weiler, 'Integration through Fear', *European Journal of International Law*, 23 (2012), 1–5.

'executive federalism'[24] we have witnessed in the past few years of Treaty and non-Treaty reform. Yet, as Weiler claims, this is an argument from *false* necessity. It is a means by which widespread unease about European decline is exploited to assert, in denial of such decline, first, that there is only one cure – the preservation of the old order, and, secondly, that there is only one potent medicine for that cure – the bitter medicine of monetary constraint and fiscal discipline.

If Europe as a political project is in doubt, what, finally, of Europe as an intellectual project – an intellectual project that might figure in a renewal or rerouting of the political project? Can we imagine any contemporary cross-disciplinary work on the European Union having the kind of (re) framing influence and lasting impact enjoyed by *TOE*? A *TOE* twenty-five years later would be written from a decidedly more precarious place than that occupied by Joseph Weiler in 1991. It is a project which, in order to succeed, would require at least as much historical sensitivity and perspicacity as its illustrious predecessor, and, from a position where so many of his troubling prognostications have come to pass, greater attention to ways and forms of European community not yet pursued.

---

[24] See, e.g., J. Habermas, *The Crisis of the European Union: A Response* (Cambridge: Polity, 2012).

# 6

## On the Past and the Future of *The Transformation of Europe*: Law, Governance, Rights, and Politics in the EU Evolution

### GIANLUIGI PALOMBELLA

### Prologue

Twenty-five years after *The Transformation of Europe*,[1] Europeans face a deep economic and political nightmare and are called to strengthen unity again, to escape a return to the past. Left aside the word *finalité*,[2] inter-governmentalism is the driving force and *functionalism* is back in action, one that focuses on economic disease demanding further institutional measures. But ironically, it is more conservative in nature than the harshly criticised Monnetist predecessor. The latter was well sitting on the normative dimension, on shared ideals – peace and freedom, economic prosperity, solidarity. 'Consequential' integration proved even effective in affording 'simple answers to the question: what does Europe stand for?'.[3] It was clearly future-oriented, a justificatory fulcrum of innovation. Contrariwise, today new functionalism works in the backward-looking spirit, on how to safeguard the present *acquis*, *vis-à-vis* a number of challenges that the EU is presently unready to face. It reminds us of the most famous sentence pronounced (in *Il Gattopardo*), by the child of Sicilian aristocracy under the destructive wind of 1860 unification:[4] 'If we want things to remain, then things will have to change.'

---

[1] J. H. H. Weiler, 'The Transformation of Europe', *Yale Law Journal*, 100, 8 (1991).

[2] J. Fischer, 'From Confederacy to Federation: Thoughts on the Finality of European Integration', in C. Joerges, Y. Meny, and J. H. H. Weiler (eds.), *What Kind of Constitution for what Kind of Polity? Responses to Joschka Fischer* (Firenze: Robert Schuman Center, 2000).

[3] 'The coal and steel Community stood for peace and freedom, the common market for economic prosperity, and so did the single market in the 1980s' (R. Dehousse, 'Rediscovering Functionalism', *Harvard Jean Monnet Working Paper*, 7/00 (2000)). Also cf. M. Cahill, 'The Constitutional Success of Ratification Failure', *German Law Journal*, 7, 11 (2006), 947–66, stressing how functionalism was all but directionless, and criticising the *finalité* perspective as inadequate.

[4] *Il Gattopardo* is a novel by Filippo Tomasi di Lampedusa.

As it seems, new, authoritative functions – whether economic, fiscal, or redistributive – are urged to prevent monetary union from dissolution. But arguments are far from the horizon of 'messianism'[5] and also of the 'progressive' ideals of the foundation. And maybe Europe is still where it has 'reached its lowest point'.[6]

European evolution appears to be still, as the *iter* in between one functionalism and another. 'Transformation' is a delicate and troubled step, and its assessment is disputable, involving both internal and external perspectives; it depends on frames of reference. During the past two decades, the *relative* movement within the European Union boat has been intense, although sometimes, as today, the *absolute* movement seems to have been altogether too slow.[7] How do we understand this all? Where has Europe gone? *Quo isti Europa?*

## I  Three Traits

1. Parameters for such a kind of enquiry were famously fixed in *The Transformation of Europe*. It also gave the insight that both Europe's *Gestalt* and its evolutionary steps were matter for *legal* analysis, provided that the latter becomes aware of fundamental questions about community values, institutional balance, and the 'politics of European law': that in fact were masterly addressed *together*, through the comprehensive view of that essay.

   Its first feature is its self-defined legal 'purism', pointing to the autonomy of law, its distinctive service and dynamics. Law – however – is not meant as a Kelsenian disembodied skeleton of norms, but as the life of a system of institutions, in interplay with the external environment and with politics itself. Accordingly, the actual tension between supranationalism and inter-governmentalism can be studied from the legal (integration) point of view. The *approach* bore a further virtue: the re-elaboration of political categories (like Hirschman's *Exit* and *Voice*) in terms of legal structures and guarantees. In sum, irreducible to sheer political instrumentalism, law is capable of response in autonomous terms, as a peer. Not as a mechanical servant, law responded to the

---

[5] Cf. J. H. H. Weiler, 'Editorial', *European Journal of International Law (EJIL)* 22, 2 (2011), 306.

[6] J. H. H. Weiler, Festival of Europe, Florence, 2011, at www.euractiv.com/fr/avenir-europe/lue-son-plus-bas-niveau-news-504676.

[7] I am metaphorically referring to Galileian 'relative motion' and similar records depending on the previous definition of the system of observation.

crisis of political allegiance in the 1960s: it answered in 'federal' terms to a 'disintegrating confederal *political* development'.[8] Such a step, *hardening law* (and closing the path to 'selective Exit') forced, thereafter, dialectical interactions: states had to rebalance by increasing *their* Voice and 'hardening law-making'.

European *law* creativity cannot be explained as the causal product of 'external' politics. The rule of law faces with its own commitments the rule of power. But it does coexist with it: 'Had no veto power existed, had inter-governmentalism not become the order of the day', Member States would have hardly 'accepted with such equanimity what the European Court of Justice was doing'.[9]

(Un)Balance provides the interpretive key to subsequent phases as well. In the completion of the internal market, the institution of majority vote, the enlargement and finally the legal expansion of competences, Member States face 'binding norms adopted wholly or partially against their will, with direct effect in their national orders'.[10] In the new setting – once the internationalist consensus model is abandoned – the novelty is the loss of equilibrium between constitutional legitimacy and institutional dynamics.

2. A second trait follows: the interpretation of the 'democracy deficit', that is, the absence of democratic process in the European enterprise led by international civil servants (the Commission) and the Council of National Executives (Council of Ministers), all of them legislating without parliamentary scrutiny (either European or national). Despite the common belief that democracy can be brought about by increasing the powers of the European Parliament, the approach of *The Transformation of Europe* places lighter accent on the sheer procedural vehicles of 'democracy': however refined, they would not *per se* make up for the *loss of direct influence* that integration generates *due to the larger boundaries* of Europe. The long-run auspice is that a supportive European political culture possibly amends the loss of *reflexivity*, actually perceived when *peoples* are asked to obey decisions whose authority does not derive from *their* autonomy, but from the will of a large number of 'others'. It is likely that more democratised procedures are established and that still they do not overcome the lack of

---

8   Weiler, 'Transformation of Europe', *supra* note 1, at 2425.
9   Ibid., 2429.
10  Ibid., 2462.

democracy, legitimacy, and 'political' involvement. So the matter shifts from democracy to *social legitimacy*.

Needless to say, twenty-five years after, even the Lisbon Treaty's empowering of majoritarianism and of the European Parliament shall fail to trigger the awaited political mobilisation.

3. The third trait that I wish to suggest is twofold. *On the one hand*, it must be observed that the rhetoric of 'ideological neutrality' had been a feature of European practice and culture, and that in 1992, the prospects for such a sign of political immaturity were less acceptable than ever. It was expected to fade due to the single market strategy, to the consequences of the monetary Union, to the new ambitions towards a vague *political* unity. Commitment to the market – so went the note – has in fact more than a technocratic (favouring undistorted competition) nature; it presupposes 'philosophy', choice, 'pressure in shaping the political culture of the Community'.[11] *On the other hand*, what is the Community like? How is it a 'promised land'? The *1992* programme's weakness was lying in a resurgent idea of unity, rather than of 'community' (in the peculiar definition that *The Transformation of Europe* provides of it). For Weiler, the *unity* ethos should *not* be the mobilising force, because in conjunction with the rhetoric of the single market, as he wrote, it would corrode the 'community' values, that is, those values treasuring the *diversity* of states and peoples (instead of hinting at a super-state), equally allowing transnational human intercourses, unencumbered with the barriers of nationalities.

4. Among other things, the first trait, the institutional approach *through law*, and the third, the peculiar idea of *community*, are both necessary to understand the later-on developed proposal of 'constitutional tolerance':[12] one that is hardly comprehensible on a sheer legalistic plane (whether Kelsenian or otherwise). Coexistence and harmony can only originate by avoiding formalistic, state-centred hierarchies and *substantively* recognising the common choice for Europe, as a pluralities' equilibrium.[13]

---

[11] Ibid., 2478.

[12] J. H. H. Weiler, 'Federalism and Constitutionalism. Europe's *Sonderweg*', *Harvard Jean Monnet Working Paper*, 10/00 (2001).

[13] 'Neither Kelsen nor Schmitt', Weiler writes in his 'Federalism and Constitutionalism' (*supra* note 12).

On a further plane, the contention that legitimacy does not always come from *process* (and also that just *outputs* might poorly serve democratic improvements) remains today a lighthouse possibly pointing to the hollowness of deracinated forms of (not-democratically tested) juridification. What Weiler calls today the *alienation* of Europe from its founding values is itself in line with his stress on the categorical difference between social legitimacy and democratic procedures, and with the caveat that their relation might be deceptive. As I would resume the argument, the two terms were suspected to engender in the future a vicious circle. In fact, the present corrosion of the founding values originates from *institutional self-understanding and behaviours, choices and interpretive practices* that are preventing European actors/peoples from developing the necessary *virtues* for those founding values to be pursued.[14]

Indeed, changing European realities still show the continuity of many 'fundamentals' illuminated at the start of the 1990s. Despite the huge progress in the famous 'deepening and widening', some knots are unsolved, as if no motion had taken place. As in Alexandre Dumas's *Twenty Years After*, the first page does not even engage in bridging the time-gap; it simply goes on as from the day before.[15]

## II   Three Domains

### 1   The European Public

I wish to suggest now three among the *domains* from which 'twenty-five years after' realities can better be seen, namely, the European 'public' (law), rights, and new governance. On them all, the *traits* in the foregoing should be made to bear, because these domains provide for the key questions in appraising persistence, failures, and promises.

The narrative established by *The Transformation of Europe* deeply relates, albeit implicitly, with the European public legality domain.

Despite exceeding the *statist* mind-set, Weiler's concern for the 'public' did not square either with a horizontal civil ('economic') society or

---

[14] J. H. H. Weiler, 'On the Distinction between Values and Virtues in the Process of European Integration', available at www.iilj.org/courses/ documents/2010Colloquium.Weiler.pdf. Cf. also J. H. H. Weiler, 'The Political and Legal Culture of European Integration: An Exploratory Essay', *International Journal of Constitutional Law*, 9, 3-4 (2011), 678–94.
[15] A. Dumas *Twenty Years After*, D. Coward (ed.) (Oxford: Oxford University Press, 2008).

with the vertical federal state. It did not match either a (ultra)Kantian cosmopolitanism of politically dis-embedded individuals or the problem-solving regulatory state – not even a thin Europe as a transnational arbiter of fairness (justice), among interdependent polities.[16] Nonetheless, I believe, it has to do with the values of a resilient idea of public law that belongs in the constitutional traditions[17] of the Europeans.

Such an idea, I submit, embodies a dual core, the tension between two different streams, political and legal: on one side, public (law) as the pre-positive material/spiritual determinants generating the political form of governmental power[18]; on the other, the modern *legal* nature of authority: for it the birth of law posits the condition for any possible 'public'[19] (not vice versa) enabling coexistence and coordination.

The first strand resonates in the demos(cratic)-centred state constitutionalism, and resists its ultra-state extension.[20] The second strand – in the Enlightenment tradition – takes the *form of law* as constitutive, and contrasts unlimited power, its claim of omnipotence, and the alleged fidelity to the deep soul of the people. European history has experienced

---

[16] J. Neyer, 'Justice, Not Democracy: Legitimacy in the European Union', *Journal of Common Market Studies,* 48, 4 (2010), 903–21.

[17] Maastricht Treaty upheld Member States' constitutional traditions (Art. 6/2); the ECJ treated them as community general source 'of inspiration'. See the interesting elaboration in W. Sadurski, 'European Constitutional Identity?', *Sydney Law School Research Paper,* 06/37 (2006).

[18] This tradition – visible through Bodin, Rousseau, and Hegel – identifies fully public law as political law, *droit politique,* as described by M. Loughlin's, *Foundations of Public Law* (Oxford: Oxford University Press, 2010). For the elaboration of public law as endowed with a *dual* core, that includes a 'public through law' as its second stream, G. Palombella, 'The (re-)Constitution of the Public', in A. McCormack, C. Michelon, and N. Walker (eds.), *After Public Law?* (Oxford: Oxford University Press, 2013).

[19] It is the 'public' instituted as a third standpoint, beyond private judgments and disagreements, as with Bentham; it is the imperative of 'public law' that with Kant overcomes a state (of nature) where injustice is *unobjectionable.* See J. Bentham, *Of Laws in General,* J. H. Burns and H. L. A. Hart (eds.) (London: The Athlone Press, 1970), 192. In Kant's view, unless man 'wants to renounce any concepts of Right, the first thing it has to resolve upon is the principle that it must leave the state of nature, in which each follows its own judgment, unite itself with all others (with which it cannot avoid interacting), subject itself to a public lawful external coercion, and so enter into a condition in which what is to be recognized as belonging to it is determined by law' ('Metaphysical First Principles of the Doctrine of Right', *The Metaphysics of Morals* [1797], M. Gregor trans. (Cambridge: Cambridge University Press, 1996) (repr. 2003), 33, § 44, 90.

[20] For example, see D. Grimm, 'The Achievement of Constitutionalism and Its Prospects in a Changed World', and on the contrary, see U. K. Preuss, 'Disconnecting Constitutions from Statehood: Is Global Constitutionalism a Viable Concept?', both in M. Loughlin and P. Dobner (eds.), *The Twilight of Constitutionalism?* (Oxford: Oxford University Press, 2010).

divergence between the two strands, and some more reliable convergence in post–World War II constitutional traditions.

If something in the 'public law' of the European community is constantly *under construction*, it is the duality of its core. In the contemporary *supranational* endeavours, the two components of public law are split on different organisational levels (respectively on the national and community levels, or even further to global orders).[21] The performative – treaty or judicial – construction of the new legal order, the famous *integration through law*, are moments belonging to the *public through law* component.

As I understand its spirit, *The Transformation of Europe* took issue with something much closer to rescuing the *dual* core of the public than to (the false friend of) *constitutionalising* the Union. It provides no basis for the cyclic appeal to the thaumaturgy of a constitution: a culture of shared, legitimate government for a common fate hardly stems from legal bootstraps and inflationary *reconstituting of constitutions*. The issues of legitimacy[22] and political faith are thought of as inherent in the threads of trust and action, in the mentioned path of 'constitutional tolerance', the Community *Sonderweg*: one that shall build on existing 'legalities', without deleting either previous constitutional commitments or their substantive interplay. That is consistent with the latent concern for what I would call the importance of *recoupling* (in a fashion appropriate to the multi-layered European dimension) the dual core of the public.[23]

Twenty-five years bring new complexity, however: the enlargements necessarily question the fabric of the European public and the recurrent questionnaire turns even less easy: what is the social and political Eros genuinely allocated on the supranational plane; does the EU work towards a thick, overriding, common *good*, or is its rationale sheer prevention of arbitrary interference;[24] what is the content of the 'European public' like? Such a frame-domain of the public deserves renovated attention, even more so after the constitutional failure, the doubts on EU economic

---

[21] See Palombella, 'The (re-)Constitution of the Public', *supra* note 18.

[22] 'It is largely since the Maastricht process that the debate on the European Union has been in terms of a "crisis" of legitimacy': G. de Búrca, 'The Quest for Legitimacy in the European Union', *Modern Law Review*, 59, 3 (1996), 349.

[23] Preserving a two-pronged allegiance: i) political and legal components of the public, ii) national/supranational levels. I framed the issue at length in Palombella, 'The (re-) Constitution of the Public', *supra* note 18.

[24] The root of this trend is in the approach to comitology by C. Joerges and J. Neyer, 'From Intergovernmental Bargaining to Deliberative Political Processes: The Constitutionalization of Comitology', *European Law Journal*, 3, 3 (1997), 273–99.

authority, the increasing nationalist and sovereigntist protest against the Union, and the overt rejection by some Member States of the liberal pillars of democracy.

## 2  Rights

Two protagonists of the European public, namely, *rights* and *governance*, can be seen as children of a further transformation, whose direction is controversial (whether fostering the political Europe, compensating for its lack, or even preventing its realisation).

In Euro-continental traditions, often rights had to partake in the structure of public law, not to play an anti-institutional (or sheer anti-political) role: once comprised of the common weal, they cannot fit the idea of unencumbered individualist autonomy. Their 'public' nature discloses 'duties' as irreducible to side effects on *others* of one individual's right.[25]

The known drive towards *European rights* is of course detached from that older continental background. The rise of post-war constitutional liberalism, the civilising pressure towards *human* rights, in their deontological momentum, the enhancement of *economic* freedoms at the core of European enterprise can broadly explain.

Now, beyond the older roots, but given their (national, evolving) constitutional persistence, oscillation between the European and the Member States' constitutional views on rights should always be expected. And it is implicit in the current dispute over the financial crisis, the national social rights undermined by the severity of European economic governance of the euro, the national resistance against further waves of immigration, and so forth.

European action has been so often described as offering universalised 'rights' and soulless technocracy. Thus, rights are less common goals that would require a solidarity context of mutual social commitments, than individual trumps contrasting the resilience of states' protectionist action: a line that has so far made Europe the realm of universalisation of the 'private'.

This fundamental question is what I would take as the general background to the disappointed note that Joseph Weiler wrote more recently: rights have become a means for furthering the 'tendency of

---

[25] Cf. G. Palombella, 'Politics and Rights in European Perspective', *Ratio Juris*, 18, 3 (2005), 400–9. And also G. Palombella, 'Diritti', in U. Pomarici (ed.), *Filosofia del diritto. Concetti fondamentali* (Torino: Giappichelli, 2007).

Citizen-as-Consumer (of political outcomes), and a consumer who is subtly conditioned to make his choices not on the basis of principle, but self-interest. Accordingly, while the legal system 'places the individual in the centre', on the other hand, it 'renders him a self-centred individual – in strong tension with the spiritual ideal of human integration'.[26]

On a different detail, and the same orientation, further dissatisfaction has been lamented in the context that generically refers to *human rights in Europe*. Gráinne de Búrca[27] stressed the weakness of the rights scene in Europe: the lack of provisions mandating monitoring of rights, intervention, and review (despite the FRA); separation *vis-à-vis* the institutional autonomy of the ECHR; a *double standard* asking external interlocutors for commitments that the EU scarcely takes on itself. Together with the risk of a human rights isolationism of the EU, it is maintained that even the judgment and reasoning of the ECJ in the famous *Kadi*[28] case concurred in this picture, by showing closure *vis-à-vis* international law obligations, and an American-style *exceptionalism*,[29] contradicting the original attitudes in the 1950s.[30]

Eventually, someone has even thought that the legal force gained by the Charter of Nice is itself a rather cheap obligation, given the high level of protection granted in the constitutional traditions of the advanced countries of the European Union: so that Lisbon deception might seem to have given us what we had already got.[31]

---

[26] Weiler, 'On the Distinction between Values and Virtues in the Process of European Integration', *supra* note 14, at 24.

[27] G. de Búrca, 'The Road Not Taken: The EU as a Global Human Rights Actor', *American Journal of International Law*, 105 (2011), 649 ff.

[28] Joined cases C-402/05 P, *Yassin Abdullah Kadi and Al Barakaat International Foundation v. Council of the European Union and Commission of the European Communities* [2008] ECR. II-3649.

[29] G. de Búrca, 'The European Court of Justice and the International Legal Order after *Kadi*, *Harvard International Law Journal*, 51, 1 (2010), 1–49.

[30] de Búrca, 'The Road Not Taken' *supra* note 27. See also Weiler, 'On the Distinction between Values and Virtues in the Process of European Integration', cit. *supra* note 14, at 38. And: 'Much of the human rights story, and its abuse, takes place far from the august halls of courts. Most of those whose rights are violated have neither knowledge or means to seek judicial vindication. The Union does not need more rights on its lists, or more lists of rights. What is mostly needed are programs and agencies to make rights real, not simply negative interdictions which courts can enforce' (at 39).

[31] J. Baquero Cruz, 'What's Left of the Charter? Reflections on Law and Political Mythology', *Maastricht Journal of European and Comparative Law*, 15, 1 (2008) at 74; F. Rubio Llorente, 'A Charter of Dubious Utility', *International Journal of Constitutional Law*, 1, 3 (2003), 405–26.

However, my sense is that the domain of rights should be taken as a core issue, that it is today of higher import and strong potential, that it is open to a less stringent fate and to being recast on a richer register than the economic liberties and the 'self-centred individual'. Prospects are theoretically better seen through the lens of the *fundamental* rights of the Charter (after Lisbon), that is, rights that are institutionally connected to the meanings and values available in the thick European context and in the social and political traditions of EU constitutional Member States. They should better be viewed as something more perspicuous than the thinner scrutiny of *human* rights compliance, although, of course, the EU has still to prove its capacity to take human rights seriously. Let me recall, then, some countervailing points. Again, the new situation has to account for the perspectives of almost thirty countries in Europe, and it is also on this plane that the *substantive* role of the Nice Charter must be appreciated, a plane on which rights (think of minorities' protection, the non-discrimination principle, social welfare, democratic process, civil and political rights and liberties, or the environment, together with the controversy about modernisation in Eastern countries, etc.) are triggering constant re-elaboration, bear a daily shifting extent and content, and are a challenge even within old European Member States.

In many ways, the Charter's reference to 'fundamental' rights certainly brings a larger series of contents/commitments than those that the 'human' rights deontology in the ECHR should normatively allow. The *fundamental* rights deeper domain includes more than those rights basically meant to a universalisable and essential measure of respect for humanity. It involves more advanced, demanding, and complex contents, requiring higher institutional and social commitments, and ongoing confrontation of assessments between ethical and political cultures. To this extent, the *human* rights more basic reference is as necessary as it is insufficient in itself to let us know about the place of rights in Europe, through the even deeper and larger import of *fundamental* rights in the Charter. Conversely, the commitments of the latter are a higher challenge for the prospects of European *identity*. Here lies the issue as to turning rights into a vehicle of 'human integration'.

Lamented Europe's lukewarm attitude towards human rights should not be underestimated, but seen in the long run, and a bit beyond some formal provisos (that is what *The Transformation of Europe* would have taught).

Even if we were (hypothetically) to agree that the reasoning of the ECJ in *Kadi* was self-referential and thus betraying true internationalism (like the United States in *Medellín*[32] and elsewhere), still we could not make this to square with (or contribute a basis for) the warning about Europe's sensitivity on human rights: all conceded, the criticised self-referentiality of the ECJ was making the protection of rights, at least in that case, the bedrock in the European order.

Moreover, even the lamented institutional separation from the ECHR might have less impact in practice. The Charter makes the ECHR part of its own meaning, and, insofar as this holds, the Charter itself has to be interpreted also through the lens of the ECHR. At least in theory, one cannot exclude a kind of indirect-*direct effect* of the Convention as a consequence. It is said that such a situation can possibly (over-)empower the national judge. In countries like Italy, it would be reasonable to hope instead for a potential blurring of the line between i) the Charter and the Convention, that is, ii) between the *diffuse* scrutiny (disapplication) of the norms infringing the Charter, and the centralised judgment (*review*) of (un-) constitutionality[33] based instead on the Convention.

Certainly, there are predictions stressing the limitations of the legal import of the Charter in the post-Lisbon scenario. But countervailing observations might apply. A limitation like Art. 52(5) that affords direct effect to rules, not principles, can have a controversial life, up to judicial definitions. On some matters of more diffuse relevance, this can lead to reopening supranational/national discussion, and the very issue of social rights is likely to become crucial. Similarly, the general limitation of the Charter's binding nature only in the case of 'implementing Union law',[34] yes, the child of a cautious protectionism, might be weakened under the self-expanding arguments (although explicitly excluded) of 'incorporation'.[35] And in this same vein, it is of relevance that horizontal effect can be granted to general principles (as at the time of cases like *Mangold* and *Kücükdeveci*[36] with non-discrimination), despite the exclusively vertical effect of the Charter (Art. 51), as a matter of 'rules'.

Finally, due to the potential role of the national judge in managing the Charter's direct effect on fundamental rights (and in arbitrating its

---

[32] *Medellín v. Texas*, 552 U.S. 491 (2008).

[33] For the Italian Constitutional Court (decisions nn. 348 e 349 of 2007), direct effect can only be granted to the Charter. In the case of ECHR, for overcoming contrary domestic ordinary rules, referral to the Constitutional Court is needed.

[34] Art. 51(1).

[35] When something 'outside' EU competences is affecting their effectiveness.

[36] Case C-144/04 *Werner Mangold v Rüdiger Helm* [2005] ECR I-09981; Case C-555/07 Seda *Kücükdeveci v Swedex GmbH & Co. KG.* [2010] ECR I-00365.

consistency with constitutional provisions) one cannot exclude that some judicial activism might practically develop by Europeanising constitutional interpretation (and sooner or later re-expand the dialogue with the CJEU through preliminary references). One possible scenario that has been foreseen features a sort of concurrence of national cultures in mastering the Charter, a kind of bottom-up harmonisation (or confrontation), better treasuring the primacy of the Charter and at the same time the Art. 53 and 52/4 limits from national constitutions and constitutional traditions. Some known questions might have a chance of new answers: how domestic re-elaboration of rights in the light of the Charter can expand into a transnational dialogue, or retreat into a national sphere; how can they offer new modes of balancing between life worlds, social contexts, and European market priorities, other than those that triggered disagreement (e.g., in Germany or Italy).[37] Despite the absence of a full-heartedly endorsed 'finalité', the chance is that greater density of European reflection shall be engendered, and that discussion about rights shall turn into a vehicle to re-considering their *political or ethical import*, involving national theatres' contribution to shaping a less technocratic/individualistic European culture, and possibly gaining a better credibility of the EU *vis-à-vis* widespread discontents.

So one of the questions for the two decades ahead is how a course about rights might frame a 'public Europe', closer to the auspices of its transformation twenty-five years ago, relocating national and supranational, legal discretion and political deliberation, and reversing the turn that led from positing 'the rights of the individual at the centre' to centring Europe on an individualistic interpretation of rights.

### 3    Governance

While the prospects of 1992 Europe were focusing on the institutional *governmental* structures, their tuning, and their accountability credentials, today and significantly, those credentials are recurrently asked of *governance* structures. The public law of Europe was – and is – seen as *politically* unsaturated, but in the past two decades, governance increasingly

---

[37] Think of the famous ECJ trilogy of the *Laval*, *Viking*, and *Rüffert* cases: Case C-341/05 *Laval un Partneri Ltd v Svenska Byggnadsarbetareförbundet* [2007] ECR I-11767; Case C-438/05 *International Transport Workers' Federation and Finnish Seamen's Union v Viking Line ABP and OÜ Viking Line Eesti* [2007] ECR I-10779; Case C-346/06 *Dirk Rüffert v Land Niedersachsen* [2008] ECR I-1989.

came to the forefront as escaping standard *legal* control, as well as lacking social and political allegiance. Europe's 'ideological neutrality' (inspired mainly by the *super partes* profile of the Commission), the third among the traits of *The Transformation of Europe* that I have stressed, is relevant here. Such a 'neutrality' flourished most – rather than in the *governmental* dimension – through the allocation of overwhelming decision-making to a regulatory process, to a variety of implementing, monitoring, advisory bodies, and due to the shift to the technocratic register, allegedly exempt from choice disputability, in traditional political terms.

In the known story, as a first structure of governance, the comitology[38] apparatus became the core of what later on Weiler called a *mesolevel*, a dimension of *infranationalism*,[39] flanking the current supranationalism and inter-governamentalism, but emptying the political dynamics and avoiding the constitutional frame. European governance grew up, especially with two more 'structures', now institutionalised, Agencies and the Open Method of Coordination. In truth, Europe has not become the sheer regulatory state that Majone advocated;[40] nonetheless, it can hardly be imagined without the core of governance. While cyclically in a twenty-five years' stalemate, inter-governmentalism follows phases of enhanced supranationalism, governance (infranationalism) flourished anew. Interestingly, even immunised against the charge of 'ideological neutrality': far from naked efficiency or technical hubris, it claims the pursuit of substantive accountability (part of the *process* and/or *output* legitimacy discourse). The Commission itself propounded governance as a promise of participation and distance-shortening between the citizens and the European fairyland.[41] And enhanced 'deliberative' nature is considered to qualify structures of comitology;[42] the Open Method of Coordination appears an advanced experiment of alternative poliarchy-democracy,[43]

---

[38] Decision of the Council n. 87/ 373 as amended by Council 1999/468, June 8, 1999.

[39] In an essay now included in *The Constitution of Europe* (Cambridge: Cambridge University Press, 1999), 96 ff as an afterword to *The Transformation of Europe: Infranationalism*.

[40] G. Majone, 'The Rise of the Regulatory State in Europe', *West European Politics*, 14, 3 (1994), 77–101; G. Majone, 'Regulation and Its Modes', in G. Majone (ed.), *Regulating Europe* (London: Routledge, 1996).

[41] *White Paper on Governance*, COM(2001) 428, July 2001, at http://eur-lex.europa.eu/LexUriServ/site/en/com/2001/com2001_0428en01.pdf.

[42] C. Joerges and J. Neyer, 'From Intergovernmental Bargaining to Deliberative Political Process: The Constitutionalisation of Comitology', *European Law Journal*, 3 (1997), 273 ff.

[43] C. F. Sabel and J. Zeitlin (eds.), *Experimentalist Governance in the European Union; Towards a New Architecture* (Oxford: Oxford University Press, 2010).

and Majone's praise of regulatory Agencies *vis-à-vis* decisional failures of traditional politics is, of its own right, still holding.

All that has become, to the eyes of political scientists, no longer a side effect of Europe's political immaturity, but an asset, the skeleton that makes it work. The European governance mode is often praised as a 'successful pattern', despite its poor roots in the traditional idea of the 'public' within the Member States' horizon.

However, that comes from supervening novelties: European governance is involved in a wider global transformation than it has anticipated, one that originates from the increased weight of *knowledge* and *learning* in decisional choices, from the need of fragmenting high-complexity issues into sectors and specialised domains, from the functional interconnections being more relevant than territorial separations, and the like. All that shifted the analytic focus from one opposition – i.e., intergovernmental vs. community (supranational) methods – towards another – the governance–government divide. The novelty, of course, cannot be side-lined.

The functional orientation of governance offers practical gains and pursues effectively behaviour-guiding objectives, pretending to decentralise the overall political deficit and as far as possible the law type control through the template of pre-fixed rules. The underworld of governance[44] has grown up and the ghost of 'ideological neutrality' of course appears repeatedly. But it is argued that the price for a knowledge society, exposed to complexity and risk, is that one cannot define once forever the contours and contents of the public interest in a fixed way. European governance develops by defining *goods*, rather than a politically debated notion of the *good*. It also stems from the Commission's hard work in stating the benchmarks and targets: thus mirroring precisely what is often complained about, that is, the shift of the EU from politics to policies. Politics is replaced by creating 'levels of criticism' and a practice of reappraisals, solving concrete questions. It also purports to manage the anxiety arising from uncertain risk regulations: a claim that is founded 'partly on the authority of expertise', but also on the limits of scientific knowledge.[45] As aptly said, that is a European *Eudaimonia*[46] based on *inter*dependence in the *lack* of a solidarity granted by kinship and sameness.[47]

[44] J. H. H. Weiler, 'In der Unterwelt der Ausschuesse', Die Zeit, 22 October 1998.
[45] D. Chalmers, 'Gauging the Cumbersomeness of EUI Law', *LSE WP*, 2 (2009), 31.
[46] Ibid., 18 ff.
[47] Chalmers (ibid., 19) recalls Emile Durkheim's distinction between organic and mechanical solidarity. He stresses rightly this point as connected to EU governance.

Now, the many facets of EU working lines are today highly interwoven. Even inter-governmentalism that resurfaced vigorously after Lisbon is sometimes seen as a blessing (especially in times of crisis), insofar as it can stir autonomous new legislative decisions.[48] The point lies in the import of governance structures in the interplay between inter-governmentalism, supranationalism, and constitutionalism. What is the role of the *underworld* of governance in the project of an *ever closer union*? If there can be a further relation between the *meso* and the *higher* level, it would mean that a 'movement towards hybridisation of governance' can bring the 'ability for the governing dimension to provide an overall framing of the Governance Structures with hierarchical governing mechanisms', and this can be tantamount to fostering 'framework laws which retain legal ground in the form of legislative procedures and access to juridical review at the same time as safeguarding the flexibility of the Governance Structures.'[49]

Summing up, European *sui generic* governance character is perhaps still amenable to institutional embedding and to some legal-political reconciliation. Instead of an instrumental tool of global governance viability, or a transmission belt for that, it might still live up to an equilibrium between infranationalism and supranationalism, recalling some form of political responsibility and social responsiveness that its regional width might perhaps still allow. The challenge is coping with the ambiguity of governance, whether the new legalised-proceduralised track, the alternative democratic path, or still the opaque escape from political control, the apotheosis of technocratic hubris in uncharted territories. Making a more mature sense of governance internally can be of help in preventing that it becomes just a further segment of a blind *global* governance determinism: in other words, from becoming a regional instance of a self-driven new governance 'naturalism', a rulemaking, in administrative mode, thriving on lack of interlocutors and on detachment from any polities whatsoever.

## Conclusions: Back to the Future

The question of the European public is certainly about the legal and political determinants and the need for their reconnection. Future developments

---

[48] G. Amato, 'Editoriale. Quale governo per l'economia europea?' at www.italianieuropei.it/it/italianieuropei-5-2011/item/2141-editoriale-quale-governo-per-l-economia-europea.html.

[49] P. Kjaer, *Between Governing and Governance* (Oxford: Hart, 2010), 161. Kjaer has gone through extensive considerations of the evolution of comitology, OMC, and Agencies, and presents the virtues and limits of the distinctive theories sustaining each of them.

shall have to deal with fundamental rights' elaboration, dialogue among cultures, and judicial interactions. Eventually, the further issue is no longer about the emergence of the governance underworld, but its political taming and optimisation as a powerful component of integration.

Against this background, Europe's legitimacy question resurfaces. The structures of Europe are a regional intermediation that both contributes to global control of complex issues and posits Europe as a *barycentre*, one that should have played a major role, and should be expected to do so at least in the future. The service of preventing European peoples from falling prey to a globalised universe of economic determinism and un-scrutinised *managerialism* can be valuable: instead of the return of national states, a credible regional player, daring interlocution with 'global' regulatory regimes and the like.

As a barycentre of its own, Europe might work in highlighting the non-coincidence between *globalisation* and *universality*, that is, between a factual global rulemaking and the *normative* conditions for its universalisation. It can ask for testing claims of global technocracy rule by the *ought* of justification and universalisability. The EU is a privileged space to this end as well, if it preserves its culture of rights, peace, solidarity, democracy, and justice, still overcoming nationalist closures and reactive statism, and rethinking universality, ethos, and diversity *vis-à-vis*, say, the excesses of *global* governance. So far, this is a 'twenty-five years after' concern, the relocation of Europe in the post-national (and allegedly post-governmental) constellation, and launching new internal solutions,[50] capable of bridging the gap *vis-à-vis* its Peoples.

In the three domains sketched *supra*, the constitution of the public law, the transforming area of rights, and the realm of governance, one can see how relevant are the traits of *The Transformation of Europe* I have pointed out in the opening. The *legal* appraisal of institutions/politics interplay, the legitimacy problem, the ideological neutrality, and the unity/community alternative define the coordinates of our progress as well. What is at stake, though, is how to reconnect the potential that rights and governance bear *vis-à-vis* the complex political future of Europe, that is, within the path to refining Europe's public law dimension. This last question partly exceeds

---

[50] For the latter, an example of a not functionalist nature, M. Poiares Maduro, 'The Euro's Democratic Deficit' (Project Syndicate at www.project-syndicate.org/commentary/maduro1/English) suggested solving the knot of democracy while furthering economic governance: 'If the way that the EU raises money is made more democratic, deciding how to spend that money would become more democratic, too. This is crucial to ensure the legitimacy of the eurozone's economic governance.'

the frames – and visibility – of two decades ago, but can be rescued in conjunction with their fundamental notions.

Undeniably the demand of a responsible and empowered *European*
politics is on the forefront, but today it might be much more difficult to
answer, given the varied surfacing of statist attitudes, that clearly show
how the Peoples of Europe have reacted against the lack of political salience of the EU by a strong State centred idea of the 'political'.

The complex interplay between states and the Union has to be rewrit-
ten also *vis-à-vis* the European citizens, through a democratic redeter-
mination of the balance between rights and *duties*. As Weiler himself
has pointed out,[51] there is no way to make European ideals work unless
a vicious circle can be broken: one where European institutions seem
to work in such a way as to prevent European citizens from cultivating
the proper virtues that are necessary to pursue the foundational ideals.
Possibly, the fresh view of a report from a few years ago on the path of
European transformation can contribute in cutting that circle: the question of democracy – precisely in connection with a sound control of economic problems – has been understandably evoked. In introducing that
report, Miguel Poiares Maduro aptly stresses that both 'political empowerment and civic solidarity' are needed 'for the Union to be able to develop
a possibly legitimate form of economic and political governance'[52] what
requires that the absence of a European politics be overcome, by freeing
the Union from being the hostage of national politics and also providing
it with autonomous resources, especially those generated from the internal market. The accent falls thereby on choices, politics, and citizens.

Based on the solid consistence of *The Transformation of Europe*, we can
rescue the spirit of qualitatively new 'transformations' that, in truth, the
EU should better embrace.

---

[51] Cf. *supra* note 14.
[52] M. Poiares Maduro, 'Democracy and Justice: The Formula for a New EU and Euro
Governance', at 1, available at http://network.globalgovernanceprogramme.eu/democracy-
and-justice/ and see the report at http://network.globalgovernanceprogramme.eu/wp-
content/uploads/2012/10/report.pdf.

# 7

# Assessing *The Transformation of Europe*: A View from Political Science

R. DANIEL KELEMEN AND ALEC STONE SWEET

*The Transformation of Europe* (TE)[1] is arguably the most influential paper ever published on the European Court of Justice (ECJ). Read as political science, the importance of the piece is threefold. First, it laid out a subtle, reconstructive account of the Court's 'constitutional' case law. This discussion quickly became a standard reference point[2] for scholars developing new empirical research on the legal system's impact on integration. Second, Weiler described (and reflected normatively on) the steady expansion of the scope of the EU's jurisdiction, findings that would be confirmed in more systematic research to come.[3] Third, it blended doctrinal analysis with a strategic, 'political' account of why two sets of actors – Member State governments and the national courts – did not destroy the process of legal integration in its infancy, though each had the power to do so.[4] Weiler showed how the ECJ's (often conflictual) interactions with national judges had served to allocate joint authority between the supranational and national legal orders, while enhancing judicial power on both levels. The so-called judicial empowerment thesis remains a dominant approach to explaining legal integration.[5] Third, and most important

---

[1] J. H. H. Weiler, 'The Transformation of Europe', *Yale Law Journal*, 100, 8 (1991), 2403–83.

[2] Along with E. Stein, 'Lawyers, Judges, and the Making of a Transnational Constitution, *American Journal of International Law*, 75 (1981), 1–27.

[3] On the phenomenon of the EU's 'creeping competences' see M. Pollack, 'Creeping Competence: The Expanding Agenda of the European Community', *Journal of Public Policy*, 14 (1994), 95–145. Also called 'spillover' in neofunctionalist integration theory, it has been the topic of extensive empirical research, see W. Sandholtz and A. Stone Sweet (eds.), *European Integration and Supranational Governance* (Oxford: Oxford University Press, 1998).

[4] See also J. H. H. Weiler, 'A Quiet Revolution: The European Court and Its Interlocutors', *Comparative Political Studies*, 26 (1994), 510–34.

[5] Related literature reviewed in A. Stone Sweet 'The European Court of Justice and the Judicialization of EU Governance', *Living Reviews in EU Governance* (2010), section 6.1, http://europeangovernance.livingreviews.org/.

for present purposes, TE presented a theory of how the Court's doctrinal moves related to state power within the EU's system of law-making and governance.

Weiler forcefully argued that the consolidation of the various 'constitutional' doctrines (direct effect, supremacy, pre-emption, human rights, and implied powers) had 'radically' reconstituted the juridical foundations of the regime, transforming an international organisation into something akin to a federal arrangement.[6] At the same time, he stressed the fact that the Member States had resisted the move to supranationalism within legislative processes, which he conceived as majority voting in the Council of Ministers to enact EU measures to complete the common market. Spurred by this paradox, Weiler developed the following thesis:

> The 'harder' the law in terms of its binding effect both on and within States, the less willing States are to give up their prerogative to control the emergence of such law.... When the international law is 'real', when it is 'hard' in the sense of being binding not only on but also in States, and when there are effective remedies to enforce it, [State control of] decisionmaking suddenly becomes important, indeed crucial.[7]

In this account, governments had tolerated the legal transformation of the regime only because each retained a veto over important new policy.

The equilibrium thesis is the overarching theoretical construct of TE, weighing heavily on how the transformation is to be appraised, both before and after the 1986 Single European Act (SEA). The SEA had, after all, 'shattered' the equilibrium.[8] Henceforth, every Member State would at times be required to enforce EU market rules that its government had opposed in the Council of Ministers, a situation that 'threatens [the EU's] very constitutional foundation.'[9] If a major crossroads in the history of European integration had been reached, Weiler was unsure as to which the direction the system would take.[10] In the post-SEA, the constitutional settlement might unravel, if governments chose to exit the system. On the other hand, the Member States might leave it intact, if they had learned to value its benefits (an outcome noted, but left untheorised). Nonetheless, two strong implications flow from the theoretical framework (that the

---

[6] To describe the transformation, Weiler uses variations on the word 'radical' no fewer than fourteen times.

[7] Weiler, 'The Transformation of Europe', 2426.

[8] Ibid., 2459–62.

[9] Ibid., 2465.

[10] Ibid., 2465.

political legitimacy of constitutionalisation rested on a specific equilibrium between a *supranational* legal system and an *intergovernmental* legislative system). First, the SEA would provide a strong test of the viability of the supranational order; the Member States could, after all, destroy or reconfigure it. Second, liberating the legislature from the veto would reduce the need for strong law-making and catalytic court. The ECJ might, accordingly, be led to constrain its supranational, integrationist impulses on its own.

In this chapter, we assess TE as political science, in light of research that has taken place since the article's publication. We do so in order to honour the article's immense contributions to our discipline. In TE, Weiler contrasted the European lawyers' view of Europe, which was 'becoming more and more federal', with the political scientists' then pessimism about the future of supranationalism.[11] In fact, TE appeared at the beginning of an important revival of political science research on European integration, after a long period of hibernation. Indeed, over the past twenty years, political scientists have produced more empirical research on the ECJ and its impact than on any other court in the world.[12]

We proceed as follows. In Part I, we briefly discuss the equilibrium thesis in light of alternative theory and relevant empirical results. The equilibrium thesis may well explain the Court's success during what TE labels the 'foundational period' (1958–73). Nonetheless, once the Court's caseload took off in the 1970s, the Court's dominance over Treaty interpretation, coupled with majoritarian and federalist dynamics, overwhelmed the capacity of any state or consortium of states to resist the steady expansion of supranationalism. In Part II, we consider legislative politics and outcomes after the SEA.[13] As we will show, the Member States did not roll back constitutionalisation, or curtail the authority of the courts, nor did the ECJ abandon its constitutional commitments and stage a retreat. Instead, with the completion of the internal market, the EU became even more rule-oriented, legalistic, procedurally complex, and adversarial (in an American sense), all factors that bolstered the centrality of the courts.[14]

---

[11] Ibid., 2410–11.

[12] Scholarship reviewed in A. Stone Sweet, 'The European Court of Justice and the Judicialization of EU Governance'.

[13] Weiler himself devoted roughly half of his text to considering the SEA and its potential ramifications.

[14] R. D. Kelemen, *Eurolegalism: The Transformation of Law and Regulation in the European Union* (Cambridge, MA: Harvard University Press, 2011).

The EU's legislative organs themselves chose to reinforce these features, notably, by delegating to the courts the charge of monitoring and enforcing EU market regulations, as they emerged. The mechanism they chose – to govern through establishing judicially enforceable rights – makes sense in a multilevel system with weak command and control features. But it also constitutes massive delegation to the courts and, with delegation, state legitimation of judicial governance.

The fact that the supranational-intergovernmental equilibrium did not long survive is powerful evidence for the view that TE underestimated how transformative the move to juridical federalism actually was.

I

TE paved the way for the political science to come. Weiler had shown that the legal system had, in effect, become the nervous system of the EU. The empirical challenge, then, was to chart and assess the legal system's impact on the overall course of integration, and on policy outcomes in specific domains. TE also forced scholars to confront a set of fundamental political questions. Why did the Member States permit constitutionalisation? To what extent were governments able to constrain the Court's supranationalist biases beyond the foundational period? Political scientists have since produced a significant quantity of systematic research that bears on these issues, based on both quantitative analysis of comprehensive data and detailed case studies of the impact of judicial rulings on policy-making at both the EU and national levels.

If one considers the equilibrium hypothesised to be an empirical benchmark *ex ante* for the assessment of later developments, then it is clear that the equilibrium began to erode immediately after the foundational period. In the second period (1973–85), Weiler rightly emphasises, EU competences steadily expanded to new areas.[15] Social scientists showed that the Court was instrumental in facilitating such 'spillover', then and afterwards, through constructing causal connections – positive feedback loops – between transnational activity, litigating EU law in the courts, and lobbying and legislating in Brussels.[16] It was also during this period that the Court's expansive, and politically intrusive, free movement of goods case law (the *Dassonville-Cassis*

---

[15] Weiler, 'The Transformation of Europe', 2442–52.
[16] W. Sandholtz and A. Stone Sweet, *European Integration and Supranational Governance*; A. Stone Sweet, N. Fligstein and W. Sandholtz (eds.), *The Institutionalization of Europe* (Oxford: Oxford University Press, 2001).

*de Dijon* framework) steadily undermined national capacity to regulate intra-EU trade, which was rapidly expanding. As has been conclusively demonstrated, this jurisprudence powerfully linked processes of 'negative integration' (the Treaty-mandated removal of barriers to intra-EU exchange) and 'positive integration' (legislating EU market rules to replace national regulations), fatally undermining national control. In the end, it was the interactions between litigants, the courts, the Commission, and a newly cohesive European business lobby that constructed the context for the intergovernmental decision to revise the treaty with the SEA.[17] Weiler knows these facts well, as he elegantly demonstrated in a later paper.[18]

It is today obvious that the dice were loaded in favour of the supranational side of the equation. Of the many important elements that weighed in favour of enhanced supranationalism, we will emphasise two. The first is the Court's status as the authoritative interpreter of the Treaty which, among other things, gave it *de jure* authority over the exercise of legislative authority. Unanimity decision rules underpinned legislative inter-governmentalism prior to the SEA, Weiler stressed, but unanimity rules also grounded and protected the Court's supranational authority. The Court's pro-integrationist, supranationalist interpretations of the Treaty were insulated, *de facto*, from reversal by the Member States.[19] If it had been otherwise, the various constitutionalist doctrines and the free movement jurisprudence might not have stuck. Rather than retreat in the post-SEA period, the Court in fact continued to interpret the Treaty aggressively. In the legal basis cases, for example, it extended majoritarian voting to policy domains that the Council of Ministers considered subject to unanimity (the veto), thereby bolstering the authority of the Parliament and the Commission.[20] And in 1991, the Court famously

---

[17] A. Stone Sweet, *The Judicial Construction of Europe* (Oxford: Oxford University Press, 2004), chapter 3.

[18] J. H. H. Weiler, 'The Constitution of the Common Marketplace: Text and Context in the Evolution of the Free Movement of Goods', in P. Craig and G. de Búrca (eds.), *The Evolution of EU Law* (Oxford: Oxford University Press, 1999).

[19] As we discuss later in this chapter, the relationship between decision-making gridlock and judicial empowerment in the EU reflects more general findings from judicial politics research about the relationship between political fragmentation and judicial power. See, for instance, M. Shapiro, *Courts: A Comparative and Political Analysis* (Chicago: University of Chicago Press, 1981); T. Ginsburg, *Judicial Review in New Democracies* (Cambridge: Cambridge University Press, 2003); G. Vanberg, 'Establishing and Maintaining Judicial Independence', in K. Whittington, R. D. Kelemen and G. Caldeira (eds.), *The Oxford Handbook of Law and Politics* (Oxford: Oxford University Press, 2008), 99–118.

[20] The judicial politics of such disputes have been the subject of systematic research. M. McCown, 'The European Parliament before the Bench: ECJ Precedent and European

moved to develop a new constitutional doctrine, of state liability, making EU law even more 'real' and 'hard', in TE's terms, providing a strong judicial remedy for harms related to compliance failures on the part of states (*Francovich*; *Brasserie du Pêcheur*). The ECJ did so through treaty interpretation, without any express basis in the Treaty, and in the face of strong and explicit Member State opposition.[21]

Second, beginning in the 1970s, the Court developed a strategic disposition that aligned it with the majority of Member States on key issues, further securing its position as lawmaker and agenda setter. Maduro examined every ruling subjected to the *Cassis de Dijon* framework in the free movement of goods domain. The ECJ, he found, engaged systematically in what he called 'majoritarian activism'.[22] Once the ECJ had determined that the national measure in question was more unlike than akin to equivalent measures in place in a majority of states, the ECJ would strike it down as a violation of the Treaty (ex-Art. 30). On its own initiative, the ECJ had begun, in the early 1980s, to ask the Commission to provide such information. Strikingly, Maduro found no exception to this rule. In contrast, the court tended to uphold national measures (under ex-Article 36 and its case law on ex-Article 30) in areas where no dominant type of regulation existed. 'Majoritarian activism' also appropriately describes cases in which the Court enacts, through Treaty interpretation, policy that would have been adopted under majoritarian rules, while being blocked under unanimity. In the post-SEA period, the court regularly enacted, as constitutionally mandated, important legislation that was supported by the Commission and a majority of governments in the Council of Ministers, but which had stalled under the veto.[23]

In sum, the Court's moves in favour of strong supranationalism made the legislative process a sub-system of EU decision-making (albeit one

Parliament Litigation Strategies', *Journal of European Public Policy*, 10 (2003), 974-95 and J. Jupille, *Procedural Politics: Influence and Institutional Choice in the European Union* (New York: Cambridge University Press, 2004) found that the Court's rulings on legal basis served to strengthen majoritarianism, and to reduce the Council of Minister's dominance in the legislative process.

[21] Stone Sweet, *The Judicial Construction of Europe*, 95–6.

[22] M. Poiares Maduro, *We, the Court: The European Court of Justice and the European Economic Constitution* (Oxford: Hart, 1998).

[23] The so-called constitutionalisation of sex equality and the non-discrimination principle more generally has been heavily documented. R. Cichowski, 'Women's Rights, the European Court, and Supranational Constitutionalism', *Law and Society Review*, 38 (2004), 489–512; Stone Sweet, *The Judicial Construction of Europe*, chapter 4.

that was often crucial to outcomes), within a greater constitutional system, the evolution of which the Court (not the states) dominated.

From a theoretical standpoint, Weiler's equilibrium thesis suffers from having been built from static, binary oppositions: the 'Intergovernmental-Supranational' and 'Exit-Voice'. A 'radical mutation of the Treaty' was effected,[24] but the underlying logics and constraints posited by the theory somehow remain in place over time. Presupposing the equilibrium beyond the foundational period, however, leads one to downplay or miss altogether how transformative the transformation really was.

In contrast, the most successful theories of how the legal system operates all (at least implicitly) predicted the demise of the supranational-intergovernmental equilibrium.[25] These approaches suggested that given a steady a caseload, the commitment of the Court to supranationalism, and the inability of reluctant Member States to meet the high decision-making threshold necessary to rein in expansive Court jurisprudence, integration would move past Weiler's equilibrium. While the theories differ in important ways, what they have in common is a conception of integration as an inherently expansive, self-sustaining process. The most comprehensive account demonstrated that the activities of market actors, lobbyists, legislators, litigators, and judges became causally connected to one another in important ways. The analysis also showed that two parameter shifts – whereby important qualitative events generated quantitatively significant transformations in the relationships among variables – had occurred, and these roughly map on to Weiler's periodisation scheme. The first shift began in the early 1970s, the second in the mid-1980s. The EU's evolving legal system was implicated in both transitions, first, through constitutionalisation, and, then, through supervising Member State compliance with EU law, especially with regard to rules governing the common market (Part II).[26]

Political scientists also addressed the question of why governments acquiesced to the transformation, and why they were not able to constrain the Court and the legal system even when they tried to do so.[27] The

[24]  Weiler, 'The Transformation of Europe', 2428.
[25]  A. Burley and W. Mattli, 'Europe before the Court: A Political Theory of Legal Integration', *International Organization*, 47 (1993), 41–76; Stone Sweet, *The Judicial Construction of Europe*; R. Cichowski, *The European Court and Civil Society* (New York: Cambridge University Press, 2007).
[26]  Fligstein and Stone Sweet (2002).
[27]  For a detailed quantitative analysis, see A. Stone Sweet and T. Brunell, 'The European Court of Justice, State Non-compliance, and the Politics of Override', *American Political Science Review*, 106 (2012), 204–13. See also K. Alter, *Establishing the Supremacy of European Law*

dominant type of explanation[28] is rooted in the logics of delegation – the role of courts in making credible state commitments to be governed by law – factorsthat Weiler largely ignored in TE. It is now broadly understood that the constitutionalisation of the EU succeeded because it enabled the states to overcome tenacious collective action problems associated with integration in federal arrangements more generally.[29] Once constitutionalised, the legal system provided a powerful mechanism for making the commitment to building a single market credible, for example. Without the court's active pursuit of market building in the 1970s, the SEA would not have been adopted in 1986. The states, after all, had utterly failed to complete the common market by the deadlines stipulated in the Treaty. After the SEA, as the corpus of EU secondary legislation grew exponentially, states harnessed the courts as a central mode of governing the Union.

## II

The equilibrium thesis posited that Member States were only willing to accept the ECJ's constitutionalisation of the Treaties and its expansion of EU competences insofar as they maintained veto power over Community decision-making. Weiler warned that the shattering of this equilibrium by the SEA presented profound dangers for the Community, in particular with regard to compliance and legitimacy, and he worried that the elimination of the veto might lead states to seek to roll back constitutionalisation and to constrain judicial power in EU governance. But in the subsequent two decades, this has not come to pass. The shift to qualified

(Oxford: Oxford University Press, 2001); F. Scharpf, 'The Joint-Decision Trap Revisited', *Journal of Common Market Studies*, 44 (2006), 845–64; Cichowski, *The European Court and Civil Society*; and R. D. Kelemen, 'The Political Foundations of Judicial Independence in the European Union', *Journal of European Public Policy*, 19 (2012), 43-58.

[28] J. Tallberg, 'Delegation to Supranational Institutions: Why, How, and with What Consequences?' *West European Politics*, 25 (2002), 23–46; M. Pollack, *The Engines of Integration: Delegation, Agency, and Agency Setting in the European Union* (Oxford: Oxford University Press, 2003); W. Mattli and A. Stone Sweet, 'Regional Integration and the Evolution of the European Polity: On the 50th Anniversary of the *Journal of Common Market Studies*', *Journal of Common Market Studies*, 50 (2012), 1–17.

[29] W. Mattli, *The Logic of Regional Integration: Europe and Beyond* (New York: Cambridge University Press, 1999); M. Shapiro, 'The European Court of Justice', in P. Craig and G. de Búrca (eds.), *The Evolution of EU Law* (Oxford: Oxford University Press, 1999); R. D. Kelemen, *The Rules of Federalism: Institutions and Regulatory Politics in the EU and Beyond* (Cambridge, MA: Harvard University Press, 2004).

majority voting in the SEA and the subsequent 'unblocking' of legislative decision-making did not herald an end to the judicial construction of Europe. Quite to the contrary, the period after the introduction of the SEA saw the EU embrace a highly judicialised approach to governance. To understand why, we must consider the political and legal dynamics involved in completing the Single Market.

Weiler emphasised that the more binding law was on Member States, the less willing they would be to give up control over the production of such law. While states may be reluctant to give up control over the crafting of 'hard' law, another set of considerations pushes in just the opposite direction. The establishment of the SEA involved both negative integration – the elimination of national barriers to trade – and positive integration – the introduction of common norms that establish a 'level playing field' for the Single Market.[30] Much of the hard law the Court imposed on Member States took the form of 'negative integration': 'deregulatory' judicial rulings that declared invalid national measures constituting barriers to free movement. But in many areas of policy-making, purely deregulatory, negative market integration is politically unacceptable to Member States. For instance, it would be politically unacceptable to create a single market in agricultural products simply by eliminating all national food safety regulations, or to create a single financial market simply by eliminating all national regulations designed to protect investors against fraud and malfeasance. In such cases, the elimination of national regulatory barriers to trade must, politically speaking, be coupled with the establishment of common, EU-wide regulations.

These realities suggest a rather contradictory corollary to Weiler's thesis.[31] The more binding the negative integration law imposed by European courts, the more Member States would need positive integration – the adoption of common EU norms – to reregulate the Single Market. In such a situation, inter-governmentalism, defined as the veto, may well become too costly to maintain. In fact, the harder the treaty law governing negative integration became, the *more* states proved willing to give up a veto over the emergence of EU legislation – in stark contrast to Weiler's thesis.

New, common EU market regulations governments help to produce must be suitable to the liberalised, continental-scale Single Market.[32] And

---

[30] On the concepts of negative and positive integration in the EU context, see Scharpf, 'The Joint Decision-Trap Revisited'.

[31] See Stone Sweet, *The Judicial Construction of Europe*, chapter 3.

[32] The following paragraphs draw heavily on Kelemen, *Eurolegalism*.

what sort of regulation is suitable to a large, liberalised market, with a diversity of players and political demands for a 'level playing field'? The answer: highly judicialised regulation. As Steven Vogel[33] has explained, economic deregulation is often coupled with 'juridical reregulation', as freer markets actually require more, not fewer rules. Where governments limit entry into national markets, they may rely on less formal modes of governance, and trust between a limited circle of stakeholders. With liberalisation, these more opaque modes of governance become untenable. In the EU, market integration entailed the replacement of opaque, informal systems of regulation at the national level with highly formal, legalistic, and judicialised modes of governance at the EU level. This cycle of national deregulation and EU juridical reregulation served to empower both EU-level and national courts, increasing judicial involvement in many areas where courts had previously played little role.

The structure of EU political institutions also encouraged this trend. Political authority in the EU has always been highly fragmented and has become increasingly so over time, with power today divided vertically between the EU and national organs and horizontally at the EU level between the Council, the European Parliament, the Commission, and the Court. And as an abundant literature demonstrates, fragmentation encourages judicial empowerment.[34] In the EU, fragmentation has chronically generated gridlock, which has given courts the space to play an assertive role without fear of override, as Weiler recognised in TE. It also creates principal-agent problems, for example, between EU lawmakers (the Commission, the Council, the Parliament) and those who implement EU law (national administrations, EU-level regulatory officials). The European Parliament understandably fears that governments may not live up to their commitments, and even governments represented in the Council may doubt one another's commitment to implementation of EU norms. To control their agents and to enhance the credibility of their commitments to implement EU law, EU lawmakers have been led to fill laws with detailed requirements, typically framed as justiciable rights, and to invite public authorities (including the Commission) and private actors to enforce these norms before national and European courts. In other words, the judicialisation of EU governance has not simply been

---

[33] S. Vogel, 'Why Freer Markets Need More Rules', in *Creating Competitive Markets: The Politics of Regulatory Reform*, M. Landy, M. Levin and M. Shapiro (eds.) (Washington, DC: Brookings Institution Press), 25–42.

[34] See *supra* note 19 and Kelemen, *Eurolegalism*, 24–5.

the product of self-assertion by the ECJ (though there certainly has been a good deal of that). Government themselves have repeatedly backed legislation requiring the ECJ, national courts, and private litigants to play a central role in governance.

The EU's extremely weak administrative capacity has also encouraged reliance on judicialised modes of governance. Courts and litigation have become the EU's substitutes for a developed, effective administrative state. The EU's bureaucracy is tiny, and Member States have continually made clear that they will not permit the construction of a centralised administrative apparatus on the scale necessary to enforce EU law effectively across the Union. Relying on private actors and national courts to enforce EU norms means loading legislation with justiciable provisions, framing policies in the language of individual rights, and promoting 'access to justice' initiatives.

In the second half of TE, Weiler expressed two main concerns with regard to the shattering of the equilibrium. First, he feared that reducing 'Voice' might lead states to 'selective Exit', through the adoption of a 'strategy' of 'noncompliance'.[35] Second, Weiler worried that the shift to majority voting would worsen the democratic deficit and further undermine the legitimacy of EU policy-making.[36] Both concerns seem well-founded, but we can now see that – rather ironically – the EU sought to address them by enhancing the role of law and courts.

Post-SEA developments actually made noncompliance a less tenable strategy than it had been in earlier periods. Throughout the 1990s and into the 2000s, the Commission took an increasingly tough stance on enforcement and promoted decentralised enforcement of EU law by private actors. These developments were part and parcel of the judicialisation of EU governance described earlier. The Commission had barely used 'infringement proceedings' before the 1980s, and many EU directives were viewed then more as statements of aspirations than as strict legal obligations. As concern over uneven implementation grew, the Commission began to deploy the infringement procedure more aggressively, beginning in the mid-1980s – just as it was launching the 1992 initiative.[37] In the 1990s, the Court moved on state liability, while the Commission further intensified its use of the infringement procedure. It did so not simply on its own initiative, but with the endorsement of the Member States, who gave the Commission new

---

[35] Weiler, 'The Transformation of Europe', 2465.
[36] Ibid., 2466–77.
[37] Kelemen, *The Rules of Federalism*, 31–4.

enforcement powers in the Maastricht Treaty, including the authority to request the ECJ to impose penalty payments on states that failed to comply with infringement rulings. EU lawmakers, too, encouraged the intensification of decentralised enforcement by private parties, establishing a host of new substantive economic, social, and political rights for private parties and establishing procedural right and remedies in EU administrative law to facilitate private enforcement.[38] Together, these measures significantly increased the likelihood and the cost of litigation in response to member state noncompliance, raising the cost of 'selective exit' just at the moment when governments might have been tempted to engage in it.

Weiler focused heavily on legitimacy problems facing the Community. While a full discussion of the democratic deficit is beyond the scope of this chapter, one aspect of the EU's response to the problem directly relates to our argument. With the dramatic expansion of EU powers that accompanied the SEA and the Maastricht Treaty, EU leaders grew sensitive to critics who questioned the EU's expansion into a wide range of increasingly sensitive policy fields. To address these concerns, the EU leaders put in place stronger, Treaty-based guarantees that the EU would act to protect fundamental rights (such as Articles 2 and 6 of the Maastricht Treaty). More generally, they embraced a language of rights across a host of policy areas ranging from free movement, to anti-discrimination, to social policy, to consumer protection, to securities regulation.[39] In these fields and many more, EU policy-makers have crafted Treaty provisions, directives, and regulations that grant private parties substantive and procedural rights and encourage them to enforce them before national and sometimes European courts. They have sought to back this 'Europe of rights' with a 'Genuine European Area of Justice', promoting various access to justice initiatives to ensure that European citizens and firms can enjoy equal and effective access to justice to enforce their EU rights across the Union.[40] And therein lies a final irony: in order to address the

---

[38] Kelemen, *Eurolegalism*, 45–56. See also G. de Búrca, 'The Language of Rights and European Integration', in G. More and J. Shaw (eds.), *New Legal Dynamics of European Union* (Oxford: Clarendon Press, 1995), 24–54; C. Harlow, 'A Common European Law of Remedies?', in C. Kilpatrick, T. Novitz and P. Skidmore (eds.), *The Future of Remedies in Europe* (Oxford: Hart Publishing, 2000), 69–83; M. Shapiro, 'The Institutionalization of the European Administrative Space', in A. Stone Sweet, W. Sandholtz, and N. Fligstein (eds.), *The Institutionalization of Europe* (Oxford: Oxford University Press, 2001), 94–112.

[39] de Búrca, 'The Language of Rights and European Integration'.

[40] Kelemen, *Eurolegalism*, 58–62. See also H. E. Hartnell, 'EUstitia: Institutionalizing Justice in the European Union', *Northwestern Journal of International Law and Business*, 23 (2002), 65–138.

perceived legitimacy deficit associated with the EU's expansive powers, EU lawmakers have sought to create a Europe of rights, expanding the protection of individual rights and opportunities to enforce those rights under European law. The legitimacy deficit they are seeking to address was in part the product of a judicially driven process of integration, and yet the Europe of rights they are promoting as a partial remedy will serve to encourage even more judicially driven integration.

## Conclusion

The impact of TE on political science scholarship has been pervasive and enduring. The article's central positive claims regarding the relationship between political and legal integration in the EU helped to set the agenda for a generation of research on the ECJ. We have focused primarily on the positive claims made in TE, rather than on the important normative questions addressed in TE, which others in this volume discuss at length. With the benefit of hindsight, and on the basis of a wealth of subsequent research, we have argued that the core claims Weiler derived from his theory of equilibrium, and the resulting concerns expressed about the impact of the SEA, have not been borne out by subsequent developments. TE illuminated the dynamics of the foundational period but underestimated just how transformative the constitutionalisation of the EU legal system really was. Judicially driven integration proved self-reinforcing. The ECJ, coordinating with EU organs and the national courts, strengthened its capacities to manage the complexities of supranational governance, despite the controversies that recurrently attend many of its important rulings. Today, many scholars voice concerns that echo those raised in TE, warning that the ECJ must constrain its supranational impulses, or risk undermining its authority. And yet, to date, the ECJ appears unbowed, presiding over a system of judicialised governance that continues to widen and deepen.[41]

---

[41] See Kelemen, 'The Political Foundations of Judicial Independence in the European Union'; S. Schmidt and R. D. Kelemen (eds.), 'Perpetual Momentum? Reconsidering the Power of the European Court of Justice', *Journal of European Public Policy*, Special Issue, 19, 1 (2012).

# 8

# The Lisbon Treaty as a Response to
# *Transformation's* Democratic Skepticism

### ARMIN VON BOGDANDY

Joseph Weiler's *The Transformation of Europe* shows what systematic legal thought can mean today. The work synthesizes positive texts, core judgements, legal doctrines, common knowledge, and mainstream insights from political science. These well-known bits and pieces are reined in by powerful concepts and brought into an order that makes sense of them by *showing their interrelatedness*. This is the essence of a true system.[1] Moreover, *Transformation* is exemplary of legal scholarship's claim to inform not just about law, but about society at large. *Transformation*, similar to pieces by G. W. F. Hegel, Santi Romano, Carl Schmitt, Sabino Cassese, Paul Kirchhof, or Bruce Ackerman, is an influential theory of social and political order. Such scholarship aiming at revealing the law's basic structure and role in society often helps a society to become aware of itself and provides reference points and key words for public debate. Indeed, *Transformation*, along with later pieces that elaborate its approach, has deeply influenced the debate on democracy in Europe. My claim is that much of Title II of the Treaty on European Union, as set by the Lisbon Treaty, can be read as a plausible political response to thoughts laid down in *Transformation*.

## I   *Transformation's* Take on European Democracy

*Transformation* attributes the so-called democratic deficit[2] mainly to three features. The first consists of the dominance of domestic governments in the political processes of the Community and the weakness of European parliamentary control over such processes.[3] Parliamentary control is weak

---

[1] No wonder that the Italian book which lays the groundwork carries 'system' in its title. J. H. H. Weiler, *Il sistema comunitario europeo. Struttura giuridica e processo politico* [*The European Community System: Legal Structure and Political Process*] (Bologna: Il mulino, 1985).
[2] J. H. H. Weiler, 'The Transformation of Europe', *Yale Law Journal*, 100 (1991), 2403, 2430.
[3] Ibid.

because a) the European Parliament wields no instrument to hold these institutions accountable; and b) the domestic parliaments can control only the members of the Council, but not the institution as such, and even this mediated control does not work properly. The empowerment of executive institutions by the process of European integration thus poses a problem for a certain concept of democracy. This concept refers to 'direct democratic accountability' to parliaments. At the same time, *Transformation* reveals a concept of 'rationalised' parliamentarism. It understands the great transformation of parliamentary government in Europe in the past fifty years has left behind unworkable ideas of parliamentary centrality.[4] It accepts that the executive is usually the moving force of the political process; the main role of parliaments in legislation is not to guide, but to control. *Transformation* therefore does not consider democracy to mean grand schemes of self-government or self-determination.

This parliamentary control-oriented understanding of democracy is supplemented a few pages later with pluralist or corporatist elements. Thus, *Transformation* considers as the second problem of democracy the fact that diffuse and fragmented interests are being largely 'squeezed out' by European politics, thereby altering the balance established between the various social, political, and economic forces in the Member States.[5] The third element of democratic stress is due to majority voting in the Council. Though governments are viewed with suspicion, *Transformation* does not dispute that their consent provides democratic legitimation for a European act.

So what should be done? *Transformation*'s impact is due in no small amount to the fact that a pro-integration author questions the traditional pro-integration answer.[6] The traditional answer is that giving 'increased powers to the [European] Parliament, directly elected by universal suffrage, would ... substantially reduce the Democratic Deficit and restore legitimacy to the Community decisionmaking process'.[7] *Transformation* reveals this proposal as insufficient, as it does not address democratic qualities such as 'closeness, responsiveness, representativeness, and

---

[4] In the 1970s and 1980s Italy made the last great attempt in Europe to put parliamentary centrality to practice, with disastrous results. See *Presidenza del Consiglio dei Ministri, Rapporto sulle condizioni delle pubbliche amministrazioni* 23 (1993); U. de Siervo, 'Il complesso universo degli atti secondari del Governo', in U. de Siervo (ed.), *Norme secondarie e direzione dell'amministrazione* (Bolgona: Il Mulino, 1992), 11, 21 et seq.

[5] Weiler, 'The Transformation of Europe', *supra* note 2, at 2452.

[6] Ibid.

[7] Ibid., at 2467.

accountability of the governors to the governed',[8] and, above all, social legitimacy that flows from a feeling of belonging to the governing organization and polity.[9] 'The legitimacy crisis does not derive principally from the accountability issue at the European level, but from the very redefinition of the European polity.'[10]

But how are we to define this European polity? Weiler distinguishes a unity vision, a federal United States of Europe, where the feeling of belonging mainly shifts to the Union, and a community vision that 'does not extinguish the separate actors who are fated to live in an uneasy tension with two competing senses of the polity's self, the autonomous self and the self as part of a larger community'.[11] How does that translate into legal and institutional arrangements? *Transformation* is wisely silent of this institutional issue, such that its analytical prowess and ethical thrust will not be weakened with proposals that usually age quickly.

## II   European Democracy According to the Lisbon Treaty

*Transformation* is one of the most visible pieces in the broad, ongoing European discussion in which social sciences, legal scholarship, political theory, and the European public in general have debated the issue of democracy in European integration.[12] This discussion, I contend, has led to good results. To be sure, the current European Union is not a democratic showcase. However, an innovative concept of post-national democracy, which, while neither utopian nor apologetic, responds to the concerns and insights voiced in *Transformation*, has found its way into the EU's founding Treaty.[13]

---

[8]  Ibid., at 2470.

[9]  Ibid., at 2471.

[10]  Ibid., at 2473.

[11]  Ibid., at 2480.

[12]  F. Schimmelpfennig, 'Legitimate Rule in the European Union', 27, Tübinger Arbeitspapiere zur Internationalen Politik und Friedensforschung (1996), available at www.uni-tuebingen.de/uni/spi/taps/tap27.htm; H. Bauer et al. (eds.), *Demokratie in Europa* (Tübingen: Mohr Siebeck, 2005); B. Kohler-Koch and B. Rittberger (eds.), *Debating the Democratic Legitimacy of the European Union* (Lanham, MD; Plymouth: Rowman & Littlefield 2007); and on the legal debate in historical retrospective, see A. von Komorowski, *Demokratieprinzip und Europäische Union. Staatsverfassungsrechtliche Anforderungen an die demokratische Legitimation der EG-Normsetzung*, Schriften zum Europäischen Recht, Band 148 (Berlin: Duncker and Humblot, 2010), 155-68.

[13]  In that respect, it can also inform the debate on global governance. See A. von Bogdandy, 'The European Lesson for International Democracy: The Significance of Articles 9 to 12 EU Treaty for International Organizations', *Jean Monnet Working Paper* (2011).

## 1   Dual Citizenship as the Vanishing Point of European Democracy in Article 9 of the EU Treaty

As Joseph Weiler states in a later piece, the 'Union belongs to its citizens.'[14] This axiom informs Article 9 of the EU Treaty and it settles, at least legally, the vexing question of the European democratic subject.[15] Citizenship is the defining legal institution.[16] Notwithstanding somewhat unfortunate paternalistic overtones, this provision clearly stands in the tradition of republican equality that reaches back to Kant and Rousseau. In a way, the Treaty gives a similar response to the *demos* question as Richard Thomas gave to Triepel and Schmitt during the Weimar period: 'Der Staat, das sind wir', meaning that a state consists of its citizens, and of no other substance or entity.[17] The democratic subjects are the European citizens, hence the idea of a singular democratic 'subject' is misleading.

Citizenship can certainly also be framed within grand schemes of a people or a nation, i.e., in holistic terms. European citizenship does not follow such schemes. The concept 'people' is reserved for the polities of the Member States, as specified in Article 1 (2) of the EU Treaty. The individualistic understanding of citizenship is confirmed by Title V of the Charter of Fundamental Rights of the European Union, which lays down citizenship rights as individual rights. European democracy is to be conceived from the perspective of the individual citizens, as confirmed by Articles 10 (2) and 14 (2) of the EU Treaty. The jurisprudence of the ECJ, which strengthens the rights of European citizenship, stresses this cornerstone of European democracy.[18]

Yet it would be a misunderstanding of the Union's principle of democracy to place *only* the individual Union citizen in the centre. The Union does not negate the democratic organisation of citizens in and by the Member

---

[14]  J. H. H. Weiler, U. R. Haltern and F. C. Mayer, 'European Democracy and Its Critique', *West European Politics*, 18 (1995) 4, 20.

[15]  For a more sceptical take, see J. H. H. Weiler, 'Citizenship and Human Rights', in J. A. Winter et al. (eds.), *Reforming the Treaty on European Union* (The Hague; London: Kluwer Law International, 1996), 57, 65.

[16]  On federal citizenship, see C. Schönberger, 'European Citizenship as Federal Citizenship', *Revue Européenne de Droit Public*, 19 (2007), 61.

[17]  R. Thoma, 'Das Reich als Demokratie', in G. Anschütz and R. Thoma (eds.), *Handbuch des Deutschen Staatsrechts*, 2 (Tübingen: 1930), 187.

[18]  See Case C-184/99 *Grzelczyk v. Centre public d'aide sociale d'Ottignies-Louvain-la-Neuve* [2001] ECR I-6193; Case C-135/08 *Rottmann v. Freistaat*, [2009] ECR I-0000; Case C-34/09 *Zambrano v. Office national de l'emploi* [2011] I-01177.

States; it follows, in the terminology of *Transformation*, the community vision, not the unity vision. Thus, alongside the Union citizens, the Member States' democratically organised peoples act in the Union's decision-making process as organised associations. The Union's principle of democracy builds on these two elements: the current Treaties speak, on the one hand, of the peoples of the Member States, and, on the other hand, of the Union's citizens, insofar as the principle of democracy is at issue. The central elements which determine the Union's principle of democracy at this basic level are thus named. The Union rests on a *dual structure of democratic legitimation*: the totality of the Union's citizens *and* the peoples in the European Union as organised by their respective Member States' constitutions.[19] This conception can be seen clearly in Article 10 (2) of the EU Treaty; it reflects the community vision exposited in *Transformation*.

Another element that follows the community vision is that democracy beyond the state does not substitute for, but rather complements domestic forms. This entails a further important element of post-national democracy. Many theories of democracy put the rule of the (simple or absolute, but never qualified) majority and the contest between competing parties at the very heart of their understanding.[20] This idea of Westminster democracy, where the citizens in national elections can 'throw the scoundrels out',[21] is almost impossible to reconcile with a developed dual structure of democratic legitimation in complex polities; this can be seen in federal states such as Belgium, Germany, and the United States. Hence the rule of the majority cannot be the defining element of post-national democracy. Post-national democracy can far better be conceptualised by theories centred on the search for broad consensus.[22]

This issue of consensus leads to the question: what exactly is the object of such consensus? Some authors understand European democracy as a way of political self-determination,[23] but not so Weiler. European democracy

---

[19] Concerning the model of dual legitimation, see S. Oeter, 'Federalism and Democracy', and P. Dann, 'The Political Institutions', in A. von Bogdandy & J. Bast (eds.), 2nd edition, *Principles of European Constitutionalism* (2009), 55, 237; and A. Peters, *Elemente einer Theorie der Verfassung Europas* (Berlin: Duncker and Humblot, 2001), 209, 219.

[20] Seminal C. Schönberger, 'Die Europäische Union zwischen "Demokratiedefizit" und Bundesstaatsverbot', *Der Staat*, 48 (2009), 535, 550.

[21] Weiler, Haltern and Mayer, 'European Democracy and Its Critique', *supra* note 14, at 4, 8.

[22] Ibid., at 4, 28; M. G. Schmidt, *Demokratietheorien*, 4th edition (Wiesbaden: Verlag für Sozialwissenschaften, 2008), 306.

[23] C. Lord, 'Parliamentary Representation in a Decentered Polity', in *Debating the Democratic Legitimacy of the European Union supra* note 12, at 160; C. Möllers, *Gewaltengliederung*

as self-determination is a non-starter. The notion of self-determination can be understood, firstly, in the sense of *individual* self-determination. To interpret the complex procedures of the Union in this sense, however, exceeds conventional imagination, or at least that of the present author. Furthermore, such an understanding might encourage intolerance and tends to exclude marginal or oppositional political subjectivity. The alternative is to interpret democracy as *collective* self-determination. This appears viable in a nation-state on the basis of a strong concept of nation or people. However, it is not transposable to the European level, because precisely such a collective, such a form of political unity, such a 'We', is missing. The consequence of this conception can therefore only be to perceive the Union as currently not capable of democracy. Although this conclusion can certainly be argued theoretically, it is useless for legal doctrine since it is unable to give meaning to a term of positive law – 'democracy' in Article 2 of the EU Treaty. Europeans who endorsed the Treaty hold a different understanding. Article 9 of the EU Treaty, read together with Articles 10 to 12, suggests that the cornerstones of European democracy are civic equality and representation, supplemented with participation, deliberation, and control, very much in line with the concept presented in *Transformation*.

### 2    The Idea of Representation in Article 10 of the EU Treaty

As set out in the Federalist Papers and in *Transformation*, the principle of democracy finds its most important expression in representative institutions; Article 10 (1) of the EU Treaty builds on this. Almost twenty years of discussion have revealed that parliamentarianism is without an alternative for the EU, but has to be adapted to its specific needs. In accordance with the basic premise of dual legitimation and the community vision, elections provide two lines of democratic legitimation. These lines are institutionally represented by the European Parliament, which is based on elections by the totality of the Union's citizens, and by the Council and the European Council, whose legitimation is based on the Member States' democratically organised peoples: see Article 10 (2) EU of the Treaty. In the current constitutional situation, the line of legitimation from the national parliaments is clearly dominant, as shown in particular by Article 48 of the EU Treaty and by the preponderance of the Council and

(Mohr Siebeck, 2005) at 28; and, most prominently, J. Habermas, *Between Facts and Norms*, 98–128 and *passim*, trans. W. Rehg (Cambridge, MA: MIT Press, 1996) (1992).

the European Council in the Union's procedures. Viewed in this light, one understands the Treaty of Lisbon as positing requirements for national parliaments in Article 12 EU of the Treaty.

The implications of this scheme are enormous. A transnational parliament can confer democratic legitimation even though it does not represent a people or a nation and does not fully live up to the principle of electoral equality.[24] The respect for diversity justifies this modification, as in other federal polities, such as Switzerland, the United States, and India. Moreover, an *executive* institution may provide a certain kind of democracy, to the extent that its membership is selected by the constituent political units of the federation. European executive federalism has its own democratic significance in light of the Union's democracy principle.[25] This notion of federalist executive democracy contrasts sharply with national constitutional law, but also with the position taken in *Transformation*.[26] In light of what is said in *Transformation*, this qualification of executive power (and its scholarly endorsement) might appear apologetic: isn't it a trick to suggest that the main cause of the problem, executive dominance, might help to solve it by attributing executive institutions democratic representativeness? My view is twofold: the contemporary constitutions of all European countries construe the institution of the executive as a democratic institution that has a role of representing in other fora the interests and values domestically defined. At the same time, the European Council and the Council should have to earn its democratic credentials. Relevant standards for assessment are laid down in Article 11 EU Treaty. One needs to investigate whether such institutions operate in a transparent and deliberative way, embedded in and responsive to the affected publics.

### 3 Participatory and Deliberative Democracy According to Article 11 of the EU Treaty

Democracy needs representation, but goes beyond it. This insight informs *Transformation* and finds support in Article 11 of the EU Treaty.

---

[24] On this latter point, for a critique of the Lisbon judgement of the German Federal Constitutional Court, see Schönberger, 'Die Europäische Union zwischen "Demokratiedefizit" und Bundesstaatsverbot', 535, 548.

[25] Oeter, 'Federalism and Democracy', *supra* note 19, at 55 and Dann, 'The Political Institutions', *supra* note 19, at 237.

[26] A. Hanebeck, *Der demokratische Bundesstaat des Grundgesetzes* (Berlin: Duncker and Humblot, 2004), 199, 279.

Of particular significance are transparency, the participation of those affected, deliberation, and flexibility.[27] Article 11, in particular, is informed by ideas of deliberative democracy, insofar as it requires that institutions shall operate in a deliberative way embedded in and responsive to the affected publics. Participation and deliberation can inform decisions in a variety of ways. What is essential is the transparency of public action, that is, its comprehensibility and the possibility of attributing accountability. European constitutional law places itself at the forefront of constitutional development when it requires that decisions be 'taken as openly as possible', i.e., transparently. The specifically democratic meaning of transparency in European law is confirmed by Article 11 (1) and (2) of the EU Treaty.

Transparency requires knowledge of the motives. From the beginning, Community law has enshrined a duty to provide reasons even for legislative acts (Article 296 TFEU), something which is hardly known in national legal orders. Its relevance for the principle of democracy enjoys general acknowledgement.[28] Access to documents, laid down in primary law in Article 15 TFEU and Article 42 of the Charter of Fundamental Rights of the European Union, is also of great importance to the realization of transparency. It has further become the subject of a considerable body of case law.[29] Another aspect is the openness of the Council's voting record on legislative measures: Article 16 (8) of the EU Treaty.[30]

The second complex of issues concerns forms of deliberation and political participation beyond elections. Popular consultations appear to be an obvious instrument, and referenda have occasionally been used to legitimise national decisions on European issues (such as accession to the Union or the ratification of amending Treaties). Extending such instruments to the European level has been proposed for some time.[31] The restrictively designed citizens' initiative of the Treaty of Lisbon (Article

---

[27] Concepts of participatory and deliberative democracy have by now been mainstreamed into democratic thought. See A. Peters, 'Dual Democracy', in J. Klabbers, A. Peters and G. Ulfstein, *The Constitutionalization of International Law* (Oxford: Oxford University Press, 2009), 263.

[28] Case C-64/05 P *Sweden v. Commission* [2007] ECR I-11389, 54, 64.

[29] J. Heliskoski and P. Leino, 'Darkness at the Break of Noon', *Common Market Law Review*, 43 (2006), 735.

[30] C. Sobotta, *Transparenz in den Rechtsetzungsverfahren der Europäischen Union* (Baden-Baden: Nomos, 2001), 144 et seq, 198 et seq.

[31] H. Abromeit, 'Ein Vorschlag zur Demokratisierung des europäischen Entscheidungssystems', *Politische Vierteljahresschrift*, 39 (1998), 80; J. Habermas, *Ach, Europa* (Frankfurt am Main: Suhrkamp, 2008), 105.

11 (4) of the EU Treaty) falls short of this, but nevertheless shows some potential.[32]

Whereas the Union has no experience with popular consultations, it has a lot of experience in allowing individual interests to intervene in the political process, as noted in *Transformation*. Research indicates that such participation of interested and affected parties might be a further avenue to realising the democratic principle.[33] Article 11 (2) of the EU Treaty is based on this understanding. However, the principle of political equality must be respected and participation has to be designed so as to avoid political gridlock or the so-called agency capture by strong, organised groups.

Making the Union more flexible is also of democratic relevance.[34] It allows a democratic national majority to be respected, without, however, permitting this national majority, which is a European minority, to frustrate the will of the European majority. However, there are difficult questions of competitive equality in the internal market as well as of democratic transparency in an ever more complex decision-making process.[35] The possibility of leaving the Union, as foreseen in Article 50 of the EU Treaty, also serves the democratic principle, since it upholds the prospect of national self-determination in the event that Union rule should appear to national public as illegitimate heteronomy.[36] On this point, we should recall the famous example of Denmark and Germany.[37]

## III Three Reasons Why the Response Should Be Taken Seriously

These innovations have so far not improved the image of European democracy with the public at large, and so the social legitimacy of the European Union continues to be weak. This should not be surprising. The impact of norms

---

[32] A. Epiney, 'Europäische Verfassung und Legitimation durch die Unionsbürger', in S. Kadelbach (ed.), *Europäische Verfassung und direkte Demokratie* (Baden-Baden: Nomos, 2006), 33.

[33] B. Kohler-Koch, 'The Organization of Interests and Democracy', in *Debating the Democratic Legitimacy of the European Union supra* note 12, at 255.

[34] D. Thym, 'Supranationale Ungleichzeitigkeit im Recht der europäischen Integration', *Europarecht*, 5 (2006), 637.

[35] J. Wouters, 'Constitutional Limits of Differentiation', in *The Many Faces of Differentiation in EU Law*, in B. de Witte, D. Hanf and E. Vos, (eds.) (Antwerpen; Oxford; New York: Intersentia, 2001), 299, 301.

[36] J. Louis, 'Le droit de retrait de l'Union européenne', *Cahiers de Droit Européen*, 42 (2006), 293.

[37] Weiler, Haltern and Mayer, 'European Democracy and Its Critique', *supra* note 14, at 4, 12.

on social perceptions and the build-up of social legitimacy, in particular, is a long-term process. And this cannot occur without education. Citizens' knowledge of how the EU operates is often crude, even outright wrong. Simple, but meaningful schemes are needed, as with the domestic systems of government. The same is true for the idea of what democracy should mean for the EU. Nothing better depicts the uncertainties of how to understand the Union's principle of democracy even at the expert level than Part I Title VI and Part II Title V of the Constitutional Treaty. Under the headings 'The Democratic Life of the Union' and 'Citizens' Rights', respectively, a number of heterogeneous provisions were amassed. The Treaty of Lisbon takes a big step forward: Its four articles in the topic are rather clear-cut and can be interpreted to convey an idea of post-national democracy that is simple enough for the public at large. It can be explained as a plausible path for a more democratic polity that follows – in *Transformation*'s terms – a community vision. Three more reasons provide support for this democratic agenda.

## 1   Its Democratic Credentials

Articles 9 to 12 of the EU Treaty are based on the two main positions advanced in twenty years of debate: (1) that which mainly looks at the powers of domestic parliaments; and (2) that which considers the European Parliament as well as deliberative and participatory understandings of democracy. Much of the best scholarly imagination has flown into efforts to unfold the European Union in a democratic way, and public opinion has participated in these efforts. As has been pointed out, Articles 9 to 12 of the EU Treaty can be construed as bringing these main positions into a forward-looking synthesis.

To evaluate the democratic credentials of those articles, one has to look not only at their content, but also at process and procedure. This synthesis has been elaborated in one of the most complex political processes that the European continent has ever seen. Moreover, its enactment has gone through the most burdensome procedures, often the procedures of constitutional amendment. Through this process, politicians and the public have become well aware of the importance of that Treaty, not least after the failure of the Constitutional Treaty of 2004. The provisions have also been the object of detailed judicial review.[38]

---

[38] Spanish Constitutional Court, Case Rs. 1/2004, Judgement of 13 December 2004; German Federal Constitutional Court, Judgement of 30 June 2009, BVerfGE 123, 267, 353; Czech Constitutional Court, Case Pl. ÚS 50/04, Judgement of 8 March 2006; Case Pl. ÚS 66/04, Judgement of 3 May 2006, 53; Case Pl. ÚS 19/08, Judgement of 22 November 2008, 97.

Accordingly, the concept of democracy as laid down in these articles enjoys the consent of the vast majority of European citizens and high legitimacy. To refute this conclusion would be to deny that the procedures of constitutional amendment have democratic relevance. It is impossible to dismiss those articles as technocratic fiat from Brussels. As a lawyer, one has to build on this. Certainly, any scholar or citizen is free to snub it on theoretical or emotional grounds, as one can always reasonably wish to live in a different polity. But this does not shake the democratic credentials of those articles which provide the first legal concept of post-national democracy. If one holds dear the principle of democracy, these articles are imposing. They put legal conceptions of democracy for Europe which cannot be reconciled with them under severe stress.

## 2    The Limits and Focus of the Citizens' Political Interest

In a faculty seminar at NYU law school in 2008, a US colleague presented his work on democracy (and corruption) on the level of US states. His core argument was that democratic institutions, in order to work properly, need to be the subject of sufficient public interest. Otherwise, democracy cannot flourish because a lack of public interest leads to civic disenchantment, a lack of democratic legitimacy – notwithstanding all formal credentials – and possibly corruption. In such a setting, the elections cannot fully deliver what they should for democratic legitimacy. One important root of the problem, according to the American colleague, is that the limited resource of citizens' political attention is mostly absorbed by the political processes at the federal level. There is a national public opinion in the United States, but it comes with heavy costs for public opinion on state issues. Accordingly, as Joseph Weiler also points out, 'State elections [in the United States] are frequently a mid-term signal to the federal government.' This is just the opposite of what is going on in Europe.[39] The U.S. colleague saw this as a deplorable development for democracy, because, for reasons of electoral size and propinquity, true participation and individual impact are far more likely on the state level.

I take from this the plausible hypothesis that in contemporary Western societies there is a rather fixed amount of political attention by average citizens. Framing democracy in federal system has to consider where that valuable resource should go, and how to divide it. Seen in this light, a

---

[39]  Weiler, Haltern and Mayer, 'European Democracy and Its Critique', *supra* note 14, at 4, 8.

little noticed but potentially significant advantage of European democracy compared with American democracy comes to the fore. European democracy maintains as the dominant focus of democratic attentions those institutions which are closer to the citizen, and in all likelihood more responsive and accountable. The European system based on executive federalism[40] hence has a specific democratic advantage that over all democratic participation remains more meaningful (and hence probably more alive) than under the U.S. system. This provides further credentials to Articles 9 – 12 EU Treaty and the community vision they endorse.

### 3   Manifesto Character

The European Union, as it operates today, is not a democratic showcase. For anyone who cares about democracy, there is no reason to be satisfied with the *status quo*. In this respect, a further reason to support Articles 9 to 12 of the EU Treaty emerges: these articles provide meaningful yardsticks for critique and indicate how to enhance the democratic content of European politics. That is to say, they constitute a manifesto for what should be done.

Remarkable tension exists between the conception of these articles, as of Titles I to III of the EU Treaty in general, and the jagged normative material in the rest of primary law. While, for example, Art. 10 (2) of the EU Treaty defines the Union as bicameral, many important exceptions remain, as in competition law (Article 103 TFEU) or in the fixing of prices in the agricultural area (Article 43 TFEU). Even though such special provisions make it impossible to categorically classify a certain practice of the EU or of the combined Member States as illegal, Articles 9 to 12 of the EU Treaty allow for substantiated critique and indicate what should be done.

Similarly, in many policy areas it is easy to show that European politics is not living up to the representative, deliberative, and participatory ideals of Articles 10 and 11 (1 to 3) of the EU Treaty, but follow a tactical logic, concerned with the efficient exercise of power. A most obvious example, although at the edges of Union competence, is provided by the crisis in Greece: the democratic standards laid down in Articles 9 to 12 of the EU Treaty were not observed by the policy response at the European level. In light of Article 9, the idea of a common citizenship is not respected. As Habermas puts it, the mechanisms give the citizens a perspective of 'us against them', a zero-sum game where the idea of a common problem

---

[40]   See Dann, 'The Political Institutions', *supra* note 19.

requiring joint effort got lost.[41] Articles 10 and 11 of the EU Treaty support Habermas's critique of the informality and non-transparency of this process, which exhibits an informal and irregular method of political coordination that destroys democratic credibility.

Articles 9 to 12 of the EU Treaty call for the further constitutionalisation and hence transformation of European public law. This requires meaningful constructions of these provisions and hermeneutic, legal, and political strategies for its realization. Such transformation is not uncommon. Under Germany's Basic Law, the constitutional organisation of the state has been substantially transformed by the impact of the principles in the first two parts of the Basic Law.[42] The French example is similarly instructive: there, the republican tradition, in the form of the universality of law and the parliament's general legislative competence, has prevailed over the text of the Constitution of the Fifth Republic.[43] Articles 9 to 12 EU Treaty give far more guidance as to what should be done. Last but not least, they support the spirit of *Transformation* not to be smug and satisfied with what has been achieved, but to challenge it on principled grounds. The nagging doubt as to whether Europe is democratic enough might be European democracy's greatest asset.

---

[41] J. Habermas, 'Rettet die Würde der Demokratie', Frankfurter Allgemeine Zeitung, 11. November 2011, available at www.faz.net/aktuell/feuilleton/euro-krise-rettet-die-wuerde-der-demokratie-11517735.html.

[42] K. Ladeur, 'Sources and Categories of Legal Acts – Germany', in G. Winter (ed.), *Sources and Categories of European Law: A Comparative and Reform Perspective* (Baden-Baden: Nomos, 1996), 235, 241 ff.

[43] J. Boulouis, 'L'influence des articles 34 et 37 sur l'équilibre politique entre les pouvoirs. L'application des articles 34 et 37 par le Conseil d'Etat', in L. Favoreu (ed.), *Le domaine de la loi et du règlement* (1982), 195ff.

# 9

# Joseph Weiler, Eric Stein, and the Transformation of Constitutional Law

### DANIEL HALBERSTAM

*The Transformation of Europe*,[1] the foundational article that we justly celebrate with this volume in honour of Joseph Weiler, is deeply bound up with an important development that reaches far beyond the European Union: the transformation of constitutional law.

This chapter pursues that idea in three parts. Part I reviews the key contributions of *The Transformation of Europe*. Part II takes us back for a critical analysis of the idea of 'constitutionalism' as first developed by Eric Stein and then deployed by Joseph Weiler. On closer inspection, we shall see here that *The Transformation of Europe* may have neglected a core element of constitutional law, something this chapter terms a 'generative space' for law and politics. As this part further explains, recognising this generative element of constitutionalism lies at the heart of the struggle to make sense both practically and conceptually of European integration to this day. Part III then briefly outlines an emerging response to this challenge, and relates this response more broadly to the transformation of constitutional law.

## I *The Transformation of Europe*

*The Transformation of Europe* lays down a unified theory of the law and politics of European integration. It proposes a comprehensive theory for making sense of important developments over long stretches of time. It also teaches. It provides the reader with much history, law, and politics of European integration, allowing us to make up our own mind about all these events as we take in Weiler's path-breaking ideas.

At its core, the article mediates an interdisciplinary tension – Weiler called it a 'paradox'[2] – that had existed in scholarship about the European

[1] J. H. H. Weiler, 'The Transformation of Europe', *Yale Law Journal*, 100 (1991), 2403.
[2] Ibid., at 2411.

Union. Especially in the first two decades of the Community, political scientists had become disillusioned with the project of integration. Predictions based on Ernst Haas's neo-functionalism had not materialised.[3] Functional spillover had promised an increase in European powers as interconnected areas of economic life would be drawn into Jean Monnet's technocratic decision-making machine in Brussels. But political scientists saw just the opposite: Member State governments reasserting their national voices and watering down supposedly supranational majoritarian institutions. European integration was thought to be in peril.[4]

Lawyers, by contrast, emphasised the great strides towards a supranational legal framework.[5] They emphasised the advances on the legal side of the enterprise by pointing to the European Court of Justice, its creation of supremacy and direct effect, and the strengthening of these doctrines over time. Where political scientists complained about the Community sliding back towards 'inter-governmentalism', lawyers noted the success of Europe's 'supranational' endeavour.

Reminiscent of the rabbi in that old joke,[6] Joseph Weiler hears the two sides of the dispute and concludes, 'You're both right.' To show why, Weiler develops an equilibrium theory of the law and politics of European integration.[7] On the one hand, Member States increased their demands for a veto because the law as developed by the ECJ would hold them to the policies Brussels passed. On the other hand, the existence of a veto made Member States agree to an expansive use of central powers that suited each of their separately determined preferences. The equilibrium thesis thus dissolved the supposed paradox and the interdisciplinary squabble.[8]

Weiler's article does not end with the founding period. He shows that Member States became willing over time to weaken their veto powers to

---

[3] See E. B. Haas, *Beyond the Nation State* (Stanford, CA: Stanford University Press, 1964).

[4] See, e.g., N. Heathcote, 'The Crisis of Supranationality', *Journal of Common Market Studies*, 5 (1966), 140.

[5] E.g., A. Wilson Green, *Political Integration by Jurisprudence* (Leyden: A. W. Sijthoff, 1969).

[6] Two people bring a case to the rabbi. After listening to the first, the rabbi says, 'You're right.' After listening to the second, the rabbi says, 'Yes, you're right.' At that point, the rabbi's spouse intervenes: 'Dear, but they can't *both* be right.' Whereupon the rabbi thinks hard, and answers, 'Yes, my dear, you're right, too.'

[7] Drawing on A. O. Hirschman, *Exit, Voice, and Loyalty* (Cambridge, MA: Harvard University Press, 1970).

[8] C.f. J. H. H. Weiler, 'The Community System: The Dual Character of Supranationalism', *Year Book of European Law*, 1 (1981), 267.

get important things done in an expanding union in which unanimity could not easily be reached.[9] Weiler points out that even the ambitious Single European Act formally preserved the balance between binding Member States and allowing them to escape from a European rule that threatened their core interests.[10] He also provides an early critical assessment of the democratic deficit by analysing formal and social legitimacy of European integration.[11] And he predicts the emergence of left/right politics in the Union after 1992.[12] Perhaps most important, he lays out two competing visions for the future of the Union – one, of a tolerant, pluralist 'community', and another, of a more traditionally conceived federal 'unity'.[13] The article closes with a passionate argument in favour of community over unity.

The article became an instant classic – and rightly so. Even the redoubtable Henry Schermers, who along with Eric Stein had served on Weiler's dissertation committee back in Florence, could find 'no fundamental mistakes in the piece'.[14] Several of the concerns anticipated in the piece, such as those regarding the emergence of left-right politics, proved prescient. Most impressive, the structure of analysis regarding the equilibrium of the founding era and the democratic deficit has defined mainstream thinking of the discipline ever since.

## II    The Challenge: Constitutionalism and European Union

Let us focus on the challenge that 'community' versus 'unity' poses for the discipline of constitutional law. Despite the changes occasioned by real-world developments that may make Weiler's insistence on 'community' sound dated, the principal divide between these two conceptions of European integration is still very much alive. What is more, this challenge has begun to transform our understanding of constitutional law in and beyond Europe. To understand the challenge, however, we must first understand how *The Transformation of Europe* itself treats one of the key elements of constitutionalism.

---

[9]    Weiler, 'The Transformation of Europe', *supra* note 1, 2431–53.
[10]   Ibid., at 2458–9.
[11]   Ibid., at 2468.
[12]   Ibid., at 2476–8.
[13]   Ibid., at 2479.
[14]   H. G. Schermers, 'Comment on Weiler's *The Transformation of Europe*', *Yale Law Journal*, 100 (1991), 2525.

## A   Constitutionalism in *The Transformation of Europe?*

There is a deep tension in *The Transformation of Europe*'s discussion of constitutionalism. Although Weiler seems to embrace the idea of constitutionalism in Europe, he might also be read as explaining it away. Put differently, Weiler's account may well amount to a denial of the very constitutionalism he purports to explain.

This is where Eric Stein comes into – or, rather, precedes – our current story. As is well known, Stein pioneered the legal study of European integration. He wrote the first English-language article on the European Court of Justice decisions in 1955,[15] taught the first law course on European integration in 1956, and published the first casebook on the subject in 1963.[16] More important for present purposes, in 1981, Eric Stein transformed that field again with his article *Lawyers, Judges, and the Making of a Transnational Constitution*.[17] In that piece, Stein coined the concept of 'constitutionalisation' and thereby changed the way legal scholars – and many others – have thought about European integration ever since.

Stein inaugurated what is now a dominant legal perception of European integration, as some kind of 'constitutional' entity. Stein also cut a path for European lawyers beyond the consideration of formal legal doctrine in understanding the legal aspects of integration. Stein's project was eclectic in that it included consideration of the surrounding professional, institutional, and social dynamics that contributed to the creation of what he termed 'a constitutional framework for a federal-type structure in Europe'.[18]

Joseph Weiler's *Transformation of Europe* builds on this work of our mutual colleague, mentor, and dear late friend. Following Stein's article, Weiler presents the classic elements of direct effect, supremacy, implied powers, and human rights as forming the core principles of constitutionalism.[19] Weiler elaborates, in particular, on an institutional element that Stein had discussed only in passing: the preliminary reference action under what was then Article 177.

---

[15] E. Stein, 'The European Coal and Steel Community: The Beginning of Its Judicial Process', *Columbia Law Review*, 55 (1955), 985.

[16] See *supra* note 6 and accompanying text.

[17] E. Stein, 'Lawyers, Judges, and the Making of a Transnational Constitution', *American Journal of International Law*, 75 (1981), 1.

[18] Ibid.

[19] Weiler, 'The Transformation of Europe', *supra* note 1, 2413–19.

Having embraced Stein's elements of 'constitutionalism', Weiler pauses to justify the use of that term, especially as a way to distinguish all this from the classic workings of public international law. Weiler explains:

> The combined effect of constitutionalization and the evolution of the system of remedies results ... in the removal from the Community legal order of the most central legal artifact of international law: the notion (and doctrinal apparatus) of exclusive state responsibility with its concomitant principles of reciprocity and countermeasures.[20]

As a result, 'there can be no argument', according to Weiler, 'that the Community legal order as it emerged from the Foundational Period appeared in its operation much closer to a working constitutional order' than to an entity functioning under public international law.[21]

Then follows Weiler's signal contribution – the unified theory of law and politics based on equilibrium. Weiler shows in terms of voice and exit how Member States gave up their prerogative of exclusive state responsibility and crossed over into this brave new world where constitutionalism reigns. Moving beyond the founding period, Weiler argues that constitutionalism has more recently come under attack because the equilibrium between voice and exit – although formally preserved – has, in practice, been 'shattered' by the introduction of majority voting in the Single European Act.[22]

An important aspect of this account is that it equates 'constitutionalism' with the hardening and broadening of European law. The danger, as Weiler points out, is that the hardening and broadening once took place in the service of the Member State government interests, but no longer does. Hence, on Weiler's account, constitutionalism has come under attack.

This account, however, raises a question about constitutionalism itself. Is the account of 'constitutionalism' in *The Transformation of Europe* complete? If we take constitutionalism – in contrast to, say, a simple understanding of delegation or administration – as the lens through which to understand European integration, would we not expect more?

### B    Constitutionalism and the 'Generative Space' of European Governance

A 'constitutional' vision of European integration suggests the creation of something we might call a 'generative space' of governance at the

---

[20] Ibid., at 2422.
[21] Ibid.
[22] Ibid., at 2460.

European level. In a constitutional – as opposed to, say, a simple administrative – vision of European integration, the European level of governance provides a distinct space in which political and legal decisions can be *created*, not merely carried out. Europe, on this view, is not merely an agent of Member States who reach their political decisions back home. The concept of a 'generative space' of European governance is meant to capture this fact, i.e., that political and legal decisions can be generated at the European level in the first instance.

Without using this terminology, Weiler does address something similar in the second part of his article. But he presents this development *as a threat to*, not *as an element of*, constitutionalism in Europe. Recall Weiler's discussion of the Single European Act.[23] The most significant element of this change was then-Article 100a (now Art. 114 TFEU), which introduced qualified majority voting for measures aimed at improving the functioning of the common market. As Weiler notes, the fourth paragraph of that provision formally restored what the opening provision had given up: the Member State veto. Article 100a(4) authorised any Member State dissenting from a particular approximation measure to file an objection and preclude application of that provision in its territory. On its face, then, this provision seemed to preserve the equilibrium of the foundational era. And yet, as Weiler explains, Article 100a did not play out that way. Member States soon found that invoking the exception was politically difficult and only feasible as an option of last resort. Negotiations were now conducted, as Weiler says, 'under the shadow of the vote' as opposed to the way they had been in the past, 'under the shadow of the veto'.[24] The Commission became more empowered as an independent actor setting the agenda, and Member States lost more control than the treaty language suggested. Weiler expressly warned that this loss of control threatened the constitutionalisation of the founding era.[25]

I suggest, by contrast, that constitutionalisation of the Union critically depends on just this loss of Member State control. In addition to the hardening and broadening of the law, constitutionalism of the European Union lies in the emancipation of the Union from Member State political (and legal) processes. We need not invoke any grand ideas of EU sovereignty or insist on some formal idea of complete autonomy or complete independence of the European level of governance. Those rather unhelpful

[23] Ibid., at 2456–74.
[24] Ibid., at 2461.
[25] See, e.g., ibid., at 2465.

concepts have proven fluid, not binary, even in more conventional federal systems. Nor is the suggestion here that the Union has become as independent from the Member States as the central government in a classic modern federal system (such as the United States). But we need to recognise that an essential part of constitutionalism in Europe lies in the shift away from, say, a principal-agent model of the relationship between the Member States and the European Union. If we take the account of 'constitutionalism' in *The Transformation of Europe*, however, the existence of any such generative aspect of European governance is not part of, but a threat to, European constitutionalism.

Focusing on the existence of a *generative space* of law and politics at the supranational level as core to constitutionalism, then, means that shattering the equilibrium between voice and exit is part and parcel of introducing constitutionalism in the Union. Weiler's threat to constitutionalism turns out to be the core of constitutionalism itself. And any story that focuses on the 'exit' and 'voice' options of Member States, Member State governments, or Member State polities taken as abiding and cohesive units of governance with exogenously determined preferences does not really explain the existence of constitutionalism; instead, it explains constitutionalism away.

To see why, let us turn back briefly to Eric Stein. Recall Stein's account in *Lawyers, Judges, and the Making of a Transnational Constitution*. In going through the foundational legal battles, Stein showed that the European Court of Justice defied the wishes of the Member State governments by ruling in favour of direct effect, supremacy, implied powers, and foreign affairs powers of the Community. In each case, as Stein points out, the Court ruled against the submitted filings of the Member State governments.

What should we make of this supposed defiance of Member State government wishes?[26] An equilibrium story focused on Member State governments' options of exit and voice sets out to show how the supposed supranational 'autonomy' worked, in fact, to further the interests of the Member State governments. That is, after all, the punch of the equilibrium idea. The perception of autonomy, so the equilibrium theory holds, was an illusion. In hardening and broadening the law, the Union was acting in the service of the Member State governments all along. Purporting to

---

[26] Even in Stein's story, the defiance of Member State wishes was not highlighted as an essential part of constitutionalism – only the hardening of the law was. So we must build beyond Stein as well.

explain constitutionalism, the equilibrium theory thus destroys constitutionalism along the way.

My point here is not merely semantic. Indeed, it has taken on greater significance since the writing of *The Transformation of Europe*. An account of 'constitutionalism' as hardening and broadening of the law sounds not all that different from the international relations story of pooling and delegation that other scholars have elaborated since then.[27] Such an 'intergovernmental' account is often suggested as an antidote to constitutional conceits. The intergovernmental argument holds that because something like the equilibrium that Weiler set out with regard to the founding period has largely continued beyond that period, the Union should still not properly be viewed as constitutional.

A host of significant corollaries flow from the rejection of a constitutional vision. It changes, for example, whether we view the Union as democratically problematic. If the Member State governments continue to get what they want, most democratic deficit claims dissolve. This is a simple but counterfactual consequence.

More important, if Member State governments are not getting what they want, the different perspectives call for different paths to reform. If Member State governments have lost some control over EU governance, a constitutional vision would focus on making Union processes and politics more accessible to individuals and to the various European publics affected by those decisions. An intergovernmental vision, by contrast, would seek to address this concern by tightening the Member State governments' grip on their wayward agent.

A difference in perspective would also change the interpretive approach of a variety of actors as they consider and deploy the foundational treaties for normative action. An intergovernmental vision would, for instance, have counselled the Court against taking a number of decisions in the way it did – from granting the European Parliament powers that were not specifically defined in the Rome Treaty[28] to the expansion of European citizenship beyond what might have been originally contemplated by the signatories to the Maastricht Treaty.[29] Whether we view these decisions as

---

[27] See, e.g., A. Moravcsik, 'Preferences and Power in the European Community: A Liberal Intergovernmentalist Approach', *Journal of Common Market Studies*, 31 (1993), 473; G. Tsebelis and G. Garrett, 'The Institutional Foundations of Intergovernmentalism and Supranationalism in the European Union', *International Organization*, 55 (2001).

[28] See, e.g., Case C-302/87 *Parliament v. Council* [1988] ECR 5615.

[29] See, e.g., Case C-34/09 *Ruiz Zambrano v. Office national de l'emploi (ONEm)* [2011] ECR I-01177; Case C-200/02 *Zhu and Chen v Secretary of State for the Home Department* [2004]

right or wrong often depends on whether we consider the Union to be a constitutional or an intergovernmental entity.

Note that the anti-constitutional account of international relations theory does not negate the hardening and broadening of EU law. It comfortably accepts all the rule-of-law features that Weiler claimed as evidence of constitutionalism back in 1991. But the intergovernmental account ultimately explains these rule-of-law features (much as Weiler did back then) in non-constitutional terms. The commitment to a binding system of law (the hardening and broadening of law at the European level), according to the international relations account, merely serves the separate Member States' preferences as these preferences emerge from the various national processes of aggregation.

To account for constitutionalism as including a *generative space* for governance, as I argue here, we must take up the story where the equilibrium is shattered. Better yet, we must reach back into the founding era to see how the equilibrium slowly eroded and constitutionalism emerged. We need an account, then, of how supranational governance successfully outpaced the equilibrium, i.e., how supranational governance challenged, changed, shaped, or even ignored Member State preferences over time.

C   *The Emergence of Constitutionalism in European Governance*

This is not the place to spell out a complete theory that accounts for the creation of a *generative space* of supranational governance in Europe. Elsewhere, I have taken more sustained aim at developing this aspect of constitutionalism in the European Union.[30] Briefly, however, some of the argument runs along the following lines.

Several institutional features of the European system of governance – not least the unanimity among Member State governments required to change the capacious treaties as interpreted by the Court – allow for a certain degree of decisional autonomy of actors at the European Union level of governance. The Court of Justice has exploited this decisional space, as have the European Parliament, the European Commission, and many other actors, including private economic actors and ordinary citizens. But

---

ECR I-09925; Case C-184/99 *Grzelczyk v Centre public d'aide sociale d'Ottignies-Louvain-la-Neuve* [2001] ECR I-6193; Case C-85/96, *Martinez Sala v Freistaat Bayern* [1998] ECR I-2691.

[30] See D. Halberstam, 'The Bride of Messina: Constitutionalism and Democracy in Europe', *Eur. L. Rev*, 30 (2005), 775.

they have often done so in a principled manner. With the Court of Justice often in the lead, these various actors have exploited their strategic space for action to 'recalibrate' the European enterprise away from Member States as the exclusive locus of normative concern. This means the Court, the Parliament, and others have interpreted the treaties to recognise individuals (and groups of individuals) as bearers of legal interests that are not necessarily mediated by Member State governments.

This 'democratic recalibration'[31] began long before the Single European Act. A host of decisions, actions, and processes systematically lifted individuals out of their national confines by providing access to a generative arena of law and politics at the European level of governance. We find national actors redirecting their interests and forging communities – even if only thin ones – across Member State lines. Supremacy and direct effect (and the formal recognition of individuals alongside Member States as rights-bearers within the Union) are just the beginning of this democratic recalibration. At the European Court of Justice (now the CJEU), other dimensions of this democratic recalibration involve the substantive conception of human rights as pan-European (as opposed to honouring exclusively Member-State-specific conceptions of rights), the creation of European citizenship beyond what Member States seem to have imagined, and the development of various social aspects of economic freedoms. Especially the Court's recognition of the European Parliament as a self-standing institution in supranational governance reveals the broad nature of this normative recalibration. Here, the Court moved beyond legal claims of individuals and recalibrated the institutional architecture to allow for the possibility of genuinely supranational politics.[32]

The Parliament's own emancipatory actions have contributed to this democratic recalibration as well. Through negotiations in successive stages of Treaty reform, bold public action challenging the existing or proposed composition of the European Commission, as well as the emergence of left-right politics in the Parliament itself, that institution has bootstrapped itself into a forum for European politics that is not controlled by the Member State governments.

All this is only the beginning of a story that involves the actions and the self-conceptions of a host of actors from judges, parliamentarians, and other officials to citizens over time.[33]

---

[31] E.g., ibid., at 777.
[32] For the five dimensions of this recalibration, see ibid. at 782–5.
[33] Ibid., at 785–8.

Understanding the constitutionalisation as including this kind of democratic recalibration in the creation and use of a generative space of supranational governance provides the legal counterpart to various political and sociological accounts that emphasise the genuinely transnational aspects of European integration.[34] It comes, perhaps, as no surprise that these theories chiefly developed after 1992 (and, in countless ways, owe their own debt to Weiler's writings). At the same time, the new claims we find here are not limited to describing a category shift that only began with the Single European Act or in a post-Maastricht world. They present a more comprehensive and gradual picture that reaches well back into the founding era.

### III    The Transformation of Constitutional Law

Is this generative space of Union governance, along with its normative recalibration, legal or legitimate? How can all this coexist with the constitutional law of the Member States? Returning to Joseph Weiler's concern in *The Transformation of Europe*, we might ask: how is the emergence of a 'constitutional' Union (which we shall now take not only in Weiler's rule-of-law sense, but in the generative sense just laid out) compatible with the vision of 'community, not unity'? Recognising constitutionalism at the level of European governance to include a *generative space* of supranational governance, and at the same time insisting on the continued existence of Member State constitutional law, seems at first blush rather incoherent – a hodgepodge of legality run wild.

The basic concern derives from the fact that constitutions are traditionally taken to stand for legal hierarchy and settlement. In a common narrative,[35] the modern tradition of constitutionalism begins in England where law is used to temper and ultimately frame politics. From there constitutionalism travels to the United States and revolutionary France where constitutionalism becomes radicalised. Politics there ground the

---

[34] See, e.g., T. Risse, 'Social Constructivism and European Integration', in A. Wiener and T. Diez (eds.), *European Integration Theory* (Oxford: Oxford University Press, 2004), 159; N. Fligstein and A. Stone Sweet, 'Constructing Polities and Markets: An Institutionalist Account of European Integration', *American Journal of Sociology*, 107 (2002), 1206–43; T. Christiansen, K. E. Jørgensen, and A. Wiener, 'The Social Construction of Europe', *Journal of European Public Policy*, 6, 4 (1999), 528-43; L. Hooghe and G. Marks, *Multilevel Governance and European Integration* (Lanham, MD: Rowman & Littlefield, 2001).

[35] See, e.g., D. Grimm, 'Verfassung II', in O. Brunner, W. Conze, and R. Koselleck (eds.), *Geschichtliche Grundbegriffe* (Stuttgart: Klett, 1990), at 859.

supreme and foundational law, which comes to be seen as 'antecedent' to the exercise of all legitimate public authority.[36] But in terms of internal institutional hierarchy and judicial review, the United States and France are seen as still stuck in various states of incompletion. And, so, according to this story, constitutionalism comes to fruition only in the rationalised Kelsenian systems of continental Europe.[37]

Especially in Europe, where this narrative of constitutional progress has great appeal, constitutionalism seems to leave little room for Weiler's 'separate actors who are fated to live in an uneasy tension with two competing senses of the polity's self, the autonomous self and the self as part of a larger community, and committed to an elusive search for an optimal balance of goals and behavior between the community and its actors'.[38] Instead, the traditional understanding of constitutional law as hierarchy and settlement suggests that a constitutional understanding of the Union inevitably favours the idea of 'unity' over that of 'community'. The traditional view, then, would counsel for either ratcheting back European integration to preserve inter-governmentalism, or for seeking to unify the system under a more traditionally understood, federal constitutional umbrella.[39]

A different tack, sympathetic to the idea of community-not-unity, or to what Weiler a decade later called the idea of 'constitutional tolerance',[40] has been to make sense of the European Union in constitutional terms despite the apparent tension that this creates. One of the initial contributions came from Neil MacCormick:

> Where there is a plurality of institutional normative orders, each with a functioning constitution … it is possible that each acknowledge the legitimacy of every other within its own sphere, while none asserts or acknowledges constitutional superiority over another.[41]

But even Homer nods. MacCormick soon shied away from the radical nature of his initial thought and ultimately subsumed the relationship

---

[36] T. Paine, *The Rights of Man* (London: Watts & Co., 1937), 36.
[37] Cf., e.g., A. Stone Sweet, 'Why Europe Rejected American Judicial Review: and Why It May Not Matter', *Michigan Law Review*, 101 (2003), 2744.
[38] Weiler, 'The Transformation of Europe', *supra* note 1, at 2480.
[39] Cf. P. Leftheriadis, 'The Idea of European Constitution', *Oxford Journal of Legal Studies*, 27 (2007), 1.
[40] J. H. H. Weiler, 'Federalism without Constitutionalism: Europe's *Sonderweg*', in K. Nicoalidis and R. Howse (eds.), *The Federal Vision* (Oxford: Oxford University Press, 2001), 54.
[41] N. MacCormick, *Questioning Sovereignty* (Oxford: Oxford University Press, 1999), 104.

between European Union law and Member State law under the rules of public international law.[42] In the end, pluralism, constitutional tolerance, and the idea of 'community-not-union' seemed to have lost out here as well. In MacCormick's vision, public international law served as the overarching legal system that would control both the Member States and the European Union.

A new generation of scholars, more insistent on the plural and constitutional character of European integration, has forged ahead by re-examining the idea of constitutionalism itself.[43] These advances come in several varieties, and are beyond the scope of this chapter to consider in depth. Suffice it to say that they share an underlying appreciation for (a) the generative space of law and politics beyond the state; and (b) a turn, in that realm of governance, to the individual (and the multiple communities she inhabits) as a locus of normative concern. What is more, they see European governance as challenging us (c) to develop a more nuanced understanding of the practice of constitutional law – even within the state – questioning traditional notions of hierarchy and settlement.

This scholarly project sees European integration as broadly connected to the changing nature of public authority in and beyond the state. For instance, the landscape of global governance is widely seen as challenging our traditional state-based understanding of public authority.[44] Here, as the non-state global actor *par excellence*, the European Union raises the question whether its position is unique or whether other institutions, organisations, or regimes of governance beyond the state might be considered 'constitutional' as well.[45]

---

[42] Ibid., at 121.

[43] For a recent collection, including critics, see, e.g., M. Avbej and J. Komárek (eds.), *Constitutional Pluralism in the European Union and Beyond* (Oxford: Hart Publishing, 2012) (including pluralist contributions from Xavier Groussot, Daniel Halberstam, Jan Komarek, Mattias Kumm, Miguel Poiares Maduro, Daniel Sarmiento, Robert Schütze, and Neil Walker). Defining generations is never easy. Some might argue that earlier work, such as that of Ingolf Pernice, should be seen as launching this larger project as well. See Franz Mayer and Mattias Wendel in ibid. Also, this is not intended to be a comprehensive collection. Alec Stone Sweet, Anne Peters, and several others can be seen as writing in this new tradition in connection with Europe as well.

[44] See, e.g., A. Peters, 'Membership in the Global Constitutional Community,' in J. Klabbers, A. Peters, and G. Ulfstein (eds.), *The Constitutionalization of International Law* (Oxford: Oxford University Press, 2009), 153.

[45] N. Walker, 'The EU and the WTO: Constitutionalism in a New Key', in G. deBúrca and J. Scott (eds.), *The EU and the WTO: Legal and Constitutional Issues* (Oxford: Hart Publishing, 2001), 31.

In this realm, the EU irritates conceptually by sitting uncomfortably between global and national governance in ways that scholars and officials have still not been able to digest. Consider the International Law Commission's report on fragmentation.[46] The Report places the EU rather blandly – and without analysis – in a 'constitutional' category, as if that were sufficient to cast the Union as lying beyond the scope of investigation. No effort is made to consider how the relationship among the Member States, the Union, and the realm of international law might challenge the Report's general conclusions, especially those on 'self-contained regimes' (which the Report views with great scepticism). Whether or under what circumstances other regimes or organisations could be, or come to be, considered 'constitutional' – or why the European Union is considered 'constitutional' and others are not – is left unclear.

If we glance in the other direction, i.e., into the state, national constitutional processes in recent decades remind us of the shortcomings of the traditional narrative of constitutional law understood as radical popular authorship, complete consolidation of authority, and perfect institutional hierarchy. For all the success of constitutionalism in taking over the world as the dominant framework for the legitimate (or purportedly legitimate) exercise of state power,[47] constitutionalism as it exists today has rarely followed the traditional script.

Here, too, the European Union may be of help – this time as a pointed irritant to constitutional law within the state. The practical intrusion of the European Union in its specific relations and legal claims vis-à-vis the Member States surely disrupts the traditional workings of constitutional law. What is more, the European Union also invites us to rethink broadly constitutional ideas of authorship, completion, and hierarchy around the world.

The point here, as on the international side of the ledger, is not to see the European Union in all things. But the promise is nonetheless to take from a constitutional understanding of the European Union – and from the unsettling function that such an understanding may have – important lessons for rethinking law and public authority in and beyond the state.

---

[46] Int'l Law Comm'n, *Report of the Study Group of the International Law Commission, Fragmentation of International Law*, U.N. Doc. A/CN.4/L.682 (Apr. 13, 2006).

[47] See D. Grimm, 'The Achievement of Constitutionalism and Its Prospects in a Changed World', in P. Dobner and M. Loughlin (eds.), *The Twilight of Constitutionalism* (Oxford: Oxford University Press, 2010).

## IV   Conclusion

If the discourse of European constitutionalism is 'the house that Eric built' and in which 'all the new and transformative renovations take place',[48] then Joseph Weiler thoroughly remodelled the mansion. By integrating law and politics into a comprehensive critical approach to the new Europe, Weiler's transformative work has taught substance and method, and led by scholarly example.

The third-generation work outlined in this chapter builds on these achievements of Stein and Weiler. But the work discussed here does so by re-examining the foundations of the construct – the idea of constitutionalism itself. The European experience, on this view, is not representative of constitutionalism as we thought we knew it. Instead, Europe practically and conceptually challenges the traditional understanding of constitutional law.

As part of that project, it is important that we move beyond an exclusive 'rule of law' conception of constitutionalism and towards one that includes an appreciation of the 'generative space' of constitutional governance in the Union. This means that we must reconsider the various conceptions of hierarchy and settlement that traditionally accompany theories of constitutional law. In so doing, the third-generation project aims at integrating our understanding of European constitutionalism into a broader understanding of law and public authority in and beyond the state. It aims, then, at nothing less than the transformation of constitutional law.

---

[48] J. H. H. Weiler, *The Constitution of Europe* (Cambridge: Cambridge University Press, 1999), 225–6.

# 10

## Perils of Unity, Promise of Union

### KALYPSO NICOLAÏDIS

Once again at a time of transformation against the real or perceived threat of disintegration, the EU hovers dangerously between the perils of unity and the promise of union. The stakes may seem starker than two and a half decades ago, when Joseph Weiler published his path-breaking work, *The Transformation of Europe*[1] but he helped define then the terms of today's debate.

That is because his framework pioneered a way of thinking about the EU, not only by weaving into a single narrative the legal and political dimensions of this ever transforming polity, but most importantly by providing a normative imperative against which the unfolding European reality could be assessed, praised, or despaired of. With the project of completing the Single Market in full swing, Weiler offered a new analysis whereby legal supranationalism was neither a mere epiphenomenon mirroring state interests nor an autonomous phenomenon overriding them. Instead, the relationship between law and politics was constantly co-constitutive yet contested. A kind of dance between (law-related) exit and (political) voice allowed for both intergovernmental (and specifically executive) control and weak political centralisation. And this in turn had been both a precondition and a consequence of strong legal authority and enforcement – that is, the progressive foreclosing of what Weiler calls selective exit (e.g., the practice of the Member States of retaining membership but seeking to avoid their obligations under the Treaty).

Under these conditions, it was possible to say that both pessimistic political scientists, who emphasised the obstacles to political bargaining, and optimistic legal theorists, who emphasised legal integration, were right in their description of bits of the elephant. And as an added bonus, the integration project could presumably strengthen both the

---

[1] J. H. H. Weiler, 'The Transformation of Europe', *Yale Law Journal*, 100, 8 (1991).

Community and the member states. But, and this is a crucial but, such dual strengthening constituted a normative imperative as well as empirical observation. Without understanding the former, the latter could be lost. Indeed, it is such an imperative that EU elites are in danger of losing sight of today.

And that is why, at a time when we are starting to envisage disintegration in Europe, we must critically engage with a theory of equilibrium Weiler developed for a previous phase of European integration.

Each scholar of course has his or her own way of appropriating, appraising, or dismissing *The Transformation of Europe* (and the broader Weiler corpus). And for sure, the passage of time, like William James' pragmatism, tends to unstiffen all our theories, including this one. On my part, I argue that our task according to *The Transformation* is not just to ask how or to what extent the EU has failed to uphold the *original* equilibrium, but rather to assess the EU's transformative potential while remaining faithful to a certain idea of what it is about. In other words, to state it rather grandly, can scholarship move from a special theory to a *general* theory of EU equilibrium? And in doing so, both generalise the initial analysis and point to its lacunae? If so, I would like to suggest what I see as three building blocks for such a strategy.

## 1 The Transformative Compass

It would have been radical enough for *The Transformation* to offer as it did a new analytical lens bringing into focus the fundamental pattern of European politics as a dance between law and politics, judges and politicians, respectively and reflexively engaged in shaping 'exit' and 'voice' in the EC, thus progressively forging a constitutionalised arrangement between states with increasing legal bite but a bite of their own making: letting go and asserting control as the *yin* and *yang* of European politics.

### *The Virtue of 'Community'*

In my view, however, the truly inspired nature of the essay comes in the next two steps. First with *judgment*: that if European integration rests on a dynamic but fragile equilibrium between normative centralisation and political assertion of autonomy, such foundational equilibrium is precious and must be preserved albeit in different guise with changing circumstances; that we should worry about dismantling that which 'helps explain the uniqueness and stability of the Community for much of its life'; and that if we do worry, then we need to know how to read the signs on the wall, the conditions that underpin the equilibrium. Weiler identifies some, but of course with time their relative importance may change and new ones may become more prominent.

But why is such preservation so important? And so we come to Weiler's third move, his conclusion for *Transformation*, that is the offering of an explicit *normative benchmark* for European developments, the eminently *critical* and political in his vision. The point of the story is not only to ask whether and how the EU manages to move from one version of the equilibrium to the next – after all, the status quo can be stable but undesirable. But crucially, that this is not any old equilibrium. There is something at stake in *this* equilibrium – a vision, an 'ideal type' which Weiler refers to as 'community' as opposed to a 'unity' paradigm. The normative benchmark on the horizon may or not be *intended* by European actors, or it may even be the common vector of various criss-crossing intentions, but somehow until now it has been preserved by the equilibrium.

So the ultimate message of *Transformation* I take to be this: if we are not careful, the promised land of 'community' may become our Paradise Lost. This vision constitutes Joseph Weiler's normative benchmark for, in the end, the European equilibrium is not only of instrumental but also of intrinsic value.

Hence my suggestion that we read *Transformation* backwards – starting with the Community vision – and that we systematically think through the link between its analytical and its normative stance. Some have been tempted to treat the later as a footnote, a kind of ex-post *desiderata* which does not affect the analytical framework per se. In contrast, I view Weiler's demarche through a specific method – which I call *normative inductivism* – namely, extracting the norm we use to assess a phenomenon from the phenomenon itself without falling into the trap of circularity. This methodological point relates to broad debates in legal and political theory which I cannot enter here. Suffice to say that normative inductivism has much affinity with Dworkin's interpretivism – e.g., an understanding of the political practices of a community through a scheme of principles that provide the best justification of these practices, sensitive both to the facts of the practices and to the values that the practices serve. That the interpreter's hypothesis amounts to attributing a *rationale* to the relevant practices does not guarantee that such a rationale is intended, but merely that the interpreter must look for it. Akin also to Adorno's 'immanent critique', we can identify how *existing* practices can be either a source of actual or *imagined* transformations or a subversion of our interpretations.

### From Community to Union of Peoples

Before we consider the test of time, it is worth reflecting on the potential and limit of the 'community paradigm' which Weiler himself has refined ever since.[2]

For one, although Weiler presented 'Community' in binary opposition to 'Unity', I believe that it is in fact more productive to present it as a 'third way' equally opposed to 'the classical model of international law' and to 'Unity'. In my view, this allows us to make the Community model more than simply an 'in between' given that both alternatives – e.g., sovereignty/national statism and unity/EU statism – are closer to each other than they are to the ideal of community. As Weiler argues, 'with its political process set up to counter the excesses of statism ended up coming round full circle and transforming itself into a (super) state'.[3] As opposed to such mimetism, the third way which we care about is 'transformative' and needs to be analysed as a new political form requiring new concepts and insights. In a parallel register, this is what I have sought to convey with the label of 'Europe demoicracy' (see Part III).

Which leads me in turn to prefer the idea of 'Union' to that of 'Community' for a host of good and bad reasons: the communitarian and organic connotations that have tainted the term 'Community' (much abused by the likes of Petain) – even if we would like to believe that terms and ideas should not be held hostage to their contingent misuse; the use of 'Union' in the federal context and the useful contrast between federal *Union* and federal *State*.[4] And of course the requisite to yield to prevailing practices – that is if we consider that the move from European *Community*

---

[2] J. H. H. Weiler, *The Constitution of Europe: 'Do the New Clothes Have an Emperor?' and Other Essays on European Integration* ( Cambridge: Cambridge University Press, 1999); J. H. H. Weiler, 'Federalism and Constitutionalism: Europe's Sonderweg', in K. Nicolaïdis and R. Howse (eds.), *The Federal Vision: Legitimacy and Levels of Governance in the United States and the European Union* (Oxford: Oxford University Press, 2001); J. H. H. Weiler, 'Deciphering the Political and Legal DNA of European Integration: An Exploratory Essay', in J. Dickson and P. Eleftheriadis (eds.), *Philosophical Foundations of European Union Law* (Oxford: Oxford University Press, 2012).

[3] Weiler, 'The Transformation of Europe', 2481.

[4] See A. Cohen, *De Vichy à la Communauté européenne* (Paris: Presses Universitaire de France, 2012).

to *Union* with the Maastricht Treaty has managed to retain the 'community spirit'. But perhaps most importantly, the (subjective) sense that 'Union' connotes a coming together while staying other, the continued autonomy and agency of the parts not only in spite of the togetherness but perhaps most importantly as a precondition for sustainable togetherness.

Crucially, this understanding of Union (or, for Weiler, Community) depends on stripping it from its teleological connotation – the idea that a Union needs to have a *telos*, an end that is radically different from its beginning, and what else than the move from separate *demoi* to the merger into oneness? Beings that have lost and yearned for 'oneness', at one point simultaneously male and female, have stirred the human imagination and peopled our myths and religions since our beginnings. After the original sin, *Adam*, the first hermaphrodite and a self-sufficient being like his creator, is divided into two imperfect sexes incapable of reproducing on their own. As told to us by Plato, each half of the primitive *androgyn*, split into two by Zeus, will forever be looking for his or her other half to become one again. How not to see our human unions and accompanying vows ('if anything but death parts me from you') as imperfect second bests, pale approximations of the original unity? And yet, Union short of Unity is the human condition, the source of its creativity as well as pathos.

So the idea of 'ever closer union' can be read as an asymptotic notion which relies on never stating – and even less attaining – some ultimate, fixed political construct. In this light, Weiler's recent warning against the kind of political messianism which has inspired European political elites from the origins comes into full relief. Today's great danger is that this messianic drive, which early on delivered a mode of integration compatible with both *Union* and *Unity*, has now come to embrace 'Unity by stealth', an end which justifies overlooking obstacles in the way, including the immense wave of resistance emanating from European publics. And yet the difficulty is this: public discourse seems to require teleological language, statements on 'what this is all about'. The question for us is whether this can be done by simply extolling purpose and explaining that there is no other horizon than a democratically sustainable process of togetherness without some new grand and shining political construct in sight. How do you explain that a polity can have a compass without a destination?

Crucially in the contemporary twist to this story, the idea of Union implies that of choice. Unity and secession are incompatible. Community is ambiguous – one is usually born in a Community but joins a Union.

Of course, one could argue that European states had no choice but to be born rubbing against each other at the tip of Asia. But they were free to create or join a Union and are, or should be, free to leave it, if an individual *demos* so decides in a democratic fashion.[5] For Weiler, the spiritual meaning of Europe's *Sonderweg* as 'constitutional tolerance' is to make integration an autonomous and endlessly renewed voluntary act of subordination to the European other.[6] Internalising mutual constraint is thus an act of emancipation if it be understood as a version of what federal language calls 'federal liberty' or indeed the choice for mutual recognition.[7] Arguably, such a right to leave can be considered all the more precious if the option is not to be exercised. In prosperous democracies at least, an overwhelming majority of citizens, however unhappy, do not choose to vote with their feet and leave their country even if they are unhappy with their current government. But they can. Similarly, most Europeans would not choose for their state of origin to leave the EU even when a majority might be unhappy about its policies. Under such conditions –which may change – the theoretical right of exit which is part of the constitutional matrix of the EU contributes to its strength, not its weakness as proponents of *Unity* would have it. Which is also why the EU needs to make up for the relatively perfunctory nature of the freedom of exit through opt-outs and differentiated integration.

One may argue that choice is not always a good thing. 'This nothing good or bad, but thinking makes it so,' said the Bard. Indeed, most citizens of affluent states seem to suffer from the pathologies of choice, a state of permanent unhappiness brought about by the sense that some other option might have been better than the one chosen. And among peoples, it could also be argued that commitment may become more profound, humility more warranted, within a no-alternative irreversible Union. Perhaps. But at what price?

## 2   Meanings of Transformation

If *The Transformation of Europe* is constructed around the notion of 'equilibrium', it ends with doubts about its sustainability. So unsurprisingly, most commentaries seek to assess whether this projection has come to

---

[5] Editor's note: This chapter was written before the 2016 Brexit referendum.
[6] Weiler, 'Federalism and Constitutionalism', 54–72.
[7] K. Nicolaïdis and R. Howse (eds.), *The Federal Vision: Legitimacy and Levels of Governance in the United States and the European Union* ( Oxford: Oxford University Press, 2001).

pass and on what grounds would we know that it has. This task is complicated by the fact that the concept of equilibrium can be understood in different ways. As with the term itself – ισορροπία which implies the leaning
on both sides to the same extent but not necessarily at the same time – the
notion of equilibrium always involves some oscillation from one side to
the other. The dynamic character of all federal polity is an old story, poised
as all federations are between federal safeguards -for states – and federal
overstretch –by the Union.[8] Indeed, history does not generally offer stable
federal bargains. The equilibrium is forever elusive and the oscillating pattern is one of lively awareness of what is wrong with the status quo.

But in the story of *this* equilibrium, the question is not whether the
polity survives, e.g., the durability of the EU per se, but whether it survives in the form that we value normatively because we believe it is the
best warrant for its long-term sustainability. If, in the end (and recalling the expansive analysis in Weiler's first collaborative EUI 1986 project,
*Integration through Law*) a non-state *Community* or *Union* is always about
sustaining the balance between the One and the Many, the polity cannot
swing too far before that balance is deemed broken. Yet while such an
equilibrium is certainly inherently unstable, Weiler may have underestimated the durability of this particular union that is the EU.

## 'Transformation'

In my view, the argument ought to start around the dual nature of 'transformation' in the EU as both incremental ('evolution') and radical ('revolution'). The latter obtains when we use a democratic theory lens, and stems
from the innovative character of the polity in the making rather than the
degree of change imposed on each familiar category (e.g., 'sovereignty
transfers' or 'delegation'). To the extent that transformation continues to
eschew a mimetic logic from the state to supra-state, or from international
law to domestic law writ-large, then a 'transformational logic'[9] constitutes a
radical departure. Much of EU legal theory inspired by *The Transformation
of Europe* has been about the ways in which the EU's legal order calls for
a transformation of reigning legal paradigms rather than mere conceptual

[8] R. D. Kelemen, 'Built to Last? The Durability of EU Federalism', in S. Meunier and K. R.
   McNamara (eds.), *Making History: European Integration and Institutional Change at Fifty*
   (Oxford: Oxford University Press, 2007), 51.
[9] R. A. Dahl, *Democracy and Its Critics* (New Haven, CT, and London: Yale University
   Press, 1989).

tweaking, as with the constellation of variants on the idea of constitutional pluralism.[10] Nevertheless, we can doubt whether the EU can ultimately be faithful to the spirit of Dahl's third 'transformation of democracy', one that would also revolutionalise the EU's social order rather than only relying on its already revolutionary institutional foundations.[11]

But if we turn to an international relations frame and to the prehistory of Weiler's historical exploration, claims about transformation are grounded on a different ontology, a departure point that is the non-state-like, non-hierarchical structure that is the international system. In this reading, the EC third way was born from the belief held by moderate federalists that power politics could be *transformed* in Europe without *transcending* the state system itself – in contrast with federalist schemes like EDC and even ECSC. Albeit necessary to tame nationalism, supranationalism would be instrumental and regulative, not ontological. Behind Monnet, administrative planers united across Europe to seek administrative economies of scale *within*[12] and colonial economies of scale *without*.[13] So, from an international relations view point, we can argue that it is indeed incrementalism which set in motion Europe's transformation: that is the institutionalisation of balance of power through the Community method as a far cry from the 'radical federal' projects floating around in the postwar era. But this in turn opened a space within which a most radical legal, institutional, and political transformation could take place.

The virtue of a conversation about the meanings of transformation is that it is first to free us from arguments from original intent including originalist obfuscation based on the myth-making function of much of the writings by and about the 'founding fathers'. Instead, the story of the equilibrium thus set in motion has much to do with unintended consequences following from a collective purpose to fine-tune the vague peace ideal into specific forms of political 'togetherness'. If what followed was a series of experimental steps which only gradually revealed a compass[14] then the very nature of the project is *ateleological*: 'doing

---

[10] G. de Búrca and J. H. H. Weiler (eds.), *The Worlds of European Constitutionalism* (Cambridge: Cambridge University Press, 2012).

[11] Dahl, *Democracy and Its Critics*; J. Bohman, *Democracy across Borders: From* Demos *to* Demoi (Cambridge, MA: MIT Press, 2007); K. Nicolaïdis, 'European Demoicracy and Its Crisis', *Journal of Common Market Studies*, 51, 2 (2013).

[12] P. L. Lindseth, *Power and Legitimacy* (Oxford: Oxford University Press, 2010)

[13] K. Nicolaïdis, B. Sèbe, and G. Maas (eds.), *Echoes of Empire, Memory, Identity and Colonial Legacies* (London: IB Tauris, 2015).

[14] See introduction of Weiler, *The Constitution of Europe.*

before being' in the vein of continental existentialist philosophers. The 'community' spirit may have been plagued by the taken-for-grantedness of its original purpose of 'peace and prosperity' calling, in Weiler's view, for grounding the project in political values sustained by individual virtues. But I would submit that the transformative challenge is in a way more ambitious as it relies on a kind of pluralist bet: that the complex and deep social structure underpinning integration in Europe is progressively creating a space where conflict about the implications of 'togetherness' can take place not only through deliberation, but also through contestation and even ultimately peaceful self-exclusion. Isn't this the spirit of constitutional tolerance? The bet can be won if our political imagination enables us to recover the open-ended and transnational nature of *transformation*.[15]

In sum, a combination of incremental and radical transformation holds the key, I believe, to the meaning of 'equilibrium': the initial *incremental* transformation of the state system on the European continent, the subsequent transformation of the legal-political order thus created through the transformation of European nation-states into EU member states, and the *radical* but incomplete transformation of their democracies in the process.

## *'Equilibrium'*

In line with Weiler's 1999 call to explore the empirical variations on and threats to the foundational equilibrium,[16] some scholars believe that the original historic diagnosis, is just that, a function of its times, superseded *inter alia* by what they see as a more expansive transformative logic through the power of legalism (Kelemen and Lindseth, this volume). Others emphasise the continued resilience of the equilibrium, the conservative nature of transformation.[17] The very fact that each side can make a plausible case may be telling us something important, namely, that two logics that used to be mutually balancing come into tension, risking stretching the pendulum too far.

---

[15] J. Lacroix and K. Nicolaïdis (eds.), *European Stories: Intellectual Debates on Europe in National Contexts* (Oxford: Oxford University Press, 2010).

[16] Weiler, *The Constitution of Europe*.

[17] A. Moravcsik and K. Nicolaidis, 'Keynote Article: Federal Ideals vs Constitutional Realities in the Amsterdam Treaty', *Journal of Common Market Studies*, 36, Annual Review (1998), 13-38.

With the first camp, we can ascertain the various ways in which the EU has indeed superseded the foundational equilibrium through QMV in particular, but without creating the kind of disruption Weiler feared. In spite of the partial loss of state 'voice', the EU remained remarkably stable throughout the 1990s and most of the 2000s thanks to the entrenchment of its constitutional order through the 'Europeanisation' of domestic legal and regulatory systems. Such entrenchment was also the result of the priority granted to market integration combined with a fragmented institutional structure which generated political incentives to issue detailed and judicially enforceable rules framed as 'rights' backed with the threat of publicly and privately enforced litigation.[18] At least until the financial crisis, core constituencies within the member states were sufficiently powerful to define the 'national' position in ways congruent with the kind of supranational legalism that was originally conditioned on the kind of political control of the legalisation process Weiler analysed in *Transformation*. Legal functionalism seemed self-sustaining, acting as a solvent for constitutional boundaries insofar as politicians and their ideologies remained complicit in this game.

It is precisely this legalisation dynamic which Weiler denounces of late as a 'formalist self-referential concept of the rule of law'.[19] The 'immense power of self-governance' afforded by the combined doctrines of direct effect and supremacy has allowed a process of expansion of rules precisely framed as 'individual rights' to obfuscate the fundamentally skewed impact that such rights may have on the distribution of the costs and benefits of integration among European citizens. It may be that supranational law was always bound to create disruptive effects, putting the interests of 'nomads' before those of 'settlers' and that this was a good thing, indeed the Union's very purpose of intertwining. But the more what is thus served are perceived as 'private' *interests* opposed to 'public' *good*, the more socially unsustainable they become. When rules-as-rights come to supersede deeply seated social rationalities, as Joerges would put it, the large sways of populations who find themselves outside the benign value-creating impact of market integration are prone to reject all 'movers' and indeed sacrifices incurred in the name of integration.[20] In this sense, the

---

[18] R. D. Kelemen, *Eurolegalism: The Transformation of Law and Regulation in the European Union* (Cambridge, MA: Harvard University Press, 2010).

[19] Weiler, 'Deciphering the Political and Legal DNA of European Integration, 137–58.

[20] C. Joerges, 'Integration Through Law and the Crisis of Law in Europe's Emergency,' in D. Chalmers, M. Jachtenfuchs and C. Joerges (eds.), *The End of the Eurocrat's Dream* (Cambridge: Cambridge University Press, 2016).

socialising of private risks during the sovereign debt crisis is an extension of the same logic.

On what grounds, then, should we believe in the capacity of the Union to adapt, indeed, reinvent some version of the equilibrium along the way? Arguably, (re)balancing need not depend on some providential 'loyalty' *a la* Hirschman's but rather on a kind of meta-equilibrium whereby both law and politics come to better internalise the balancing constraint of the other side: law correcting its own penchant for uniformity, states correcting their own penchant for ignoring externalities. This in turn implies considering the political agency of the social, outside classic aggregative political structures. If so, the triangle between law, politics, *and* society remains under-theorised.

Much of the legal scholarship (including Weiler's) has shown that the original constitutional compromise between EU competence and member states' autonomy could be sustained through a subtle interaction between EU law making and CJEU jurisprudence sensitive to 'the perils of Unity' brought about by unreflexive legalism. Arguably for instance, much of the internal market jurisprudence has avoided addressing regulatory burdens to free movement by reducing regulatory diversity, seeking instead the same result by changing the baseline in conflict of laws to the country-of-origin jurisdiction, and then, crucially, retreating from the extreme version of such a choice, on a case-by-case, sector-by-sector basis, grounded on the constructive ambiguity of words like 'legitimate' or 'proportional' regulations.[21] Flirtation with the Unity paradigm in secondary law-making and enforcement may thus be subject to difficult interpretation as to what constitutes the 'writing on the wall', hints or decisive moves. In my view, the six-pack legislation of 2012 aimed at enforcing EMU rules on national economies has crossed the fine line between financial crisis management and the engineering of convergence for its own sake.

When it comes to the Treaty-making realm, whether the decade-long attempt at formal constitutionalisation (adopting an actual Constitution) was indeed an attempt to cross the line between the promise of *Union* and the perils of *Unity* is mute, at least for the time being. The question that remains is whether the conceptual apparatus offered by the scholarship on constitutional pluralism and the praxis it is meant to capture succeeds

---

[21] K. Nicolaïdis, 'Trusting the Poles, Mark 2: Towards a Regulatory Peace Theory in a World of Mutual Recognition', in I. Lianos and O. Odudu (eds.), *Regulating Trade in Services in the EU and the WTO: Trust, Distrust and Economic Integration* (Cambridge: Cambridge University Press, 2012).

in fully operationalising the constraining virtues of Weiler's constitutional tolerance.[22] A powerful pluralist argument can be made that the constitutional paradigm, however amended to embrace the non-hierarchical nature of the EU polity, simply cannot accommodate the kind of deep diversity characterising the social-political realities of our the current era.[23] Any form of formal constitutionalism, in this view, comes to adopt overarching norms, like subsidiarity, meant to direct the solution of conflicts or the contribution of each level, to the coherence of the overall order. In contrast, systemic pluralism calls for the decentralised management of diversity all the way down, mutual accommodation without guidance except for perhaps from the self-limiting virtue which comes from the permanent possibility of contestation and the impossibility to freeze deals imposed by the powers of the day.[24] Such pluralist arguments go a long way in grounding normatively the case against *Unity* in the EU. But they may not entirely serve the *Union* paradigm insofar as they rely overwhelmingly on the social third leg of the triangle, overlooking the question of the political per se. If, on the contrary, the *Community* or *Union* is one of peoples whose self-determination is channelled primarily through their own liberal democratic states as well as secondarily through their myriads of modes of citizenship allegiance to the Union, then systemic pluralists echo constitutionalists, by painting a politically impoverished world where 'movements', 'forces', and 'networks' have replaced *la place publique* of territorially constituted peoples. To ascertain the fate of Weiler's equilibrium in today's EU, we need to come back to the transformation of the member states and the way they manage their democratic interdependence.[25]

Can there be much doubt that, even when veto-less, the member states have continued to direct the EU show over the past twenty-five years? And that this matters to citizens? There are clearly many ways in which 'voice proxies' have served to maintain some version of Weiler's equilibrium. Institutionally, the collective reassertion of state power alongside supranational legality over the past decade has been remarkable, including in the

---

[22] Weiler, 'Federalism and Constitutionalism, *op cit.*
[23] R. Howse and K. Nicolaïdis, 'Legitimacy through "Higher Law?" Why Constitutionalizing the WTO Is a Step Too Far,' in T. Cottier, P. C. Mavroidis, and P. Blatter (eds.), *The Role of the Judge: Lessons for the WTO* (Bern: The World Trade Forum, 2002), Volume 4.
[24] N. Krisch, Beyond Constitutionalism: the Pluralist Structure of Postnational Law (Oxford: Oxford University Press, 2010).
[25] C. J. Bickerton, *European integration: From nation-states to member states.* (Oxford: Oxford University Press, 2012).

crowning of the European Council as the institutional apex of the EU in a constitutional convention presumably dominated by parliamentarians.[26] Moreover, enlargement has not meant an abandonment of 'consensus democracy' suggesting that the equilibrium can cope with the pressures from scale;[27] and the (now headless) rotating presidency remains a tool of small state balancing. Moreover, the EU machinery increasingly balances an *inter*-governmental with an inter-*state* logic. Arguably, that states *qua* states sustain their structural involvement in supranational institutions through informal modes of governance and national fiefdoms can constitute a more effective voice than voting mechanisms.[28] The real concern with the kind of transnational interventionism brought about by the financial crisis is less with the reassertion of state power – which in truth had never disappeared – than with the incapacity of governments to involve in their horizontal dealings political and crucially *social* forces beyond temporary majorities, as well as the disregard of legal supranationalism for the fundamental value of state autonomy.

To be sure, when proxies for voice have been found wanting, member states have perfected the recourse to 'negotiated' partial exit as long as they find it in their collective interest to let each other do so – as illustrated most spectacularly in the context of EMU. Paradoxically, that differentiated integration has become so prevalent of late may be less a sign of fragmentation than of a commitment to legality. This may mean in turn that we will need to analyse more systematically the sustainability of another sort of meta-equilibrium between different version of the voice-exit continuum, operationalised by different groupings of states. Ultimately, we may still question the *de facto* feasibility of the highly symbolic 'exit clause' introduced by the Lisbon Treaty, but the very fact that the exercise of this option has now become part of mainstream electoral templates may mean that bargaining 'in the shadow of exit' will serve as a voice proxy in the EU political landscape.

In the end, the more profound problem in the EU today is not that of disenfranchised governments in Brussels, but that of discredited governments at home. The currency of power inside the EU is no longer between

---

[26] P. Magnette and K. Nicolaidis, 'The European Convention: Bargaining in the Shadow of Rhetoric', *West European Politics* (April 2004).

[27] R. Dehousse, F. Deloche-Gaudez, and O. Duhamel, *Elargissement – Comment l'Europe s'adapte* (Paris: Presses de Sciences Po, 2006).

[28] M. Kleine, *Informal Governance in the European Union: How Governments Make International Organizations Work* (Ithaca, NY: Cornell University Press, 2013).

big and small countries or even creditor and debtors, but between the haves and have nots of self-ascribed political virtues like openness, a divide which in turn threatens the kind of political mutual recognition which underpins the *Community* or *Union* paradigm. The euro crisis has stretched the potential for EU transformation *within* its parameters to its limits. But we must refrain from wholly inferring from emergency management the shape of things to come.

### 3   Transformation as Democratic Mutation

The question of the democratic anchoring of the EU has become both the deepest source of Europe's current malaise and the potential source of its most transformative promise yet. Weiler's express preoccupation twenty-five years ago with the lack of democratic foundation for the EU was prescient and the key to grounding the promise of *Union* against the perils of *Unity*. If the development of majoritarian legislative authority combined with the granting of competences to bodies with limited capacity to deliver on the expectations created by such competences was the root of the problem then, this gap has been dramatically amplified by the management of the euro crisis. And Weiler's argument at the time that such gap would not be bridged by further empowering a body like the European Parliament or adopting democratic recipes borrowed from statehood is certainly more relevant than ever, although the EP is now entrenched in the Union's democratic landscape. But alternative albeit partial solutions are at hand which did not present themselves twenty-five years ago. This is where the transformative promise lies.[29]

For one, whether or not fears of EU pre-emption of national autonomy and democratic self-government will turn out to be warranted in the long run, we have started to witness a 'democratisation of national vetoes' through referenda, parliamentary action, and, ultimately, national electoral processes. But it will take more than a respect for such democratic vetoes to sell the EU's democratic credential to increasingly sceptical publics. The idea of European demoicracy is meant to translate the regulative principles of constitutional tolerance and mutual recognition at the heart of *Community* into the language of democracy.[30] It is meant to provide a

---

[29] K. Nicolaïdis and R. Youngs, 'Europe's Democratic Trilemma', *International Affairs* (November 2014).

[30] K. Nicolaïdis, 'We the Peoples of Europe', *Foreign Affairs*, 83, 6 (2004); K. Nicolaïdis, 'The Idea of European Demoicracy', in J. Dickson and P. Eleftheriadis (eds.), *Philosophical Foundations of European Union Law* (Oxford: Oxford University Press, 2012); Nicolaïdis, 'European Demoicracy and Its Crisis'.

normative benchmark both to defend the EU-as-is against a statist reading that would pin EU democracy to the mast of classic legislative-executive designs and to criticise the EU for its lack of democratic ambition. In this light, the EU's transformation has created the legal-institutional foundation for the EU as a demoicracy, but the latter depends and builds on a fragile yet sustained equilibrium. While the imperative was and still is not to cross the Rubicon and change the EU's political nature from voluntary to coercive association, this leaves us with quite a margin of manoeuver. This Rubicon is a large river and its shores – the political orders of 'unity' and 'anarchy' on either side – are not clear lines in the sand. As an open-ended process of transformation, Europe's demoicracy in the making may yet be saved from continued elite capture by the horizontal and fluid nature of the new 'crowd-sourced' politics of the twenty-first century.

This is in my view the paradigm that should inspire democratic renewal in the EU today consistent with *Union* rather than *Unity*: a demoicratic system, focused on a) the European respect for as well as rescue of national democratic processes, avoiding the drift from technocratic recommendations to supranational democratic pre-emption; b) a supranational consensus democracy resting on the equal ownership of EU decisions by states and citizens; c) and above all a true transnational ambition towards the progressive maturing of European citizens inspired by the virtues of transnational mutuality and capacity to own others' plights and democratic traditions.

If we are to get there, however, Europeans need to call the bluff of those politicians and pundits whose messianism continues to reflect a long-standing elite continental tradition of conceiving democratic politics as a means to a particular end, rather than embracing the 'untidiness' of pluralist political liberalism as an ethos in and of itself. Hopefully, European citizens will thus reinvent a new kind of European idealism affirming that *convergence, homogeneity, and Unity* by stealth has now run its course. Hopefully, they will instil existing EU institutions with such an ethos. If not, the fallout from the crisis will be to shatter the social and political contract at the heart of the late twentieth-century European project of *Community* or *Union*.

# 11

# Unity and Community: A Tale of Two Monsters and One Unanswered Question

ALEXANDER SOMEK

### Thank You, Massimo!

It must have been shortly before Austria's accession to the European Union in 1995 that I had taken it upon myself to study its legal system. I began reading a book that offered a short introduction. Its author was a former fellow student of mine who had made a remarkable career in the foreign office. His work offered a quite sensible introduction to the sources and structures of European Union law. What I encountered was, nonetheless, surprisingly off-putting. The law of the Union appeared to me as Ulrich Haltern would describe it only a few years later: an assemblage of lifeless texts, 'empty shells with no roots', dissociated from the evolution of a political community.[1] It all appeared haphazard to me, as a product of change and circumstance rather than of grand designs. From the pillar structure all the way down to the exposition of the co-decision procedure, I felt reminded of the most insufferable quarters of administrative law or commercial law. Not a trace of constitutional ideals, not even the cosmopolitan spirit of public international law. All that I encountered was the grey in grey of bureaucracy.

Fortunately, at about the same time that I tried to find my bearings in Union law, I agreed to participate in a conference in Graz, Austria, which was attended by my friend and colleague Massimo LaTorre. Over lunch I described to him my experience with studying European Union law and implored him to help me find something appealing. He replied by asking me whether I had read any of Joseph Weiler's writings. I had to pass since I had never heard the name before. 'Would there be anything else?' I asked, and Massimo replied, 'No, there is just Weiler.'

---

[1] See U. Haltern, 'Pathos and Patina: The Failure and Promise of Constitutionalism in the European Union', *European Law Journal*, 9 (2002), 19–38.

Such exclusiveness intrigued me. This is how I discovered *The Transformation of Europe* and began viewing the Union from the perspective of political philosophy.

In what follows I would like to engage with the article's concluding observation concerning the unity and the community vision. It goes to the heart of Weiler's contention that supranationality is a new and defensible form of human association. As much as I wanted to believe his claim upon first encounter, I sense that experience has in the meanwhile taught us that there are reasons for doubt.

## Unity and Community Vision

The concluding sections of *Transformation* observe that after 1992, Europe will no longer be able to steer clear of ideological controversy; more so, it will also have to capture its own ethos. While it took roughly another fifteen years for ideological conflict to become salient in instances such as the Takeover or the Service Directive,[2] the question concerning Europe's ethos became sadly eclipsed by the constitutionalisation spectacle and the Union's insatiable geopolitical appetite for growth.

As is well known, in his own attempt to determine this ethos, Weiler distinguishes between the unity and the community vision.[3] While the unity vision remains faithful to the dream of a European federal state, the community vision aspires to something different. While Weiler is still somewhat struggling with articulating this different vision in *Transformation*, the major themes, which are going to be unpacked in subsequent writings, are already in place. Weiler claims that, as a community, Europe is based on the 'self-limitation' of its constituent units and their readiness to struggle continuously with a 'new discipline of solidarity'. Far from superseding states, the Union qua community involves them in an 'increasing', however uneasy, embrace.[4] The practice of limiting, pooling, and sharing sovereignty is the most salient mark of such international communitarianism. The supranational

---

[2] For an account, see M. Höpner, 'Eine neue Phase der europäischen Integration: Legitimitätsdefizite europäischer Liberalisierungspolitik', in M. Höpner and A. Schäfer (eds.), *Die Politische Ökonomie der europäischen Integration* (Frankfurt aM: Campus Verlag, 2008), 130–56.

[3] See J. H. H. Weiler, *The Constitution of Europe: "Do The New Clothes Have an Emperor?" And Other Essays on European Integration* (Cambridge: Cambridge University Press, 1999), at 90–1.

[4] See ibid., at 93.

entity is not supposed to replace the state, but merely to complement and to 'tame' it.

The community vision, as expounded in *Transformation*, nonetheless perceives states from an international perspective. The Member States no longer figure as independent sovereign actors, but appear to be interdependent elements of a larger whole. This international communitarianism, which has in the meanwhile become the tiresome darling token of 'constitutionalists' in international law,[5] is ever more intriguing, however, when examined from below, that is, from the perspective of nations. It was in subsequent writings that Weiler tried to explain more thoroughly how the community vision is linked to the full realisation of nationality. We are told, then, that a supranational entity is supposed to rescue the nation from its asphyxiating embrace by the state. Such an ethos suggests, indeed, that the Union is to serve, rather than supersede, nationality.

## Behemoth: Boundary Abuse

This is a sophisticated idea. It begins with recognising that nations provide each of us with a social home and make us special without being aloof. But since much libidinous energy is invested in national pride, nations are prone to give rise to oppression. The means thereto is the state, which Weiler casts in the position of the Behemoth, the monstrous land animal.[6] Seduced by its prowess, nations succumb to evil. When fused with state power, nations engage in violent conquest, appropriate culture for ideological ends, or discriminate against others out of a misguided sense of superiority.

Establishing a supranational entity is an attempt at avoiding these ills. Indeed, in a manner reminiscent of pre-modern constitutional discourse, Weiler asserts that 'supranationalism aspires to keep the values of the nation-state pure and uncorrupted.'[7] The interposition of institutions that make nations yield to one another preserves what is good about nations

---

[5] For a recent introduction, see S. Wheatley, *The Democratic Legitimacy of International Law* (Oxford: Hart Publishing, 2010), 163–210.

[6] As is well known, the monsters Behemoth and Leviathan make their appearance in the Book of Job 40, 15–24, and 41, 1–34. Thomas Hobbes used the name 'Behemoth' as the title for his historical dialogues on the history of the English civil war, apparently in order to avail of a signifier that was ambiguous enough to designate the Church of England, the Roman Catholic Church, and the Long Parliament. See P. Seaward, 'General Introduction', in P. Seaward (ed.), *Thomas Hobbes, Behemoth, Or The Long Parliament* (Oxford: Oxford University Press, 2010), 1–70 at 64.

[7] Weiler, *The Constitution of Europe*, supra note 3, at 250.

while holding their unruly ambitions in check.[8] In other words, supra-nationality is the nation's mode of developing a superego so that states become capable of behaving responsibly. Responsible states, that is, do not abuse their boundaries – neither territorial lines nor limits vis-à-vis civil society. Supranational discipline takes away the means of aggression, roots out discrimination, and weakens the power of intervention in the social sphere. When the state becomes weaker, the nation can flourish. More so, when a supranational arrangement is effective, aggressive national prejudice is taken out of personal dealings. People come to experience and to respect one another as 'others'.

### Leviathan: Abuse or Existence?

This is, in a nutshell, Weiler's reconstruction of the community ethos. It is quite impossible not to be taken with it at first impression. Unwittingly, however, it partakes of an ambivalence that is written into the genetic code of the Union.

Let me begin with Weiler. The ambivalence is revealed in the course of his normative rejection of the unity vision. It would be 'more than ironic', he says, if an entity created to contain the ills of statehood were to grow into a 'superstate'.[9] Little progress would have been made if at the end of the day the 'us' were European and the 'them' those outside the Union.[10]

The concern articulated here is that a reintroduction of boundaries would be inconsistent with the community vision. Surreptitiously, the national ill alters its shape. It no longer appears to be the *abuse* of the boundary in contrast to its mere existence; most surprisingly, the very *existence* of the boundary seems to constitute the abuse.

---

[8] For an excellent document that explains how a mixed constitution accomplished the objectives of preserving the good aspects of its constituent units while checking their ills, see King Charles I, 'Answer to the Nineteen Propositions of June 18, 1642', in J. P. Kenyon (ed.), *The Stuart Constitution 1608–1688*, 2nd edition (Cambridge: Cambridge University Press, 1986), 19–20. For a recent resuscitation of this idea, see J. McCormick, *Machiavellian Democracy* (Cambridge: Cambridge University Press, 2011).

[9] A note on semantics is in order here. Our culture does not have much of a problem with identifying 'superstars', selecting 'supermodels', celebrating 'superman', and pursuing the ambition of being a 'superpower'. Even the supernatural incites gripping anxiety. By contrast, the 'superstate' gives European Union scholars the creeps. When it comes to the state, 'super' is not better. This bespeaks a characteristically liberal anxiety. The state is a necessary evil. This much is conceded. But a 'superstate' would bring only evil.

[10] Weiler, *The Constitution of Europe*, supra note 3, at 95.

Whether one or the other is inconsistent with the community vision is the unanswered question.

Remarkably, this unanswered question is not merely a gap in Weiler's theory. It is a social fact. More precisely, the question *appears* to be left unanswered while in many cases the answer is given *tacitly* against boundaries as such. Hence, it is a social fact that the European Union sustains, on the surface, a certain level of openness with regard to what is to become of boundaries while below this surface these same boundaries are incessantly under attack. Weiler's work is, however unwittingly, part of the social reality that it purports to describe.

The tacit answer to the unanswered question explains why the Union – even though by virtue of its own territorial growth always tempted to behave as the Behemoth – has turned out to be such a colossal Leviathan.[11] The latter, as is well known, is a sea monster. The sea is the element in which commercial empires realise their existence (apologies to Hobbes for an obvious Schmittianism, but Schmitt was, despite being obnoxious, also a learned man).[12] Commercial empires transcend boundaries through colonisation or, more peacefully, through creating zones of economic interpenetration. While the Behemoth lurking underneath the unity vision strives for enlargement, the Leviathan of the community vision gobbles up boundaries.

Per my remarks that follow, I should like to explain in which respect the unanswered question reveals the *true* ethos of the community vision and why, dialectically, the unity vision therefore retains its appeal. The question remains at which level political boundaries have to be established in Europe.

### Yes, I *Can* Be More Specific

The legal form of fundamental freedoms lends to the unanswered question its social appearance: is what matters the abuse of existing boundaries or is their sheer existence already an abuse?

---

[11] I am, of course, using the contrast between the two monsters differently than Franz Neumann, who used the Leviathan as a symbol for the state and the Behemoth as symbol for the non-state and a situation of lawlessness. See F. Neumann, *Behemoth: The Structure and Practice of National Socialism 1933–1944*, 3rd edition (New York: Octagon Books, 1963).

[12] See C. Schmitt, *Land und Meer: Eine weltgeschichtliche Betrachtung* (Leipzig: Philipp Reclam jun., 1942).

It all begins with protection from discrimination on the grounds of nationality.[13] This is indeed consistent with pre-empting boundary *abuse*. Political boundaries among nations may be maintained so long as they are not used to confer an unfair advantage on your own folk.

The obstacle approach takes the examination of boundaries one step further. It focuses on inhibitions of commercial flows that arise *systematically* from the very co-existence of nation-states. The co-existence of different nations is deemed a problem (and not the premeditated abuse of a political power to exclude). The existence of boundaries constitutes the abuse unless it can be shown that measures taken by the national authorities satisfy the principle of proportionality. Passing the proportionality test *indirectly* reaffirms the boundary. As a result, the boundary no longer is a given. No longer do boundaries reflect the existence of the national polity. Rather, in their reaffirmed form they signal the presence of a regulator that is capable of effective problem-solving. It does not matter whether a nation-state is doing the regulating. Cast in Hegelian terms, boundaries are 'sublated' into the wider sphere of European public reason, that is, the reasons sufficient to sustain market intervention regardless of who is actually in charge of it.[14] Not surprisingly, the regulations that survive the Court's scrutiny may legitimately become a target of harmonisation. The existence of boundaries turns out to be the problem that needs to be addressed.

The sublation of boundaries is followed by a reversal of their thrust. Originally, public power exercised within a political space is insuperable. In the course of their reconstitution on the basis of European public reason they can be transformed into vehicles for the cunning exercise of private power. The Union's variety of economic substantive due process[15]

---

[13] On the following, see my brief reconstruction of the form of fundamental freedoms in A. Somek, *Engineering Equality: An Essay on European Antidiscrimination Law* (Oxford: Oxford University Press, 2011), at 47–50.

[14] On the loss of concreteness implicit on 'sublation', see the perspective comments by S. Žižek, *The Sublime Object of Ideology, 2nd edition* (London: Verso, 2008), xiv–xv.

[15] The description 'economic substantive due process' designates a period in the history of the application of the Fourteenth Amendment of the American constitution that protected 'freedom of contract' vis-à-vis state regulation that pursued social objectives. See *Lochner v. State of New York*, 198 US 45 (1905). For different perspectives on the significance of this case in American constitutional history, see B. Ackerman, *We the People*, vol. 1: *Foundations* (Cambridge, MA: Harvard University Press, 1991), at 63–6; A. R. Amar, *The American Constitution: A Biography* (New York: Random House, 2005), at 475; M. J. Horwitz, *The Transformation of American Law 1870–1960: The Crisis of Legal Orthodoxy* (Oxford: Oxford University Press, 1992), 9–31.

endorses boundaries inasmuch as they help to facilitate liberalisation and to put pressure on states to converge on business-friendly standards. Economic substantive due process introduces the portability of relatively more business-friendly laws into the jurisdiction of one's choice. You create a company in A but do business in B, thereby avoiding application of local company law. *Centros*[16] and *Cartesio*[17] may come to mind. The boundary poses a problem for those with a craving for more economic liberty. But Union law eliminates the boundary's exclusionary effect. B has to accept A-style companies. Boundaries are turned against themselves. At best, they are transformed into markers of variety that may well be sustained in order to enhance the menu of options.[18] They become commodified. No longer are they a manifestation of the sovereignty of the state.

Finally, institutions of 'social market economies'[19] – corporate governance structures and industrial relations – have come under attack by Court and Commission. Countries with Anglo-American philosophies have escaped censure while others experience pressures to adapt.[20] Boundaries are threatened with erasure where they matter the most, namely, when it comes to the institutions that embed markets into a larger social background.

The conclusion that needs to be drawn from these developments is that already with the endorsement of the obstacle approach the boundaries themselves have been under attack. That the existence of boundaries is the problem is the *tacit* answer to the unanswered question. It remains latent not least because boundaries continue to play an important role in the commodified format of economic substantive due process. Nevertheless, sublation and commodification are the means by which Leviathan, who 'esteemeth iron as straw, and brass as rotten wood',[21] emerges victorious over Behemoth.

---

[16] Case C-212/97 *Centros Ltd. v. Erhvervs- og Selskabsstyrelsen* [1999] ECR I-1459.
[17] Case C-210/06 *Cartesio Oktató és Szolgáltató bt* [2008] ECR I-000000.
[18] See S. Deakin, 'Two Types of Regulatory Competition: Competitive Federalism versus Reflexive Harmonisation. A Law and Economics Perspective on Centros', *Cambridge Yearbook of European Legal Studies* (1999), 231–60.
[19] On the simplification involved in using this term in the context of the varieties of capitalism, see F. W. Scharpf, 'The Double Asymmetry of European Integration, Or: Why the EU Cannot Be a Social Market Economy', 09/12 *MPIfG Working Paper* (2009).
[20] See M. Höpner and A. Schäfer, 'A New Phase of European Integration: Organized Capitalism in Post-Ricardian Europe', 07/4 *MPIfG Discussion Paper* (2007).
[21] Job 41, 27.

Our German friends would likely reply to my observations that none of these examples demonstrates that Union law is incapable of drawing a line between abuse and existence. On the contrary, the line is drawn all the time with the aid of the proportionality principle. Where regulations pass muster, the boundary is reaffirmed.

But this is an optical illusion, which is created by the application of a public law standard. It casts all problems as problems of an 'abuse' of state power, even where the problem concerns the *existence* of boundaries. Taking a closer look at the obstacle approach reveals the distortion. State A may have more stringent standards than state B. The proportionality principle says that A's standard is unnecessarily restrictive and that from now on A needs to recognise the standard of B. Using an unnecessarily restrictive standard, however, is not tantamount to abusing a boundary. If the standard sweeps too broadly it simply diminishes liberty as understood by liberalism.[22] The use of an unnecessarily restrictive standard can be taken to be *boundary* 'abuse' only if a norm says that the less restrictive standard of the country of origin is to be given precedence. The underlying norm introduces a presumption in favour of economic liberty as a result of which *national differences* are experienced as requiring a justification. Hence, in every single instance the *existence* of the national boundary is at stake vis-à-vis transnational liberty. Existence is cast as an 'abuse' of state power.

## The Stranger: Client of the Unanswered Question

The tacit answer to the unanswered question remains latent. The Member States do not disappear. The boundaries are only intermittently overridden in the interest of those availing themselves of the benefits of mobility.

It is in this context that one realises that the communitarianism among states – the nice image of the Union as an international community – is not replicated at the individual level. The clients of supranationality are individuals for whom others are strangers.[23] The Union is the place where the small-cap other is respected as the large-cap Other. This is unsurprising. The type of place where people encounter one another as strangers is a market (and not a polity). They remain unknown to one another – large-cap Others – because the relationship is abstract.[24]

---

[22] Liberty as understood by liberalism is liberty qua absence of impediments to motion. See Q. Skinner, *Liberty before Liberalism* (Cambridge: Cambridge University Press, 1998).

[23] See Weiler, *The Constitution of Europe, supra* note 3, at 343.

[24] See A. Sohn-Rethel, *Warenform und Denkform* (Frankfurt aM: Suhrkamp, 1978), at 114.

While the existence of political boundaries is notoriously suspect of constituting abuse, the clients of the community vision enjoy the benefits of a liberalism without nations. It is the type of liberalism where the question can be *left open* whether individuals are conjoined by common sympathies.[25] The Union liberates a transnational civil society – a system of needs and mutual dependence[26] – from the confines of the state.

From the perspective of this zone of unencumbered encounters, what states offer to nationals are services. The recurrent question is, therefore whether such services should be available to all regardless of nationality.[27] The *corpus mysticum Europaeum* is composed of individuals busying themselves with the pursuit of individual projects. The smarter specimens among them have fully internalised the maxims of self-improvement and self-management.[28] Those who are not self-activating are eligible to benefit from the Union's efforts to 'empower' individuals.[29] The Union is right for those who are active and smart. Its legal order assists them in extracting their activities from the social context in which they take place. Sadly, this does not look at all like rescuing the nation from the embrace of the state. It looks more like dumping the nation from the template of the market.

## From Liberalism without Nations to the State without Sovereignty

What remains of the state once one tames the state in the Bodinian and Hobbesian sense? This question admits of a simple answer: the most important component of the state in the Weberian sense.

---

[25] See F. A. von Hayek, *Individualism and Economic Order* (Chicago: University of Chicago Press, 1948).

[26] This is the classical nineteenth-century understanding of civil society. See G. W. F. Hegel, *Elements of the Philosophy of Right*, trans. H. B. Nisbet (Cambridge: Cambridge University Press, 1991), at § 189, at 227.

[27] Not surprisingly, this has become a very prominent theme of the jurisprudence on European citizenship. See, for example, C. Barnard, *The Substantive Law of the EU: The Four Freedoms, 2nd edition* (Oxford: Oxford University Press, 2008), at 430–41.

[28] See M. Foucault, 'Governmentality', in his *Power*, J. D. Faubion (ed.), trans. R. Hurley et al. (New York: New Press, 2000), 201–22; B. Cruikshank, *The Will to Empower: Democratic Citizens and Other Subjects* (Ithaca, NY, and London: Cornell University Press, 1999).

[29] See European Commission, 'Consumer Empowerment in the EU', http://ec.europa.eu/consumers/consumer_empowerment/docs/swd_consumer_empowerment_eu_en.pdf. See also the study prepared by the Bureau of European Policy Advisers, which is part of the Commission bureaucracy, titled '*Empowering People, Driving Change: Social Innovation in the European Union*', http://ec.europa.eu/bepa/pdf/publications_pdf/social_innovation.pdf.

What Weiler has come to analyse so brilliantly under the name of 'infranationalism'[30] is Weber's *rationale Staatsanstalt* (rational state-organisation)[31] upgraded to the twenty-first century. Infranationalism is all about administrators talking to other administrators and listening to well-informed private actors. Within a multilevel system, manifestations of this state in the Weberian sense can be encountered everywhere. It is a more perfect embodiment of administrative rationality that has outgrown the confines of legality because it no longer generates legitimacy. Effective regulation is supposed to do the job. It is all about sound economic policy along with a high standard of consumer, health, and environmental protection.

Again, just as there is a link between the tacit answer to the unanswered question and the clients of supranationality, there is a link between the liberalism without nations and the state without sovereignty. What individuals for whom political self-determination has become too cumbersome really want is sound expertise, reliable risk management, resolute crisis management, and protection of their civil rights. They demand a type of administrative self-monitoring that is adapted to the complexities of a transnational economy. It does not have to be law. It could be management, too.[32]

Surprisingly, in this light, the 'beyond the state' mantra turns out to be rather idle. What one encounters beyond the state is the same that one encounters within the state, namely, the state in charge of the rational administration of things. Beyond and below the nation, the state continues to be a state. The Leviathan of the twenty-first century does not offer protection in exchange for obedience;[33] it provides incentives in order to stimulate activities that might find reward on markets.

One can easily dispense with sovereignty when one no longer governs. States appear then like monarchies with an incompetent monarch. Metternich once memorably remarked that Austria was not governed,

---

[30] See J. H. H. Weiler, 'Prologue: Amsterdam and the Quest for Constitutional Democracy', in D. O'Keeffe and P. Twomey (eds.) *Legal Issues of the Amsterdam Treaty* (Oxford and Portland: Hart Publications, 1999), 9–19.

[31] See M. Weber, *Wirtschaft und Gesellschaft: Grundriss der verstehenden Soziologie*, J. Winckelmann (ed.), 5th edition (Tübingen: Mohr, 1976), 29, 825–43.

[32] See, most recently, C. F. Sable and J. Zeitlin, 'Experimentalism in the EU: Common Ground and Persistent Differences', *Regulation & Governance*, 6 (2012), 410–26.

[33] See C. Schmitt, *Der Begriff des Politischen* (Berlin: Duncker und Humblot, 1963), at 53, who took the idea from Hobbes.

but administered. It may be time to study history and to rethink what we mean when we say 'governance without government'.

The community vision is consistent with the emancipation of administration from politics.

## Nozick Lives

The founders of the European communities believed that the type of organisation that they were about to create would cure the ills of the nation-state. But they did not act on this belief in an institutional vacuum. I guess that it must have been understood by the founders that the national welfare state had to play a key role in keeping aggressive nationalist movements at bay.

The problem of nationalism, then and now, is not the frenzied appropriation of state power by ethnic groups, but rather how fellow-feeling can fuel mass support for authoritarian governments. It can have many causes, not the least of which are social cleavages and the enduring impression of disempowerment.

Aside from Stalinism, militarism and fascism have been the great curse of the twentieth century. The juxtaposition of nation and state is far too abstract in order to capture one root of the problem, namely, the absorption of parts of the working class and the petty bourgeoisie by mobilising passions that combine a religious obsession with the purity of the group with the licence to use any means, including violence, for the sake of collective self-assertion.[34] Historically, nothing is more dangerous for Europe than voters turning away from the more temperate designs of social and Christian democracy.[35] The Union may not have contributed to the decline of these ideologies, but it has done nothing to halt the recrudescence of authoritarian nationalism. Sadly, it is now part of the normal situation: Haider (R.I.P.), Le Pen, Orban.

The erosion of its Christian social and social democratic ethos is perhaps Europe's most pressing problem. Undoubtedly, the Union's liberalism without nations has benefitted from its demise. As is well known, the Euro crisis gave rise to a governance structure that is strangely reminiscent of

---

[34] See R. O. Paxton, *The Anatomy of Fascism* (New York: Vintage Books, 2004), at 41, 219.

[35] See, generally, T. Judt, *Ill Fares the Land* (New York: Penguin Press, 2010). See also A. Somek, 'The Social Question in a Transnational Context', *LSE European Institute Working Paper*, www2.lse.ac.uk/europeanInstitute/LEQS/LEQSPapers.aspx.

what Hermann Heller described in the 1930s under the name of authoritarian liberalism.[36] Governments take charge of maintaining a 'healthy economy' even against the resistance of their peoples.[37] Sustaining inequality is achieved in tandem with austerity. It seems as though the Union has done its bid to assist modern capitalism in withdrawing from its historical truce with democracy.[38]

It is to be feared, however, that an entity without boundaries cannot protect ordinary people against the perceived necessities of fiscal and economic stabilisation. The only model of justice that can be realised in a polity without boundaries is a model that comprises the Nozickian principles of justice in acquisition, transfer, and rectification.[39] Rejecting closure is a high-minded idea. But in practice, it means abdicating social responsibility. Worse still, it speaks niceness to a libertarian anti-statist ideology. It seems as though we have to realise now that supranationality as an ideal provided a comforting veneer covering a harsh world where capitalism is hijacking democracy. It was able to perform this ideological role because even the most elaborate conception presented by Weiler shied away from answering the unanswered question while a tacit answer exists in practice. Arguably, abuse is what should have mattered. But what supranationality amounted to in practice was the repeated overriding of the boundaries' existence. What disappears, concomitant to boundaries, is political control.

## Unity

Where the market is in charge of distribution it does not matter, legally, if people go away after they have made their gain or whether they decide to spend part of their earning on charity. With regard to the latter, they are free, for example, to donate vast amounts of money to an opera house while an appreciable number of their fellow citizens lack heat and adequate nutrition. In fact, engraving the donor's name on the face of this or that building rewards such generous gestures. This type of reward is

---

[36] See H. Heller, 'Autoritärer Liberalismus?' (1933), reprinted in *Gesammelte Schriften*, vol. 2 (Leiden: A. W. Sijthoff, 1971), 643–53. See the contribution by M. Wilkinson, forthcoming in *German Law Journal*.

[37] See C. Schmitt, 'Starker Staat und gesunde Wirtschaft' (1932), reprinted in idem, *Staat, Großraum, Nomos. Arbeiten aus den Jahren 1916–1969*, G. Maschke (ed.) (Berlin: Duncker & Humblot, 1995), 71–85.

[38] See W. Streeck, 'The Crises of Democratic Capitalism', *New Left Review*, 71 (2011), 5–29.

[39] See R. Nozick, *Anarchy, State, and Utopia* (New York: Basic Books, 1974), at 150–5.

usually not forthcoming for paying one's taxes. Libertarianism caters to the most individual of all human interests, namely, the desire to rise above mortality.

Any conception of justice that wishes to move beyond a mere libertarian framework requires boundaries. The effectiveness of distributive justice presupposes mandatory contributions and the absence of incentives to evade responsibility. Realising solidarity requires centralisation or, heaven forbid, unity.

From the perspective of Europe's most enduring problem – the social question[40] – boundaries are not the problem. They are necessary in order to arrive at a solution. The existential question confronting the Union is where the relevant lines will be drawn. Will the Union matter more than the states? Or are the units that provide protection going to reassert their priority?

Be that as it may, today Weiler's community vision must appear to us like a noble dream. It is a witty intellectual testament to a period when the European integration process was so successful that it even seemed to give rise to new philosophical ideas.

Even though that's all over now, not least owing to the dazzling brilliance of its author, Weiler's conception of supranationality is highly likely to find a lasting place in the annals of European intellectual history.

---

[40] See T. Judt, 'The Social Question Redivivus', in his *Reappraisals: Reflections on the Forgotten Twentieth Century* (New York: Penguin Books, 2009), 411–32.

# 12

# How Transformative Is the European Project?

### TÜRKÜLER ISIKSEL

Professor Weiler's seminal 1991 essay poses two bold, enduring questions.[1] Can we view European integration as a transformative project? And if so, has it achieved the transformation it set out to achieve? The questions are deceptive in their simplicity, not least because *transformation* is a notoriously inconstant metric. The difficulty of grasping the nature of transformative politics might explain why the topic has inspired so much philosophical reflection. Emblematically, Jean-Jacques Rousseau opens *Of the Social Contract* with a promise to investigate whether 'taking men as they are and laws as they can be made to be, it is possible to establish some just and reliable rule of administration in civil affairs'.[2] Though Rousseau betrays this promise almost as soon as he makes it, it might as well be the mantra of contemporary political science: we believe that through shrewd institutional design, we can sustain cooperation among political actors who espouse disparate values, persuasions, and motives. Following Robert Wokler, I will call this the Procrustean view of political transformation, because its horizons are truncated by a modest sense of the possible.[3] Accordingly, our reformist ambitions must conform to what

---

[1] J. H. H. Weiler, 'The Transformation of Europe', *Yale Law Journal*, 100 (1991), 2403–83.

[2] J. Rousseau, *The Social Contract and the First and Second Discourses*, S. Dunn (ed.) (New Haven, CT: Yale University Press, 2002), Preface to Book I, at 155.

  The ambition voiced by Rousseau is symptomatic of modern European political thought rather than transformative: Before him, Machiavelli prided himself in tending to the 'effectual truth of things' rather than 'imaginary republics and monarchies'. Similarly, Hobbes premised the *Leviathan* on an accounting of man as a complex circuit of appetites and aversions, which he proposed not to rewire, but to surround with the right kind of institutional insulation.

[3] In referring to Procrustean and Promethean approaches to political transformation, Wokler seeks to capture two distinct ways of construing 'the relation between human nature and politics'. According to Wokler, those who espouse a Procrustean approach are 'inclined ... to believe that there are inescapable features of human nature which governments must somehow both control and accommodate'. By contrast, the Promethean attitude tends 'to suppose human nature malleable or perfective and governments, correspondingly, as at least potentially capable of improving their subjects'. Thus, according to Wokler, 'Ancient

is given to us in the world. We do not need to transform citizens; we only need good laws and institutions.

It is ironic that such a prudent maxim should be articulated by Rousseau, whose own social contract has been taken to task for requiring a great deal more than merely good laws. Above all, critics argue, the Rousseauian social contract calls for a wholesale moral rehabilitation of human nature, particularly as Rousseau understands the latter.[4] In Rousseau's words,

> He who dares undertake to give institutions to a nation ought to feel himself capable, as it were, of changing human nature; of transforming every individual, who in himself is a complete and independent whole, into part of a greater whole ... of altering man's constitution in order to strengthen it.[5]

It is precisely because he does not expect ordinary mortals to pull off such Promethean feats that Rousseau wheels out the sublime figure of The Legislator whose own origins are, alas, never fully specified.[6] For who can give laws that 'change human nature' without himself being subject to the frailties of human nature? This approach to political transformation contrasts sharply with the Procrustean one insofar as its horizons extend beyond the existing world of human institutions, propensities, and desires.[7]

Is the transformation treated in Professor Weiler's eponymous essay of a Promethean or Procrustean sort? How far does the European integration

---

constitutions, like those of Lycurgus for Sparta and Solon for Athens, as well of course as of Moses for the Jews, were conceived as predominantly Promethean gifts of divine inspiration brought by great legislators to man. Modern constitutions, like the Federalists' for America, have been more sharply tailored for a close fit to human nature, more Procrustean.' See R. Wokler, 'Democracy's Mythical Ordeals: The Procrustean and Promethean Paths to Popular Self-Rule', in G. Parry and M. Morran (eds.), *Democracy and Democratization* (New York: Routledge, 1994), 38–42.

[4] Most notably, J. N. Shklar, *Men and Citizens: A Study of Rousseau's Social Theory* (Cambridge: Cambridge University Press, 1969). For a contrasting view, see R. Wokler, *Rousseau* (Oxford: Oxford University Press, 1995).

[5] Rousseau, *The Social Contract*, Book II, Ch. 7, 181.

[6] '[H]ow would a blind multitude, which often knows not what it wishes because it rarely knows what is good for it, execute by itself an enterprise so great, so difficult, as a system of legislation? By themselves, the people always desire what is good, but do not always discern it ... the public must be taught to understand what they want. Then from the public enlightenment results the union of understanding and will in the social body; and from that the close cooperation of the parts, and lastly, the maximum power of the whole. Hence arises the need of a legislator.' ibid, Book II, Ch. 6, 180.

[7] Wokler, 'Democracy's Mythical Ordeals'.

project aspire to alter the political landscape from which it arose? How far has it, in fact, altered it? These questions frame my short reflection. I will argue that both *The Transformation of Europe* and the transformation of Europe oscillate between two tendencies,[8] one transformative and the other circumspect, reaching for one without quite letting go of the other.

## Three Visions of *Finalité Politique*: Unity, Community, Sovereignty

*The Transformation of Europe* draws a deep and lasting contrast between two competing visions of European integration, which Professor Weiler terms the 'unity' and 'community' models. The transformative quality of each of these models is thrown into high relief when considered against a third model, which is the *ex ante* of European integration: an unruly, mutually distrustful batch of states packed into a dense continent, each concerned to further their national interests. According to what I will refer to as the default 'sovereigntist' attitude, the selling point of supranationalism is that it promises to supply member states with auxiliary 'problem-solving' capacity in unwieldy policy domains. At the outset, then, European integration was designed to appeal to states as nothing more than 'an arrangement, elaborate and sophisticated, of achieving long-term maximization of the national interest in an interdependent world.'[9]

Competing visions of European integration can either work around the sovereigntist attitude or try to transform it. Here, the 'unity' and 'community' models each offer up different answers. In Professor Weiler's formulation, unity denotes the forging of a comprehensive supranational polity through the gradual withering away of national political institutions and the assimilation of salient national particularity. Proponents of the unity model hope for a 'United States of Europe' conceived in the traditional statist mould; that is, they see a 'full political union' on the continental scale as the *finalité politique* of integration.[10] By contrast, the community vision entails 'limiting, or sharing sovereignty in a select albeit growing number of fields' without dissipating it altogether.[11] On this view, shared sovereignty is no mere *modus vivendi*; to the contrary, it is a transformative ideal that demands, in Weiler's words, 'a

---

[8] In this chapter, *The Transformation of Europe* will refer to Professor Weiler's 1991 essay. The same phrase without italics will refer to the historical process itself.
[9] Weiler, 'The Transformation of Europe', 2481.
[10] Ibid., 2479.
[11] Ibid., 2479.

type of self-limitation in [states'] self-perception, a redefined self-interest, and hence, redefined policy goals'.[12] It is guided by a principled commitment to creating a composite and variegated 'community of states and peoples sharing values and aspirations'.[13]

Although unity may seem at first glance like the more far-fetched of the two alternative scenarios for the transformation of Europe, Professor Weiler argues that the community vision is more imaginative, riskier, and perhaps more utopian than unity, which merely scales up the familiar statist blueprint. By contrast, the community model rejects enforced uniformity. Instead, it would create a supranational political sphere that must simultaneously pursue two tasks that are in tension with one another, serving both as a counterweight to, and a guardian of, the diverse and distinct national communities of Europe.[14] The community model does not ultimately aim to 'extinguish' the national self but sets out to rehabilitate, or, in Professor Weiler's terms, 'civilise' or 'tame' it through 'new modes of discourse and a new discipline of solidarity'.[15] While unity would replace one kind of state with another, community seeks to alter the reflexes, discursive structures, and self-perceptions of sovereign states. More than this, it requires patient reconstruction and de-essentialisation of our ideas about the nature of political community.

As Professor Weiler has noted in *The Transformation of Europe* and subsequent writings, the community vision entails a perpetually unresolved tension between universalistic values and national particularity. While many post-war federalists hoped for a sudden epiphany on the part of European nation-states that would eliminate this tension for good in favour of European unity, Jean Monnet opted for prudent incrementalism. The success of the transformative project would depend not on the superhuman virtue of a Rousseauean lawgiver, but on the maintenance of a quotidian discipline of togetherness by member states and supranational institutions. As the Schuman Declaration famously put it, 'Europe will not be made all at once.... It will be built through concrete achievements which first create a de facto solidarity'.[16] The very fact that

---

[12] Ibid., 2480. See also K. Nicolaïdis, 'European Demoicracy and Its Crisis', *Journal of Common Market Studies*, 51, 2 (2013), 351–69; F. Cheneval and F. Schimmelfennig, 'The Case for Demoicracy in the European Union', *Journal of Common Market Studies*, 51, 2 (2013), 334–50.

[13] Weiler, 'The Transformation of Europe', 2479.

[14] Ibid., 2480.

[15] Ibid.

[16] Robert Schuman, *Declaration of 9 May 1950*.

the phrase 'founding fathers', borrowed from American constitutional lore, translates uneasily into the European context is because Monnet, Schuman, Spaak, Spinelli, et al. were pragmatists rather than prophets.[17]

Although the European project was designed to be compatible with the traditional calculus of national interest, however, the project itself was never intended to stop at 'de facto solidarity'. If it had, we would not consider its ambitions transformative. In addition, the regimen of supranationalism was meant to sublimate the belligerence and egoism of nation-states without abolishing either the nation or the state. What Professor Weiler terms the 'community model' has a Promethean aspect insofar as it requires imagining a new, composite form of political ordering with a distinctive ethos. Like an Aristotelian virtue, supranationalism would initially be practised by member states out of self-regarding motives. Through sustained engagement in collective decision-making, however, member states would acquire a universalist orientation in their exercise of public power. The core of the transformative ambition of supranationalism is therefore to rework the idea of self-interest – and indeed the very idea of self – by expanding member states' scope of moral concern to include a community of peers.[18] In other words, the ambitions of incremental integration went beyond mechanically harnessing or containing the sovereigntist impulse. Rather, the aim was to cultivate a new form of political obligation whose source would be neither passion nor interest[19] but a deliberate, reasoned commitment on the part of nation-states and their citizens to abide by shared political principles and norms of reciprocity.

## 'Really Existing' Supranationalism: Calibrating Exit and Voice

The transformative thrust of Professor Weiler's community model is tempered by his attention to the dynamics that gradually expanded the scope

---

[17] One self-styled prophetic figure in the *dramatis personae* of European integration is Valéry Giscard d'Estaing, whose Philadelphian project – alas – fell embarrassingly short of its bombastic billing.

[18] In this sense, supranationalism entails a sense of what Hannah Arendt called the 'enlarged mentality' and what Tocqueville called 'self-interest well-understood'. In the *Transformation of Europe*, Professor Weiler alludes to the New England township, presumably with Tocqueville in mind. See Weiler, 'The Transformation of Europe', 2469.

[19] To borrow another well-known dichotomy of Albert Hirschman's. See A. O. Hirschman, *The Passions and the Interests: Political Arguments for Capitalism before Its Triumph* (Princeton, NJ: Princeton University Press, 1977).

of supranational governance in Europe. Although member states had allowed themselves to become enveloped in a dense web of supranational norms and institutions by the 1990s, this did not mean that they had been cured of their crude sovereigntist impulses. Rather, Professor Weiler's explanation draws on Albert Hirschman's incentive-based scheme that analyses the dynamics of organisational membership predominantly in terms of exit and voice.[20] Professor Weiler argues that member states allowed the ECJ to gradually tighten the fabric of supranational law (i.e., raise the costs of 'exit') in the founding period not because they had left their selfish motivations behind, but because they regarded their interests as being sufficiently protected by the power of veto (i.e., amplified 'voice') they retained in the formal legislative processes of the Community. This involved a relatively modest transformation, a process by which the ever-extending arm of supranational law created an equilibrium between exit and voice in the Community structure.

Nonetheless, Professor Weiler worried in 1991 that with the expansion of Community competences, the return of qualified majority voting, and the Court's stringent enforcement of legal obligations, the supranational structure was becoming claustrophobic for member states. Subsequent rounds of treaty-making have allayed some of these concerns by recalibrating the equilibrium between exit and voice, thereby implicitly reaffirming the primacy of these dynamics. For instance, the Lisbon Treaty introduced a *de jure* exit option in the form of a provision for member state withdrawal from the Union, which the United Kingdom has recently decided to exercise. However, Professor Weiler noted that the exit dynamic is also manifest in 'selective' and negotiated participation in a 'multi-speed Europe', Europe of 'variable geometry', or 'Europe à la carte'. This outcome sharply contrasts with the ECJ's endless exhortations for a uniform Community legal order.[21]

---

[20] One often-overlooked detail in this context is the subtitle of Hirschman's book, which underlines Hirschman's concern with making sense of '*decline* in firms, organizations, states'. This adds to the Owl of Minerva feel of Professor Weiler's 1991 essay. By zeroing in on the dynamics of exit and voice in the EU, as many contributions in this volume do, we are perhaps looking for ways to forestall its decline. A. O. Hirschman, *Exit, Voice, and Loyalty: Responses to Decline in Firms, Organizations, States* (Cambridge, MA: Harvard University Press, 1970).

[21] For an account that highlights the discursive role of appeals to uniformity, effectiveness, and legal certainty in the jurisprudence of the Court of Justice, see M. de S. -O. -l'E Lasser, *Judicial Deliberations: A Comparative Analysis of Transparency and Legitimacy* (Oxford: Oxford University Press, 2004).

In addition to expanding exit options, the EU has also become institutionally more multi-vocal as its competences and public profile have grown. Thanks to multiple rounds of enlargement and the widening of the Union's policy repertoire, what Professor Weiler termed Europe's 'constitutional conversation'[22] has been joined by many more voices. Moreover, member state representation is no longer the exclusive purview of national executives represented in the Council, if it ever was. En route to '[controlling] the excesses of the modern nation-state',[23] European supranationalism has to some extent disaggregated the state into its component institutions and units.[24] For the most part, when national political institutions and supreme courts foray into the European dialogue, they do so to air their concern that the EU (and often, the Court of Justice in particular) is traversing the constitutional limits it once promised to respect.[25] Anxieties over *Kompetenz-Kompetenz*, national constitutional identity, and democratic autonomy have drawn national supreme courts into an ever-louder chorus of protest against the ECJ's still resolutely federalist baritone.

It remains a matter of controversy whether greater institutional contestation confers greater legitimacy on EU decision-making by drawing upon the 'legitimacy resources'[26] of member states, or whether it creates a centrifugal dynamic that could unravel the supranational enterprise. I leave this question open. What I would like to emphasise, however, is that however they are institutionalised, neither of these two dynamics (exit or voice) requires going beyond the basic assumptions of the sovereigntist model. If what is still keeping the Union together is a canny arrangement of carrots and sticks, safety valves and patch-ups, opt-outs and side payments, then more than sixty years of integration have not been that transformative, or at least not in the way that its founders had hoped.

---

[22] J. H. H. Weiler, 'European Neo-constitutionalism: In Search of Foundations for the European Constitutional Order', *Political Studies*, 44, 3 (1996), 517–33, at 532.

[23] J. H. H. Weiler, *The Constitution of Europe* (New York: Cambridge University Press, 1999), 250.

[24] Many see the disaggregation of the state as a wider trend in world politics. See J. Mathews, 'Power Shift', *Foreign Affairs*, 76, 1 (1997), 50–67; A. Slaughter, *A New World Order* (Princeton, NJ: Princeton University Press, 2004).

[25] Professor Weiler pointed to *Van Gend en Loos* as furnishing the origins of a 'judicial-constitutional contract' that for decades kept the peace between the supranational judiciary and national supreme courts. See 'The Transformation of Europe', 2451.

[26] P. L. Lindseth, *Power and Legitimacy: Reconciling Europe and the Nation-State* (Oxford: Oxford University Press, 2010), at 11.

## Loyalty: The Missing Element of the Community Alchemy

Hirschman writes that when an organisation disappoints its members, 'loyalty holds exit at bay.'[27] In the European context, loyalty entails a long-term commitment on the part of member states and their citizens to stick with the supranational project even when it fails to deliver the goods. Although the Monnet method of integration had asked states to buy into nothing that they could not cash out of, it did so in the hope that their pragmatic transfers of sovereignty would accumulate into political allegiance over time.

In his essay, Professor Weiler gave a circumspect assessment of the extent to which supranationalism had succeeded in modifying the parochialism inherent in national sovereignty.[28] The primordial or affective sources of political allegiance on which member states draw (what Professor Weiler calls 'Eros') are unavailable to a polity organised along the lines of the community model. For this reason, normative scholarship on European integration has latched onto constitutionally driven and constitution-sustaining forms of loyalty as the best we can hope for in the supranational context.[29] In contrast to observers such as Jürgen Habermas,[30] David Held,[31] or David Beetham,[32] however, Professor Weiler's work is far less sanguine about whether the EU can engender its own democratic public or piggyback on domestic structures of legitimation.

---

[27] Hirschman, *Exit, Voice, and Loyalty*, 77.

[28] Weiler, 'The Transformation of Europe', 2465–6.

[29] The most well-known proponent of this position is Jürgen Habermas, whose idea of uniting Europe by fostering a sense of constitutional patriotism was for a time influential on academics and policy-makers alike. In his writings of the 1990s, Habermas sought to show that a European constitution would play a 'catalytic' role in creating a vibrant European *demos* capable of sustaining meaningful democratic opinion- and will-formation at the supranational level. Habermas argued that Europe needed a new 'legal institutionalization of citizens' communication' to foster a post-national 'ethical-political self-understanding' emancipated from assumptions of ethnic or cultural identity. '[T]he communicative network of a European-wide political public sphere embedded in a shared political culture' would be 'founded on a civil society composed of interest groups, nongovernmental organizations, and citizen initiatives and movements, and will be occupied by arenas in which the political parties can directly address the decisions of European institutions and go beyond mere tactical alliance to form a European party system'. J. Habermas, 'The European Nation-State: On the Past and Future of Sovereignty and Citizenship', in J. Habermas, *The Inclusion of the Other: Studies in Political Theory*, C. Cronin and P. De Greiff (eds.) (Cambridge, MA: MIT Press, 1998), 161, 153 respectively.

[30] Ibid.

[31] See, for instance, D. Held, 'Democracy and Globalization', in D. Archibugi, D. Held, and M. Koehler (eds.), *Reimagining Political Community* (Stanford, CA: Stanford University Press, 1998).

[32] See D. Beetham, 'Human Rights as a Model for Cosmopolitan Democracy', in ibid.

The failed constitutional moment of the early 2000s, the economic crisis that ensnared Europe for the better part of a decade, and the fever of Euroskeptic populism that has yet to break appear to vindicate these misgivings. Whereas grave continental crises in the past might have renewed rather than diminished faith in the European project, recent ones have revitalised the state-centred utility calculus, making the ideals of unity and community seem like noble yet naïve illusions of yesteryear. Whereas the Schuman Declaration had promised that a 'fusion of interest' would overcome 'sanguinary divisions', there is reason to fear that interests can become unfused much more rapidly than they are fused, and that it was perhaps gratuitous to assume that the fusing of interests would lead to a redirection of allegiances. In sum, the pragmatic dynamic of exit versus voice continues to be prominent in shaping the course of European integration while loyalty, whether as a citizen or elite attitude towards European integration, has made only modest headway.

In his 2005 book, Giandomenico Majone, a steadfast proponent of a contained, apolitical, and unsentimental approach to integration, threw down the gauntlet for principled *communautaires*: 'nobody has yet convincingly explicated the value-added of a European federation – what it might realistically do that could not be achieved by less far-reaching commitments.'[33] That Majone's challenge has so far largely gone unmet highlights the paucity of public and scholarly confidence in the transformative ambition of the European project. At sixty years' remove, the European project calls to mind Alasdair MacIntyre's allegory of the forgotten civilisation:[34] Even though supranational institutions have endured, they have lost the symbolic and cultural background against which they made sense. During the initial decades of European integration, citizens who had lived through Europe's grim internecine conflicts understood that the significance of economic integration went well beyond giving them access to cheap imports. The gradual fading of the rich ideal of a supranational community has left us with a market-inflected scheme of cooperation that vacillates between crude national sovereignty and an equally crude form of instrumentally rational cooperation. As a result, of the three 'founding ideals' of European integration enumerated by Professor Weiler, namely, peace, prosperity, and

[33] G. Majone, *Dilemmas of European Integration: The Ambiguities and Pitfalls of Integration by Stealth* (Oxford: Oxford University Press, 2005), vi.
[34] A. MacIntyre, *After Virtue: A Study in Moral Theory* (South Bend, IN: University of Notre Dame Press, 1984), 1-2.

supranationalism,[35] only prosperity resonates as a still-current value in European public discourse. Supranationalism is deeply unpopular, and the ideal of peace has mellowed into somnolence. Missing its once-robust normative core, what we are left with the institutional husk of the transformative ideal.

Elsewhere, Professor Weiler has extensively critiqued that loss of purpose. To take one example,

> The condition of Europe ... is not, as is often implied, that of constitutionalism without a constitution, but of a constitution without constitutionalism. What Europe needs, therefore, is not a constitution but an ethos and *telos* to justify, if they can, the constitutional order it has already embraced.[36]

Attempts to reconstruct the *telos* of European integration usually entail either an editorialized narrative of what the founding generation aimed at, or else an account of what supranationalism has to contribute to the contemporary configuration of political power. By contrast, the distinctive *telos* of Professor Weiler's idea of supranationalism is the promise of distancing the exercise of political power from parochial forms of cultural or ethnic belonging.

Although these aspirations are informed by the trauma of Europe's civil wars, supranationalism is also continuous with the tradition of modern constitutional revolutions that set out to curb the arbitrary exercise of sovereign power.[37] Insofar as it seeks to discipline the discretionary power of the nation-state vis-à-vis its 'others' (whether other states, foreigners, or domestic minorities),[38] supranationalism represents the most recent chapter in the history of the constitutional idea. What is therefore

---

[35] Weiler, 'Fin de Siècle Europe: Do the New Clothes Have an Emperor?'

[36] J. H. H. Weiler, 'European Neo-constitutionalism: in Search of Foundations for the European Constitutional Order', *Political Studies*, 44, 3 (1996), 517-33, at 518.

[37] In his classic study, Charles Howard McIlwain argues that constitutional rule originates in attempts to bring about the 'legal limitation on government' and denotes 'the antithesis of arbitrary rule'. C. Howard McIlwain, *Constitutionalism Ancient and Modern* (Ithaca, NY: Cornell University Press, 1940), 24.

[38] On this point, see C. Joerges and J. Neyer, 'From Intergovernmental Bargaining to Deliberative Political Processes: The Constitutionalisation of Comitology', *European Law Journal*, 3, 3 (1997), 273–99, at 294; M. Poiares Maduro, 'Sovereignty in Europe: The European Court of Justice and the Creation of a European Political Community', in M. L. Volcansek and J. F. Stack Jr. (eds.), *Courts Crossing Borders: Blurring the Lines of Sovereignty* (Durham, NC: Carolina Academic Press, 2005).

remarkable is not the present ubiquity of constitutional language, but its virtual absence up until the 1970s because, in a crucial sense, the European project was always a constitutional project *par excellence.*

This is not to say that every invocation of constitutional terminology in discussing European integration (or other super-national regimes) can carry this normative freight. Sometimes, that terminology is used merely to denote an institutional phenotype, a 'check list' of features that resemble a constitutional mode of political ordering.[39] At other times, the insistence that European law is not mere law, but law of a constitutional sort masks a transformative ambition (or wishful thinking). For instance, when the ECJ declared that the founding treaties furnish 'the constitutional charter' of the Community,[40] it did not merely rename existing reality but reframed it through a performative utterance. At the very least, it staked a claim to a new basis of authority for supranational law (although whether it can make good on that claim remains hotly contested).

### Beyond the Melian Dialogue: *The Transformation of Europe* as an Unfinished Epistemic Project

Although Professor Weiler graciously ceded credit for the constitutional thesis to Eric Stein,[41] *The Transformation of Europe* secured a bridgehead for constitutional scholarship in the study of European integration. During the 1990s, the European debate quickly adopted constitutionalism as a central category in debates about supranational political legitimacy. Since then, constitutional discourse has become the vernacular of studies on governance beyond the state.

Nonetheless, the pervasiveness of constitutional analysis is puzzlingly at odds with the dismal failure of the attempt to stage a Philadelphian 'constitutional moment' in Europe in the early 2000s. Why insist on constitutional language in academic scholarship if it failed to stick in the 'real world'?

---

[39] J. L. Dunoff and J. P. Trachtman, 'A Functional Approach to International Constitutionalization', in J. L. Dunoff and J. P. Trachtman (eds.), *Ruling the World? Constitutionalism, International Law, and Global Governance* (Cambridge; New York: Cambridge University Press 2009), 9.

[40] Case 294/83 *Partie Ecologiste 'Les Verts' v. Parliament* [1986] ECR 01339.

[41] See J. H. H. Weiler, 'The House that Eric Built', in J. H. H. Weiler, *The Constitution of Europe* (New York: Cambridge University Press, 1999), 225.

I suspect that the general penchant for constitutional discourse in accounting for post-national governance has something to do with epistemic empowerment. The terminological shift is symptomatic of the conquest of new territory for legal and political theory in the disciplinary turf war against classical international relations scholarship. Scholars of norms have seized on proliferation of transnational legal regimes to wear down the realist orthodoxy according to which only sovereign states and their capacity to exert violent force 'matter'.[42] Put differently, the language of constitutionalism offers traction for normative theory and legal scholarship in a domain where their insights have traditionally been dismissed as trivial and inapplicable at best, dangerous at worst.[43] It suggests that law, as a factual and normative category, can not only shape state 'behaviour', but can also help reconfigure the unquestioned categories (such as interest, preference, or power) on which international relations scholarship is built.

How long will the heyday of post-national constitutional thinking last? A note of caution might be in order. I argued earlier that part of the European project's transformative quality lies in the attempt to open up a new chapter in the history of the constitutional idea. But what exactly is transformative about constitutionalism if, as Jack Straw quipped, even golf clubs have constitutions? Before we rush to crown constitutionalism as the most apposite category for making sense of the 'post-national constellation',[44] therefore, we must first figure out how to deploy that idea without blunting its transformative edge.[45]

---

[42] As Waltz memorably put it: 'National politics is the realm of authority, of administration, and of law. International politics is the realm of power, of struggle, and of accommodation.' K. Waltz, *Theory of International Politics* (New York: McGraw-Hill, 1979), at 113.

[43] J. L. Dunoff, 'The Politics of International Constitutions', in *Ruling the World?* 204–5.

[44] To borrow Habermas' phrase.

[45] I suggest one way of doing this in T. Isiksel, *Europe's Functional Constitution. A Theory of Constitutionalism beyond the State* (Oxford: Oxford University Press, 2016).

# 13

## The Transformation of Europe: Loyalty Lost, Democracy Lost?

FRANZ C. MAYER

### I Introduction

Albert Otto Hirschman, born in 1915 in Berlin, a 'product of the Weimar republic'[1] who left his country in 1933, published *Exit, Voice, and Loyalty. Responses to Decline in Firms, Organizations and States* in 1970.[2] Twenty years later, Joseph Weiler used the concepts of Exit and Voice in *The Transformation of Europe* in order to reconstruct and analyse the first four decades of European integration. In his own words:[3]

> Exit is the mechanism of organizational abandonment in the face of unsatisfactory performance. Voice is the mechanism of intraorganizational correction and recuperation. [There is] a kind of zero-sum game between the two. ... A stronger 'outlet' for Voice reduces pressure on the Exit option. ... The closure of Exit leads to demands for enhanced Voice.

The Hirschmanian concepts are adapted to the EU context, though. The Exit option is being discussed in legal categories, Voice in political categories. One of the tricks Joseph Weiler uses here is that when it turns

---

[1] He died in December 2012. 'Exit Albert Hirschman: A Great Lateral Thinker Died on December 10th', *The Economist*, 22 December 2012. On his fascinating life – leading from Berlin to Paris, Italy, the Spanish Civil War, Berkeley, the US Army, Latin America, appointments at Yale, Columbia, Harvard, and Princeton, and back to Berlin, reflecting the turmoil of the twentieth century – see J. Adelman, *Worldly Philosopher: The Odyssey of Albert O. Hirschman* (Princeton, NJ: Princeton University Press, 2013), from whom I borrow the characterisation as 'product of the Weimar republic'.

[2] A. O. Hirschman, *Exit, Voice and Loyalty: Responses to Decline in Firms, Organizations and States* (Cambridge: Cambridge University Press, 1970).

[3] J. H. H. Weiler, 'The Transformation of Europe', *Yale Law Journal*, 100 (1991), 2403, 2411.

Chair of Public Law, European Law, Public International Law, Comparative Law, Legal Policy, Faculty of Law, University of Bielefeld, Germany, franz.mayer@uni-bielefeld.de. Parts of this text were presented at the conference in honour of Joseph H. H. Weiler on the occasion of his sixtieth birthday, Max-Planck-Institute for Comparative Public Law and International Law, Heidelberg, 1 September 2011.

out that total exit (unilateral Member State withdrawal from European integration) is not a helpful category,[4] he quickly moves on to selective exit: 'the practice of the Member States of retaining membership but seeking to avoid their obligations under the Treaty'.

Joseph Weiler introduces Hirschman's third notion, Loyalty, 'in a loose manner'.[5] Instead of destabilisation, he argues, it could also be that 'acceptance of Community discipline may have become the constitutional reflex of the Member States and their organs,' and, after two decades of enhanced voice, 'loyalty to the institution may have developed that breaks out of the need for constant equilibrium'.[6]

In *The Constitution of Europe* published in 1999, the second chapter contains an abbreviated version of *Transformation* with a new afterword.[7] The afterword is also about loyalty. It is not particularly optimistic. Loyalty, 'if it exists at all, is precarious, because there is a legitimacy dissonance between the constitutional claims of the polity and its social reality'.[8] This claim is backed up with different elements of evidence. The most important challenges, according to Joseph Weiler, are the challenges posed by general public opinion in several Member States, with Euroscepticism spreading. Europe, he says, is no longer part of a consensus: 'Politicians can no longer count on automatic approval of their architectural changes to Community and Union'; the current political processes of community governance offer 'a much less hospitable environment for the continued development or even the sustaining of the constitutional architecture. A new transformation is called for'.[9] That was in 1999. Needless to say that nearly twenty years later, with a view to the Euro crisis, the refugee crisis, and BREXIT, some of these observations appear to be everything but outdated.

---

[4] See Art. 50 TEU, introduced with the Treaty of Lisbon in 2009, though. The Polish Constitutional Court stresses that withdrawal ('exit') is one of the possibilities to deal with conflicts between EU law and national law arising out of the primacy principle, Case K 18/04 Accession Treaty, judgement of 11 May 2005, www.trybunal.gov.pl/eng/summaries/documents/K_18_04_GB.pdf. Following a referendum on the British exit from the EU ('BREXIT') on 23 June 2016, the British government submitted a letter triggering the procedure under Art. 50 TEU on 29 March 2017.

[5] Weiler, 'The Transformation of Europe', 2403, 2465.

[6] Ibid.

[7] J. H. H. Weiler, *The Constitution of Europe: 'Do the New Clothes Have an Emperor?' and Other Essays on European Integration* (Cambridge: Cambridge University Press, 1999), 96 et seq.

[8] Ibid., 99.

[9] Ibid., 101.

The concept of loyalty and the question of a democratic deficit are at the core of *Transformation*, and the two issues seem to be interrelated. What about loyalty (see infra, part II) and the democracy deficit (see infra, part III) today, and what does it all mean for EU law and EU law scholars (see infra, part IV)?

## II   What Happened to Loyalty?

Joseph Weiler considered loyalty to be precarious in 1999 already, in the afterword. At first glance, things do not seem to have improved since then. The test is whether acceptance of Union discipline has become the constitutional reflex of the Member States and their organs. With negative referenda in France, the Netherlands (2005), and Ireland (2008), and the rise of populist Eurosceptics in several countries, the challenges posed by general public opinion seem to be increasing. Many people read the German *Lisbon* decision[10] as an attack on European integration. And then the Euro crisis.

### 1   Examples of Loyalty

On the other hand, there may also be indications of the opposite: isn't the way the Eurogroup members accept the decisions and measures suggested to stabilise the Euro evidence for the loyalty reflex mentioned? And wasn't it the overwhelming majority of Member States that joined the Fiscal Treaty in 2012 after the Euro states had to turn to a solution outside the founding treaties because of the British? Sure, some Member States participate in these measures only grudgingly. Nevertheless: they do participate and help.

Some of the highest courts at the Member State level are displaying a remarkable calm and good timing for symbolic measures. The German Constitutional Court is not the best example here. But in 2013 the Austrian Constitutional Court, in a measured decision, stressed the difference and the border between law and politics in the Euro crisis.[11] Also in 2013, the French Constitutional Council submitted a preliminary reference to the ECJ for the first time in history.[12] Moreover, a closer look at

---

[10]  BVerfGE 123, 267 – *Lisbon*.
[11]  ÖVerfGH, SV 2/12–18, 16 March 2013 – *ESM decision*.
[12]  CC, 2013-314P QPC, 4 April 2013 – *Jeremy F.*

the recent decisions of the German Constitutional Court also leads to a more nuanced assessment even for this court. Sure, the 2009 *Lisbon* decision has its ugly parts where it insists on sovereignty as if Germany was the tiniest of all Member States, permanently marginalised and abused by the others.[13] But there is also the principle of *Europarechtsfreundlichkeit*. Difficult to translate ('EU law friendliness'), but it does have to do with loyalty to the European construct. The 2010 *Honeywell* decision[14] is even more explicit on this. The cause of this new constitutional principle, European integration friendliness, may be derived from the *Grundgesetz*, and not from EU constitutional law, but that does not matter in the present context.

Still, what about the more or less open and more or less credible threats by the *Bundesverfassungsgericht* to confront the European legal order head-on, using fundamental rights control (*Solange*), *ultra vires*-control, or identity control?[15]

## 2 Loyalty Is not about Faith

Here, it is helpful to go back to Albert O. Hirschman's conceptualisation of loyalty:

According to Hirschman, loyalty may be functional. Exit, Voice, and loyalty are about discontent with the way things are going, for example within an organisation. In Hirschman's words: 'That paradigm of loyalty, 'our country, right or wrong', surely makes no sense whatever if it were expected that 'our' country were to continue forever to do nothing but wrong.'[16]

---

[13] BVerfGE 123, 267 (346 et seq., 357) paras. 223 et seq., 248 et seq. – *Lisbon*. See on that F. C. Mayer, 'Rashomon in Karlsruhe: A Reflection on Democracy and Identity in the European Union,' *International Journal of Constitutional Law*, 9 (2011), 757.

[14] BVerfGE 126, 286 – *Honeywell*. See also F. C. Mayer and M. Walter, 'Die Europarechtsfreundlichkeit des BVerfG nach dem Honeywell-Beschluss', *Jura*, 33 (2011), 532.

[15] BVerfGE 37, 271 – *Solange I*; BVerfGE 73, 339 – *Solange II*; BVerfGE 89, 155 (188) para. 106 – *Maastricht*; BVerfGE 123, 267 (350) paras. 234 et seq. – *Lisbon*. See for a more recent example of 'turf defence' the German Constitutional Court's First Senate's reaction to ECJ, 26 February 2013, Case C-617/10, *Åklagaren v Åkerberg Fransson*, in BVerfG, First Senate, 1 BvR 1215/07, judgement of 24 April 2013 – Counter-terrorism Database, threatening to declare ECJ decisions *ultra vires*. See in that context F. C. Mayer, 'Defiance by a Constitutional Court – Germany', in A. Jakab und D. Kochenov (eds.), *The Enforcement of EU Law and Values: Ensuring Member States' Compliance* (Oxford: Oxford University Press 2017), 403 et seq.

[16] Hirschman, *Exit, Voice and Loyalty*, 78.

So there is an assumption of influence and improvement. This expectation, Hirschman writes, that over time the right turns will more than balance the wrong ones, profoundly distinguishes loyalty from faith.[17] Thus, the German Constitutional Court and many other players at the Member State level may not have faith in European integration. But there is loyalty. There should be.

## III  The Democracy Deficit

In *Transformation*, Joseph Weiler calls the democracy deficit 'a permanent feature of the Community'.[18] In a nutshell: hardening EC law (constitutionalisation) made it extremely difficult for national parliaments to control things at the national, implementing level, and an ex ante control proved largely not feasible. Taking a closer look, it was not exactly the Voice of the Member States that was enhanced, but the power of governments, the Voice of the executive branch. Where do we stand with this 'permanent feature'?

### 1  Scoundrels: Out!

An initial reflex is to say that today things are even worse than what *Transformation* anticipated. Consider the 'scoundrels argument', copyright Joseph Weiler: isn't it true that democracy is about throwing the scoundrels out – and in the EU it is still impossible to 'throw the scoundrels out',[19] still impossible to hold individuals responsible for European decisions, no matter how much the EP insists on its ever-increasing powers? This rather simple observation is difficult to argue away. Of course, it is a typical problem of multilevel polities that it is not that easy to detect who the actual scoundrels are.[20] But the perception of a European democracy deficit is just there, and it will not go away simply with a clever new theory of European democracy.

### 2  The National Parliaments' Role and the Factor Time

Still, things may be in a better democratic shape than expected. And this may be due to elements that are both addressed in *Transformation* already:

---

[17]  Ibid.
[18]  Weiler, *The Constitution of Europe*, 37.
[19]  Ibid., 329. See also K. Nicolaïdis, 'We the Peoples of Europe ..', *Foreign Affairs*, 83 (2004), 97.
[20]  See the joint decision trap literature by Scharpf and others in this context: F. W. Scharpf, 'The Joint Decision Trap. Lessons from German Federalism and European Integration', *Public Administration*, 66 (1988), 239.

the role of national parliaments and the factor time. Both elements have to be read together.

The first element is the role of national parliaments in upholding the democracy and legitimacy of European integration. *Transformation* is pessimistic on the abilities of national parliaments to make a meaningful contribution here. Surely, the provisions introduced by the Lisbon Treaty on the role of national parliaments, i.a. concerning subsidiarity control, may appear as some kind of constitutional law placebo to many people.

But looking closer, taking the example of Germany, there is more to it and there is a potential for further development. The German debate about the *Bundestag's* role in controlling the government's action in safeguarding the stability of the Euro is just the latest step in a development where a national parliament is increasingly building up capacities, expertise, and political sensitivity in order to be a European parliament, too. This development in part overrides political party affiliations with the president of the *Bundestag* confronting the chancellor, both members of the same political party. There may even be a potential for transforming or loosening the grip of political parties on the political process in Germany here.

This development does take time.[21] But *Transformation* already suggests that there has to be an 'adjustment period' for the new democratic settlement.[22] What if we still are in the middle or even at the beginning of that adjustment period?

## 3   The Subjective Side of Democracy: Perceptions

*Transformation* insists on social legitimacy, as opposed to formal legitimacy. It does not explain where social legitimacy comes from. Maybe social legitimacy is to a large extent about perceptions.

Isn't it striking that sometimes an institutional configuration is not questioned and accepted as democratic, whereas a similar institutional configuration elsewhere is challenged? Consider the legislative process in Germany, which involves an opaque committee, the *Vermittlungsausschuss*, coming in at the end of the process when there is a disagreement between federal government and the *Länder* (states), which in reality is often

---

[21] And there are backlashes; just consider the German Parliament's major *gaffe* when introducing an opaque, anti-democratic, obscure committee in order to deal with urgent Euro matters. The idea was struck down by the BVerfG, see BVerfG, Second Senate, 2 BvE 8/11, judgement of 28 February 2012 – '9er-Gremium' (nine-member committee).

[22] Weiler, 'The Transformation of Europe', 2403, 2471.

enough a disagreement between different political parties and not a genuinely federal conflict. Is this much more democratic than the law-making process at the European level? Probably not,[23] but the social legitimacy is there, some kind of trust that 'things are in order'. If this is an example of the power of perceptions, this raises the question: who is responsible for perceptions and for the social legitimacy?

One possible answer is: the media. The *Lisbon* proceedings in Germany were an example that illustrated how the media do not quite succeed in explaining the political process when it comes to European integration. With the Euro issue being even more complex and technical, the quality of media coverage was even more depressing: uninformed at best, pursuing their own agenda at worst.

Obviously, to blame the media alone would be too easy. Because even with a more comprehensive and less biased media coverage and a general level of knowledge of European affairs in the population, there would still be no difference in that fundamental flaw: beyond perceptions, it is difficult to affect European politics by a vote.

### 4  Democracy Deficit – the Wrong Debate: From Democracy Talk to Identity Talk

But the democracy debate may be the wrong debate anyway. Twenty-five years ago in *The Transformation of Europe*, Joseph Weiler pointed to all the issues that triggered the democracy deficit during the foundational period. Maybe it is time for Exit in this debate. It seems to me that I am not alone with the assessment that the democracy debate does not lead anywhere. The most visible indication of this, I believe, is the shift from democracy talk to identity talk. Increasingly, the defence of national identity seems to be the core issue. Consider Article 4 para. 2 TEU.[24] According to this provision, the European Union shall respect the national identities of the Member States. National identity includes constitutional identity, as it refers to 'fundamental structures, political and constitutional'.

The German Constitutional Court mentions identity in the context of national identity or national constitutional identity roughly thirty

---

[23] The evidence is that the German Constitutional Court strikes down decisions taken in that committee on a regular basis; see BVerfG, Second Senate, 2 BvR 758/07, judgement of 8 December 2009.

[24] There was an identity provision in the treaties before (Art. 6 TEU), but it was beefed up substantially in the Lisbon Treaty.

times in the Lisbon decision. The core statement is the following one: 'integration into a free community neither requires submission that is removed from constitutional limitation and control nor forgoing one's own identity.'[25]

Again: could it be that, to some extent, most people have given up on democracy at the European level? Isn't it striking that the democracy deficit arguments have been around for the past twenty years or so and they keep coming back, but there is no tangible progress in the debate?

Joseph Weiler wrote of the democracy deficit as a 'permanent feature' in *Transformation*. Well, there may be an understanding – maybe just a feeling – that there are limits to what can be achieved in terms of democracy at the European level. Hence, the turn to identity. With endless debates on a real or perceived democracy deficit not having had any significant effect on perceptions, despite all kinds of modifications of institutional settings and treaty text design,[26] identity may be the new central issue of European integration.

This shift is also a shift from a proactive attitude (reaching out for participation) towards European integration to taking a defensive attitude. Insisting on democracy at the European level means that you still want to be a part of the process, exercise control, and also shape the process. Safeguarding national identity, on the other hand, is a different approach, as it is defensive. It insists on a 'them and us' perspective.

This is not per se a problem. Joseph Weiler's concept of constitutional tolerance rests on the idea that you may accept difference:

> The alternative strategy of dealing with the alien is to acknowledge the validity of certain forms of non-ethnic bounded identity but simultaneously to reach across boundaries. We acknowledge and respect difference, and what is special and unique about ourselves as individuals and groups; and yet we reach across differences in recognition of our essential humanity. ... On the one hand, the identity of the alien, as such, is maintained. One is not invited to go out and, say, 'save him' by inviting him to be one of you. One is not invited to recast the boundary. On the other hand, despite the boundaries which are maintained, and constitute the I and the Alien, one is commanded to reach over the boundary and accept him, in his alienship, as oneself. The alien is accorded human dignity. The soul of the I is

---

[25] BVerfGE 123, 267 (347) para. 228 – *Lisbon*.

[26] Remember how Title VI of the Treaty establishing a Constitution for Europe displays that the Convention (or its president) got carried away, at times: 'The democratic life of [!] the Union'. Title II of TEU-Lisbon went back to a more sober style; it reads 'Provisions on Democratic Principles'.

tended to not by eliminating the temptation to oppress but by learning humility and overcoming it.[27]

Identity-related arguments are not very new in EU constitutional law. The identity issue, however, has gained new momentum with Member States' courts beginning to use the idea of national constitutional identity to build a bridge between European and national constitutional law.

The national identity mentioned in Article 4 TEU-Lisbon or in the *Lisbon* decision is *prima facie* not related to individual identity, referring primarily to some sort of collective identity, inter alia the identity of the national constitution.[28]

But obviously, the identity of an individual living in, say, Germany is not unaffected by a claim that there is such a thing as a national identity and a national constitutional identity. This is where a core issue of the democracy debate, the question of multiple *demoi*, comes back: can one belong to more than one polity? Probably yes, but national identity and national constitutional identity override any other kind of allegiance.

It is probably not a coincidence that identity as a topic of European constitutional law gains momentum at this time, at the beginning of the twenty-first century and with the Treaty of Lisbon.

One of the most important institutional novelties of the Lisbon Treaty, if not *the* most important one, considering the ever increasing number of Member States, is the introduction of qualified majority voting in many areas that, so far, were in the realm of unanimity. What can you do if you find yourself in a minority? Invoke national identity.

Then, there seems to be a link between national identity and sovereignty. Remember that ten out of twelve of the newest Member States plus Germany have gained full sovereignty at the beginning of the 1990s only. In these countries, which comprise more than a third of the EU population, the longing to define something that under no condition may be determined by 'outsiders' is probably (still) particularly strong.[29]

Finally, there has been a general debate on identity in several Member States, which was unrelated to European integration. In Germany, the

---

[27] J. H. H. Weiler, 'In Defense of the Status Quo: Europe's Constitutional *Sonderweg*', in J. H. H. Weiler and M. Wind (eds.), *European Constitutionalism Beyond the State* (Cambridge: Cambridge University Press, 2003), 7, 19.

[28] See CONV 375/1/02 REV 1 at 11 for the discussion on the identity clause in Working Group V of the European Convention.

[29] The ugly and malicious version of this legitimate perspective is the equation of the European Union and Soviet Union, suggested i.a. by Czech President V. Klaus, *The Times*, 20 February 2009.

question of 'Who are we?' led to a debate on the concept of *Leitkultur*.[30] In France, where the government sponsored a 'Grand débat sur l'identité nationale'[31] in 2009 and in the UK,[32] the debate on national identity is much more recent. One may add other states such as the Netherlands or Belgium.

What is the problem with national identity and the European constitutional order? Allowing the concept to have a substantial function in legal terms may turn out to be a Pandora's Box. Member States will be tempted to declare all kinds of issues to be part of their national identity in order to shield themselves from European law.

On the other hand, if the identity issue is dealt with within the framework of European law, i.e., by using the preliminary reference procedure and by establishing a constitutional discourse between the European level and the Member State level on a given identity issue, the concept may even help to pursue the aim of any multilevel polity: as much unity as necessary, as much multiplicity as possible.

In any event, holding up national identity may serve as a functional equivalent to what democracy used to be about: self-determination.

## 5    Re-establishing the Equilibrium?

In fact, all of this is reminiscent of what took place in the foundational period with the establishment of an equilibrium according to *Transformation*: selective Exit is increasingly blocked because of majority voting.

However, instead of leading to an enhanced Voice, this time, another way of selective Exit seems to have been found: invoking national identity could be read as a new selective Exit option. This interpretation of identity claims as selective Exit may not be plausible, though, if a unilateral invocation of national identity is not allowed, and if the identity claim is only possible as part of a process and a conversation that takes place between the highest courts of the Member States and the ECJ.

The *Bundesverfassungsgericht* in its *Lisbon* and *Honeywell* decisions and the ECJ in its *Sayn-Wittgenstein*[33] judgement seem to indicate that we are

---

[30] See S. Manz, 'Constructing a Normative National Identity: The Leitkultur Debate in Germany, 2000/2001', *Journal of Multilingual and Multicultural Development*, 25 (2004), 481.

[31] See the government website: www.debatidentitenationale.fr.

[32] See 'Britain "Needs National Identity" to Get through Recession, says Gordon Brown', *The Guardian*, 25 March 2009.

[33] Case C-208/09, judgement of 22 November 2010, [2010] ECR I-13693 – *Ilonka Sayn-Wittgenstein v. Landeshauptmann von Wien*.

not in a unilateral action mode here. Loyalty has to do with this. At the same time, note who is in charge of the exit decision nowadays: not politics, but courts.

## IV    Conclusion: EU Law and EU Lawyers – the Transformation of Loyalty?

*Transformation* also deals with the position of law in the evolution of the Community.[34] Where do we stand with European integration law?

There are two ways to look at the current situation. One perspective is the perspective of the depressed lawyer. The other one is the perspective of the optimistic lawyer.

### 1    Depression

The depressed lawyer looks at the reality of European integration and can only see decay. It is not only the fact that increasingly, European Council conclusions seem to replace legislation: all major institutions seem to simply ignore the law.

- The European Parliament imposes an interinstitutional agreement that boldly overturns the institutional balance laid down in primary law.[35]
- Commission and Council ignore the rules of the monetary union. The no bail-out clause, some people say, is violated by the bilateral financial help given to Greece, as well as by the EFSF and ESM constructs.[36]
- The ECB buys trashy Member State bonds against the rules laid down in the treaties, it is said.[37]
- And the ECJ? It does what it experienced itself with the German Constitutional Court and refuses to accept a distinct legal order's claim

---

[34] Weiler, 'The Transformation of Europe', 2403, 2409.

[35] European Parliament/Council/Commission, Interinstitutional agreement between the European Parliament, the Council and the Commission on budgetary discipline and sound financial management (2006/C 139/01), Official Journal C 139, 14/6/2006, p. 1; Framework Agreement on relations between the European Parliament and the European Commission, Official Journal L 304, 20/11/2010, p. 47.

[36] H. Kube and E. Reimer, 'Grenzen des Europäischen Stabilisierungsmechanismus', *NJW*, 63 (2010), 1911.

[37] M. Seidel, 'Der Ankauf nicht markt- und börsengängiger Staatsanleihen, namentlich Griechenlands, durch die Europäische Zentralbank und durch nationale Zentralbanken', *EuZW*, 21 (2010), 521. This issue was dealt with in the category of a potential *ultra vires* act of the ECB in the main proceedings of the second Euro case. See for the interim measures decision BVerfG, Second Senate, 2 BvE 6/12 et al., 12 September 2012, para. 202. The case

of superiority – remember the *Kadi* case.[38] It also seems to be looking for allies to fend off the ECtHR.

Moreover, isn't the substance of European law also a reason to be depressed? Remember the services directive[39] and its horrible drafting style. Turning to regulations instead of directives does not seem to improve things, as the debate on the data protection regulation seemed to indicate.[40] However, it is not just about secondary law. Primary law is a mess as well: the Treaties have undergone a tantalising reform process that began with the Maastricht Treaty and ended with the Treaty of Lisbon after more than fifteen years, yet nobody even tried to codify the ECJ case law on the four freedoms. It is still all judge-made law, from *Dassonville* to *Keck* and *Cassis de Dijon*.

Speaking of substituting EU law: in the Euro crisis, we saw how the Member States established structures – entailing law as well – outside the Treaties, because they were too afraid to modify the Treaties. *Schengen* and *Prüm*[41] were not exceptions; they do it on a regular basis now. The EFSF was not even a public law structure, it was an entity incorporated under Luxemburg law, operating under English law. The ESM is at least established by means of a public international treaty, but the European Parliament and to a large extent national parliaments are marginalised wherever such intergovernmental constructs are used.

An eminent authority, Jürgen Habermas, speaking at Humboldt University in 2011 and in his subsequent writings,[42] probably expressed what is obvious to the non-lawyer. Here I am paraphrasing: If the Euro problem is real and big and threatening, and if the right thing

---

went on to become the first one to lead to a preliminary reference of the German constitutional court, BVerfG, Second Senate, 2 BvR 2728/13, 14 January 2014. See the ECJ's answer in Case C-62/14 *Gauweiler and Others v Deutscher Bundestag* [2015] ECLI:EU:C:2015:400 and the final decision BVerfG, Second Senate, 2 BvR 2728/13, 21 June 2016.

38 ECJ Joined cases C-402/05 P and C-415/05 P – *Yassin Abdullah Kadi and Al Barakaat International Foundation v Council of the European Union and Commission of the European Communities* [2008] ECR I-6351. See also ECJ Opinion 2/13, EU accession to the ECHR, ECLI:EU:C:2014:2454.

39 Directive 2006/123/EC of the European Parliament and the Council of 12 December 2006 on services in the internal market, Official Journal L 376, 27/12/2006, p. 36.

40 Proposal for a regulation of the European Parliament and the Council on the protection of individuals with regard to the processing of personal data and on the free movement of such data (General Data Protection Regulation), COM(2012) 11 final, see for the final piece of legislation Regulation 2016/679, OJ L 119, 4 May 2016, p. 1.

41 Schengen Agreement Official Journal L 239, 22/09/2000, p. 13; Prüm Convention 27 May 2005, Council Doc. 10900/05.

42 J. Habermas, *Zur Verfassung Europas* (Berlin: Suhrkamp, 2011).

to do would be to engage in EU action (because there is a European Parliament that, unlike national parliaments dealing with Euro measures, is the one parliament that puts some kind of European common interest first and not a German or a French interest), why is it that the EU does not act?

The lawyer's answer to Habermas: it is because of a lack of competence (principle of conferral), Article 352 TFEU not being applicable. Then, the argument goes, EU law as such is not part of the solution. Law is part of the problem.

## 2  Optimism

However, maybe all of this is just part of the picture. The optimistic lawyer looks at the recent events and sees a confirmation of the role and importance of law.

What is true is that the rules of the stability pact were bent, by Germany and France, some time ago.[43] On the other hand, there has been a tremendous effort to keep the Euro measures compatible with primary law. The Member States really went out of their way and even turned to Treaty amendment, if considered unavoidable.[44] Moreover, as European law, in particular, is not static, the interpretation given to the bailout rule in Article 125 TFEU, to Article 122 TFEU and to Article 123 TFEU seems to be at least defendable in legal categories.[45]

The fact that entities were created outside the: Treaty framework may be read as evidence that the law is indeed effective: governments are afraid to turn to substantial Treaty revision because they know that EU law is for real. This is a legal-effectiveness trap.

And, as far as the Euro crisis is concerned, it appears that the choice is not to abandon law, it is to introduce even more law:

- Wasn't one of the problems that the rules of the stability pact were not subject to the jurisdiction of the ECJ? In this logic – the absence of law is the problem, we need more law – there was a debate about bringing in the ECJ and giving it full jurisdiction over the rules governing the

---

[43] 'Loosening those Bonds – Europe's Governments are Wriggling Free of the Stability Pact's Constraints', *The Economist*, 17 July 2003.

[44] Consider the example of Art. 136 para. 3 TFEU.

[45] See in that context ECJ Case C-370/12 *Thomas Pringle v Government of Ireland and Others* [2012].

monetary union. This led to the Fiscal Compact that does foresee a role for the ECJ.

- The Merkel Pact – officially called the Euro Plus Pact – initially suggested that all other Member States introduce a debt brake in their respective constitutions the way the Germans have it. This debate led to a debt brake being introduced by the Fiscal Treaty.
- Article 136 para. 3 TFEU was introduced in order to clarify that it is compatible with EU law to set up the ESM outside the EU Treaty framework: again, this constitutes an attempt to stay within the legal playing field, not evidence of the players leaving the playing field.

What would it actually mean if the alternative reading was to some extent more convincing and if there were illegal acts or at least some decline in the quality and relevance of EU law? Of course, for the lawyer, this is the worst case, as it threatens the very basis of his power and influence.

However, if we are taking a step back: wouldn't an occasional decoupling of the *Rechtsgemeinschaft* (community of law) and the EU be evidence of an enhanced degree of maturity of European integration? It could be read as proof of the fact that the EU is increasingly a political union and not only a creature of law, a European Union that does not immediately collapse without the *Rechtsgemeinschaft*. Of course, this argument must not be pushed too far, being potentially dangerous. It must not be misunderstood as waving the *Rechtsgemeinschaft* farewell. However, it may still help to explain why it makes sense to leave certain issues to the political realm and why a political question approach is useful, sometimes – not only because it also limits the reach of the courts.[46] Considering this, imposing a constitutional law debt brake on all Member States does not appear as convincing anymore.

What are the consequences of all of this for the EU law scholar? In a very loose way, the concepts of Exit, Voice, and Loyalty may help to explain the options. Exit is abandonment. The EU law scholar turns to other topics and issues, such as football law, Internet law, and so forth. What could be Voice here? Defending and explaining the law – but also its limits. This is what *The Transformation of Europe* was about in 1991.

---

[46] This is the approach taken by the Austrian Constitutional Court in its ESM decision, ÖVerfGH, SV 2/12–18, 16 March 2013, para. 57.

Albert O. Hirschman emphasised that Loyalty holds Exit at bay and activates Voice. So it is not 'EU law, right or wrong'. Again I quote Hirschman:

> [The] intimation of some influence and the expectation that, over a period of time, the right turns will more than balance the wrong ones, profoundly distinguishes loyalty from faith.[47]

Let us be loyal, then.

---

[47] Hirschman, *Exit, Voice and Loyalty*, 78.

# 14

# The Transformation of Private Law

HANS W. MICKLITZ

## I A Note on 'Transformation' and 'Private Law'

I first met Joseph Weiler when he came as a visiting professor to the Centre for European Legal Policy at the University of Bremen, as early as 1985. The Centre, established in 1982 in stark contrast to the then mainstream scepticism against Europe's future, was still seeking its intellectual identity. Regularly held discussion on key texts dealing with the foundations of Europe laid the ground for its future profile. Here I came into contact with Walter Hallstein, *Europa als Rechtsgemeinschaft*; Hans-Peter Ipsen, *Europäische Gemeinschaft als Zweckgemeinschaft*; Ernst-Joachim Mestmäcker, *Die Wirtschaftsverfassung der Europäischen Gemeinschaft*, the economic constitution – and with an early text of Joseph Weiler in which he presented his theory that the Member States were ready to accept the driving force of the European Court of Justice in understanding the EU legal order as an autonomous legal order because they were able to control the political process of decision making in the Council.[1]

Roughly twenty years after Joseph Weiler's sojourn in Bremen, I applied to the European University Institute. The research project which I presented was later published in the *Yearbook of European Law* under the title of the 'Visible Hand of European Private Law'.[2] The subtitle tells the story: 'The Transformation of European Private Law from Autonomy to Functionalism in Competition and Regulation'. The article breathes the language of 'transformation', a process which was triggered and shaped

---

[1] J. H. H. Weiler, 'The Community System: The Dual Character of Supranationalism', *Yearbook of European Law*, 2 (1981), 267.

[2] H. W. Micklitz, 'The Visible Hand of European Private Law', *Yearbook of European Law*, 28, P. Eeckhout and T. Tridimas (eds.) (2010), 3–60.

This chapter has been written in the context of the ERC project on European Regulatory Private Law http://blogs.eui.eu/erc-erpl/?doing_wp_cron=1362126691.69594907760620117 18750. The footnotes are cut to a minimum. This chapter has been written in 2012.

by the constitutional rhetoric of the ECJ and which then impinged upon private law. Europe is disembedding private law from its national constitutive public legal background, a development which is as dramatic as the transformation of national constitutions.

In *The Transformation of Europe*, Joseph Weiler does not discuss private law. He was interested in the analysis of the 'principal characteristics of the new operating system in a historical frame', 'in the two key structural dimensions of constitutionalism in a nonunitary polity' (2408),[3] in 'the structure and process of the Community ... rather than substantive policy and content' (2408). In such a view private law could play a role only at an abstract conceptual level, like in the writings of Ernst Böhm and Ernst Joachim Mestmäcker on the 'European Economic Constitution' where private law served as a placeholder for the constituting of a European private law society (*Privatrechtsgesellschaft*).[4] The first major piece of scholarly research on the impact of *primary* EU law on private law and its long-term implications for the conceptualisation of private law in the European context dates back to 1995 and is linked to Ernst Steindorff's seminal work which still stands like a lighthouse in the darkness of private law research. My focus is different. European private law is first and foremost *secondary* community law, subject to agreement in the Council and the Parliament. Such an undertaking changes the focus of the exit/voice model at least in two ways. Firstly, private law is about substance, a dimension Joseph Weiler explicitly set aside, and secondly, private law-making and private law enforcement internalises, so to speak, the exit/voice rhetoric. This deserves to be explained.

## II  On the Transferability of the Exit/Voice Model to Private Law

In looking into private law I will distinguish between the *traditional* private law enshrined in national codifications (the French Code Civil, the German BGB, the Italian Codice Civile) or in the common law system and the *regulatory* private law which became visible first in the *regulatory* state of the early twentieth century and later in the *welfare* state of the second half of the twentieth century through an assemblage of particular laws and regulations dealing either with *horizontal* status–related issues

---

[3] The numbers in brackets refer to J. H. H. Weiler, 'The Transformation of Europe', *The Yale Law Journal*, 100 (1991), 2403.

[4] D. Gerber, 'Constitutionalising the Economy: German Neo-liberalism, Competition Law and the "New" Europe', *American Journal of Comparative Law*, 42 (1994), 25.

such as the rights of workers, tenants, or consumers and *vertical* topic or sector-related issues in the field of regulated markets, such as telecom, energy, postal services, transport, financial services, health care, and education, just to name the most important ones.

My hypothesis is the following: Member States are ready in their overwhelming majority to promote European integration in the Council of Ministers through the development of European *regulatory* private law aimed at laying down ground rules for contract-making and product liability to the benefit of particular right holders as well as to shape sectorial markets. However, the very same Member States voice critique and resistance whenever the EU via law-making or via judicial interference tends to Europeanise *traditional* private law, thereby touching on the national 'identity' of the Member States (Art. 4 TEU). The distinction between the two areas of private law and their linkage to the exit/voice paradigm explains why the process of European integration through *regulatory* private law continues smoothly, steadily, and overall rather quietly whereas the political project of a European Civil Code seems to lead to deadlock.

Does such a transfer remain within the limits of the explanatory power of the exit/voice model? The European Court of Justice is shaping the economic constitution of Europe via the four freedoms and competition law rules, which influences the basic concepts behind any understanding of private law, such as 'autonomy' or 'freedom to do business', 'the concept of contract' and of 'state (and private) liability'; however, the major players are the political institutions, the European Commission, the European Parliament, the European Council, and the Member States. Before 1986 the Member States controlled the political process, in the field of private law via the adoption of the two (1976 and 1981) consumer policy programmes by a unanimous decision taken of what is today Art. 352 TFEU. After 1986 the European Commission turned into the major political driver in pushing for European private law-making. Gradually, the Member States lost control of the political process in the Council, not only because of the increased importance of the European Commission, but due to the empowerment of the European Parliament. The emphasis shifted from form – unanimity and consensual political control – to substance – conflicts over 'what' is private law and 'which parts' of private law could and should be submitted to secondary Community law. This is what I mean by 'internalised'. The exit/voice model can no longer be construed in the structural dimension of constitutionalism – the ECJ as the motor of European legal integration and the Member States as those which control the political process in the Council. Exit vs. voice has become an integral part of the private law-making process and what has to be shown next of the interplay between the judiciaries and the regulatory agencies.

This implies that the role of the ECJ in private law has to be reconsidered. In two landmark decisions of the early 1990s – *Alstom Atlantique*[5] and *CMC Motorradcenter*[6] – the ECJ made clear that it is not ready to use *primary* community law to decide over the substance of national private law. This was a message sent to the political institutions which should take the lead via secondary community law-making if they so decide. In private law the ECJ is largely operating on the basis of *secondary* community law, which means on private law rules which have been submitted to the process of exit and voice, where the Member States had to strike deals in order not be outvoted or where as a means of last resort Member States in a minority position abstained or refused to accept the majority vote. The ECJ when interpreting secondary private law rules is not safeguarded by a unanimously agreed treaty, howsoever boldly interpreted, but by simple majority voting in the Council (plus approval in the European Parliament). Despite the more difficult legitimating basis the ECJ upholds supremacy and direct effect in private law, gradually turning into a European civil court which is contributing in its interpretation of secondary community law rules to the development of an 'autonomous' understanding of key private law concepts. This is very much in line with the role and function Joseph Weiler attributes to the ECJ in the constitutive phase of European integration. The rather unsafe political ground on which the ECJ is operating in private law makes its judgments more open to political critique (voice).

In regulatory law a new player enters the scene, regulatory agencies, which monitor and survey the markets using private law as a means to shape markets. As each of the markets is governed by different rules and different regulatory agencies, the rise of regulatory private law goes hand in hand with the fragmentation of horizontally applicable private law and the emergence of self-standing sectorial legal orders.

The exit/voice model changes its outlook in private law, in that the model is integrated into the law-making (the political process) and the application and enforcement (the judicial interpretation), but it remains a powerful device to explain the shaky balance between politics and law in the Europeanisation of private law. In the following I will

---

[5] Case C-339/89 *Alsthom Atlantique SA v Compagnie de construction mécanique Sulzer SA* [1991] ECR I-00107.

[6] Case C-93/92 *CMC Motorradcenter GmbH v Pelin Baskiciogullari* [1993] ECR I-05009.

distinguish between the exit/voice paradigm in the *political* making of private law (III) and the *legal* enforcement of private law via the judiciary and the executive (IV). In each of the two, the *political* making and the *legal* enforcement, I will contrast European regulatory private law with traditional private law. The internalisation of the exit/voice model in the law-making and the enforcement procedure establish a kind of a balance, which holds the integration process together. In the last part (V) I will argue that the European Union is developing European regulatory private law as an autonomous legal order, largely distinct from traditional national private law systems. This 'transformation' not only erodes the exit/voice paradigm, but endangers the whole architecture of the European Union as a non-unitary polity.

### III   Exit/Voice in European Private Law-Making

European regulatory private law can be grouped around the division of horizontal and vertical regulatory private law. Horizontal rules cut across different markets and set common standards for European consumers, European workers, European travellers, etc.

I will try to show how horizontal consumer law which triggered the development of European private law turned from a harmonious into a highly conflictual field of politics, when the European Parliament and the European Commission instrumentalised consumer law as a building block for the envisaged European Civil Code, thereby challenging the national identity of the Member States as enshrined in their traditional private legal orders. The closure of selected exit turned into overt resistance. On the other side are vertical rules mainly shaped to establish and regulate sectorial markets. Here harmony and widespread consensus drive the development of European private law. Largely unnoticed though highly effective, the EU – the EU institutions and the Member States – are building a genuine law on services outside the traditional bodies of national private legal orders.

### *Horizontal Private Law – From Harmony to Conflict*

Consumer law developed in three steps. The first is characterised by a harmonious development supported by nearly unanimous support, the second by rising conflicts between the European Commission and the Member States as well as between the Member States, the third by growing tendencies of the majority of the Member States to reject the introduction of a self-standing set of European contract law rules which supplement consumer contract law.

Consumer law has made a remarkable career in the EU exactly at the moment when it was on the decline in the Member States. The reason has been often described and analysed. The European Commission, more precisely the *Sutherland* report, discovered the consumer as a construct, which could be instrumentalised for the building and the 'completion of the Internal Market'. The Single European Act led to the adoption of long-pending projects in the field of consumer contract law by way of its new competence rule, Art. 114 TFEU. In the two consumer programs of 1976 and 1981 the Member States had, jointly and unanimously, laid the ground for the development of a consumer policy and thereby for the elaboration and the adoption of consumer contract law directives. The spirit governing the discussion in the aftermath of the Single European Act can be characterised by the dominating ideal of finding consensus. It is true that Member States were negotiating in the shadow of the majority principles. Recalcitrant Member States could be outvoted, but the policy in the early days was different.

The common spirit enshrined in the unanimous adoption of the two consumer policy programmes paved the way for the completion of all those regulatory projects, which have their roots in the two consumer policy programmes. Before the entry into force of the Maastricht Treaty, there was no formal legal obligation to publish Member States' voting results. That is why for these years only the preparatory documents are available. However, these suggest that all the consumer law directives adopted between 1986 and 1994 were adopted with the unanimous support of all Member States.

How was it possible for the European Commission to gain support for its policy to take away competences from the Member States? The explanation may be found in the long-dominating principle of minimum harmonisation which allowed the Member States to support the adoption of consumer private law directives whilst maintaining and defending national particularities. The Member States were ready to give way to the development of a common platform of consumer rights, but they were unwilling to leave the field entirely to the European Commission.

The second much more conflictual stage of development started in the late 1990s, when the European Commission tried ever harder to shift the focus from minimum to full harmonisation. The European Commission based its new policy on the Lisbon Declaration in 2000, which paved the way for the adoption of the consumer policy programme 2002–6 by the

Council, in which full harmonisation of consumer law was promoted as an appropriate means of the further development of consumer law. The Member States developed different strategies in fields where they felt their sovereignty was endangered; half harmonisation in the consumer credit directive 2008/48/EC or reductionism in the Consumer Rights Directive 2011/83/EC.

The third, still ongoing step is linked to the project so strongly promoted by the European Parliament: the elaboration of a European Civil Code as the second pillar standing side by side with the (failed) European constitution. In 2001, the Communication of the European Commission on European Contract law[7] triggered a European, if not worldwide debate on the feasibility of the making of a European Civil Code. The European Commission set aside the traditional path of coordinating different national private law systems which has led to a strong Europeanisation of the law on jurisdiction (Reg. 44/2001) and of the applicable law in contract law (Reg. 593/2008) and tort law (Reg. 423/2007). There is no need to reconstruct the blossoming debate.

What matters is the link between harmonised horizontal consumer law and general contract if not civil law. By now consumer law remains the only relevant area of harmonised private law rules. A European contract law in whatever outlook would reach deep into the national private legal orders, much deeper than the still remote pieces of consumer contract law will ever do. The so-called Academic Draft of Reference elaborated by the study group and the acquis group encouraged the European Commission to first publish a so-called Feasibility Study in 2011 which led to the presentation of the highly controversial optional code on contract law, in EU parlance the CESL – the Common European Sales Law, based on Art. 114 TFEU.

Since *Societas Europaea*[8] the EU can no longer avoid a debate on competence. Several national parliaments have objected to the Commission proposal expressly based on the argument that it does not meet the subsidiarity and proportionality requirements of the Treaty. They have invoked the procedure according to Art. 6/7 of the Protocol on the 'Application of the Principles of Subsidiarity and Proportionality'. So far only the UK has taken a clear-cut position against the project whilst the European Parliament keeps on pushing for a European solution.[9]

---

[7] COM (2011) 635 final of 11.10.2011.

[8] Case C-436/03 *European Parliament v Council of the European Union* [2006] ECR I-03733.

[9] See St. Weatherill, 'The Consumer Rights Directive: How and Why a Quest for "Coherence" has (Largely) Failed', CMLR 2012, 49.

## Vertical Private Law – Smooth Harmonisation
## without Major Conflicts

The common basis for deregulating and re-regulating public services – telecom, energy (gas and electricity), transport, postal services – as well as the establishment of a European financial market dates back to the Single European Act, respectively the White Paper on the Completion of the Internal Market which contained a comprehensive programme of ca. 300 regulatory measures aimed at completing the internal market. The Single European Act provided the necessary legitimacy for setting the legislative machinery into motion, through the introduction of Art. 100 a) (today Art. 114 (TFEU) and the majority principle.

Where is the link to private law? The overall idea was to liberalise – not necessarily to privatise – the former public services, to substitute statutory monopolies for competitive markets, to the benefit of customers, be they companies or final consumers. The liberalisation occurred in steps, each linked to a particular wave of regulation. In the telecom, energy, and transport sectors it has become common to speak about the first, second, and third generations of directives. In the first ten years emphasis was put on the establishment of competitive market structures, to separate the networks from the supply, and to empower new entrants who could compete with the former statutory monopoly. Regulatory agencies were set up at the national level to establish competitive market structures and to monitor and supervise their workability. The more advanced the markets turned out to be, the more obvious were the deficiencies in the shaping of the private law relations in the newly established markets. The third generation in particular is meant to remedy deficiencies in private law relations. Today the dense set of secondary community law covers the entire field of the respective regulated markets. From the making of the law in the respective community institutions, over its fine-tuning in regulatory agencies, up to the establishment of alternative dispute settlement mechanisms, for b2b and b2c, secondary community law has largely replaced the former national rules on public services.

Again the question is how is it possible that the Member States were and are ready to support the transformation of public services into private companies, the elaboration of sector-related private law rules, often even fully harmonised? Clearly, the Member States are not willing to accept European regulatory agencies with large decision-making powers, which would downgrade national agencies to executive agents. These reservations did not prevent them from supporting the overall liberalisation policy which lies in the hands of the European Commission as the major driving force (2455).

Seen through the lenses of private law, two reasons seem to be of outstanding importance. Regulated markets are markets for services. National private legal orders are traditionally weak with regard to service contracts. The whole private law systems are largely designed after the model of sales contracts. Therefore the new European directives and regulations adopted in the field of regulated markets did not clash with an established body of national private law rules. The second reason reaches deeper. It is related to the overall phenomenon that the European integration process strengthened and is still strengthening the power of the executive in the rule-making procedure. The invention of the comitology procedure and later the *Lamfalussy* procedure is witness to how the liberalisation of the public services led to a major increase of delegated rule-making via the executive. Such a reading of the liberalisation process illustrates how the Member States were able to extend political control far beyond the law-making process into the management of the respective regulated markets. The result is a European domestic policy which circumvents European and national parliaments and which yields a nearly unnoticed and unprecedented rise of regulatory private law, instrumentalised to serve the needs of the different rationalities governing the respective sectors.

## IV Exit/Voice in the Application and Enforcement of European Private Law

Adjudication in horizontal private law differs considerably from adjudication in vertical private law. In the former the ECJ turns into a key player which is shaping horizontal European consumer law via a growing number of preliminary references. The deeper the ECJ intervenes, the more often there is resistance in academia, but not so much in the national judiciaries and national politics. In the latter area of vertical private law we can observe a process of de-judicialisation. The ECJ is not the key player in the application and enforcement of vertical private law; these are the national regulatory agencies as coordinated at the European level.

### Horizontal Private Law – From Harmony to Ever More Conflicts?

Since the mid-1990s, preliminary references procedures brought the ECJ into the picture. At the time of writing there are 101 judgments, most of them dealing with unfair contract terms (20), doorstep selling (17), air passenger regulation, and consumer credit (12), and fewer with time sharing (3), distant selling (7), consumer sales (5), and consumer credit (3). Quantity does not necessarily tell us anything about the importance of the preliminary references. The few cases decided under the consumer sales directive have a far-reaching impact on the national legal systems. A relevant number of references is the result of strategic use of European law, mainly by organised groups of claimants or by consumer entities which benefit from legal standing but choose the right claimant and the right conflict to bring a case before the ECJ.[10] The rising number of preliminary references from the new Member States gives consumer law drafted according to the Western cultural ideology a new twist in that the referring courts challenge the established thinking of Western European law in legal categories.

The steadily rising flow of references enables the ECJ to actively and forcefully, though not necessarily consistently, enter the scene, using the main devices of European constitution-building to interpret the consumer law directives: supremacy and direct effect – with two major differences. In secondary community law, the ECJ does not use the doctrine of preemption, but speaks instead of preclusion, and it does not recognise the horizontal direct effect of secondary community law, although it comes relatively close to it. In substance, the ECJ is defining the legal concept of the consumer and the supplier, is elaborating appropriate consumer law remedies, and is shaping the role and function of national judges as guardian of consumer rights *ex officio*.[11]

Most of the judgments have raised concern only in circles dealing with the relevant substantive legal issues. Quite a few, through a growing number of judgments, have and are raising concern outside the legal

---

[10] Case C-404/06 *Quelle AG v Bundesverband der Verbraucherzentralen und Verbraucherverbände* [2008] ECR I-02685; Joined cases C-65/09 and C-87/09 *Gebr. Weber GmbH v Jürgen Wittmer and Ingrid Putz v Mediapress Electronics GmbH* [2011] ECR I-05257.

[11] Overview V. Trstenjak and E. Beysen, 'European Consumer Protection Law: *Curia emer dabit remedium?*', *Common Market Law Review*, 48 (2011), 95–124.

environment in which the case is embedded: *Gonzalés Sanchez*[12] holding that the product liability directive provides for full harmonisation, *Mangold*[13] and *Kücükdevici*[14] prohibiting age discrimination in employment contracts, *Test Achats*[15] introducing unisex premiums in insurance contracts and *Putz/Weber*[16] obliging Member States to provide for non-negligent compensation of damages resulting from defective products.

Why do the Member States and their courts by and large accept the judgments of the ECJ? Is there really a growing resistance against the judicial activism of the ECJ or even 'judicial romanticism' on behalf of the Luxemburg court?

Two explanations might be given for the broad acceptance, each pointing into a different direction. The first lies in the fact that the ECJ does not decide the case, but provides guidance to the referring court by interpreting the relevant consumer law directives. The distinction between the law and the facts, the law rooted in EU law and the facts grounded in the particular national circumstances, gives way to various strategies reaching from loyalty to blatant rejection. It is hard to impossible to assess whether and to what extent the Member State courts are following, following half-heartedly, or not following at all the guidance provided from Luxemburg. The Member States rejected the attempt of the ECJ to publish the final decision of the referring court taken in light of the findings in the preliminary reference procedure. Public access would have considerably facilitated assess to the potential impact of the judgments. What remains are case studies in various fields of consumer law, each requiring serious and time-consuming research. The risk should not be overestimated. Blatant rejection in hard cases would certainly come to be known to the European Commission, the Member States and – in particular – the European citizens who are behind the court procedure.

The second reason prevents the Member States from challenging the authority of the ECJ via the exit option. Just like in the field of equal treatment the ECJ has become a court of last resort – and last hope – for those

[12] Case C-183/00 *María Victoria González Sánchez v Medicina Asturiana SA* [2002] ECR I-03907.

[13] Case C-144/04 *Werner Mangold v Rüdiger Helm* [2005] ECR I-9981.

[14] Case C-586/10 *Bianca Kücük v Land Nordrhein-Westfalen* [2012] ECR I-nyr.

[15] Case C-236/09 *Association Belge des Consommateurs Test-Achats ASBL and Others v Conseil des ministres* [2011] ECR I-00773.

[16] Joined cases C-65/09 and C-87/09 *Gebr. Weber GmbH v Jürgen Wittmer and Ingrid Putz v Medianess Electronics GmbH* [2011] ECR I-05257.

consumers who failed in hard cases before national courts. The so-called *Heininger* saga demonstrates just like *Smith v. Advel*[17] and others that the claimants overestimate the capacities of the ECJ to 'direct' Member States' courts so as to overcome 'deficiencies' in the national private law systems. However, the rather limited positive experiences do not prevent e.g. over-indebted consumers in Spain[18] who suffer from the effects of the economic crisis to set all their hopes on the ECJ. For the good or the bad the ECJ has turned into a court which finds itself in the position of social engineering. The ECJ is perceived as the sole and remaining European institution which is in a position to balance out the negative impact of a market-driven policy which deepens the cleavage between the 'included' and the 'excluded'. The excluded are those who seek 'justice' before the ECJ. The nearly unlimited reach of application of EU law, subject to critique from a constitutional point of view, demonstrates its political potential in the field of consumer law.

One might argue that the ECJ faces more resistance in recent years. A closer analysis shows, however, that the resistance mainly derives from parts of national academia and much less from national judges and in particular not from Member States politicians. There is only one notable exception to be reported. *Gonzales Sanchez* led to a Decision of the Council[19] in which the Member States unanimously criticised the judgment in relatively harsh words, however with no consequences, as the ECJ confirmed its controversial position in later judgments. The national judges implemented the guidance from Luxemburg even in hard cases like *Mangold* or *Putz/Weber*. There is a strong difference between the excitement of parts of legal academia and the apathy of politics. It remains to be seen whether and to what extent Cameron's plea for a referendum will affect the authority of the ECJ, perhaps not primarily but also in private law matters.

## *Vertical Private Law – De-judicialisation – How Far Can It Go?*

The key actors in vertical private law – the so-called regulated markets – are not courts, national and European courts, but national and European agencies. It suffices to contrast the extremely limited number

---

[17]  Case C-408/92 *Constance Christina Ellen Smith and Others v Avdel Systems Ltd* [1994] ECR I-04435.

[18]  Case C-415/11 *Mohamed Aziz v Caixa d'Estalvis de Catalunya, Tarragona i Manresa (Catalunyacaixa)* [2013].

[19]  OJ C 26, 4.2.2003, 2.

of preliminary references in vertical private law with the much higher number of cases in horizontal consumer law. The number is even lower if one directs attention to those cases which demonstrate a direct link to contractual matters. In private law it is mainly *Alassini*,[20] a case in which the ECJ had to decide over the mandatory character of alternative dispute resolution prior to having access to normal courts.

The liberalisation of the former public services and the establishment of a European capital market have led to vertically separated bodies of rules, in which the private law dimension forms an integral part of the overall regulatory setting. This implies that regulatory agencies use private law as a means to shape markets, even if this is neither formally foreseen nor necessarily in line with the respective EU law requirements. The role of the European regulatory agencies is not yet clear. Notwithstanding the fact that the outlook of the European agencies differs from market to market, it is plain that the European agencies benefit mainly from a coordinating role. Much research needs to be done to evaluate what exactly the national agencies are doing and whether and to what extent their individual or policy decisions affect private law relations. Individual decisions are not public. If any national reports provide for limited information and only in few countries, concrete knowledge is available on cases in which national agencies had to decide on private law matters. The same holds true for the role and function of European agencies. It might well be that their coordinating role, though limited in legal terms, has a strong harmonising impact on the way in which national agencies decide. This laboratory of administrative decision-making and its potential fragmenting effect on the private law system needs to be disclosed and made accessible to private law theory.

Why are the Member States ready to accept the de-judicialisation of the regulated market? Why are the Member States ready to coordinate the administrative enforcement between themselves and with the European Commission? I would identify two reasons. The first is mainly rooted in institutional choice. It was much easier for the European Commission than for the Member States to initiate the liberalisation of public services. Member States faced and are still facing strong critique at the national level, although none of the Member States seems ready to turn the clock back. They could blame Europe for the potential negative impact resulting from the liberalisation although they were silently supporting the European policy. The second has to do with the increasing globalisation

---

[20] Case C-317/08 *Rosalba Alassini v Telecom Italia SpA* [2010] ECR I-02213.

of regulated markets. The Member States recognised not only the need to coordinate and bundle their activities in the making of the technical rules which govern sectorial markets, but also to put more emphasis on coordinated law enforcement in the hands of regulatory agencies.

Where are the limits to the de-judicialisation and the overall tendency to keep the law enforcement in the hands of regulatory agencies and dispute settlement bodies? Just as in consumer law, the ECJ is faced with preliminary references which bear a strong social outlook, where private parties who feel more victims than beneficiaries of liberalised (if not) privatised markets invoke the ECJ as the court of last resort. *Belov*[21] might serve as an example. Here the state electricity distribution companies had placed meters to measure electricity consumption at a height of seven metres above the ground on posts situated on the outside of houses connected to the electricity network in a certain number of urban districts in Bulgaria which were known to be inhabited primarily by members of the Roma community.

## V   The Consequences of the Internalisation of Exit/Voice

My hypothesis is that the European Union is developing out of regulatory private law a largely autonomous European private law which is managed by regulatory agencies and where the courts have only a limited say, be they national or European. The strong impact of globalisation on regulated markets – think of financial services, transport (airlines, shipping), and telecommunication – promotes the process of detachment and of independentalisation[22] from the national private law systems. Member States' private legal orders are threatened by the risk of provincialisation, being bound to deal only with conflicts of minor economic and therefore also of minor legal relevance. If my hypothesis turns out to be correct, the legitimacy of European private law as such is in jeopardy.

---

[21] Case C-394/11 *Valeri Hariev Belov v CHEZ Elektro Balgaria AD and Others* [2013] ECR I-nyr.
[22] This means the process of becoming independent = independentalisation.

# 15

# *The Transformation of Europe* and of Selective Exit Twenty-Five Years After

MARLENE WIND

I first came across *The Transformation of Europe* (ToE) in 1993 when I had just started as a PhD candidate at the EUI in Florence. As a political scientist, I was admitted to the institute on a project about the changes in sovereignty in light of the European integration process, but was rather unsure how I should go about studying this phenomenon empirically. Many political scientists had at the time produced bookshelves theorising about 'the post-sovereign condition' (see Held et al. among others), but very few (if any) were able to delineate *empirically* what kind of transformation(s) Europe had actually been undergoing. Joseph Weiler's ToE was therefore an eye opener of dimensions to me, and I knew right from the very moment I first read it that I had found what I was looking for. Not because *The Transformation* represented a deep, empirical study of the 'post-sovereign condition'; nor was it a philosophical piece about the destiny of the European nation-state. But it made intelligible how those dramatic changes we had all been witnessing in Europe since the establishment of the Common Market could be comprehended as an intimate – though not always intentional – interplay between the political and the legal spheres. European legal integration was not only presented in a way that was easily digestible for a political scientist. More importantly, ToE represented a fascinating narrative of the European constitutional development as a dynamic and creative field which otherwise rent-seeking member states were gradually seduced by.

With ToE I also discovered a legal scholar who was in reality a semi-political scientist and whose splendid teaching of European law I was so lucky to be able to follow both at the EUI, where Weiler occasionally taught after having left for the States, and some years later when I visited him at Harvard Law School, where we were editing a book together.[1]

---

[1] J. H. H. Weiler and M. Wind (eds.), *European Constitutionalism Beyond the State* (Cambridge: Cambridge University Press, 2003).

What I did not know in the early and mid-1990s but was to discover later, however, was that ToE not only ended up delivering the frame for my PhD dissertation, but also turned out to influence my entire academic career as a political scientist studying law and courts.

In the following pages, I have decided to focus primarily on what I believe to be the most important insights of ToE and, perhaps more importantly, how these ended up inspiring my own work on law and politics in the EU. I have thus divided the following sections into 'four personal lessons learned'. None of the issues raised here will, however, in any way attempt to pay tribute to the entire scholarly value of ToE nor to Weiler's many other writings, i.e., on democracy. Hence, the following should merely be read as my take on the 1991 article and how it impacted my own thinking on: interdisciplinarity, law-politics theories of European integration, selective-exit – understood here (perhaps wrongly?) – as non-compliance, and finally the dialogue between national courts and the CJEU.[2]

## Lesson 1: Interdisciplinarity at Heart

Albert Hirschman's[3] book *Exit, Voice and Loyalty: Responses to Decline in Firms, Organizations and States* from 1970 is absolutely central to ToE. By using Hirshman's theory to explain the essence and dilemmas of the integration process, Weiler demonstrated in a nutshell why Europe cannot be studied by lawyers or political scientists in splendid isolation from each other. While most political science scholarship on Europe neglected law entirely at the time when ToE was written (and even until fairly recently), Community lawyers also completely neglected politics, as Weiler puts it:

> This characterization [of a pure law approach to Community law] might, however, lead to a flawed analysis. It might be read (and has been read) as suggesting that the cardinal material locus of change has been the realm of law and that the principal actor has been the European Court. But this would be deceptive. Legal and constitutional structural change have been crucial, but only in their interaction with the Community political process.[4]

---

[2] For simplicity, I use CJEU for the European Court in the following.

[3] A. O. Hirschman, *Exit, Voice, and Loyalty – Responses to Decline in Firms, Organizations and States* (Cambridge, MA: Harvard University Press, 1970).

[4] J. H. H Weiler, 'The Transformation of Europe', *Yale Law Journal*, 100, 8 (1991), 2407.

I couldn't agree more. Situated as I was in the beginning of the 1990s in a world of inter-governmentalism with leading scholars like Andrew Moravscik in political science and Alan Milward in history (who both somehow depicted the entire integration process as 'A Rescue of the Nation-State'), it was a relief to encounter the almost entirely opposite story in ToE. It was not that lawyers, as Weiler rightly points out, carried the truth about Europe. They certainly did not. But their narrative was refreshingly different and fundamentally challenged the classical political science analysis of states as the only important drivers of integration. Thus, while the inter-governmentalists saw the European integration process as something that could be reduced to national interests and transaction costs, lawyers depicted a gradually emerging constitutional structure embracing more and more of political life. Weiler notes this himself:

> It is not surprising ... that lawyers were characterising the Community of that epoch [the foundational period MW] as a 'constitutional framework' for a federal-type structure, whereas political scientists were speculating about the survival of supranationalism.[5]

The lawyers' bias could, according to Weiler, be attributed to the fact that a majority came from international law. They were thus both surprised and thrilled by bearing witness to an emerging legal structure that hardened into 'real binding law' almost by the day.[6] Political scientists, on the other hand, focused entirely on the decision-making processes in the Council and later with liberal inter-governmentalism at the national decision-making processes and how these determined how much sovereignty could be 'given up'. What political scientists observed in the 1960s was the veto-practise of President Charles de Gaulle and the agony of his empty chair policy. No surprise, then, that the two camps, while speaking of the same phenomenon, saw entirely different things. One cannot help thinking of Puchala's 'Of Blind Men, Elephants and the Study of International Integration', in which he argues that whether you see an elephant or something entirely different out there depends on what part of the elephant's body you are looking at.[7] For this reason alone Joseph Weiler's article

---

[5] Ibid., 2411.

[6] See ibid., 2403.

[7] D. J. Puchala, 'Of Blind Men, Elephants and International Integration', Journal of Common Market Studies, 10 (1972), 268. As he puts it: '[D]ifferent schools of researchers have exalted different parts of the integration "elephant". They have claimed either that their parts were in fact the whole beasts, or that their parts were the most important ones, the others being of marginal interest. No model describes the integration phenomenon with

filled out a lacuna in both political science and law. Law was the structure which encapsulated narrow political interests, taking both law and politics to places which were not in advance anticipated by either of the two disciplines. Taking both narratives into account on their own terms and showing their interrelatedness theoretically as well as empirically was probably one of the largest accomplishments of ToE. Today I can thus hardly imagine any introductory or advanced course on the EU – across the globe – in political science or law, where *The Transformation* is not included on the curriculum.

## Lesson 2: The Unintended Consequences of European Integration?

In 'Sovereignty and European Integration' from 2001, which builds on my PhD thesis and includes a preface by Joseph Weiler,[8] I tried to extract the law-politics dynamics from ToE by combining it with Anthony Giddens' theory of structuration.[9] Giddens argues that all human acts can be regarded as rational (and even self-maximising). However, because structures mould, bend, and encapsulate rational actors in their pursuits, they (whether individuals or states) will never be able to completely control, predict, or even firmly calculate the future effects of their own actions. The result is, according to Giddens, that rational or intentional deeds will produce unintended effects which then inevitably become the structural basis for future decisions[10] (1984). The logic is pretty banal, but nevertheless insightful, as it challenges in a quite fundamental way the classical dogma (still taught in most introductory IR courses) that states never give up sovereignty, and if they do, they will be able to foresee and make a rational calculation of all future consequences.

I was precisely searching for a sophisticated theory which could account for the sometimes unintended structural power of law as it moulds and creates new conditions for states in the integration process, a theory that could prove the political science dogmatists wrong and explain how and why a number of sovereignty-loving European states over time agreed to no longer ultimately decide about the laws of their own land. It thus

---

complete accuracy because all models present images of what integration should be or could be rather than here and now' (ibid., 276).

[8] Published as M. Wind, *Sovereignty and European Integration: Towards a Post-Hobbesian Order* (London & New York: Palgrave Macmillan, 2001).

[9] A. Giddens, *The Constitution of Society* (Cambridge: Polity Press, 1984).

[10] Ibid.

struck me how Giddens' micro theory of human (or in this case state behaviour) combined with ToE's basic law-politics logic fitted so beautifully into this narrative.

In sum, what we were witnessing in the European integration process in the 1960s – as I saw it and described it in my book – was exactly a story of a group of more or less self-interested member states who, in the pursuit of their own post-war survival, gradually were locked in by an irreversible European legal structure, a structure whose strength they might not have anticipated from the start, but which they eventually had to accept, internalise, build on, and even defend for decades to come. The acceptance of EU law supremacy and direct effect from the 1960s and onwards could in this way be seen as a rational and down-to-earth problem-solving devise ensuring that all member states abided by the same laws, making the internal market more efficient and its rules more predictable. But it was at the same time a story about the adoption of an incredibly powerful legal structure, which over the years turned into an effective legal framework embracing almost all parts of European political life, perhaps with the exception of the EU's Foreign and Security Policy. In transcending both the narrow-minded, actor-based rationalist approach on the one hand and the more deterministic legal approach on the other, ToE inspired generations to much better understand the closely linked law-politics dynamics in the European Union.[11] But would this structured and socialising equilibrium continue after the introduction of majority voting? Weiler predicted that it might not, and lots of studies in political science actually ended up proving him right in this prediction, as we are to see.

## Lesson 3: Selective Exit Rehearsed?

In *The Transformation of Europe*, as in Hirschman's book, three parameters are as mentioned earlier central: 'exit, voice, and loyalty'. The thesis in the original Hirschman text was that you may respond in one of two ways if you believe that the quality of an organisation, of which you are a member, decreases: you can either *exit* (leave the organisation) or you can use your *voice* and try to reform it. In ToE, Weiler transfers this dilemma

---

[11] For a newer study trying to link the law and political science approaches to Europe, see U. Neergaard and M. Wind, 'Studying the EU in Legal and Political Science Scholarship', in U. Neergaard and R. Nielsen (eds.), *European Legal Method in a Multilevel EU Legal Order* (Copenhagen: Djøf Publishing, 2012), 263–93.

to the EC in its foundational period. As a real exit from the Community quickly was considered a non-option for the unsatisfied member states, the interesting thing was whether the members (the states) would choose to collaborate (use their voice) or cheat (make use of some kind of 'selective exit') if they wanted to change the state of affairs. Due to the constitutionalisation of the treaties and the decision-making process by consensus in the Council 'selective exit', or non-compliance, was, however, also considered a rare phenomenon. As Weiler puts it:

> A principal feature of the Foundational Period has been the closure, albeit incomplete, of Selective Exit with obvious consequences for the decisional behaviour of the Member States.[12]

In this understanding it was the constitutionalisation and the consensus mechanism in the Council which, in themselves, turned the member states into obedient compliers and provided for 'more sophisticated processes of self-correction' than 'selective exit'.[13] The hypothesis was that when law became 'hard' and binding, there would be an increased incentive to actually take the decision-making process seriously. Weiler himself puts it in this way as a more general thesis of international law-making:

> The 'harder' the law in terms of its binding effect both on and within states, the less willing states are to give up their prerogative to control the emergence of such law or the law's 'opposability' to them. When international law is 'real', when it is 'hard' in the sense of being binding not only on but also in states, and when there are effective legal remedies to enforce it, decision making suddenly becomes important, indeed crucial.[14]

Weiler also made clear that he feared that when majority voting, and the expansion of the single market after 1992, became a reality, the mutual trust and understanding obtained though this mechanism could be undermined. The reason was that member states could risk being voted down, a fact that might delegitimise the entire project. Until very recently, we have not had any systematic studies of whether this fear or prediction in fact materialised.

Did member states in fact make increased use of 'selective exit' in terms of cheating and non-compliance, or did they start refusing the constitutionalisation by going against or challenging the hard constitutionalisation by the European Court? Several recent studies in political science

[12] Weiler, 'The Transformation of Europe', 2412.
[13] Ibid., 2411.
[14] Ibid., 2426.

show that we need a more nuanced view of what 'selective exit', or as we could call it today: 'member states non-compliance strategies', really consists of. In much of the legal literature there has been an enormous faith in the actual effectiveness of Community law simply due to the supremacy and direct-effect doctrines. Weiler was aware of this problem and of the fact that supremacy and direct effect were far from 'self-executing' when he in ToE warned against any naïve attempt to deduce compliance directly from the treaties or the Court's case law.

In ToE, Weiler did not spend much time explaining how 'selective exit' in light of majority voting would play out. More refined theories of Europeanisation were needed in order to capture how member states could avoid their Community obligations in a more refined and sophisticated way by not obviously breaking the law. Political scientists thus approached 'selective exit' as outright or more subtle non-compliance. When directives, and to some degree even regulations, are disregarded or deliberately implemented too late or wrongly, it is a form of 'selective exit', and citizens and private enterprises pay the price because it often results in a very uneven European rights protection. And very often, member states' non-compliance strategies are difficult to detect as they dress up as 'narrow' or strict interpretations of European rules and regulations. Take an environmental regulation such as the water framework directive as an example. If national authorities either implement the directive very narrowly or not at all, it can be seen as 'selective exit'. Or (as one study has shown), if the culture in the national ministry of the environment sets out to nurse environmental groups and punish farmers, a specific directive will easily be 'over-implemented' to the disadvantage of those who depend on equal competition rules in the internal market.

Studies have also shown that narrow or under- implementation can go on for years without any consequences – even in what is normally considered 'law-abiding member states'. Whether deliberate or non-deliberate, non-compliance can have serious consequences. A study of cultural inertia and reluctance in national administrations towards CJEU case law and the citizenship directive thus showed that thousands of citizens in Denmark were deprived of their specific rights to family unification under EU law simply because the EU rules was not communicated to citizens on the Ministry's website. Instead, the Ministry of Integration – for years – chose only to inform about the much stricter national family unification rules which made unification a mere fiction to many families. It took five years before this mal-administration was disclosed in the media and even then without any consequences for the administration and public authorities.[15] It is important to emphasise that the two examples of 'selective exit' sketched here happened *despite* the directives being *formally* implemented on time by the national government. The problem is exactly that formal or 'legally correct' implementation (that is, directives which reportedly are implemented on time) tells us very little about what is actually happening on the ground when EU law meets the European citizen. Only solid, empirical implementation studies into the needy, giddy details of national law-making can help us here.

There is no doubt that the research on 'selective exit' or 'implementation barriers' has exploded recently, in particular in political science. It is, however, impossible to say whether there is, or has been, an increase in non-compliance in the member states as such. This is precisely because official data and the earliest research on national compliance were based on statistics where the national governments themselves reported in to the Commission about their compliance record.[16] Formal transposition statistics based on aggregated data from the member states or the Commission are, however, often useless, not to say directly misguiding. If we want to know anything meaningful about the actual relationship between the EU's decision-making process and non-compliance, we thus need to look at how the law works on the ground.[17] However, because a 'law on the ground approach' is a very recent phenomenon, we know very little about whether increasing non-compliance cases may be attributable to increased voice and 'a hardening of the law' in the decision-making processes, as suggested by ToE.

In my opinion there is little doubt that the new wave of compliance/implementation studies could be seen as the 'modern' version of 'selective exit' in ToE's understanding. When discussing 'selective exit', both ToE and more recent versions are exactly *not* dealing with an outright rejection of EU law at the national level. Outright rejection would be much easier to study in terms of infringement cases before the Court and number of

---

[15] See M. Wind, 'The European "Rights Revolution" and the (Non) implementation of the Citizen Directive in Denmark', in L. Miles and A. Wivel (eds.), *Denmark and the European Union* (London: Routledge, 2014).

[16] This also goes for this now-famous book: G. Falkner et al., *Complying with Europe: EU Harmonization and Soft Law in the Member States* (Cambridge: Cambridge University Press, 2005).

[17] See M. Wind, 'Law on the Ground: Can Culture Explain the Successes and Failures of Enforcement of European Law?, in A. Wechsler and H. Micklitz (eds.), *The Transformation of Enforcement: European Economic Law in a Global Perspective* (Oxford: Hart Publishing, 2016).

'opening letters' from the Commission. Studies into how administrative, political, and legal culture influences and impacts the actual implementation of EU law and how it meets the citizen are much more subtle and difficult to conduct. A research project on 'selective exit' of EU law could, however, be carried out as presented in the scheme that follows. Note that it is the intermediate variables – the study of the 'barriers' or 'gate keepers to correct and timely implementation' – which are the most interesting to focus on in such a modern case study of 'selective exit':

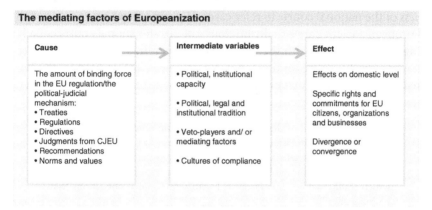

**The mediating factors of Europeanization**

| Cause | Intermediate variables | Effect |
|---|---|---|
| The amount of binding force in the EU regulation/the political-judicial mechanism: <br> • Treaties <br> • Regulations <br> • Directives <br> • Judgments from CJEU <br> • Recommendations <br> • Norms and values | • Political, institutional capacity <br><br> • Political, legal and institutional tradition <br><br> • Veto-players and/ or mediating factors <br><br> • Cultures of compliance | Effects on domestic level <br><br> Specific rights and commitments for EU citizens, organizations and businesses <br><br> Divergence or convergence |

## Lesson 4: Non-compliance and the Relationship between National Courts and the CJEU

The issue of non-compliance and selective exit could, however, also be about the collaboration between CJEU and the national courts. In this final 'Lessons Learned Section', I shall touch a bit on this. In ToE, Weiler underscores the relationship and dialogue between the national courts and the CJEU. In fact, it would be no exaggeration to say that ToE was the first to emphasise just what a crucial role the national courts played in the successful transformation of Europe. Had national courts (and litigants) not taken up the challenge given to them in the treaties and by the CJEU, it is doubtful whether Europe would have moved very far away from a traditional international law regime in which states are the sole masters of the treaties. After having explained the functioning of Art. 267 (former 177), Weiler argues in ToE that:

> The national courts and the European Court are thus integrated into a unitary system of judicial review. The European Court and national courts have made good use of this procedure. On its face the purpose of Article 177 is simply to ensure uniform interpretation of Community law

throughout the Member States. ... However, very often the factual situation in which art 177 comes into play involves an individual litigant pleading in a national court that a rule, measure, or national practice should not be applied because it violates the Community obligations of the Member State. In this manner the attempts of Member States to practice selective Community membership by disregarding their obligations have become regularly adjudicated before their own national courts.[18]

Weiler thus clearly asserts that the successful mechanism not only depends on active litigants who are aware of their rights, but also on the *willingness* of the national courts to refer cases. However, as we are to see, not all European societies are equally litigious nor are all national courts equally eager to collaborate with the CJEU, even though this is often assumed in the broader literature on this topic. Nevertheless, ToE is right in emphasising that the preliminary ruling system is not just important, but, in fact, revolutionised the system, or as Weiler puts it:

> [T]he overall effect of the judicial remedies cannot be denied. The combination of 'constitutionalization' and the system of judicial remedies to a large extent nationalized Community obligations and introduces on the Community level the habit of obedience and the respect for the rule of law which traditionally is less associated with international obligations than national ones.[19]

Few scholars would today deny that the combined effect of constitutionalisation and the CJEU's powers, both the preliminary ruling system, but also the other remedies like the infringement procedures, have been eminent in transforming Europe from a simple international law system to a true constitutional order.

It is thus not surprising that most EU law textbooks and academic legal articles have described the preliminary reference procedure as an effective instrument in cajoling in particular lower national courts into loyal European courts. The problem is, however, that this perspective for years resulted in a collective neglect or even denial of the *variance* among national courts when it comes to actually engaging in a dialogue with the CJEU. However, as recent studies have shown far from all lower (or indeed supreme) national courts have been eager to forward cases to the European Court. While in particular many law researchers have taken the collaboration between national courts and the CJEU for granted, some political science studies have questioned that things would work

---

[18]  Weiler, 'The Transformation of Europe', 2420–1.
[19]  Ibid., 2421–2.

so smoothly. In fact, Weiler himself was one of the first to pose the very basic question: why would national judges at all be interested in cooperating with a supranational court like the CJEU and thus bypass their own colleagues in the national supreme court? Intuitively – not least from a classical dualist perspective – this is actually a puzzle. Already ToE hinted rather clearly at this issue, but Weiler also rather explicitly pointed to the potential interest on part of national court judges in getting direct access to a supranational court, without first having to ask higher up in the system, so to speak.[20]

Nevertheless, these quite essential issues on the role of national and European courts soon sparked an enormous scientific activity, tests, and hypothesis-tracing, perhaps in particular among American political scientists. One author, Karen Alter, for instance, wanted to understand whether it indeed was personal and institutional incentives which drove the lower-ranked national judges in Germany and France to refer cases to the CJEU. From a political science perspective, it was a quite fundamental puzzle why lower-ranked judges might want not only to bypass their senior colleagues in the supreme courts, but also their national governments, which then clearly had to accept judicial review by a supranational body.[21] Another political science study argued that the increasing number of preliminary references could be explained by the trade density in Europe; hypothesising that more trade between countries would lead to more dispute settlements represented here by cases raised by national courts at the CJEU.[22]

None of these studies have, however, been confirmed in later work on variance among national courts and their referral practice. My own work on national courts and the preliminary reference procedure has shown that the two studies mentioned earlier are both problematic as they claim to be able to generalise about national court behaviour across the board. Lower courts have certainly collaborated

---

[20] J. H. H. Weiler, 'A Quiet Revolution: The European Court of Justice and its Interlocutors', *Comparative Political Studies*, 26, 4 (1994), 510–34.

[21] K. J. Alter, *Establishing the Supremacy of European Law: The Making of an International Rule of Law in Europe*, 1st edition (New York: Oxford University Press, 2001). See also A. Slaughter, A. Stone Sweet, and J. H. H Weiler, *The European Courts and National Courts – Doctrine and Jurisprudence: Legal Changes in Its Social Context* (Oxford: Hart Publishing, 1998).

[22] A. Stone Sweet and T. L. Brunell, 'The European Court and the National Courts: a Statistical Analysis of Preliminary References, 1961–95', *Journal of European Public Policy*, 5, 1 (1998), 66–97.

with the CJEU, which ToE and Weiler's other work has convincingly demonstrated. However, not all national courts' judges have been equally eager to do so nor to bypass national supreme courts and governments. There is, in other words, a rather cemented 'Uneven Legal Push for Europe'[23] when looking at the national courts' willingness to forward cases to the CJEU.

The Nordic courts are a very good example of a group of courts and judges who at times clearly prefer not to engage with CJEU.[24] Thus, a systematic study drawing on statistics, interviews, and surveys among Danish and Swedish judges shows that Nordic judges prefer to refer as few cases as possible to the CJEU and, contrary to the findings of Alter (2001), close to none of the lower courts referred a case to the CJEU during the first thirty years! The study shows that should a case eventually reach the CJEU today, it has most likely been referred by the national supreme court and has, often, been sanctioned by the Ministry of Justice.[25] These studies suggest, in other words, that one should be incredibly careful when generalising about judge incentives across the board or when predicting judicial activity on the basis of trade statistics. One could argue that the Nordic study is yet another example of 'selective exit' since fewer cases forwarded often implies that citizens' European rights will not be as efficiently protected, in particular because the study also demonstrates that Nordic judges know little about EU law. The fact that Nordic citizens almost never take their governments to court only adds to this picture of an uneven legal protection.[26] The literature predicting adversarial

---

[23] See M. Wind, D. S. Martinsen and G. P. Rotger, 'The Uneven Legal Push for Europe: Questioning Variations When National Courts go to Europe', *European Union Politics*, 10, 1 (2009), 63–88.

[24] M. Wind, 'The Nordic Reluctance Towards Supranational Judicial Review', *Journal of Common Market Studies*, 48, 4 (2010), 1039–63.

[25] Wind, Martinsen and Rotger, 'The Uneven Legal Push for Europe'; Wind, 'The Nordic Reluctance Towards Supranational Judicial Review'. See also P. Pagh 'Præjudicielle forelæggelser og Juridisk Specialudvalg, *Ugeskrift for retsvæsen*, 41 (2004), 305–14 who has shown that in twenty out of twenty-two cases, the Ministry of Justice recommended to the state attorney that the cases should not be forwarded to the CJEU. In all cases, this recommendation was followed by the national judges. See P. Pagh, 'Juridisk Special Udvalg og præjudicialle forelæggelser for EF-domstolen' [The Judicial Commitee and the preliminary references to the European Court of Justice], in B. Egelund Olsen and K. Engsig Sørensen (eds.), *Europæiseringen af dansk ret* (Copenhagen: Djøf/Jurist- og Økonomforbundet, 2008), 475–511.

[26] See also J. Mayoral, K. Schaldemose, and M. Wind, *National High Courts as Gate-Keepers*, forthcoming.

legalism[27] as a new way of enforcing the law in Europe certainly is not supported by data from the Nordic part of Europe.

The interesting question is, of course, how we are then to explain the 'Uneven Push for Europe' or the 'Reluctance to Supranational Judicial Review' among some courts? I argue in my research that it all comes down to legal and political culture. As the Nordic countries are all majoritarian democracies with no tradition for judicial review at the national level, they will be very reluctant to forward cases to a supranational body primarily because this would resemble introducing judicial review nationally through the back door.[28] Doing so in any systematic manner would, in other words, challenge the privileged status of the parliament, which is regarded, also by national judges and ordinary citizens, as elevated above the other branches of government. In sum, in the Nordic countries, judicial review has traditionally been regarded as incompatible with majoritarian democracy and 'government by the people'.

The interesting question is, then, in my opinion, what consequences it has for the ordinary citizen if the reluctance to forward cases is a result of a legal 'protectionist culture'. There is probably little doubt that the issue on the research agenda for the future is not just differences in legal compliance culture and (lacking?) judicial dialogue, but also the crucial question of how we make sure that EU citizens have equal access to justice.

## Conclusion

*The Transformation of Europe* is still one of the most important pieces ever written on the EU – even twenty-five years after. What made ToE specifically valuable for political scientists was its explicit attempt to theorise law and political science in conjunction to offer a genuine theory of European integration. Theory aside, Weiler's most profound preoccupation for the past two decades has not been theorising but, I would argue, the issue of democracy and the EU's problems when

---

[27] See R. D. Kelemen, 'The Americansation of European law? Adversarial Legalism a la Européenne', *European Political Science*, 7 (2008), 32–42.

[28] See M. Wind, 'When Parliament Comes First - The Danish Concept of Democracy Meets the European Union', *Nordic Journal of Human Rights*, 27, 2 (2009); J. Elo Rytter and M. Wind, 'In Need of Juristocracy? The Silence of Denmark in the Development of European Legal Morms', *International Journal of Constitutional Law* 9, 2 (2011); see also M. Wind, 'Who Is Afraid of European Constitutionalism? The Nordic Distress with Judicial Review and Constitutional Democracy', *iCourts Working Paper*, 12, 2246–4891 (2014), 1–20.

it comes to delivering on this particular aspect vis-à-vis its citizens. Constitutionalism beyond the state[29] rather than statehood has been the answer to the Union's problems in Weilers 'book': constitutional tolerance and a union of several *demoi*. In ToE, he expressed a sincere worry that the constitutional balance might be undermined through majority voting and transfer of more member state competences to the EU level. A healthy constitutional indeterminacy that works was throughout Weiler's preferred option – or as he cunningly put it: if it ain't broke – why fix it? Nevertheless, while I agree with Weiler that the continued drive towards a federal constitutional settlement may be problematic, we still face the fundamental difficulty of making sure that citizens not only feel their individual (constitutional) culture is respected, *but also* trust that their rights are being equally protected across Europe. May not too much 'tolerance' lead to an uneven legal rights development, i.e., if narrow-minded local judges, politicians, or civil servants administrating EU rules, regulations, and CJEU case law interpret rights according to local mores instead of universal European standards? We have seen so much of exactly this in recent years. This does not mean that we should go back to the constitutional messianism of the past, but it does remind us that our deepest responsibility – also as theorists – goes not only to the celebration of a messy and wonderfully pluralist European ethos, but also to the citizen and her faith in Europe as a project of equal treatment. As the transformation of Europe has been the transformation of statehood, it should also be a true transformation of citizenship which is free, non-discriminatory, and no longer locked into traditional discretionary rights spheres.

---

[29]  See Weiler and Wind, *European Constitutionalism Beyond the State.*

# 16

# Europe Transformed. Exit, Voice ... and Loyalty?

MIGUEL POIARES MADURO

*The Transformation of Europe* transformed EU legal scholarship. Its transformative impact can perhaps only be rivalled by that of Eric Stein's piece *Lawyers, Judges and the Making of a Transnational Constitution,*[1] which effectively introduced the constitutional lexicon into EU legal scholarship.

The power of Weiler's piece lies in its many original ideas, but, above all, in presenting a simple but powerful analytical framework to explain how the transformation of Europe occurred and in the association made between that framework and a new methodological paradigm to study EU law and integration. One of the remarkable aspects of the article is the way in which Weiler links the originality of his substantive thesis with the originality of his methodology. Weiler departs by highlighting a paradox: two very different scholarly narratives of the founding period of European integration (that Weiler identifies until the mid-1970s). One was a narrative of increased integration; the other a narrative of stagnation and even retreat in integration. The explanation for the opposing narratives rested on different disciplines: lawyers looked at the process of European integration and saw the emergence of a federal or quasi-federal legal order; political scientists focused on the decision-making process and saw increased inter-governmentalism (in particular by new unanimity requirements). For Weiler, it was not simply a question of needing to know both in order to understand European integration; it was also that you could not really make sense of each of those narratives if you did not know the other. Lawyers could effectively understand and explain the success of legal integration only by looking at the world of politics and

Director, School of Transnational Governance, European University Institute. I would like to thank all the participants at the workshops at the European University Institute and Yale Law School for comments on a previous version. Thanks to Leonardo Pierdominici for research assistance in revising and editing the footnotes.

[1] E. Stein, 'Lawyers, Judges and the Making of a Transnational Constitution', *American Journal of International Law*, 75 (1981), 1.

noticing the increased intergovernmental control over decision-making, and vice versa. In this way, Weiler's substantive thesis is inextricably linked to his methodological claim towards a more interdisciplinary European legal scholarship.

In order to explain the interaction between the legal and the political, Weiler made use of the concepts of voice and exit originally developed by Albert Hirschman.[2] As is well known, in the use Weiler made of those concepts, exit (specifically selective exit) refers to 'the practice of the Member States of retaining membership of the Treaties but seeking to avoid their obligations under the Treaty, be it by omission or commission',[3] while voice refers to state control over decision-making.[4] The core of Weiler's thesis is the equilibrium between exit and voice. The emergence of a constitutional, federal type of legal order, decreasing the possibility for selective exit for States, was possible because of their increased voice in the processes of decision-making at the European level. It is this that explains the success of legal integration. But it is also on this equilibrium that Joseph Weiler seems to base much of the legitimacy of European integration. The tension inherent in it reflects the tension inherent in Weiler's preferred model of integration: the 'community vision', which is to be preferred to a union model copying the State, and which envisions a permanent, uneasy co-existence among States and each State and the Community.[5]

It is at this point that, with the skill of a screenwriter, Weiler leaves a seed of discomfort and suspense in his story of successful integration. Weiler alerts readers to the risk that the founding equilibrium could be put into question as a consequence of the growing powers and majority decision-making that followed the creation of the European single market in the late 1980s and early 1990s. Could Europe become a victim of its success? Has Europe, in fact, become a victim of its own success? And was there an alternative? Weiler presents the tension inherent in the founding equilibrium almost like an existential requirement of the project of European integration. At the same time, however, he presents the project as having a permanent incremental nature. This amounts to a tension in Weiler's

[2] A. O. Hirschman, *Exit, Voice, and Loyalty – Responses to Decline in Firms, Organizations and States* (Cambridge, MA: Harvard University Press, 1970).
[3] J. H. H. Weiler, 'The Transformation of Europe', *Yale Law Journal*, 100 (1991), 2403, at 2412.
[4] Ibid., at 2423.
[5] Ibid., at 2480.

approach itself that is wonderfully depicted by one of the final sentences of *The Transformation of Europe*:

> The *community* vision sees as its 'ideal type' a political union in which the Community and Member States continue their uneasy co-existence, although with an ever-increasing embrace.[6]

Weiler does not really articulate a theory of how to arbitrate the conflicts arising from that co-existence, nor does he say how that existential tension can be preserved in the face of its own internal logic of continuous increased integration. It's clear, particularly in subsequent works, that he sees with great suspicion any attempt to embark in any form of grand constitutional moment that would try to shortcut the incremental character of the *community* vision and risk its delicate balance. On the other hand, his most recent works put great emphasis on the need to embody the process of integration with values capable of liberating it from what he perceives as an equally dangerous technocratic ethos. How these different aspects can be reconciled is an open question.

To a large extent, Weiler's community vision seems to anticipate constitutional pluralism.[7] The latter departs from the recognition that in Europe's constitutional practice there are equal constitutional claims of final authority made by both the EU and national constitutional orders. For many constitutional pluralists, like myself, this reality of competing constitutional claims of final authority reflects the particular nature of the EU constitutional legitimacy. In this light, a normative claim is made that the question of final authority ought to be left open. Heterarchy[8] is superior to hierarchy as a normative ideal for the European Union. This normative thesis implies, in practice, another: that those competing constitutional claims are of equal legitimacy or, at least, cannot be balanced against each other in general terms.

---

[6] Ibid., at 2481.

[7] A connection that is reinforced by how he articulates his principle of constitutional tolerance in J. H. H. Weiler, 'Federalism and Constitutionalism: Europe's *Sonderweg*', *Harvard Jean Monnet Working Paper*, 10/00 (2001). For an overview of the constitutional pluralism scholarship in Europe, see M. Avbelj and J. Komarek (eds.), *Constitutional Pluralism in the European Union and Beyond* (Oxford: Hart Publishing, 2012).

[8] To use the expression of D. Halberstam, 'Constitutional Heterarchy: The Centrality of Conflict in the European Union and the United States', in J. Dunoff and J. Trachtman (eds.), *Ruling the World? Constitutionalism, International Law and Global Governance* (Cambridge: Cambridge University Press, 2009), 326.

The parallel with Weiler's notion of EU legitimacy founded on an equilibrium between voice and exit that, in turn, reflects a permanent existential tension between the Community (now the Union) and the States is obvious. It is not surprising, therefore, for one of the most common challenges to constitutional pluralism to be similar to that faced by Weiler's: how to preserve that permanent tension between equal claims of final normative authority. The assertion is that the nature of those claims is such that ultimately one of them must prevail. My answer, in the context of constitutional pluralism, has been that there is no point in discussing if one will prevail and, if so, which one. Instead, what is important is to discuss how to frame the current context of constitutional pluralism in a way that is supportive of EU legitimacy. Whether there will be a final answer to the question of ultimate constitutional authority between state and EU law will be itself the product of the practice of constitutional pluralism. At the moment, instead, it is that practice of constitutional pluralism that is itself constitutive of the legitimacy of EU law.

What is not necessary, both for constitutional pluralism and, I would argue, for Weiler's *community* vision is for its existential and legitimating tension to always be preserved by the particular equilibrium between voice and exit of its foundational period. EU legitimacy will continue to require, at least in the foreseeable future, that that existential tension between EU and state authority be preserved, but the way that is guaranteed may change. The core of my chapter will identify how a transformed European Union can still secure such legitimacy.

### Europe Transformed: Constitutionalisation and Europeanisation

In *The Transformation of Europe*, Weiler announced that the founding equilibrium was likely to be destabilised by the expansion of the Community jurisdiction and the reintroduction of majority voting following the European single market. In my chapter, I will argue that such destabilisation has been even bigger than Weiler predicted. For that purpose, I will build on a description of Europeanisation that I have put forward in a previous work. My starting point is that there is actually a much closer link between the two periods of the transformation of Europe described by Weiler than one might initially think.

For Weiler, what explains the radical departure of Community law from international law is the combined effect of constitutionalisation with the evolution of the system of legal remedies.[9] But the constitutionalisation's

---

[9] Weiler, 'The Transformation of Europe', 2422.

transformative impact is presented more as a consequence of its quantitative impact than of an inherent qualitative difference. For Weiler, some doctrines such as direct effect and supremacy, could, as well, be presented as international law doctrines, only their application in the Community had assumed such magnitude that it amounted to a qualitative difference.[10] What mattered is that the Community legal order resulting from the foundational period operated like a constitutional order.[11]

I would like to argue, however, that the constitutionalisation of Community law had a much deeper foundation, one that was qualitative in nature from its beginnings in the Court's case law. Moreover, if understood in this way, the constitutionalisation of Community law already embodies the seeds of Europeanisation. In other words, the second period of the transformation of Europe is a direct result of the first.

The basis of my argument is the conception of the normative authority of Community law underpinning the judgments of the ECJ on direct effect and supremacy. That conception assumed a direct relation between Community rules and the peoples of Europe. The treaty is presented as more than an agreement between States; it is an agreement between the peoples of Europe that established a direct relationship between EC law and those peoples.[12] In practice, and simultaneously, the treaties were constituted by and constituted a new sovereign authority, distinct from the States but founded on the peoples of those States. It is this that also explains the autonomy of the Community legal order (from both State and international legal orders).[13] This corresponded, in fact, to a claim

---

[10] Ibid., at 2418. See also B. de Witte, 'The European Union as an International Legal Experiment', in G. de Búrca and J. H. H. Weiler (eds.), *The Worlds of European Constitutionalism* (Cambridge: Cambridge University Press, 2012), 19.

[11] Weiler, 'The Transformation of Europe', 2422.

[12] Case C-26/62 *NV Algemene Transport- en Expeditie Onderneming van Gend & Loos v Netherlands Inland Revenue Administration* [1963] ECR 3.

[13] See the link between Case C-26/62 *NV Algemene Transport- en Expeditie Onderneming van Gend & Loos v Netherlands Inland Revenue Administration* [1963] ECR 3 and Joined Cases 402/05 and 415/05 *Kadi and Al Barakaat International Foundation v Council and Commission* [2008] ECR I-6351, also suggested by G. Martinico, 'The Autonomy of EU Law: A Joint Kadi II – Van Gend en Loos Celebration', in M. Avbelj, F. Fontanelli and G. Martinico (eds.), *Kadi on Trial: A Multifaceted Analysis of the Kadi Trial* (Abingdon: Routledge, 2014), 157. See also the common thread among cases such as Judgment of 4 February 1959, Stork & Cie. / ECSC High Authority (1/58, ECR 1959 p. 17), Judgment of 17 December 1970, Internationale Handelsgesellschaft mbH / Einfuhr- und Vorratsstelle für Getreide und Futtermittel (11/70, ECR 1970 p. 1125), Judgment of 26 February 2013, Melloni (C-399/11) ECLI:EU:C:2013:107, Opinion 2/13, of 18 December 2014 (ECLI:EU:C:2014:2454).

of independent normative authority that also meant that the European Communities were, in the words of the Court, endowed with sovereign rights.[14] This normative authority and its autonomy also entitled (required) the Community legal order to set its borders with regard to national and international legal orders.

The assumption of independent normative authority required the adoption of further constitutional doctrines to constrain and legitimise that authority such as the protection of fundamental rights. This created a self-feeding dynamic on the part of European constitutionalism. The stronger the constitutional claim of authority, the deeper the form of constitutionalism necessary. But it also limited it to a constitutionalism instrumental to and defined by that claim of constitutional authority. Law was constitutionalised, but politics remained intergovernmental.[15]

Nevertheless, the normative autonomy of Community law, founded on a source of legitimacy flowing directly from the peoples of Europe and, therefore, not dependent on the States, also allowed the expansion of the political ambitions inherent in the process of European integration. This has been reinforced by the functional dynamics of the process of economic integration and by the progressive shift of political action from the national to the European arena. As a consequence, independent normative authority has been complemented by increased independent political authority (the autonomy to define the forms and goals of its political action). This is visible in a series of phenomena that can be classified under the general heading of Europeanisation.

The first element of Europeanisation relates to the growth of Community and now EU competences. This has expanded well beyond what Weiler already identified in *The Transformation*. Any analysis of the extension of EU powers will emphasise the growth of its competencies through successive Treaty revisions, the use of the internal market and

---

[14] See the famous jargon adopted in Case C-26/62 *NV Algemene Transporten Expeditie Onderneming van Gend & Loos v Netherlands Inland Revenue Administration* [1963] ECR 3, part II/B: 'The objective of the EEC Treaty, which is to establish a common market, the functioning of which is of direct concern to interested parties in the Community, implies that this Treaty is more than an agreement which merely creates mutual obligations between the contracting states. This view is confirmed by the preamble to the Treaty which refers not only to governments but to peoples. It is also confirmed more specifically by the establishment of institutions endowed with sovereign rights, the exercise of which affects Member States and also their citizens.'

[15] I develop and explain the risks of this in M. Poiares Maduro, 'The Importance of Being Called a Constitution: Constitutional Authority and the Authority of Constitutionalism', *International Journal of Constitutional Law*, 3 (2005), 332.

implied powers provisions of the Treaty of Rome by the political process, and the expansive interpretation of those and other Treaty provisions made by the European Court of Justice. These developments have turned the European Union into a new space for political action with respect to largely open and undetermined goals. The borders of the Union action are no longer defined by the explicit competences that the States have attributed to it. They result instead from the political action of a broad variety of European, State, and infra-State actors that attempt to promote their interests in a new level of decision-making whose political authority is such as to allow for the pursuit of almost any set of policy goals. Inherent in this is the emergence of the European Union as a political community where many of the traditional functions of governance are now exercised.

A second element of the process of Europeanisation is related, instead, to the degree of EU control and impact on those policies that continue to be pursued by the States (either exclusively or concurrently with the Union). A key role in the Europeanisation of the States has been played by market integration rules of the Treaty and the simple dynamics generated by economic integration itself. The Europeanisation of national policies through market integration can, in the first place, be seen in the way in which the Court of Justice and the Commission control the exercise of many national competences through the application of the rules of market integration. A good example regards the interpretation of the free movement rules. The broad scope of application conferred to these rules meant that they could, *de facto*, be used to challenge almost any area of national legislation that impacts the market. This led to a spill-over of EU law and its rationale of market integration into other political and social spheres at the national level.[16] National legislation regulating the market became subject to review under EU law and assessed under its criteria of necessity and proportionality, independent of any protectionism intent or effects. This meant that EU law often second-guesses the reasonableness of national policies on areas such as consumer, environmental, or health protection. In addition, this soft Europeanisation often triggers hard Europeanisation (in the form of EU legislation on those issues).

Finally, Europeanisation did not take place only with regard to the extent of competences transferred from the States to the European Union. Also the way in which such competences are exercised has been progressively Europeanised, in the sense of being the product of a European

---

[16] See M. Poiares Maduro, *We The Court: The European Court of Justice and the European Economic Constitution* (Oxford: Hart Publishing, 1997).

majority. This is so, first of all, because of the move from unanimous decision-making to majoritarian decision-making in the Council. Also in this respect, the move towards majoritarian decision-making has extended well beyond the internal market area Weiler discussed in *The Transformation of Europe*. But furthermore, the majoritarian character of the Union has been strongly (perhaps too strongly) reinforced by the fact that proportional representation to the population now dominates both the Parliament and the Council.

All this means that the European Union is today, to a large extent, a majoritarian polity. Such a polity entails an open and undetermined field of competences and policy choices, a system of decision-making dominated by majority vote, proportional dominated criteria of representation, and a certain degree of closure.

In such a context, how could one prevent the legitimacy crisis that Weiler, in practice, already anticipated in a much more limited set of circumstances? Is there a way to reinstate the founding equilibrium albeit in a different form, or is the tension and equilibrium inherent in the original form of European constitutionalism simply unsustainable? The last two parts of this chapter are devoted to highlight both that the legitimacy crisis is here and how to answer it.

## The Crisis of Legitimacy

I will highlight at least four dimensions of the crisis.

The first dimension is a cognitive one. It is expressed, notably, in the increased tension between, on the one side, the political scope of the European Union and the expectations that it creates in its citizens and, on the other side, its existing policies and politics. Citizens have expectations with regard to the Union that the Union cannot, in light of its current competences, politics, and means of action, fulfil. If one looks at the Eurobarometer surveys, we discover – perhaps surprisingly, perhaps not – that among the goals and policies indicated by citizens as those from which they expect more from the Union are matters such as economic growth, social solidarity, promotion of peace and democracy, and fighting crime and unemployment, all areas where the European Union either has no competences or has only limited instruments to intervene.[17] A second

---

[17] This disparity between what the Union can do and what citizens expect leads them to develop an almost schizophrenic perspective of the European Union, one that reminds me of an anecdote told at the end of Woody Allen's movie *Annie Hall*. A couple goes out for dinner in New York and spends the entire meal complaining of how bad the food is. 'It is

aspect is the strong asymmetry between the diffuse character of the larger benefits of European integration (economic growth, peace, etc.) and the concentrated character of its perceived costs (like reforms of deep-rooted national policies benefitting particular social groups). This is reinforced, in the increasingly important financial domain, by the absence of any revenues capable of signalling to citizens the wealth created by the Union itself. Instead of the Union distributing at least part of the wealth it generates, it is perceived as transferring the wealth of some states to other states.

The second dimension is a political gap. First, there is a gap between the policy impact of the EU and its politics. The European Union is perceived by citizens as shaping the economic and social model of Europe without the corresponding policy instruments or political debate. This is, in large part, a consequence of the well-known gap between negative integration (economic integration through national markets' deregulation: elimination of national measures restrictive of free movement) and positive integration (economic integration through Community-wide reregulation: adoption of harmonised legislative measures by the EU political process).[18] Jürgen Habermas has argued that this social gap results from globalisation and that the European Union is, instead, best conceived as a solution to it.[19] But that view is yet to prevail and the EU is increasingly presented as an instrument of a particular ideological agenda. Both in *The Transformation of Europe* and in subsequent works, Weiler himself alerted to the risks involved in assuming the project of economic integration as ideological or value neutral. Increasing the capacity for regulatory intervention of the EU will not, by itself, solve this problem. Depoliticising EU action is no longer a solution and is, instead, perceived as a form of hiding the ideological agenda. The deeper problem is that even if the Union would develop the necessary policies it does not seem to have the politics. In fact, the absence of such politics is the main reason for the absence of the policies. The second dimension of its political gap is therefore the lack of the politics necessary to support the political scope of the Union. As the Euro crisis so clearly illustrates, European politics are still national politics that have not even adequately internalised the European dimension of policies. The incapacity of national politics to

---

terrible, the worst food we ever had.' 'Yes, it is uneatable but, more importantly, the portions are so small.'

[18] See the well-known remarks by F. Scharpf, *Governing in Europe: Effective and Democratic?* (Oxford: Oxford University Press, 1999), in particular in chapter 2.

[19] J. Habermas, *The Post-national Constellation* (Cambridge: Polity Press, 2000).

internalise interdependence leads to a failure of European policies in the absence of genuine European politics.[20]

The third dimension is the paradox of inclusion and its impact in the internal and external borders of the Union. I have argued elsewhere that the Union is, at its core, a project of inclusion.[21] This has an internal and external dimension. Internally, the Union promotes the inclusion of the interests of the citizens of one Member State in the polity of another Member State. But an ever-extended inclusion would lead to a dissolution of State polities into the European polity. St. Tomas of Aquinas once said that if all are my friends, then no one is my friend. Having friends entails differentiating. A successful political community is also found in preferring our own. To deny to national political communities the right, in some respects, to still prefer their own would deny their existence. This would put into question the existential tension that both Weiler and constitutional pluralists identify as still necessary for the legitimacy of the project of European integration. In fact, the situation is even more complex in the EU since we can identify risks of both over-inclusion (mostly by the Union overreaching in shaping national political determinations) and sub-inclusion (because many European citizens do not effectively benefit from integration and because many externalities are still being imposed by some States on other States). The external dimension of the inclusion crisis is enlargement. Enlargement is the best example of the philosophy of inclusion that defines, to a great extent, the process of European integration. But the paradox is that over-inclusion may also here become a threat to the process of integration. The increased instability of the EU polity is affecting the empirical conditions supportive of integration. This does not exclude further integration, but requires a deeper debate about the balance between the closure and openness to be achieved in the EU polity.

---

[20] I develop this point in M. Poiares Maduro, 'A New Governance for the European Union and the Euro: Democracy and Justice', Robert Schuman Centre for Advanced Studies Policy Paper No. 2012/11.

[21] Weiler's principle of constitutional tolerance is very similar to this: see J. H. H. Weiler, 'Federalism without Constitutionalism: Europe's *Sonderweg*', in K. Nicolaïdis and R. Howse (eds.), *The Federal Vision* (Oxford: Oxford University Press, 2001), 54. For my own vision, see Poiares Maduro, 'We the Court: The European Court of Justice and the European Economic Constitution', op. Cit., at 174 ff. In particular, see M. Poiares Maduro, 'Europe and the Constitution: What If This Is as Good as It Gets?', in M. Wind and J. H. H. Weiler (eds.), *European Constitutionalism Beyond the State* (Cambridge: Cambridge University Press, 2003), 74.

The fourth dimension is a constitutional gap. It is a product of the tension between normative constitutionalism and political intergovernmentalism inherent in the foundational equilibrium identified by Weiler. As stated, law in the European Union is constitutional, but politics remains predominantly (though not exclusively) intergovernmental. Policy decisions continue to be primarily a product of intergovernmental bargaining. More importantly, they continue to be often framed in intergovernmental terms. National governments aggregate the preferences of their citizens and EU policies strike a balance between those aggregated preferences.

The results of these intergovernmental bargainings take the form, however, of European 'universal' rules addressed to all EU citizens. This raises important problems. First, it interferes with the mechanisms for political accountability at both the national and European levels. National governments may, for example, transfer unpopular decisions from the national to the European level as a way of transferring the political costs for those decisions. More importantly, it raises deep questions as to the extent of constitutionalism in the European Union. When States negotiate national quotas for certain products, often trading the interests of some of their producers for the interests of others (as in any international negotiation), can the producers from a particular State claim before the Union that they are being discriminated against because they are less well treated than those in another Member State? We are often being asked to derogate from the true standards of constitutionalism in order to respect the intergovernmental nature of EU decision-making.

This intergovernmental challenge to constitutionalism is severely aggravated by the increased majoritarian character of the EU polity highlighted earlier. There could be nothing worse than a form of intergovernmental majoritarianism, one where majorities are defined along national boundaries. Unfortunately, as I have argued elsewhere, that is a real risk resulting from the current evolution of the EU institutional system.[22]

## Loyalty

The mapping of these different dimensions of the EU legitimacy crisis highlights similarities but also differences with what Joseph Weiler

[22] M. Poiares Maduro, 'The New Form of Majoritarianism in the EU', *European Law Review*, 28 (2003), 900–4.

anticipated. More importantly, however, these dimensions share the tension that I have identified in Weiler's work: they appear to pull in different directions. Requiring more European powers and politics but also a stronger protection of national powers and politics. Claiming for more European constitutionalism but also for a protection of the claims of national constitutionalism. Demanding inclusion but also a certain degree of closure. To a large extent this is a reflection of the constitutional pluralism on which the Union is founded. The problem is that the foundational equilibrium supporting that constitutional pluralism has disappeared.

Reconciling these different pulls requires a new foundational equilibrium, one where loyalty will have to play a much more important role. Loyalty is the third concept Hirschman uses. Weiler mentions it only briefly but does so to highlight what will be necessary once the foundational equilibrium will be put into question. He appears, however, to expect loyalty to replace the equilibrium and not to be an element of a new equilibrium. He also appears to conceive loyalty from a purely empirical perspective. It will be there or not.[23] This is reinforced by the idea that it will depend on a sense of belonging, to be determined, on a long-term basis, by factors such as political continuity, social, cultural, and linguistic affinity.[24] Weiler does not seem to look at it favourably from a normative point of view.

In the last part of my chapter, I want to argue, departing from Hirschman's own use of the concept of loyalty, that it can, first, be used as part of a new equilibrium with voice and exit and not as a substitute to them and, second, that being the case, it should also be constructed in normative terms (in other words, we ought to discuss what we ought to do to secure loyalty).

For Hirschman, loyalty is not really a substitute for voice and exit. Loyalty activates voice. When we commit to an organisation or polity, we are encouraged to use voice to shape it. But loyalty is also a function of exit. The easier it will be to exit, the less relevant voice becomes. However, paradoxically, that same possibility renders voice more effective. This is so because of the threat of exit.[25]

As Hirschman puts it: 'loyalty is a key concept in the battle between voice and exit.'[26] But it is so because it is the product of a rational choice.

---

[23] Weiler, 'The Transformation of Europe', 2464.
[24] Ibid., at 2470; Hirschman, *Exit, Voice and Loyalty*, at 77 and ff.
[25] Ibid., at 82–83.
[26] Ibid., at 82.

Hirschman is very clear in distinguishing loyalty from faith.[27] Loyalty is the result of the extent to which a member estimates his or her possible influence.[28] This opens the door to make a normative construction of loyalty for the EU without incurring the risks of cultural, religious, or ethnic exclusivity that Joseph Weiler, mostly in his post-ToE work, worked so much to combat at the national level and to prevent from emerging at the EU level.

What kind of rules, values, or processes are necessary to secure to all EU citizens an equal estimation of influence? This should be the inquiry. At the same time, this conception of loyalty must be part of a new equilibrium on voice and exit, and not a substitute for where that equilibrium is missing. This allows us to place loyalty in the context of the preservation of the existential tension that both Weiler and constitutional pluralists still consider crucial for the legitimacy of European integration. How is this to be done in the European Union? By reconstructing voice and exit in light of loyalty.

One of the interesting aspects of Hirschman's construction of loyalty is its link to voice. How else to interpret making loyalty depend on our estimation of influence? Loyalty does not require, however, one to be influential himself or herself but, in the words of Hirschman, 'the expectation that *someone* will act or *something* will happen to improve matters'. This provides a powerful insight into the role of voice as an element securing loyalty in a political community. It is possible to move from a system based on individual voice (veto power) to a system based on what we could define as systemic voice. In other words, the replacement of voice for loyalty is largely a replacement between two different forms of voice: one focuses on individual decisions, the other on systemic voice.

In my view, securing loyalty in the EU requires a move towards systemic voice. But what does this mean? As stated, Hirschman measures the expectation of influence by the likelihood that *someone will act* (not necessarily us) or *something will happen* (not necessarily now and not necessarily directly on each specific issue). Voice can therefore be exercised by proxies; it can vary and take place at different moments; and it can result from compensation through other actions. This, I argue, is how we should construct a concept of systemic voice supportive of loyalty.

---

[27] 'In comparison to the act of pure faith, the most loyalist behavior retains an enormous dose of reasoned calculation': ibid., at 78–9.

[28] The estimate of their ability to influence the organisation (in our case, the EU polity): ibid., at 77.

I can't get into details in this short chapter, but I can state what are, in my view, the basic conditions necessary for systemic voice in the EU. First, systemic identity. In other words, that the fundamental values of the Union coincide with the fundamental values of the member states. Second, a deliberative and institutional system favouring proxy politics (where national majorities can be, more often than not, replaced by cross-national ideological majorities). In other words, a form of politics where your representation is not limited to your State and you know that, in most issues, even if you are part of a small State you will be equally represented by others in larger States. Third, a majoritarian system where majorities and minorities are not rigid but instead of fluid composition. A system preventing the emergence of permanent and insulated minorities (*net losers*) and the aggregation of individuals in rigid majorities, or the creation of pivotal players. This guarantees to any citizen part of the minority in a particular decision a chance to be part of the majority in a different decision. At the same time, it limits zero-sum decisions (since those that compose the majority know that they can, in the next deliberation, be part of the minority and have, therefore, an incentive to internalise some of the interests of the losing minority). Unfortunately, I fear that the current institutional system may not satisfy all these conditions.

This may render even more important the other side of the equilibrium: exit. Again, in here I can only limit myself to state that threats of selective exit are likely to increase in the EU but may also face stronger instruments of enforcement on the part of EU law. As such, it is likely that threats of selective exit may be fewer but be *upgraded* into national constitutional challenges. It is unclear at this point if this will end in conflict or a new form of constitutional accommodation. The consequence may not be a de facto increase on selective exit. Instead a new form of exit may develop, one resulting from that new constitutional accommodation taking place between the claims of supremacy of the ECJ and national constitutional courts. I would call this *internal exit*. It will be managed by the ECJ, under the pressure of national constitutional courts, by making use of two legal concepts. First, there would be an increased recourse to the concept of national constitutional identity to allow national derogations from EU law. Second, the Court would increase its counter-majoritarian role, notably in the review of EU competences when subject to majority decision-making.

Times are not appropriate, however, to end in an optimist tone. I therefore want to end by making explicit a deep discomfort that permeates my search for loyalty in the EU. I have been discussing loyalty on the assumption that exit is still possible. The Treaty now expressly allows it,[29] and the outcome of the UK referendum on Brexit makes that legal possibility concrete. This apparently contradicts the idea that full exit is not economically and politically viable for a State for the reasons Weiler already highlighted in *The Transformation of Europe*.[30] In fact, however, the discussions on the possible alternatives to UK membership already highlight the extent to which full exit is unlikely. The UK is fast realising the high (if not unbearable) costs of exiting the EU. It will discover that one can exit EU governance but not European interdependence.

The degree of interdependence between European states is such that the situation becomes similar to what Hirschman identifies with respect to the production of public goods and evils (producing positive and negative externalities): it does not matter if you exit since you will remain subject to the organisation choices.[31] There may be areas where a state could, by successful selective exit, avoid contributing to the production of a public good, but it will still be affected by how that public good (or evil) will be produced by others.[32] Furthermore, selective exit in one area may lead to exclusion from another area. In other words, the extent of interdependence both between States and between EU policies is such that it renders increasingly difficult any effective form of exit for States. As Hirschman notes with respect to public goods and evils, the paradox is that the more you may want to exit, the more difficult the decision to exit becomes.[33] In that case, loyalty is no longer a choice; it's the only option that you have. This is the real risk, if perceived as such, for the EU. What makes us a different kind of polity is that we were not born into it. It was our choice. It

---

[29] See the exit clause for Members which wish to withdraw from the Union introduced by the Treaty of Lisbon, i.e., TEU Article 50, according to which (par. 1), 'Any Member State may decide to withdraw from the Union in accordance with its own constitutional requirements.'

[30] See Weiler, 'The Transformation of Europe', 2412 ff. and 2465.

[31] Hirschman, *Exit, Voice and Loyalty*, at 100 ff.

[32] The Euro is a good example. Being in or being out does not fully exclude a State from its consequences. Even if not part of the Euro, a State can be both the subject and the producer of externalities resulting from currency exchange fluctuations. It can also be directly affected by its crisis and have to intervene financially in its support, as the UK has recently found out. Similarly, to a large extent, it is the mismatch between voice and exit that explains both the emergence of the Euro crisis and the incapacity to effectively address it. It is the dangerous mix of strong potential for mutual externalities (arising from interdependence) with insufficient voice that explains the current crisis.

[33] Hirschman, *Exit, Voice and Loyalty*, at 103. At a certain point, as he notes, the alternative is no longer one between voice and exit but between voice from within and voice from without.

needs to stay our choice. Its voluntary character needs to be constantly reasserted in order for the Union to preserve its legitimacy. But at the same time, that will only be possible if we take seriously the choice for interdependence that we have made. Ultimately, the question we face is how to legitimately govern the consequences of the interdependence we have entered into.

# 17

# The Transformation of Europe Revisited: The Things that Do Not Transform

## J. H. H. WEILER

*The Transformation of Europe*, published in 1991 in the *Yale Law Journal*, was ten years in the making. Its infant version was in EUI Working Paper No 2 from 1981 titled 'Supranationalism Revisited: Retrospective and Prospective – The European Communities after Thirty Years'. It went through various iterations such as 'The Community System: The Dual Character of Supranationalism', which appeared in the recently born *Yearbook of European Law*,[1] later in *Il Sistema Comunitario Europeo – Struttura Giuridica e Processo Politico* (Il Mulino, 1985), and then, in its final and mature version in 1991 as *Transformation*, after which I had had enough and moved on to other themes.

Given the immodest ambition of that project, to revisit *Transformation* is to revisit the European system and in a sense to revisit the transformation of my own thinking of that system.

*Transformation* has had no shortage of critics – Daniela Caruso's spectacular *The Missing View of the Cathedral*[2] being a memorable early legal critique, and ending with Alec Stone Sweet and Dan Kelemen's very generous critique in this volume.[3] No one to circle the wagon, my own work subsequent to *Transformation* could be read as a slow dismantling of what was left of cathedral. Even on such foundational notions such as how to read *Van Gend en Loos* I have come to understand (and teach) things differently.[4]

---

[1] I recall being sorely disappointed that it did not win the prize that Oxford University Press awarded to the best paper published in the *Yearbook*. *Vanitas Vanitatum*. It did become the most cited article in the history of the *Yearbook* – *Vanitas Vanitatum Omnia Vanitas!*

[2] D. Caruso, 'The Missing View of the Cathedral: The Private Law Paradigm of European Legal Integration', *European Law Journal*, 3 (1997), 3.

[3] I think the real difference between Alec, Dan and me has to do with the methodology of 'proof' in the social sciences than in our understanding of Europe.

[4] J. H. H. Weiler, 'Rewriting Van Gend & Loos: Towards a Normative Theory of ECJ Hermeneutics', in O. Wiklund (ed.) *Judicial Discretion in European Perspective* (The Hague: Norstedts Juridik, Stockholm/Kluwer, 2003).

But some things have remained untransformed in my own thinking and, I believe, in European integration.

*Transformation* posited as its foundational explanatory key to understanding the success of the European construct, the equilibrium between legal structure (as a proxy for the institutional edifice of European integration) and legitimation rooted in national polities.

When in subsequent work I proposed a normative theory of European integration ('To Be a European Citizen';[5] 'Constitutional Tolerance'[6]), the robust 'survival' of the of the national demos in a system of multiple demoi, and legitimation in national polities and politics was posited not as a necessary evil, but as the defining element in the normative originality and nobility of European integration, and its distinguishing feature from all other federalisms in which the federal demos tends to dominate legally and oftentimes even to obliterate culturally and socially all others.

I still believe that that woefully underspecified concept of 'legitimacy' is an indispensable element of any understanding of the European construct since it is the indispensable oxygen, the political reservoir to which we reach out in times of crisis for it is that which allows the adoption of policies which are not popular and go outside the normal cycles of democratic politics.

The quest for understanding legitimacy in the context of European integration is thus another untransformed element in my intellectual wanderings. In my current work I have come to understand the tragic nature of the European construct. A satisfactory democratic legitimation will, I have come to think, necessarily come at the expense of the normative nobility of constitutional tolerance.

Turning then (yet again[7]) to legitimacy, European discourse employs two principal concepts: input (process) legitimacy and output (result) legitimacy. I wish to add a third, less explored, but in my view central legitimating feature of Europe – political messianism. I propose to explore, in turn, each of these forms of legitimacy in their European context, and in relation to each show why, in my view, they are exhausted, inoperable in

---

[5] J. H. H. Weiler, 'To Be a European Citizen: Eros and Civilization', *Journal of European Public Policy*, 4 (1997), 495.

[6] J. H. H. Weiler, 'Federalism without Constitutionalism: Europe's *Sonderweg*', in K. Nicolaïdis and R. Howse (eds.), *The Federal Vision: Legitimacy and Levels of Governance in the United States and the European Union* (Oxford/New York: Oxford University Press, 2001).

[7] I develop here some ideas first explored in J. H. H. Weiler, 'The Political and Legal Culture of European Integration: An Exploratory Essay', *International Journal of Constitutional Law (ICON)*, 9, 3-4 (2011), 678–94.

the current circumstance. The current crisis overwhelms current thinking of European integration. A larger perspective may, thus, be of some utility. But even in the context of the current crisis, whereas Europe requires *European* solutions, if these are to be successfully adopted, they will require an employment of legitimacy resources to be found within *national* communities. To the extent that these national resources will be found to be depleted, the crisis we are facing will remain not only insoluble but existential.

## I   On Two Genres and Three Types of Legitimacy

There are two basic genres – languages, vocabularies – of legitimacy: normative and social. The vocabulary of normative legitimacy is moral, ethical, and it is informed by political theory. It is an objective measure even though there will be obvious ideological differences as to what should be considered legitimate governance. Social legitimacy is empirical, assessed or measured with the tools of social science. It is a subjective measure, reflecting social attitudes. It is not a measurement of popularity, but of a deeper form of acceptance of the political regime.

The two types of legitimacy often inform each other and may even conflate, but not necessarily so. A series of examples will clarify. By our liberal pluralist normative yardstick, German National Socialism of the 1930s and 1940s was a horrible aberration, the negation of legitimate governance. Yet, socially and empirically, for most Germans almost until the defeat in 1945 it was not only popular, but considered deeply legitimate leadership. By contrast, Weimer democracy would pass our normative test of legitimate government, yet for a very large number of Germans it was not merely unpopular, but considered illegitimate leadership, a betrayal of Germany.

However, in less extreme situations, we do expect some measure of conflation between the two. One hopes that if a regime is normatively legitimate, because, say, it practises constitutional democracy, it will enjoy widespread social legitimacy, and that the opposite will be true too: in a regime which fails the normative tests, one hopes that the social legitimacy will be low too. One can imagine complicated permutations of these parameters.

Legitimacy, normative or social, should not be conflated with legality. Forbidding blacks to sit in the front of the bus was perfectly legal, but would fail many a test of normative legitimacy, and with time lost its social legitimacy as well. There are illegal measures which are considered, normatively and/or socially, as legitimate, and legal measures which are considered illegitimate.

For the purpose of this chapter, it is worth exploring briefly the relationship between popularity and legitimacy. If I am a lifelong adherent of the Labour Party in the UK, I might be appalled by the election of the Tories and abhor every single measure adopted by the government of the Tory prime minister. But it would never enter my mind to consider such measures 'illegitimate'. In fact, and this is critical for one of the principal propositions of this chapter, the deeper the legitimacy resources of a regime, the better able it is to adopt *unpopular* measures critical in the time of crisis when exactly such measures may be necessary.

There is something peculiar about the current crisis. Even if there are big differences between the austerity and immediate growth camps, everyone knows that a solution has to be European, within a European framework. And yet, it has become self-evident that crafting a European solution has become so difficult, that the institutions and the Union decision-making process do not seem to be engaging satisfactorily and effectively with the crisis, even when employing the intergovernmental methodology, and that it is governments, national leaders, of a small club, who seem to be calling the shots. The problem is European, but Europe as such, its own Institutions, is finding it difficult to craft the remedies.

I would like to argue that in the present circumstance, the legitimacy resources of the European Union – referring here mostly to social legitimacy – are depleted, and that is why the Union has had to turn to the Member States for salvation.

Alan Milward famously and convincingly wrote on the European rescue of the nation-state.[8] The pendulum has swung, and in the present crisis it will be the nation-state rescue of the European Union. The complicating factor, which makes the present crisis unprecedented, is the legitimacy crisis in which several of our Member States find themselves, with large sectors of the electorate turning to populist/extremist parties on the left and right. These parties often offer policies which are of limited credibility to an objective observer. Their appeal is precisely in that they give an outlet to a deep dissatisfaction with the institutions of democracy and with democracy as an institution. National democratic legitimacy is also reaching crisis levels.

---

[8] A. Milward, *The European Rescue of the Nation State*, 2nd edition (London and New York: Routledge, 2000).

Moving from the genres of legitimacy to a typology of legitimacy, I would like to suggest the three most important types or forms of legitimacy which have been central to the discussion of European integration. The most ubiquitous have been various variations on the theme of input and output legitimacy.[9]

> Process (or Input) Legitimacy – which in the current circumstance can, with some simplification, be synonymised with democracy. It is easier put in the negative: To the extent that the European mode of governance departs from the habits and practices of democracy as understood in the Member States, its legitimacy, in this case both normative and social will be compromised.
>
> Result (or Output) Legitimacy – which, again simplifying somewhat, would be all modern versions of Bread and Circus. As long as the Union delivers 'the goods' – prosperity, stability, security – it will enjoy a legitimacy that derives from a subtle combination of success *per se*, of success in realising its objectives and of contentment with those results. There is no better way to legitimate a war than win it. This variant of legitimacy is part of the very ethos of the Commission.
>
> Telos Legitimacy or Political Messianism whereby legitimacy is gained neither by process nor output but by promise, the promise of an attractive Promised Land. I will elaborate on this later.

I will now try and illustrate the collapse of all three forms of legitimacy in the current European circumstance.

## II   Europe, the Current Circumstances

This is an interesting time to be reflecting on the European construct. Europe is at a nadir which one cannot remember for many decades and which, various brave or pompous or self-serving statements notwithstanding,[10] the Treaty of Lisbon has not been able to redress. The surface manifestations of

---

[9] I have found helpful M. Boedeltje and J. Cornips, 'Input and Output Legitimacy in Interactive Governance'. Technical report, October 2004; K. Lindgren and T. Persson, 'Input and Output Legitimacy: Synergy or Trade-Off? Empirical Evidence from an EU Survey', *Journal of European Public Policy*, 17, 4 (2010).

[10] See, for example, 'Plenary Session of the European Parliament, Strasbourg, 20 February 2008: Treaty of Lisbon', which includes various statements from the members of the European Parliament, Janez Lenarcic, President of the Council and Margot Wallström, Vice-President of the European Commission, as well as the European Parliament resolution of 20 February 2008 on the Treaty of Lisbon (2007/2286(INI)); 'Brussels European Council 14 December 2007', Brussels, 14 February 2008, 16616/1/07 REV 1, including the EU declaration on globalisation; European Commission, 'Your Guide to the Lisbon Treaty', http://ec.europa.eu/publications/booklets/others/84/en.pdf, President Buzek, News of the

crisis are with us every day on the front pages: the Euro crisis[11] being the most current. Beneath this surface, at the structural level, lurk more profound and long term signs of enduring challenge and even dysfunction and malaise. Let us refract them through the lens of legitimacy.[12]

First, as regards process legitimacy, there is the persistent, chronic, troubling democracy deficit, which cannot be talked away.

First, although the 'no demos' thesis seems to have receded in recent discourse, its relevance is suddenly more acute than ever. The difficulties, as will be seen, of constructing all manner of 'fiscal union' type solutions for the Euro crisis are in no small measure the result of – yes, 'no demos' – a lack of transcendent responsibility for the lot of one's fellow citizens and nationals. Germans and Dutch and Finns are not saying: 'A bailout is the wrong policy.' They are saying, why should we Germans, or Dutch, or Finns help those lazy Italians or Portuguese or Greeks? A very visible manifestation of the no-demos thesis of Europe's democracy crisis.

Second, there are failures of democracy which simply make it difficult to speak of governance 'by and of' the people. The manifestations of the so-called democracy deficit are persistent and no endless repetition of the powers of the European Parliament will remove them. In essence it is the inability of the Union to develop structures and processes which adequately replicate or, 'translate',[13] at the Union level even the imperfect

European Parliament, 1 December 2009, www.europarl.europa.eu/president/ressource/static/newsletter/newsletter-3/newsletter.html?ts=1277465318672; José Manuel Durao Barroso, President of the European Commission, 'The European Union after the Lisbon Treaty', 4th Joint Parliamentary meeting on the Future of Europe, Brussels, 4 December 2007, SPEECH/07/793, 7 December 2007.

[11] D. Dinan, 'Governance and Institutions: Implementing the Lisbon Treaty in the Shadow of the Euro Crisis', *Journal of Common Market Studies*, 49, S1 (2011), 103.

[12] The literature is rich. Here is a partial sample of some truly helpful studies: J. Thomassen (ed.), *The Legitimacy of the European Union after Enlargement* (Oxford: Oxford University Press, 2009); J. Thomassen and H. Schmitt, 'Introduction: Political Legitimacy and Representation in the European Union', in H. Schmitt and J. Thomassen (eds.), *Political Representation and Legitimacy in the European Union* (New York/Oxford: Oxford University Press, 1999), 3–21; D. Beetham and C. Lord, *Legitimacy and the European Union* (London/New York: Longman, 1998); M. Haller, 'Is the European Union Legitimate? To What Extent?', *International Social Science Journal*, 60 (1999), 223–34; A. Moravcsik, 'Reassessing Legitimacy in the European Union', *Journal of Common Market Studies*, 40 (2002), 603–24; B. Guastaferro and M. Moschella, 'The EU, the IMF, and the Representative Turn: Addressing the Challenge of Legitimacy', *Swiss Political Science Review*, 18 (2012), 199–219.

[13] N. Walker, 'Postnational Constitutionalism and the Problem of Translation', in J. H. H. Weiler and M. Wind (eds.), *European Constitutionalism Beyond the State* (Cambridge: Cambridge University Press, 2003), 29.

habits of governmental control, parliamentary accountability, and administrative responsibility that are practised with different modalities in the various Member States. Make no mistake: it is perfectly understood that the Union is not a State. But it is in the business of governance and has taken over extensive areas previously in the hands of the Member States. In some critical areas, such as the interface of the Union with the international trading system, the competences of the Union are exclusive. In others they are dominant. Democracy is not about States. Democracy is about the exercise of public power – and the Union exercises a huge amount of public power. We live by the credo that any exercise of public power has to be legitimated democratically and it is exactly here that process legitimacy fails.

In essence, the two primordial features of any functioning democracy are missing – the grand principles of accountability[14] and representation.[15]

As regards accountability,[16] even the basic condition of representative democracy that at election time the citizens 'can throw the scoundrels out'[17] – that is, replace the government – does not operate in Europe.[18] The form of European governance,[19] governance without government, is, and will remain for considerable time, perhaps forever, such that there is no 'government' to throw out. Dismissing the Commission by Parliament (or approving the appointment of the Commission president) is not quite the same, not even remotely so.

Startlingly, but not surprisingly, political accountability of Europe is remarkably weak. There have been some spectacular political failures of European governance: the embarrassing Copenhagen climate fiasco[20];

---

[14] A. Przeworski, S. C. Stokes and B. Manin (eds.), *Democracy, Accountability and Representation* (Cambridge: Cambridge University Press, 1999); P. C. Schmitter and T. L. Karl, 'What Democracy Is … and Is Not', *Journal of Democracy* (Summer 1991), 67.

[15] P. Mair, 'Popular Democracy and the European Union Polity', *European Governance Papers* (EUROGOV), nG. C-05-03 (2005), 4.

[16] C. Harlow, *Accountability in the European Union* (Oxford: Oxford University Press, 2003).

[17] I. Shapiro, *Democracy's Place* (Ithaca, NY: Cornell University Press, 1996), 96; J. H. H. Weiler, 'To Be a European Citizen: Eros and Civilization', in J. H. H. Weiler (ed.), *The Constitution of Europe 'Do the New Clothes Have an Emperor?' and Other Essays on European Integration* (Cambridge: Cambridge University Press, 1999), 329.

[18] R. Dehousse, 'Constitutional Reform in the EC', in J. Hayward (ed.), *The Crisis of Representation in Europe* (Abingdon: Frank Cass, 1995), 118, at 123.

[19] P. Allott, 'European Governance and the Re-branding of Democracy', *European Law Review*, 1, 27 (2002), 60.

[20] See European Parliament resolution of 10 February 2010 on the outcome of the Copenhagen Conference on Climate Change (COP 15), P78TA(2010)0019, Wednesday, 10 February 2010, especially points 5-Se.

the weak (at best) realisation of the much-touted Lisbon Agenda (aka Lisbon Strategy or Lisbon Process);[21] the very story of the defunct 'Constitution',[22] to mention but three. It is hard to point in these instances to any measure of political accountability, of someone paying a political price as would be the case in national politics. In fact, it is difficult to point to a single instance of accountability for political failure as distinct from personal accountability for misconduct in the annals of European integration. This is not, decidedly not, a story of corruption or malfeasance.[23] My argument is that this failure is rooted in the very structure of European governance. It is not designed for political accountability. In a similar vein, it is impossible to link in any meaningful way the results of elections to the European Parliament to the performance of the political groups within the preceding parliamentary session, in a way that is part of the mainstay of political accountability within the Member States.[24] Structurally, dissatisfaction with 'Europe' when it exists has no channel to affect, at the European level, the agents of European governance. The Spitzenkandidaten exercise has only marginally corrected this anomaly. Depressingly, Parliament has reverted to its 'rotation exercise' among the two big centre-left, centre-right blocs, and the European Council has made its dissatisfaction with the Spitzenkandidaten exercise quite clear with a determination not to allow a repetition of the exercise.

Likewise, at the most primitive level of democracy, there is simply no moment in the civic calendar of Europe when the citizen can influence directly the outcome of any policy choice facing the Community and Union in the way that citizens can when choosing between parties which offer sharply distinct programmes at the national level. The political

---

[21] I. Begg, 'Is there a Convincing Rationale for the Lisbon Strategy', *Journal of Common Market Studies*, 46, 2 (2008), 427; 'Facing the Challenge. The Lisbon Strategy for Growth and Employment', Report from the High Level Group Chaired by Wim Kok, November 2004.

[22] I. Ward, 'Bill and the Fall of the Constitutional Treaty', *European Public Law*, 13, 3 (2007), 461; Editorial Comments, 'What Should Replace the Constitutional Treaty?', *Common Market Law Review*, 44 (2007), 561.

[23] On this aspect, see V. Mehde, 'Responsibility and Accountability in the European Commission', *Common Market Law Review*, 40 (2003), 423.

[24] J. Priestley, 'European Political Parties: The Missing Link', *Notre Europe*, Policy Paper 41 (2010); F. Roa Bastos, 'Des partis politiques au niveau européen? Etat des lieux á la veille des élections européennes de juin 2009', *Etudes et Recherches*, 71 (2009); O. Audeoud, 'Les partis politiques au niveau européen: fédération de partis nationaux', *Les cahiers du GERSE*, Nancy, 3 février 1999.

colour of the European Parliament only very weakly gets translated into the legislative and administrative output of the Union.[25]

The political deficit, to use the felicitous phrase of Renaud Dehousse,[26] is at the core of the democracy deficit. The Commission, by its self-understanding linked to its very ontology, cannot be 'partisan' in a right-left sense, neither can the Council, by virtue of the haphazard political nature of its composition. Democracy normally must have some meaningful mechanism for expression of voter preference predicated on choice among options, typically informed by stronger or weaker ideological orientation.[27] That is an indispensable component of politics. Democracy without Politics is an oxymoron.[28] And yet that is not only Europe, but it is a feature of Europe – the 'non-partisan' nature of the Commission – which is celebrated. The stock phrase found in endless student textbooks and the like, that the supranational Commission vindicates the 'European Interest', whereas the intergovernmental Council is a clearinghouse for Member State interest, is, at best, naïve. Does the European Interest not necessarily involve political and ideological choices? At times explicit, but always implicit? Again, the formidable Mr. Juncker has been able only marginally or in a Machiavellian way (I use this term in the best sense of the word) to redress this problem in the selection of his Commission. He could allocate portfolios with imagination but could not choose candidates of Member States based on programmatic commitment.

Thus the two most primordial norms of democracy, the principle of accountability and the principle of representation, are compromised in the very structure and process of the Union.

The second manifestation of the current European circumstance is evident in a continued slide in the legitimacy and mobilising force of the European construct and its institutions. I pass over some of the uglier manifestations of European 'solidarity' both at governmental and popular levels as regards the Euro crisis or the near abandonment of Italy to deal with the influx of migrants from North Africa as if this was an Italian problem

---

[25] V. Bogdanor, 'Legitimacy, Accountability and Democracy in the European Union', *A Federal Trust Report* (2007), 7; A. Follesdal and S. Hix, 'Why There Is a Democratic Deficit in the EU: A Response to Majone and Moravcsik', *Journal of Common Market Studies*, 44 (2006), *op. cit.*, 545.

[26] R. Dehousse, 'Constitutional Reform in the EC', *op. cit.*, at 124. See also J.-M. Ferry and P. Thibaud, *Discussion sur l'Europe* (Paris: Calmann-Lévy, 1992).

[27] Follesdal and Hix, 'Why There Is a Democratic Deficit in the EU', *op cit.*, 545.

[28] See P. Manent, *La raison des nations, réflexions sur la démocratie en Europe* (Paris: Gallimard, 2006), 59.

and not a problem for Europe as a whole. I look instead at two deeper and longer-term trends. The first is the extraordinary decline in voter participation in elections for the European Parliament. In Europe as a whole the rate of participation is below 45 per cent, with several countries, notably in the East, with a rate below 30 per cent. The correct comparison is, of course, with political elections to national parliaments where the numbers are considerably higher.[29] What is striking about these figures is that the decline coincides with a continuous shift in powers to the European Parliament, which today is a veritable co-legislator with the Council. The more powers the European Parliament, supposedly the *Vox Populi*, has gained, the greater popular indifference to it seems to have developed.[30] The past elections saw the lowest turnout of voters in the history of direct elections. It is sobering but not surprising to note the absence of the European Parliament as a major player in the current crisis. But the institutional crisis runs deeper. The Commission has excelled as a creative secretariat and implementor and monitor, but neither as the sources of ideas or veritable political leadership. It has been faithful and effective as His Master's Voice. But most striking has been the disappearing act of the Council. No longer the proud leader of Europe according to the Giscardian design, but an elaborate rubber stamp to the Union's presidents – Merkel and whomever else is around. A double failure of institutional legitimacy, of Parliament and of Council. Of supranationalism and inter-governmentalism. The resort to an extra-Union treaty as a centrepiece of the reconstruction is but the poignant legal manifestation of this political reality.

The critique of the democracy deficit of the Union has itself been subjected to two types of critique. The first has simply contested the reality of the democracy deficit by essentially claiming that wrong criteria have been applied to the Union.[31] The lines of debate are well known.[32] For what it is worth, I have staked my position previously. But

---

[29] A. Menon and J. Peet, 'Beyond the European Parliament: Rethinking the EU's Democratic Legitimacy', *Center for European Reform Essays* (2010); P. Magnette, 'European Governance and Civic Participation: Can the European Union Be Politicised?', *Jean Monnet Working Paper*, 6/01 (2001).

[30] J. Buzek, 'State of the Union: Three Cheers for the Lisbon Treaty and Two Warnings for Political Parties', *Journal of Common Market Studies*, 49 (2011), 7 at 15; see also Weiler, *The Constitution of Europe*, 266.

[31] J. H. H. Weiler, 'Does Europe Need a Constitution? Demos, Telos and the German Maastricht Decision', *European Law Journal*, 1, 3 (1995), 219, especially 225 *et seq.*

[32] P. Craig, 'The Nature of the Community: Integration, Democracy, and Legitimacy', in P. Craig and G. de Búrca (eds.), *The Evolution of EU Law* (Oxford: Oxford University Press, 1999), 25.

I am more interested in the second type of critique, which implicitly is an invocation of result or output legitimacy. Since the Union, not being a State, cannot replicate or adequately translate the habits and practices of statal democratic governance, its legitimacy may be found elsewhere.[33]

In analysing the legitimacy (and mobilising force) of the European Union, in particular against the background of its persistent democracy deficit, political and social science has indeed long used the distinction between process legitimacy and outcome legitimacy (aka input/output, process/result etc.).[34] The legitimacy of the Union more generally and the Commission more specifically, even if suffering from deficiencies in the state democratic sense, are said to rest on the results achieved – in the economic, social, and, ultimately, political realms.[35] The idea hearkens back to the most classic functionalist and neo-functionalist theories.[36]

I do not want to take issue with the implied normativity of this position – a latter day *Panem et circenses* approach to democracy, which at some level at least could be considered quite troubling. It is with its empirical reality that I want to take some issue. I do not think that outcome legitimacy explains all or perhaps even most of the mobilising force of the European construct. But whatever role it played it is dependent on the *Panem*. Rightly or wrongly, the economic woes of Europe, which are manifest in the Euro crisis, are attributed to the European construct. So when there suddenly is no bread, and certainly no cake, we are treated to a

---

[33] N. MacCormick, 'Democracy, Subsidiarity, and Citizenship in the "European Commonwealth"', *Law and Philosophy*, 16 (1997), 331–56.

[34] See, for example, C. R. Beitz, *Political Equality: An Essay in Democratic Theory* (Princeton; Guildford: Princeton University Press, 1989), chapters 2 and 4; R. A. Dahl, *Democracy and Its Critics* (New Haven, CT: Yale University Press, 1991), 163. See also more specifically, G. Majone(ed.), *Regulating Europe* (London: Routledge, 1996); F. W. Scharpf, *Governing in Europe: Effective and Democratic?* (Oxford: Oxford University Press, 1999), 7 *et seq.*

[35] K. Featherstone, 'Jean Monnet and the Democratic Deficit in the European Union', *Journal of Common Market Studies*, 32, 2 (1994), 149, at 150.

[36] Ibid., 155; C. Pentland, 'Political Theories of European Integration: Between Science and Ideology', in D. Lasok and P. Soldatos (eds.), *The European Communities in Action* (Brussels: Bruylant, 1981), 545, at 550 *et seq.*; B. Rosamond, *Theories of European Integration* (New York: Palgrave Macmillan, 2000), 20 *et seq.*; D. Mitrany, *A Working Peace System* (Chicago: Quadrangle Books, 1966); E. B. Haas, *The Uniting of Europe* (Stanford, CA: Stanford University Press, 1958); E. B. Haas, 'Trubulent Fields and the Theory of Regional Integration', *International Organization*, 30 (Spring 1976), 173; L. N. Lindberg, *The Political Dynamics of European Economic Integration* (Stanford, CA: Stanford University Press, 1963); L. N. Lindberg and S. A. Scheingold (eds.), *Regional Integration: Theory and Research* (Cambridge: Cambridge University Press, 1971).

different kind of circus whereby the citizens' growing indifference is turning to hostility and the ability of Europe to act as a political mobilising force seems not only spent, but even reversed. The worst way to legitimate a war is to lose it, and Europe is suddenly seen not as an icon of success, but as an emblem of austerity, thus in terms of its promise of prosperity, failure. If success breeds legitimacy, failure, even if wrongly allocated, leads to the opposite.

Thus, not surprisingly, there is a seemingly contagious spread of 'anti-Europeanism' in national politics.[37] What was once in the province of fringe parties on the far right and left has inched its way to more central political forces. The 'Question of Europe' as a central issue in political discourse was for long regarded as an 'English disease'. There is a growing contagion in Member States in North and South, East and West, where political capital is to be made among non-fringe parties by anti-European advocacy.[38] The spill-over effect of this phenomenon is the shift of mainstream parties in this direction as a way of countering the gains at their flanks. If we are surprised by this, it is only because we seem to have airbrushed out of our historical consciousness the rejection of the so-called European Constitution, an understandable amnesia since it represented a defeat of the collective political class in Europe by the *vox populi*,[39] albeit not speaking through, but instead giving a slap in the face to, the European Institutions.[40]

## III   Europe as Political 'Messianism'

At some level, the same could have been said ten and even twenty years ago.[41] The democracy deficit is not new – it is enduring. And how did Europe legitimate itself before it scored its great successes of the first decades?

---

[37] C. Leconte, *Understanding Euroscepticism* (Palgrave Macmillan, 2010).

[38] R. Harmsen and M. Spiering (eds.), *Euroscepticism: Party Politics, National Identity and European Integration* (Amsterdam: Rodopi, 2005), 13; A. Szczerbiak and P.A. Taggart, *Opposing Europe?* (Oxford: Oxford University Press: 2008), vol. I & II.

[39] N. Fligstein, *Euroclash. The EU, European Identity, and the Future of Europe* (Oxford: Oxford University Press, 2008).

[40] For former examples, see J. H. H. Weiler, U. R. Haltern, and F. C. Mayer, 'European Democracy and Its Critique', in J. Hayward (ed.), *The Crisis of Representation in Europe* (Abingdon: Frank Cass, 1995), 4.

[41] See, for example, European Commission, 'European Governance: A White Paper', COM (2001) 428 final, Brussels; V. Bogdanor and G. Woodcock, 'The European Community and

As I hinted previously, at the conceptual level, there is a third type of legitimation which, in my view, played for a long time a much larger role than is currently acknowledged. In fact, in my view, it has been decisive to the legitimacy of Europe and to the positive response of both the political class and citizens at large. I will also argue that it is the key to a crucial element in the Union's political culture. It is a legitimacy rooted in the *politically messianic*.

In political 'messianism', the justification for action and its mobilising force derive not from process, as in classical democracy, or from result and success, but from the ideal pursued, the destiny to be achieved, the 'Promised Land' waiting at the end of the road. Indeed, in messianic visions the end always trumps the means.

Mark Mazower, in his brilliant and original history and historiography of twentieth-century Europe,[42] insightfully shows how the Europe of monarchs and emperors which entered World War I was often rooted in a political messianic narrative in various states (in Germany, and Italy, and Russia and even Britain and France). It then oscillated after the war towards new democratic orders, that is, to process legitimacy, which then oscillated back into new forms of political messianism in fascism and communism. As the tale is usually told, after World War II, Europe of the West was said to oscillate back to democracy and process legitimacy. It is here that I want to point to an interesting quirk, not often noted.

On the one hand, the Western states, which were later to become the Member States of the European Union, became resolutely democratic, their patriotism rooted in their new constitutional values, narratives of glory abandoned and even ridiculed, and messianic notions of the State losing all appeal. Famously, former empires, once defended with repression and blood, were now abandoned with zeal.[43]

And yet, their common venture, European integration, was in my reading a political messianic venture *par excellence*, the messianic becoming a central features of its original and enduring political culture. The mobilising

Sovereignty', *Parliamentary Affairs*, 44, 4 (1991), 492: '*The shortcomings of the Community lie in the feelings of remoteness and lack of influence and involvement on the part of many of its citizens*'; D. Grimm, 'Does Europe Need a Constitution?', *European Law Journal*, 1, 3 (1995), 282, at 291 *et seq.*; C. Hill, 'European Foreign Policy: Power Bloc, Civilian Power – or Flop?', in R. Rummel (ed.), *The Evolution of an International Actor – Western Europe's New Assertiveness* (Boulder, CO: Westview, 1990), 35.

[42] M. Mazower, *Dark Continent –Europe's Twentieth Century* (London: Allen Lane, 1998).

[43] J. Lacroix, 'For a European Constitutional Patriotism', *Political Studies*, 50 (2002), 944, at 949 *et seq.*

force and principal legitimating feature was the vision offered, the dream dreamt, the promise of a better future. It is this feature which explains not only the persistent mobilising force (especially among elites and youth), but also key structural and institutional choices made. It will also give more depth to explanations of the current circumstance of Europe.

Since, unlike the democracy deficit which has been discussed and debated *ad nauseam* and *ad tedium*, political messianism is a feature of European legitimacy which has received less attention, I think it may be justified if I pay to it some more attention.

## IV The Schuman Declaration as a Manifesto of Political Messianism

The Schuman Declaration is somewhat akin to Europe's 'Declaration of Independence' in its combination of vision and blueprint. Notably, much of its text found its way into the preamble of the Treaty of Paris, the substance of which was informed by its ideas. It is interesting to re-read the Declaration through the conceptual prism of political messianism. The hallmarks are easily detected as we would expect in its constitutive, magisterial document. It is manifest in what is in the Declaration and, no less importantly, in what is not therein. *Nota bene*: European integration is nothing like its European messianic predecessors – that of monarchies and empire and later fascism and communism. It is liberal and noble, but politically messianic it is nonetheless.

The messianic feature is notable in both its rhetoric and substance. Note, first, the language used – ceremonial and 'sermonial' with plenty of pathos (and bathos).

> *World peace cannot be safeguarded without the making of creative efforts proportionate to the dangers which threaten it....*
>
> *The contribution which an organised and living Europe can bring to civilisation is indispensable ...*
>
> *... a first step in the federation of Europe [which] will change the destinies of those regions which have long been devoted to the manufacture of munitions of war....*
>
> *[A]ny war between France and Germany becomes not merely unthinkable, but materially impossible.*
>
> *This production will be offered to the world as a whole without distinction or exception....*
>
> *[I]t may be the leaven from which may grow a wider and deeper community between countries long opposed to one another by sanguinary divisions.*

It is grand, inspiring, Churchillian one might even say with a tad of irony. Some old habits, such as the White Man's Burden and the missionary tradition, die hard:

> *With increased resources Europe will be able to pursue the achievement of one of its essential tasks, namely, the development of the African continent.*

But it is not just the rhetoric. The substance itself is messianic: a compelling vision which has animated now at least three generations of European idealists where the 'ever closer union among the people of Europe', with peace and prosperity an icing on the cake, constitutes the beckoning promised land.[44]

It is worth exploring further the mobilising force of this new plan for Europe. At the level of the surface language it is its straightforward pragmatic objective of consolidating peace and reconstructing European prosperity. But there is much more within the deep structure of the Plan.

Peace, at all times an attractive desideratum, would have had its appeal in purely utilitarian terms. But it is readily apparent that in the historical context in which the Schumann Plan was put forward the notion of peace as an ideal probes a far deeper stratum than simple swords into ploughshares, sitting under ones' vines and fig trees, lambs and wolves – the classic biblical metaphor for peace. The dilemma posed was an acute example of the alleged tension between grace and justice which has taxed philosophers and theologians through the ages – from William of Ockham (pre-modern), Friedrich Nietzsche (modernist) and the repugnant but profound Martin Heidegger (post-modern).

These were, after all, the early 1950s with the horrors of war still fresh in the mind and, in particular, the memory of the unspeakable savagery of German occupation. It would take many years for the hatred in countries such as The Netherlands, Denmark, or France to subside fully. The idea, then, in 1950, of a community of equals as providing the structural underpinning for long-term peace among yesterday's enemies represented more than the wise counsel of experienced statesmen.

It was, first, a 'peace of the brave' requiring courage and audacity. At a deeper level it managed to tap into the two civilizational pillars of

---

[44] F. Piodi, 'From the Schuman Declaration to the Birth of the ECSC: The Role of Jean Monnet', Archive and Documentation Centre (CARDOC), Directorate-General for the Presidency, European Parliament, *CARDOC Journals*, nu 6 (May 2010); T. Hoerber, 'The Nature of the Beast: The Past and Future Purpose of European Integration, *L'Europe en formation*, 1 (2006), 17; Weiler, *The Constitution of Europe*, 8.

Europe: the Enlightenment and the heritage of the French Revolution and the European Christian tradition.[45]

Liberty was already achieved with the defeat of Nazi Germany – and Germans (like their Austrian brethren-in-crime) embraced with zeal the notion that they, too, were liberated from National Socialism. But here was a project, encapsulated in the Schuman Declaration, which added to the transnational level both equality and fraternity. The post-WWI Versailles version of peace was to take yesterday's enemy, diminish him, and keep his neck firmly under one's heel, with, of course, disastrous results. Here, instead was a vision in which yesteryear's enemy was regarded as an equal – Germany was to be treated as a full and equal partner in the venture – and engaged in a fraternal interdependent lock that, indeed, the thought of resolving future disputes would become unthinkable.[46] This was, in fact, the project of the Enlightenment taken to the international level as Kant himself had dreamt. To embrace the Schuman Plan was to tap into one of the most powerful idealistic seams in Europe's civilizational mines.

The Schuman Plan was also a call for forgiveness, a challenge to overcome an understandable hatred. In that particular historical context the Schumannian notion of peace resonated with, was evocative of, the distinct teaching, imagery, and values of the Christian call for forgiving one's enemies, for love, for grace – values so recently consecrated in their wholesale breach. The Schuman Plan was in this sense, evocative of both confession and expiation, and redolent with the Christian belief in the power of repentance and renewal and the ultimate goodness of humankind. This evocation is not particularly astonishing given the personal backgrounds of the founding fathers – Adenauer, De Gaspari, Schumann, Monnet himself – all seriously committed Catholics.[47]

---

[45] See, for example, J. Habermas and J. Derrida, 'February 15, or, What Binds Europeans Together: Plea for a Common Foreign Policy Beginning in Core Europe', in D. Levy et al. (eds.), *Old Europe, New Europe, Core Europe: Transatlantic Relations after the Iraq War* (London: Verso, 2005), 5, 10; A. Finkielkraut, *La défaite de la pensée* (Paris: Gallimard, 1987); J. H. H. Weiler, *L'Europe chrétienne: Une excursion* (Paris: Editions du Cerf, 2007); J. M. Ferry, *La république crépusculaire. Comprendre le projet européen in sensu cosmopolitico* (Paris: Editions du Cerf, 2010); R. Schuman, *Pour lour lch*, 55 et seq.

[46] A. Munoz, 'L'engagement européen de Robert Schuman', in S. Schirmann (ed.), *Robert Schuman et les pères de l'Europe: cultures politiques et années de formation* (Brussels: Peter Lang, 2008), 39, at 44.

[47] A. Fimister, 'Integral Humanism and the Re-unification of Europe', in S. Schirmann (ed.), *Robert Schuman et les pères de l'Europe: cultures politiques et années de formation* (Brussels: Peter Lang, 2008), 25; 'Schuman was an ardent Roman Catholic, and his views about the desirability of political unity in Western Europe owed much to the idea that

The mobilising force, especially among elites, the political classes who felt more directly responsible for the calamities of which Europe was just exiting, is not surprising given the remarkable subterranean appeal to the two most potent visions of the idyllic 'Kingdom' – the humanist and religious combined in one project.[48] This also explains how, for the most part, both right and left, conservative and progressive, could embrace the project.

It is the messianic model which explains (in part) why for so long the Union could operate without a veritable commitment to the principles it demanded of its aspiring members – democracy and human rights. Aspirant States had to become members of the European Convention of Human Rights, but the Union itself did not. They had to prove their democratic credentials, but the Union itself did not – two anomalies which hardly raised eyebrows.

Note, however, that its messianic features are reflected not only in the flowery rhetoric. In its original and unedited version the declaration is quite elaborate in operational detail. But you will find neither the word

---

*it was above all the continent's Christian heritage which gave consistence and meaning to the identity of European civilization. And the Europe he knew and loved best was the Carolingian Europe that accorded with his religious faith and his experience of French and German cultures'*; M. Sutton, 'Chapter 1: Before the Schuman Plan', *France and the Construction of Europe, 1944–2007: The Geopolitical Imperative* (New York and Oxford: Berghan Books, 2007), 34; *'It is with deep faith in our cause that I speak to you, and I am confident that through the will of our free peoples, with your support and with God's help, a new era for Europe will soon begin.'* Extracts from a speech by Alcide De Gasperi at the Consultative Assembly of the Council of Europe in Strasbourg on 16 September 1952 - Volume 3, 1952 of the *Official Reports of Debates of the Consultative Assembly of the Council of Europe.*

[48] One should add that the transnational reach of the Schuman Plan served, as one would expect, a powerful internal interest the discussion of which even today meets with resistance. The challenge of 'fraternity' and the need for forgiveness, love, and grace was even more pressing internally than internationally. For each one of the original Member States was seriously compromised internally. In post-war Germany, to put it bluntly, neither State nor society could function if all those complicit in National Socialism were to be excluded. In the other five, though ostensibly and in a real sense victims of German aggression, important social forces became complicit and were morally compromised. This was obviously true of Fascist Italy and Vichy France. But even little Luxembourg contributed one of the most criminally notorious units to the German army and Belgium distinguished itself as the country with the highest number of indigenous volunteers to the occupying German forces. The betrayal of Anne Frank and her family by their good Dutch neighbours was not an exception but emblematic of Dutch society and government who tidily handed over their entire Jewish citizenry for deportation and death. All these societies had a serious interest in 'moving on' and putting that compromised past behind them. If one were to forgive and embrace the external enemy, to turn one's back to the past and put one's faith in a better future, how much more so, how much easier, to do the same within one's own nation, society, even family?

democracy, nor human rights, a thunderous silence. It's a 'Lets-Just-Do-It'
type of programme animated by great idealism (and a goodly measure of
good old state interest, as a whole generation of historians such as Alan
Milward[49] and Charles Maier[50] among others have demonstrated).

The European double helix has from its inception been Commission
and Council: an international (supposedly) apolitical transnational
administration/executive (the Commission) collaborating not, as we
habitually say, with the Member States (Council), but with the governments, the executive branch of the Member States, which for years and
years had a forum that escaped in day-to-day matters the scrutiny of any
parliament, European or national. Democracy is simply not part of the
original vision of European integration.[51]

This observation is hardly shocking or even radical. Is it altogether fanciful to tell the narrative of Europe as one in which 'doers and believers'
(notably the most original of its institutions, the Commission, coupled
with an empowered executive branch of the Member States in the guise
of the Council and COREPER), an elitist (if well-paid) vanguard, were
the self-appointed leaders from whom grudgingly, over decades, power
had to be arrested by the European Parliament? And even the European
Parliament has been a strange *vox populi*. For hasn't it been, for most of
its life, a champion of European integration, so that to the extent that,
inevitably, when the Union and European integration inspired fear and
caution among citizens (only natural in such a radical transformation of
European politics), the European Parliament did not feel the place citizens would go to express those fears and concerns?

The political messianic was offered not only for the sake of conceptual clarification, but also as an explanation of the formidable past success
of European integration in mobilising support. It produced a culture of
praxis, achievement, ever expanding agendas. Given the noble dimensions of European integration, one ought to see and acknowledge its vir-
tuous facets.

But that is only part of the story. It also explains some of the story of
decline in European legitimacy and mobilising pull which is so obvious

---

[49] Milward, *The European Rescue of the Nation State*.

[50] C. S. Maier and G. Bischof (eds.), *The Marshall Plan and Germany: West German
Development within the Framework of the European Recovery Program* (Providence: Berg
Press, 1991).

[51] Featherstone, 'Jean Monnet and the Democratic Deficit', 150; J. Delors, *Independent*, 26
July 1993.

in the current circumstance. *Part of the very phenomenology of political messianism is that it always collapses as a mechanism for mobilisation and legitimation.* It obviously collapses when the messianic project fails. When the revolution does not come. But interestingly, and more germane to the narrative of European integration, even when successful, it sows its seeds of collapse. At one level the collapse is inevitable, part of the very phenomenology of the messianic project. Reality is always more complicated, challenging, banal, and ultimately less satisfying than the dream which preceded it. The result is not only absence of mobilisation and legitimation, but actual rancour.

Democracy was not part of the original DNA of European integration. It still feels like a foreign implant. With the collapse of its original political messianism, the alienation we are now witnessing is only to be expected. And thus, when failure hits as in the Euro crisis, when the *Panem* is gone, all sources of legitimacy suddenly, simultaneously collapse.

This collapse comes at an inopportune moment, at the very moment when Europe of the Union would need all its legitimacy resources. The problems are European and the solution has to be at the European level. But for that solution to be perceived as legitimate, for the next phase in European integration not to be driven by resentful fear, the architects will not be able to rely, sadly, on the decisional process of the Union itself. They will have to dip heavily into the political structure and decisional process of the Member States. It will be national parliaments, national judiciaries, national media, and, yes, national governments who will have to lend their legitimacy to a solution which inevitably will involve yet a higher degree of integration. It will be an entirely European phenomenon that at what will have to be a decisive moment in the evolution of the European construct, the importance, even primacy of the national communities as the deepest source of legitimacy of the integration project will be affirmed yet again. And yet, what do we do if we find that those national reservoirs are running low and in some cases even depleted?

# INDEX